The Irish World Wid
History, Heritage, Iden

Volume 5 **Religion and Identity**

The Irish World Wide
History, Heritage, Identity

Edited by Patrick O'Sullivan

The Irish World Wide
History, Heritage, Identity

Volume 5
Religion and Identity

Edited by Patrick O'Sullivan

Leicester University Press
London and New York

Leicester University Press
A Continuum imprint
The Tower Building, 11 York Road, London SE1 7NX
370 Lexington Avenue, New York NY10017-6550

First published 1996, reprinted in paperback 2000
© Editor and contributors 1996

British Library Cataloguing in Publication Data
A catalogue record for this book is available from the British Library

ISBN 0 7185 1424 6 (HB)
    0 7185 0233 7 (PB)

Library of Congress Cataloging-in-Publication Data
Religion and identity / edited by Patrick O'Sullivan.
        p.   cm. — (The Irish world wide : v. 5)
    Includes bibliographical references and index.
    ISBN 0–7185–1424–6 (Hardback) ISBN 0 7185 0233 7 (Paperback)
    1. Irish–Foreign countries—Religion. 2. Ireland—Emigration and immigration. 3. National characteristics, Irish.   I. O'Sullivan, Patrick, 1944–   . II. Series.
    BL980.I7R45   1996
    305.891´62—dc20   95–50701
                                                                                CIP

Typeset by Falcon Oast Graphic Art
Printed and bound in Great Britain by Biddles Ltd, *www.biddles.co.uk*

In memory of Sister Odile O'Sullivan,
Sisters of the Infant Jesus

Contents

List of tables

List of contributors

Bernard Aspinwall, formerly Senior Lecturer in Modern History at the University of Glasgow, is now based at the University of Strathclyde, Scotland. He is vice-chair of the British Universities Transatlantic Committee. His published books include *Portable Utopia: Glasgow and the United States, 1820–1920*, and he has published numerous articles on aspects of Scottish and Catholic history. He is currently working on a major study of Catholic attitudes to wealth creation.

James P. Cantrell, of the University of Arkansas, in the southern United States, is the descendant of Irish migrants, Catholic and Protestant. He is currently working on a major study of Irish influences in the American South, 'The Matrix and the Nexus: Celtic heritage in Southern literature'.

Barry M. Coldrey, an Australian, joined the Christian Brothers Congregation in 1958. He has taught in three Australian states, in Pakistan and in Papua New Guinea. He is the author of over twenty books including *Faith and Fatherland: the Christian Brothers and Irish Nationalism, 1838–1921*.

Mary J. Hickman is Director of the Irish Studies Centre at the University of North London, England. Her main research area is the historical and contemporary experience of the Irish in Britain. Her forthcoming book, *Religion, Class and Identity*, explores the relationship between the British state, the Catholic Church and the education of the Irish in Britain.

Paula M. Kane is assistant professor of Religious Studies at the University of Pittsburgh, USA. Her articles have appeared in *Church History* and *US Catholic Historian* and her book, *Separatism and Subculture: Boston Catholicism, 1900–1920* was published in 1994.

Leon B. Litvack is lecturer in English at the Queen's University of Belfast, Northern Ireland. He is the author of *John Mason Neale and the Quest for Sobornost*, and is a member of the executive of the Society for the Study of Nineteenth Century Ireland.

James White McAuley is Senior Lecturer in Sociology at the University of Huddersfield, England, and is secretary of the British Association for Irish Studies. He has written extensively on Northern Ireland. His book, *The Politics of Identity: a Loyalist Community in Belfast*, was recently published by Avebury Press.

Paul O'Leary lectures in history at the University of Wales, Aberystwyth. He has published, in Welsh and in English, on Irish migration and is currently preparing the first full-scale study of the Irish in Wales, 1798–1922.

Janice Tranter, Sister of St Joseph, Lochinvar, New South Wales, Australia, has written a major study of the founding of her congregation and continues research for her congregation. Her published work includes contributions to the Irish–Australia Conference and the History of Women Religious Workshop.

Anne-Maree Whitaker gained her doctorate from Macquarie University, Sydney, and is the author of *Unfinished Revolution: United Irishmen in New South Wales, 1800–1810*, published in 1994 by Crossing Press. After a twentieth-century interlude studying IRA veterans, she is now working on a biography of Lieutenant-Governor Joseph Foveaux (1767–1846).

Introduction to Volume 5: religion and identity

Patrick O'Sullivan

A consistent narrative

In the early 1560s a young lad, a boy of 13 or 14, left Ireland. His name was John Martin. His father had been sacristan in Cork Cathedral, in the period which saw English attempts to establish the reformed religion in Ireland, and John Martin had worked as a boy servant in the palace of the bishop of Cork. The boy's father died. The boy's mother married again. The new husband was a tailor called Cornelius, who renamed the boy 'William Cornelius'. ('Cornelius' is sometimes found in this period as an un-Irishing of 'Kenneally'.) The stepfather, the mother and the boy then settled in England. They lived for some years at Padstow, in the West Country. The stepfather died. The mother went blind: the young man was later to recount how he led her from door to door begging.

By 1567, we know, the lad was in work: he may have been kidnapped by a press gang. He was a lowly cabin boy on the *Jesus of Lubeck*, the flagship of John Hawkins, sailing out of Plymouth on Hawkins's third slaving voyage. John Martin, known on ship as 'Cornelius the Irishman', was soon demoted to the even more lowly position of 'sweeper' due, we are told, to laziness. After initial success in Africa (success in that hundreds of Africans were captured and sold into slavery in the New World), this expedition led by Hawkins ended in disaster in Mexico. In a battle with a Spanish fleet at San Juan de Ulua, the port of Vera Cruz, the burning flagship was abandoned, and the crew crowded into a smaller vessel. Soon, to save that overcrowded little ship, some one hundred men were put ashore, amongst them John Martin. Meanwhile Hawkins and another one hundred survivors began the painful voyage east and north, to England.

In Mexico, the marooned sailors soon fell into the hands of the Spanish colonial authorities. Some of the leaders were sent to judgement in Spain, but the majority were not too badly treated, assigned various punishments and later released under supervision. John Martin worked for a while for another Irishman resident in Mexico, the barber-surgeon Domingo Suarez, from whom he learnt the rudiments of that craft. We also hear of an episode in an inn in Pachuca: when maudlin and drunk, John Martin protested that he was an Irishman and a subject of the King of England. When a Spaniard pointed out that England did not have a King, Martin angrily replied that he had meant the Queen: and he was ready to die for her.

A sober John Martin then found his way to the remote village of La Trinidad, in Guatemala, where he established himself as a barber-surgeon. He seems to have found respect in that little community. He married, rescuing from direst poverty his bride, Juana de Barrionuevo, and her parents, Alonso de Maya and Isabel Benitez. The marriage took place on St Matthew's Day, 21 September 1573. A child, a girl to be named Isabel after her grandmother, was born in July 1574.

We know so much about this initially unpromising Irish migrant because in 1571, probably in response to the raids of Francis Drake (who had received help from contacts within the Spanish colonies), the reinvigorated Inquisition was established in Mexico, and the surviving Inquisition records have been sensitively analysed for us by P. E. H. Hair.[1] The English sailors were rounded up.[2] They were tortured, questioned and assigned punishments: punishment usually involved a period wearing the *sambenito*, confined to a monastery for religious re-education.[3] One, George Reaveley, was found guilty of heresy. In the jargon of the Inquisition he was sentenced to be 'relaxed': he was garotted and his body burned, at an *auto-da-fé* in Mexico City in 1574.

'Juan Martinez', in distant La Trinidad, was missed in that first round-up. But in 1574, just after the birth of his child, Martin was arrested and taken to Mexico City. He took with him letters of commendation from his parish priest and local magistrates. A respectful letter from Martin's brother-in-law, and a loving letter from his wife, followed him to Mexico City: these letters were preserved in the Inquisition's files, so it is doubtful if they ever reached him. Juana's letter begins, 'Hermano mio de mi corazon' . . . Little Isabel sends a loving kiss.

The English prisoners were brought in again, to be questioned about Martin. The prisoners had, for the most part, survived their first experience of the Inquisition by admitting their 'Lutherite' upbringing and beliefs, and ingloriously disowning them. Even George Reavely had made no defence of his faith. There are ways of surviving such tribunals, working out what the questioners want and providing it. Yet, in fairness to Martin's English shipmates, as they realized that the Inquisition's questions were leading to a condemnation of Martin, they stressed Martin's unimportance: he was a youth who had simply done what he was told to do, or what everyone else had done. On board ship he was regarded as a doubtful Protestant, because he was Irish. He was nicknamed 'Saint Patrick'. The Irish barber-surgeon, Diego Suarez, was question. He managed to recall a favourable piece of evidence: Martin had once told him that an Englishman had kicked his mother because she carried a rosary. She wept, saying she wanted to return to Ireland.

The Inquisition was searching out heresy. Martin's defence was that he was Irish and Catholic, and that he had taken part in Protestant services, in

England and on board Hawkins' ship, because he had to. But this defence did not allow him the escape route found by his English shipmates. The key question for his Inquisitors was this: had John Martin betrayed his Irish Catholic faith and upbringing when he settled in 'Lutherite' England? It was a question about what was going on in the mind of an Irish boy, suddenly uprooted and set down in Padstow. Really, the offences of which John Martin was accused were most probably too intellectual, too theological and too precise for his understanding. Alone, friendless, frightened, he was not even aware that some pieces of evidence might have helped his case: he denied Suarez's story of his mother's rosary. The inquisitors sought abject submission expressed in a consistent narrative; Martin's performance offended their tidy minds.[4]

After long questioning, before, during and after torture, Martin eventually admitted that, yes, 'he had believed in the doctrine of England as far as he had understood it, and had thought to be saved by it.' That was what the Inquisitors wanted. At last, a consistent narrative. It was clear that he was a heretic. He was garotted and his body burnt at the second *auto-da-fé* in Mexico City, on 6 March 1575.

> Among the scores of *sambenitos* colourfully hanging in the aisles of Mexico cathedral until the eighteenth century was one which bore this inscription: *Guillermo Corniels y por otro nombre Juan Min* [sic] *Yrlandes natural de corc vezino de la Trinidad barvero herege Lutherano relaxado en persona año de 1575* (William Cornelius, otherwise John Martin, Irishman, native of Cork, inhabitant of La Trinidad, barber, Lutheran heretic, relaxed in person, 1575).[5]

If George Reaveley has been hailed as the first Protestant martyr in America, poor John Martin can be seen as a martyr of another kind: the powerless, solitary migrant, making his way, as best he can, in a world he cannot influence. Ground between the millstones of the Reformation and the Counter-Reformation, through all his changes of name, and his confusion of loyalties, political and religious, John Martin retained a sentimental attachment to Ireland and some sort of Irish identity. So much is clear from the carefully recorded answers to the Inquisitors' questions.[6] Near the end, when he realized that he was doomed, he admitted to the drunken incident in Pachuco, but protested 'I have always had in my heart the belief in the catholic doctrine of my country that I could not forget.'[7]

An inconsistent narrative

The story of John Martin, 'Cornelius the Irishman', fits any number of demonologies. P. E. H. Hair makes the comparison with Arthur Koestler's *Darkness at Noon*. There are points of contact with the career of Galileo, John Martin's more intelligent and more fortunate contemporary.[8] The image of 'Cornelius the Irishman' hovers before us, as we enter *Religion and Identity*, the volume of *The Irish World Wide* that looks at religion. That there had to be such a volume was evident. Like John Martin, the Irish live on the fault-line between the Reformation and the Counter-Reformation, and issues of religion loom large in Irish history and in Irish migration history. The volume would necessarily touch on sensitive areas, on core beliefs about the self, the community and life's purpose. At the same time, as part of our academic project, the volume would cover some themes where there was already a massive literature, and other themes where very little had been done. There are links between the sensitivity of the subject matter and the distortions in the literature.[9]

All academic disciplines construct narratives, but, I console myself, there are times when difficulty constructing 'a consistent narrative' is a blessing rather than a failing. The disparate academic disciplines which have studied religion have certainly created a confused research record. In this Introduction, I can only briefly map that confusion, in ways that will make sense to the new scholar and to the expert, in the hope that you will talk to each other. I have taken the space to explore, in a little detail, one area of confusion, which I have centred, in a kind of academic shorthand, on the sociology of Max Weber.

The contributors to *Religion and Identity*, like all the contributors to *The Irish World Wide*, give advice about wider, background reading, and I need not repeat their advice here. Here I must place chapters in context, I must fill gaps, I must widen debates. (The notion of the devil's advocate leaps, unsummoned, to the mind.) I must build the foundation from which we can launch into a close reading of our contributors' chapters. I also want to give some flavour of the discussions and the correspondence that went into the shaping of this volume.

When those discussions began I did have 'a shopping list', some notion of themes I felt our volume on religion should cover. I wanted to give due weight to both Irish Catholic and Irish Protestant migrant traditions. This meant that at once certain developmental routes were not open: triumphalist rhetoric from any tradition would have to be placed in a context. I wanted to explore the complexities of Irish Catholic traditions, and their relationship with migration: I certainly wanted a study of a male religious order and a study of a female religious order.

What our contributors created is not simply another study of Irish religion, but something more subtle: a volume about the place of religion in the development of changing Irish migrant identities. So, appealing to our series' subtitle, the volume on religion within *The Irish World Wide* came to be called *Religion and Identity*. I would draw particular attention to the 'media studies' parts of this volume: for it is within and around the arts, particularly within and around the Irish arts of the word, that debate and negotiation about the interrelationship between religion and identity become visible. This volume is thus a background volume to the entire series: it makes more visible themes already present throughout the *The Irish World Wide*.

Let us now map out some problems at the centre of any study of religion, problems acknowledged better within some academic disciplines than others. In history the plainest acknowledgement is in John Kent's *The*

Unacceptable Face: 'If religion is to serve, rather than seduce mankind, we need to examine its historical record, its unacceptable face, much more critically than has been done by either the ecclesiastical or the social historian.'[10]

> The success of the modernists and the historical critics obscured the survival of the traditional Christian philosophy of history, according to which divine providence presided over the broad sweep of events and guided it towards its goal in the final triumph of creative love over evil, a goal which was bound to be attained because God willed it and which, in a theological sense rarely clarified for laymen, was said to have already been achieved by Christ in his death and resurrection. These ideas of Providence caused less intellectual difficulty in the late nineteenth century because it seemed as though they could be reconciled with the Victorian idea of progress, an idea which owed more to idealist philosophy than to Christian theology, and more to economic and imperial expansion than to either.[11]

The tradition within history of trying to deduce the wishes of Providence from 'the broad sweep of events' is long and strong, and, as well as making their own deductions (with Providential explanations of migration, for example), the Irish have themselves suffered from the Providentialist theologies of the powerful.[12]

The tradition within the social sciences is to approach religion with what has been called 'methodological atheism', by which is meant a belief in methodology unconnected to a belief in religion.[13] In the background is that famous summing up of the sociological approach: 'If men define situations as real, they are real in their consequences.'[14]

'Methodological atheism' solves problems, but brings its own dangers. Researchers' own beliefs may be disguised or the influence of belief not acknowledged. In this volume I have not censored belief, and I have not censored unbelief. Belief and unbelief are part of our subject matter. In research 'methodological atheism' may lead to a working assumption that when people are talking about religion they are really talking about something else. This assumption becomes, in its strongest form, an insistence that people stop talking about religion and start talking about something else. It has been noted, for example, that commentators seem reluctant to address the religious, and theological, aspects of the conflicts in Northern Ireland.[15] In the best practice we should be aware of theology, and make the theology visible. 'If theologizing means simply any systematic reflection about religion, then it would seem plausible to regard it as too important to leave to theological experts.'[16]

Affinities and differences

Let me, once again, within Irish Migration Studies, ask questions about our research agenda. Who or what is shaping our agenda? Why do we so often find ourselves following well-beaten research tracks, that somehow do not lead to greater understanding? There cannot, for example, be many academic regimes that must so resolutely explore the thinking of both Thomas Malthus *and* Max Weber. Malthus we can leave until *The Meaning of the Famine*, the last volume of *The Irish World Wide*.

Max Weber is a duly enshrined founding father of sociology.[17] He had a special interest in the sociology of religion, and a number of his observations about religion retain explanatory power.[18] But when one Weber postulate, the 'Protestant work ethic', is plugged into Irish issues there is frustration: are we again simply dealing with stereotypes, positive or negative, foisted upon the Irish, yet another sub-department of post-colonialism?[19] We must take a step back and draw on the interdisciplinary strengths of Irish Migration Studies.

> All revolutions are declared to be natural and inevitable, once they are successful, and capitalism, as the type of economic system prevailing in Western Europe and America, is clothed to-day with the unquestioned respectability of the triumphant fact. But in its youth it was a pretender...[20]

It has long been thought that there are connections between the rise of capitalism and the rise of Protestantism, but the nature and direction of those connections is obscure. Weber, musing on the connections, suggested that certain features of Protestant theology favoured the capitalist spirit. This theology, this vision of the world and of humankind's relationship with God, which Weber located in its purest form in the teachings of Calvinist divines in England in the seventeenth century, excludes mysticism and ritual, and focuses on questions of predestination: the Calvinist hopes that he is one of the 'elect', already chosen by God to be saved. 'By a tendency not logical but psychological, the Calvinist seeks signs of his election in this world. It is because of this tendency, Weber suggests, that certain Calvinist sects have ended by finding in worldly success, even economic success, a sign of election.' Work for profit becomes a 'calling', and profit is sought not for self-indulgence but for reinvestment. There is 'an amazing coincidence' between the Protestant ethic and capitalist logic: 'for capitalism is defined precisely as the pursuit of profit which is not consumed but reinvested.'[21]

So, within sociology, a theology is made visible. Weber's thesis has attracted a huge literature, and I cannot here explore that literature in detail.[22] The literature is cumulatively indecisive. One commentator, Anthony Giddens, can quickly bring together 'a formidable indictment of Weber's views'.[23] (And we can note, in passing, the critique of 'the Tawney-Weber thesis' by the historian Hugh Trevor-Roper, who suggests that capitalism developed in the sixteenth and seventeenth centuries not because the entrepreneurs were Protestant but because the entrepreneurs were *migrants*.[24])

The Weber thesis is still a standard part of undergraduate sociology courses. The traditional, and easiest, way of teaching Weber's thesis is to see Weber as reacting to Marx (or the simpler Marxists of Weber's own time): in contrast to a theoretical system that gave priority to economics in history, and thus to material things and to social class, Weber wanted to demonstrate the effect of ideas in history.[25] His work thus provides an entry point into sociological thought: 'If men define situations as real...' Weber's thesis is one of the few sociological theses that has escaped from captivity: you will regularly meet the notion of 'the Protestant work ethic' in bar-room discussion.

The thesis is important in the history of academic disciplines, for Weber's approach is an eruption by one emerging academic discipline ('sociology') into ways of understanding, and using, historical material, whilst another academic discipline, history itself, was still finding its feet. History, as an academic discipline, is curiously reluctant to engage with theory, and curiously uncritical of theory when there is engagement. These tensions can be seen in the responses to Weber's thesis of the English economic historian and social commentator, R. H. Tawney. By stressing the importance of English Calvinism to the development of the 'Protestant ethic' Weber had wandered onto Tawney's patch.[26] From cautious acknowledgement in Tawney's own *Religion and the Rise of Capitalism*, where critique of Weber is relegated to the footnotes, Tawney moves, through cautious acceptance in Tawney's 1930 'Foreword' to the Parsons translation of Weber, ultimately to cautious rejection.[27] One commentator on the 'Protestant ethic' summarizes Tawney's position:

> In his view it was the gradual abdication by religion of the spheres of economic and political activity — a secularization of the business world that is coincidental with, but not the consequence of, the Reformation — which permitted the rise of unrestricted capitalist individualism ... The 'acquisitive society' had triumphed totally over the egalitarian one. The success of capitalism is, therefore, the failure of Protestantism.[28]

The key term is, of course, 'secularization', the withdrawal, or ejection, of religion from many areas where religion had claimed dominion, not least on questions of usury.[29]

By basing his argument so much on his understanding of the English Calvinism of the seventeenth century, and by relying so much on 'Anglo-Saxon' sources, Weber placed his argument within English/Irish relationships in that century, and in subsequent centuries. And not wholly unwittingly. The example Weber gives of Cromwell's 'quite specifically capitalistic line of thought' is from Cromwell's proclamation of war against the Irish.[30]

But there is, it will be appreciated at once, a 'procrustean structural problem' when applying Weber's thesis to English and to Irish patterns: the penal code and 'the legacy of structural discrimination against the Catholics'.[31] It might be thought that the penal code, with its schematic attack on the economic power of Catholics, would have protected Catholics within England and Ireland from an unthinking application of the Weber thesis: but only to a certain extent is this true.[32]

The Weber thesis is certainly around in world-wide Irish Migration

Studies, though sometimes in a covert and confusing way. The sociology leaks uncritically into the history. For Andrew M. Greeley, Weber's thesis is one of the 'models for viewing American Catholicism', and there is irritation, throughout Greeley's works, with the ways that theses like Weber's combine with traditional American prejudices to shape and misshape research.[33] Donald Harman Akenson has carried the analysis further, seeing in Kerby Miller's *Emigrants and Exiles* a 'reincarnation' of Weber's thesis.[34]

Weber's thesis supports, and draws support from, existing prejudices, especially in the English-speaking world. A theory about a special Protestant affinity with capitalism is a theory about a specific Catholic disability.[35] The theory feeds into, and supports, that obsession, in Ireland and in Irish histories, with exploring differences between Protestant and Catholic in ways that ultimately, to the methodologically aware, take us down within statistical margins of error. In Irish Migration Studies the most significant contribution to that debate is Akenson's *Small Differences*, a book whose title efficiently sums up its conclusions.

If the research record is confusing, part of the confusion arises because, as Akenson points out, ultimately the various academic disciplines differ as to what might be regarded as evidence.[36] It follows that the full shape and size of the problem can never be made visible within only one academic discipline: we need an interdisciplinary approach, and an area of study that requires an interdisciplinary approach, as a step to mapping out the problem. We need something like Irish Migration Studies.

All this is of more than academic interest to the migrant Irish. For if the migrant Irish, Catholic and Protestant, go forth with any single world-wide task then (and I do not know whether to report this with pride or shame) that task is to disprove the Weber thesis. Greeley notes, in *The American Catholic*, 'The Catholic immigrants came with a little more than a dream of success and respectability ... The Jews have made it big in the United States; that is not a surprise. So, too, have the Irish Catholics, and that is something of a surprise.'[37] Marjorie R. Fallows, in her list of successfully challenged myths, points out that 'Irish Catholics have been successful', and adds, 'It would be as valid to attribute their success to their religion as it was to attribute their presumed failure to the same cause.'[38] Both Fellows and Akenson compare the economic success and the 'upward mobility' of Americans of Irish Protestant heritage with that of Americans of Irish Catholic heritage, and find that it is the Catholics who have done 'better'.[39]

This is simply to say that migrants emigrate in search of work, hoping to better their lot, or hoping to make a better life for their children. And the children build on the hard work of the parents. Joel Mokyr says: 'Emigration in the early nineteenth century involved considerable risk, a definite postponement of consumption in the present and the immediate future for the sake of higher earnings in the remote future (possibly only enjoyed by another generation), and in any event considerable and emotional effort.'[40]

While there is a massive literature, attacking, defending, responding to and developing Weber's thesis, there are gaps in that literature. The historian of theology sees Weber's thesis as 'a bold attempt to demonstrate the significance of a *theological* factor for the development of modern intellectual attitudes', but goes on to add that 'despite the extensive literature ... produced as a result of the "Weber syndrome", a theological discussion about it has hardly as yet begun'.[41] The theology has been made visible, but not visible enough.

Tawney comments: 'Weber wrote as a scholar, not as a propagandist, and there is no trace in his work of the historical animosities which still warp discussions of the effects of the Reformation.'[42] This is true. Yet, students of Catholic faith or heritage are, I think, often perturbed to meet, at the heart of the new academic discipline of sociology, something that looks like standard Protestant anti-Catholic polemic of the seventeenth to twentieth centuries, an unacknowledged echo of the Thirty Years War. The patterns of prejudice within Weber's own source material need to be clarified.[43] It might, for example, be pointed out that there were already strong associations, within the British cast of mind, between Catholicism, poverty and retarded progress. These associations are so pervasive that they will be met, as a matter of course, in everyday reading.[44] Let us, with Irish Migration Studies, explore one study of that British cast of mind.

Forging nations

Linda Colley's *Britons: Forging the Nation 1707–1837* deliberately ignores Ireland.[45] She has been criticized in Ireland for that:

> In omitting Ireland Colley has missed an excellent opportunity to examine, comparatively, the development of 'Britishness' in Ulster and Britain. The Ulster case is particularly relevant, given that the British 'nationality' that Colley identifies with the 18th century — centred mainly on Protestantism — still characterises the British identity of Northern Ireland today.[46]

But to the scholar of Irish history the Irish threnody is there, throughout Colley's book, like a ground bass to the main theme. For the scholar of Irish migration Colley's book has even more resonances.

Colley offers a perception of 'Great Britain as an invented nation superimposed, if only for a while, onto much older alignments and loyalties':

> It was an invention forged above all by war. Time and time again war with France brought Britons, whether they hailed from Wales or Scotland or England, into confrontation with an obviously hostile Other and encouraged them to define themselves collectively against it. They defined themselves as Protestants struggling for survival against the world's foremost Catholic power. They defined themselves against the French as they imagined them to be, superstitious, militarist, decadent and unfree.[47]

There are, within this understanding of 'Britishness', appeals to

'Providence': 'For in the end, nothing succeeds like success. And success, above all success in war, was what the men who governed Great Britain were able to hold out as legitimisation of their rule to the millions below them'.[48] This British ideology, and theology, of violence does much to explain the traditions of Irish revolutionary violence: it explains the extraordinary importance attached by Irish tradition to the Battle of Fontenoy in 1745, when the six Irish regiments in the service of France drove back the English Brigade of Guards, to create a French victory. It is not simply a matter of romantic perceptions of the 'Wild Geese'. When battle was engaged on equal terms the wishes of 'Providence' could be renegotiated.[49]

For strategic reasons England could not allow the smaller island at its back to go its own way. The fear that a foreign power might use Ireland as a base was confirmed by the landing of a Spanish army in Ireland to support the insurgent Irish in 1601, and of French armies in 1690, 1691, 1715 and 1798. There were, as well, unsuccessful attempts to land armies in Ireland, and displaced Irish élites were involved in other attacks upon the English empire.

These strategic observations are commonplaces, perhaps, but they need to be spelt out, partly because they are so rarely spelt out. They are spelt out, however, in the memorandums submitted in the 1740s to the Comte d'Argenson, King Louis XV's Minister of War, and to the Duc de Richelieu, by Pierre André O'Heguerty.[50] It was these strategic considerations that logically led O'Heguerty, Antoine Walsh and the other (*émigré* Irish or of Irish heritage) shipowners and merchants of Nantes and St Malo, to finance the invasion of Scotland in 1745 by Charles Edward Stuart, 'Bonnie Prince Charlie' of Scottish legend.[51] There was significant Irish involvement in the actual invasion force: of the seven leaders, 'the Seven Men of Moidart', two were Scottish, one was English and four were Irish. One of the Irishmen was, of course, John O'Sullivan, the Prince's tutor.[52]

In Scotland, Prince Charles gathered a Scottish army and marched south, into England. The hoped-for English rising to support his cause did not materialize, though we are told that, as his army paused in Manchester, in the north of England, it was joined by disaffected apprentices and by the Irish who lived in Manchester.[53] Prince Charles's impetus faltered in Derby, in the English Midlands, when it became clear that there would be no matching French invasion on the south coast. Then began the retreat to Scotland and destruction. Irish volunteers, the victors of Fontenoy, sailed north from France, to arrive in time to suffer the disaster of Culloden.

This Irish-financed, Irish-supported adventure of Prince Charles Stuart in 1745 is one of Linda Colley's starting-points. The Stuart invasion tested the newly forged 'Britons' and their nation. Why did England and lowland Scotland not rise to support the Stuart claims? Her answer is 'the centrality of trade in the British economy': 'large numbers of men from commercial as well as landed backgrounds took an active part in raising money and in taking arms on behalf of the existing order', the Hanoverian dynasty. The vast majority of people did nothing. Thus, 'deprived both of widespread domestic support and of substantial foreign aid, the Jacobites were defeated long before Culloden. Defeated not because their own supporters looked to the past, but rather because so many Britons had too much to lose in the present.'[54]

Fatal shores

This then was the 'Britain' that in 1787, in one of the most extraordinary events in history, sent the First Fleet to Australia, to turn a continent into a prison hulk. If the convict fleets transported England, and Britain, in miniature to Australia, they also transported English/Irish conflicts, most evidently after the Irish rebellion of 1798. In our first chapter Anne-Maree Whitaker explores the Irish Catholic dimension of the penal colony by focusing on the experiences of the convict priests, caught up in the mass arrests after 1798, and transported to the British Gulag.[55] These priests, true to their calling in terrifying circumstances, shaped the founding myths of Australian Catholicism: the story of the little ark, made by Irish Catholics to house and hide the host, is recounted in the stained glass of Sydney's Catholic cathedral.[56]

Whitaker's account of the visit of a French ship to the penal colony makes visible one of the contradictions within Irish Catholicism. The experiences of the convict priests encapsulate Irish Catholicism's vision of itself. Yet, outside Britain, Irish Catholics are members of what is most probably the largest organization in the world, the Catholic Church, and are associated with what is most probably the oldest formal organization in the world, the papacy. Throughout Western Europe, and throughout the colonies and former colonies of the Catholic powers, Catholicism is associated with rank, riches and privilege.[57]

The fear of Catholic power, as we have seen at the heart of an embattled British Protestant identity, is constantly in the background in our next chapter, James White McAuley's exploration of the emigration experiences of the Protestant peoples of Ireland and of the place of migration in the creation of Irish Protestant identities. Protestant experiences have already figured largely throughout *The Irish World Wide*, with specific chapters and acknowledgement throughout of Protestant participation in the worldwide Irish emprise.[58] As McAuley reports, those experiences remain underresearched, particularly in recent years.[59]

In the General Introduction to *The Irish World Wide* I promised opportunities to study readily available texts from an Irish Migration Studies perspective. Three chapters now look at three different arts of the word, linking with our media studies volume, Volume 3, *The Creative Migrant*, and chapters in Volume 6, *The Meaning of the Famine*. And what texts could be more readily available than the songs and hymns we carry in our own heads, Margaret Mitchell's *Gone with the Wind*, and Synge's *The Playboy of the Western World*?

The paradoxical title of Leon Litvak's chapter stresses the theology of song, making us all look again at our repertoire: sing with understanding.

I will highlight two of Litvack's observation. Irish Protestant songs and hymns draw on the shared British repertoire, and the British repertoire, of course, ignores what McAuley has shown to be a central part of Irish Protestant experience, emigration. And look at that wonderful starting-point for a discussion of similarities and differences: Faber's two versions of 'Faith of our Fathers', one for Ireland and one for England.

Through James P. Cantrell's intriguing chapter we highlight a tangled knot within Irish-American historiography: as Fallows and Akenson have both pointed out, the majority of people of Irish heritage in the United States are Protestant.[60] Further, David Noel Doyle has observed that there are too many Irish Protestants in the United States to be explained by differential immigration patterns. Akenson and Doyle suggest that, at some date, numbers of Irish Catholics changed their religion.[61] The discovery of this 'apostasy' may offend some sensibilities: it certainly embarrassed its first discoverer, that neglected figure in Irish-American historiography, Michael J. O'Brien, writing in 1919.[62]

Cantrell's end is his beginning: the apparent anomaly that the heroine of the epic of the American Civil War, the personification of the 'Protestant South', should be an Irish-American Catholic called 'Scarlett O'Hara'. The Irish elements of Margaret Mitchell's epic novel are evident: the O'Hara family name, the house called 'Tara'. Other Irish themes are present, not least, perhaps, the experience of hunger and Scarlett's curse or prayer, that she and her kin will never go hungry again. It has been suggested that Mitchell's title, *Gone with the Wind*, has Irish resonances.[63] Yet the Irish of the American South have somehow been invisible to our research: this is a problem for Irish-American historiography, for the gap in the research has distorted the synthesis. Here, in order to engage with the novels of Mitchell and Ellen Glasgow, Cantrell must first, bravely, engage with the distorted historiography, before offering a moral engagement with the world of the novels.

Paula M. Kane reveals the international dimensions of the *Playboy* debate, and the *Playboy* riots. Again, the theology is made plain: the confusion of nationalist sensibility and Catholic theology is explored in ways unavailable to an Ireland-centred study of the *Playboy* controversy. Kane shows us that it is part of the long debate within society and within theology about the role of the artist.[64]

Donald Akenson was right to direct our attention back to Gerard Connolly's essay, 'Irish and Catholic: myth or reality?': 'it opens the possibility that there is an Irish ethnic identity that is not tied to religion, but is something different, deeper.'[65] Now, in a juxtaposition that challenges monolithic views of the neighbouring island, three linked but different studies of the Irish within the three countries of Ireland's sister island raise questions about 'identity'. Thus Welsh and Scottish national identities are themselves under siege: and there is the fear in Wales and Scotland that every person of Irish heritage who asserts that heritage effectively dilutes the Welsh or Scottish identity.

Bernard Aspinwall, in a wide-ranging study of Irish Catholicism in

Scotland, shows how Catholicism, at first a marker of Irish difference, became a vehicle for assimilation. Paul O'Leary approaches the question of an Irish identity in nineteenth-century Wales by imaginatively studying the survival of Irish folk and customary practices, practices which organized religion would stamp out. His chapter links with recent developments in the sociology of memory and the sociology of religion.[66] Aspinwall's theme is reprised by Mary Hickman in her closely argued chapter. If, as is often suggested, the great achievement of the Irish Catholic diaspora is the creation of separate Catholic schools throughout the English-speaking world, Mary Hickman shows that it was an achievement with a price. In the end we find ourselves comparing the massive resources that went into keeping the Irish Catholics Catholic with the puny resources that went into keeping them Irish.

Mission statements

'Missionaries are people committed to the notion of the portability of religion.'[67] Is there some way of exploring connections between religious identities within Ireland and missionary activity outside Ireland? Two recent books, Edmund M. Hogan, *The Irish Missionary Movement*, and Norman W. Taggart, *The Irish in World Methodism*, seem to address that theme.[68] Such books turn into a consistent narrative the many Irish works of biography, or hagiography, the published lives of Weber's religious virtuosi, of which perhaps the ideal type is Jordan's life of 'Bishop Shanahan of Nigeria'.[69] But such books have become increasingly problematic, not so much for what they say as for what they do not say. One reviewer of Hogan's book was simply puzzled by these absences, and mapped out a completely different approach to the subject matter:

> My own starting point would be to consider the changing supply of missionaries — clerical, paraclerical ('religious' in Roman Catholic parlance) and lay — within the context of the professions more generally. I am inclined to view the substantial population of overseas evangelistic missionaries which existed earlier this century as a clergy surplus exported from Europe and North America to the rest of the world. For reasons why there was such a surplus, I would look into changing patterns of career opportunities for middle-class men and women both in the religious sphere and elsewhere.[70]

The notion of a 'clergy surplus' has the merit of placing Irish missionary activity within the patterns of Irish migration noted elsewhere in *The Irish World Wide*.[71] The notion also links with the wider discussion of the Irish as the 'ideal colaborators' within the expanding nineteenth-century British Empire in Akenson's *Irish Diaspora*.[72] Yet these aspects of the missionary enterprise are rarely discussed within Irish writing, nor is the concomitant effect on non-European ethnic groups. It might be thought that a nation, part of whose nation-building myth involves criticism of an invader who vilified Irish religion and culture, would at least think twice about so

happily doing precisely that to other threatened peoples. The only place in
Irish writing where I am sure I have identified a critique of Irish missionary activity is in Brian Friel's *Dancing at Lughnasa*, and there it is given to
us with dramatist's ambivalence.[73] This is clearly an area where the sensitivity of the subject matter creates gaps in the literature. Our last two contributors bring us perceptions from outside Ireland. They are certainly
aware of these world-wide debates, though the main focus of their chapters is on the ways that an Irish Catholic identity is created and maintained,
inside Ireland and outside Ireland, through the religious orders.

The influence of the Society of Jesus on the intellectual life of Catholic
Ireland has been overestimated: partly because the Jesuits were the educators of the Irish Catholic middle class, and partly because of the myth-
shaping genius of James Joyce.[74] But it is the Irish Christian Brothers who
have been, for two centuries, the major influence on Irish Catholic boys and
men. A book by our next contributor, Barry Coldrey, has mapped the complexities of the relationship between the Irish Christian Brothers and the
class (in every sense) that shaped the war of 1918–22.[75] And the influence
of the Christian Brothers has been explored, with appropriate ambivalence,
in Cathal Black's disturbing documentary film, *Our Boys*, whose main
theme is the link between violence and education.[76] Barry Coldrey, as the
historian of his order, acknowledges that there is a problem to be
addressed here, and it is a problem that spans the two centuries, and the
cultural and social changes seen in that time.

> It is scarcely surprising that the pioneers of Irish women's history have concen-
> trated on women acting together, in contexts where men appear as either adver-
> saries or outsiders. The experience of the nun, the prostitute, the servant, the
> suffragist ... was moulded by attachment to social groups or organisations par-
> ticular to women.[77]

The study of nuns has loomed large in Irish women's history: for here are
readily identifiable groups of active women, educated, creating archives
for the potential researcher.[78] Some thinkers within feminism are troubled
by this, seeing in organized religion just another form of patriarchy. But
there are inherent instabilities in this form of patriarchy. Catherine of Siena
could order the Pope to leave Avignon and return to Rome and, however
we may analyse the real politics of that decision, the woman's holiness was
part of the equation. Acknowledged holiness brings power. At the other
extreme we can cite the young woman whose behaviour is dismissed by
her family as 'incorrigibly pious'.[79]

Through women's religious orders traditional Irish Catholic culture
allows to some women a role, and a career structure, outside the family
and outside marriage. Male hierarchies are uneasy about this, and in the
histories of the women's religious orders we see a negotiation between the
needs of the work, the needs of women coming together to accomplish the
work, and structures acceptable to the hierarchy. The quandaries of
Catherine McAuley, ultimately the founder of the Sisters of Mercy, have

been chronicled, as have those of her Archbishop, Murray of Dublin: 'I did not think that founding a new order was part of your plan ... really, Miss McAuley, I had no idea that a new congregation would start up in this manner.' Yet McAuley, too, was doubtful that what she really wanted to do was found yet another women's order.[80]

In my General Introduction I said that, again and again, our research takes us to graves, to stones bearing Irish family names, there to pay our respects. Our last chapter by Sister Janice Tranter, recounts the origins of her order, the Sisters of St Joseph, the order's links with Irish Catholic families and its place in the development of Irish-Australian Catholicism. And the chapter leads us to a grave.

On 21 May 1991 armed guerillas of the Sendero Luminoso, Maoist/ Marxist revolutionaries, took over the town of Huasahuasi, in the Andes Mountains of Peru. Five people, four men and one woman, were taken from their homes and brought to the central square. The four men held minor civic positions. The woman was Sister Irene McCormack, Sister of Saint Joseph, an Australian of Irish heritage, a missionary. The five captives were shouted at and interrogated. At last they were made to lie face down on the tiles of the square, and each was shot in the back of the head. Some reports say that the executioners were very young, 15 or 16 years old, and that the killer of Sister Irene was a young girl.[81]

If, as we approach the end of our terrible century, we need a structure for study or meditation (the exercises are similar), we could, every now and then, put aside two hours, which is the time Sister Irene McCormack waited in the square for her death. And we could try to understand the forces that brought Irene McCormack to Peru, and the forces of logic and eschatology that led a child to believe that it was a reasonable and a right thing to do, to kill a 52-year-old woman.

Patrick O'Sullivan
Bradford
August 1995

Notes

1. P. E. H. Hair, 'An Irishman before the Mexican Inquisition, 1574–5', *Irish Historical Studies*, Vol. XVII, No. 67 (March 1971). Hair's essay brings to mind Emmanuel Le Roy Ladurie, *Montaillou*, translated by Bray, Penguin, Harmondsworth, 1980, where again the meticulous records of the Inquisition tell of lives otherwise hidden from history. John Martin appears briefly in David B. Quinn, *Ireland and America: Their Early Associations, 1500–1640*, Liverpool University Press, Liverpool, 1991, and Rayner Unwin, *The Defeat of John Hawkins: a Biography of His Third Slaving Voyage*, Allen and Unwin, London, 1960. Unwin's book puts the events in their English context, looking forward (p. 229) to Hawkins's and Drake's battles with the Spanish Armada of 1588.
2. Unwin (p. 265) suggests that the Spanish Viceroy, who is known to have opposed the extension of the Inquisition to Mexico, may have deliberately

directed the Inquisitor-General's attention towards the English prisoners, and away from his own people.

3. The *sambenito*, or *sanbenito*, was a yellow penitential garment, so called ironically because it resembled the habit of the monks of Saint Benedict; Henry Kamen, *The Spanish Inquisition*, Weidenfeld and Nicolson, London 1965, p. 184, derives the word from *saco bendito*.

4. Hair, p. 313.

5. Hair, p. 319.

6. Martin's answers are of interest to the historian of religion within Ireland. Prompted by the Inquisitors, he recalls the country people making their way through snow to confession and communion on Holy Friday and he sees the destruction of the monasteries as a cause of Irish hatred of the reformed religion (Hair, p. 318).

7. Hair, p. 318.

8. Hair, p. 318; the demonising of the Spanish Inquisition has been so thorough — especially within English popular novels of the nineteenth century — that it is wise to read Henry Kamen as a corrective. As we saw in Martin J. Counihan, 'Ireland and the scientific tradition', in Patrick O'Sullivan, ed., *The Creative Migrant*, Volume 3 of *The Irish World Wide*, p. 29, the Galileo affair and 'the conflict thesis' are usually seen as the starting point for discussion of faith and reason. Andrew M. Greeley, *The Persistence of Religion*, SCM Press, London, 1973, reflecting on Galileo, and the problems of communicating with Inquisitors, observes, p. 246: 'One cannot, of course, be too harsh in criticizing the theories of the churchmen of the past.' *Eppure ci muoviamo*.

9. E. Thomas Lawson and Robert N. McCauley, *Rethinking Religion: Connecting Cognition and Culture*, Cambridge University Press, Cambridge, 1990, p. 1, speak of their 'frustration with the timidity that characterizes so many scholars' discussions of religious behaviour and the contempt which characterizes many of the rest ... Both approaches are obscurantist, ultimately — the first because of its terror of theory and the second because of its restrictive view of theory.'

10. John Kent, *The Unacceptable Face: the Modern Church in the Eyes of the Historian*, SCM Press, London, 1987, p. 12.

11. Kent, *Unacceptable Face*, p. 4. Kent's observations here obviously link with the discussion of Weber and of missionary endeavour later in this Introduction.

12. I anticipate the discussion in *The Meaning of the Famine*, Volume 6 of *The Irish World Wide*. But see Peter Gray, 'Potatoes and providence: British Government's responses to the Great Famine', *Bullán*, Vol. 1, No. 1, (Spring 1994). It is not, of course, only Christians who attempt deductions from 'the broad sweep of events': thus many commentators draw attention to the eschatology of Karl Marx (see, for example, Nicholas Lash, *A Matter of Hope: a Theologian's Reflections on the Thought of Karl Marx*, Darton Longman & Todd, London, 1981, Chapter 18, especially pp. 253–5).

13. This 'suggestive term' Peter L. Berger ascribes to his former pupil, Anton C. Zijderveld: see Peter L. Berger, *The Social Reality of Religion*, Penguin, Harmondsworth, 1973, pp. 106 and 207, and the discussion under Appendix II, p. 181 onwards. See also the discussion in Robert Towler, *Homo Religiosus: Sociological Problems in the Study of Religion*, Constable, London, 1974, p. 2.

14. This, the most cited, miscited and wrongly attributed, summing-up of the endeavour that is sociology first appeared in the last chapter of W. I. Thomas and Dorothy S. Thomas, *The Child in America: Behavior Problems and Programs*, Alfred A. Knopf, New York, 1928, p. 572. It is sometimes attributed to Florian

Znaniecki, W. I. Thomas's co-worker on *The Polish Peasant* project, or to other W. I. Thomas associates and followers. See the discussion in Edmund H. Volkart (ed), *Social Behaviour and Personality: Contributions of W. I. Thomas to Theory and Social Research*, Social Science Research Council, New York, 1951, p. 14 and p. 81. For the influence of Thomas and Znaniecki on Irish Migration Studies, see Patrick O'Sullivan, 'Introduction: the Irish in the New Communities', in, *The Irish in the New Communities*, Volume 2 of *The Irish World Wide*, p. 8.

15. See Paul Badham, 'The contribution of religion to the conflict in Northern Ireland', in Dan Cohn-Sherbok (ed.), *The Canterbury Papers: Essays in Religion and Society*, Bellew, London, 1990, and see the works of Steve Bruce, for example, *The Edge of the Union: the Ulster Loyalist Political Vision*, Oxford University Press, Oxford, 1994, p. 28 and pp. 133–4.

16. Peter L. Berger, *A Rumour of Angels: Modern Society and the Rediscovery of the Supernatural*, Penguin, Harmondsworth, 1971 (original edn. 1969), pp. 10–11. This is not to say that because a problem can be defined and understood theologically it necessary has a theological solution. But we should, in the best practice, be aware of the theology.

17. Duly enshrined by Raymond Aron, *Main Currents in Sociological Thought*, 2 vols, translated by Howard and Weaver, Penguin, Harmondsworth, 1970 (Weber is discussed in Vol. 2), and by Anthony Giddens, *Capitalism and Modern Social Theory: an Analysis of the Writings of Marx, Durkheim and Max Weber*, Cambridge University Press, Cambridge, 1971.

18. I am thinking of the concepts of the 'religious virtuoso', who displays 'charisma' (a notion borrowed from theology), and of the power of bureaucracy, whose 'ideal type' is sometimes seen in the religious order. Michael Hill, *The Religious Order: a Study of Virtuoso Religion and its Legitimation in the Nineteenth Century Church of England*, Heinemann, London, 1973, remains a helpful introduction, and an application of these ideas.

19. Our source in English for this Weber thesis is the series of essays published as Max Weber, *The Protestant Ethic and the Spirit of Capitalism* translated by Talcott Parsons, Unwin, London, 1930. This text has been reprinted often, sometimes with a change of publisher name. The 1930 and subsequent Unwin editions have a 'Foreword' by R. H. Tawney; the 1976 and subsequent George Allen & Unwin editions have an 'Introduction' by Anthony Giddens. The New York publisher is Scribner. Tawney's 'Foreword' can also be found as 'Max Weber and the spirit of Capitalism', in J. M. Winter (ed.), *History and Society: Essays by R. H. Tawney*, Routledge & Kegan Paul, London, 1978.

20. Tawney, 'Foreword' to Weber, *Protestant Ethic*, p. 1(c).

21. Aron, pp. 222–3.

22. For example, American specialists will be aware of a Weber-influenced approach to the early history of the English colonies which were to form the United States of America, an approach made visible most recently in Stephen Innes, *Creating the Commonwealth: the Economic Culture of Puritan New England*, Norton, New York and London, 1995.

23. Giddens, 'Introduction' to Weber, *Protestant Ethic*, 1976, p. 12: the elements of Weber's analysis that Giddens feels are most called into question are the distinctiveness of the notion of 'calling' in Lutheranism, the supposed lack of 'affinity' between Catholicism and entrepreneurial activity, and the degree to which Calvinist ethics actually dignify the accumulation of wealth in the manner suggested by Weber.

24. See the title essay in H. R. Trevor-Roper, *Religion, the Reformation and Social*

Change, and Other Essays, Macmillan, London, 1967, p. 22: 'today few scholars believe in this sudden sixteenth-century break-through of industrial capitalism. We know too much about medieval Italian and Flemish capitalism.' Trevor-Roper suggests that many Protestants were migrants, forced to emigrate by the excesses of the Counter-Reformation, but sees this as one more example of the links between migration and entrepreneurship. There are obvious ways of integrating Trevor-Roper's thesis with wider migration theory. Trevor-Roper tells us (p. x) that this essay was first presented at a conference in Galway, where it was not well received by 'an audience powerfully reinforced by local monks and nuns': the essay first appeared in print in G. A. Hayes-McCoy, *Historical Studies IV: Papers Read Before the Fifth Irish Conference of Historians*, Bowes & Bowes, Dublin, 1963.

Braudel confesses himself 'allergic' to the Weber thesis: 'There are more things in the world than the Protestant ethic.' Fernand Braudel, *Civilisation and Capitalism, 15th–18th Century, Vol. 2, The Wheels of Commerce*, translated by Reynolds, Fontana, London, 1985, pp. 569, 570.

25. Some commentators explicitly quarrel with this approach: see Gordon Marshall, *In Search of the Spirit of Capitalism: an Essay on Max Weber's Protestant Ethic Thesis*, Hutchinson, London, 1982: Marshall's book remains a readable introduction to the complexities of the 'Protestant ethic' debate. See also Gianfranco Poggi, *Calvinism and the Capitalist Spirit: Max Weber's Protestant Ethic*, Macmillan, London, 1983.

But mentioning Marx allows us to make connections within intellectual history: for Marx, in his turn, is often seen, in his English context, with his base in London, as wishing to develop a theory that eliminated considerations of *population* from factors important in the development of history and culture, thus reacting against Malthus, and the Malthus-influenced British approach to social and class issues. And Malthus originally developed his ideas in reaction to the benign Utopianism of Godwin and Condorcet. See Marvin Harris, *Cultural Materialism*, Random House, New York, 1979, p. 70.

26. R. H. Tawney, *Religion and the Rise of Capitalism*, John Murray, London, 1926, and many times reprinted. Tawney cautiously acknowledges Weber's thesis, p. 212, and comments: 'In every human soul there is a socialist and an individualist, an authoritarian and a fanatic for liberty, as in each there is a Catholic and a Protestant.' The detailed arguments against Weber's thesis are marshalled in a long note on pp. 319–21. Tawney was here writing before the appearance of the Parsons translation of the Weber essays.

27. Tawney's 'Foreword' to Weber, *Protestant Ethic*, p. 10, concludes that Weber's conclusions 'are susceptible ... of more than one interpretation'. A later Tawney essay, 'The study of economic history' observes that 'the brilliant work of Max Weber, at any rate in the essays by which it is most widely known in England, sought in the region of ideas and psychology an interpretation of movements susceptible of simpler explanations.' See Winter (ed.), *History and Society*, p. 59.

28. Marshall, *Spirit of Capitalism* p. 202. Marshall, however, thinks that Tawney's 'changing position with respect to Weber's original argument is reducible, in the final result, to an almost identical stance'. The phrase 'acquisitive society' refers to another work by R. H. Tawney, *The Acquisitive Society*, Bell & Sons, London, 1921, and many times reprinted.

29. Roger Aubert *et al.*, *The Church in a Secularised Society*, Paulist Press, New York/Darton, Longman & Todd, London, 1978, is the title of Volume 5 of *The Christian Centuries* and covers the same period as Volume 5 of *The Irish World Wide*.

30. Weber, *Protestant Ethic*, p. 82. The clarifying Note 13, p. 213, continues: 'Cromwell, with the deepest personal conviction ... bases the moral justification of the subjection of the Irish, in calling God to witness, on the fact that English capital has taught the Irish to work.'

31. Donald Harman Akenson, *Small Differences: Irish Catholics and Irish Protestants 1815–1922*, McGill-Queen's University Press, Montreal/Gill & Macmillan, Dublin, 1988, p. 23. See also Akenson, 'The Irish in the United States', in Patrick O'Sullivan (ed.), *The Irish in the New Communities*, and Akenson, *The Irish Diaspora: a Primer*, P. D. Meany, Toronto/Institute of Irish Studies, Belfast, 1993. Though I disagree with Akenson in matters of detail and interpretation his works remain the indispensible starting-point for an exploration of these issues within Irish Migration Studies.

32. I can find little in the sociological literature that even acknowledges the existence of the penal codes.

33. 'Models for viewing American Catholicism' is Chapter 1 of Andrew M. Greeley, *The American Catholic: a Social Portrait*, Basic Books, New York, 1977. For Greeley's irritation see, for example, his Note, pp. 51–2.

34. Akenson, *Irish Diaspora*, p. 34; Akenson, *Small Differences*, pp. 48–50.

35. Matters are not helped when a simplistic, bar-room version of Weber's thesis seeps into academic discourse. Poggi is scathing about 'excessively abbreviated renderings, in the secondary literature' (p. X) and gives a glaring example from an essay on management theory (p. 114). 'Although few evangelicals will have read the German sociologist Max Weber's essay on "The Protestant Ethic and the Spirit of Capitalism", many have absorbed a popularized version of the thesis that reformed religion had the secondary consequence of promoting a "this-worldly" asceticism ... At the height of the Protestant crusades of the nineteenth century this claimed link between religion and civic virtue was developed into a vicious parody of the diligent, temperate, and honest Protestant and the gin-soaked, gambling, feckless Catholic.' Steve Bruce, *The Edge of the Union*, p. 60.

36. Akenson, *Small Differences*, p. 17. See also the conclusion of Marshall, *Spirit of Capitalism*, especially pp. 172–3.

37. Greeley, *American Catholic*, p. 66.

38. Marjorie R. Fallows, *Irish Americans: Identity and Assimilation*, Prentice-Hall, Englewood Cliffs, 1979, p. 68. It could be argued that all this gives a theological spin to the Irish migrant obsession with economic success, and that fascination with Irish millionaires: the theology is Protestant, not Catholic.

39. See the discussion in Fallows, *Irish Americans*, Chapter 5, 'Status and social mobility', pp. 60–80; Akenson, 'The Irish in the United States', p. 120.

40. Joel Mokyr, *Why Ireland Starved: a Quantitative and Analytical History of the Irish Economy. 1800–1850*, George Allen & Unwin, London, 1983, p. 234: Mokyr finds little evidence to support the hypothesis that Ireland lost its entrepreneurs through emigration. Earlier (p. 218 onwards) Mokyr discusses the postulate of the 'Protestant work ethic', without mentioning Weber, and is not particularly impressed by its application to Ireland.

41. Henning Graf Reventlow, *The Authority of the Bible and the Rise of the Modern World*, translated by John Bowden, SCM Press, London, 1984, pp. 93–4.

42. Tawney, 'Foreword' to Weber, p. 1(E).

43. I am grateful to Leo Gooch for help in thinking through this part of the Introduction. Leo Gooch, 'The Durham Catholics and Industrial Development, 1560–1850', MA thesis, University of York, 1984, is a study of English Catholic families active in coal-mining in the north-east of England, and concludes

(p. 104): 'whilst the nature of Catholic belief had no bearing on economic practice membership of the Catholic Church had. The thesis that the Catholics were disinclined to take up profit-making activities takes no account of the legal position which reduced Catholics to an economic condition that prevented them from being entrepreneurial. It cannot be argued that a Catholic is less success-ful in business than a Protestant if either is excluded from the competition.'

On the penal code in Ireland, Akenson, *Small Differences*, pp. 22–3, observes: 'the Irish penal code is one of the most puzzling problems in Irish history and, considering its importance, one which is remarkably little studied ... it is not clear what was the motivation behind its imposition.' W. N. Osborough, 'Catholics, land and the Popery Acts of Anne', in T. P. Power and Kevin Whelan (eds), *Endurance and Emergence, Catholics in Ireland in the Eighteenth Century*, Irish Academic Press Dublin, 1990, is helpful but remains puzzled by some aspects of the code (p. 22). Would it help if we read the code theologically? — the code nudges the hand of Providence.

44. In 1885 Alexander Mackay thus apostrophized 'Romanism': 'what is Italy today but what thy corrupt teaching for centuries has made it? What is Spain? What is Ireland? Even in Malta thy vileness is everywhere conspicuous. Beggary, ignorance, blackguardism, crime — these are the characteristic marks, with filth and poverty, too.' Mackay, the Scottish Calvinist representative of the Church Missionary Society, was then on his way to Buganda, to his part in the creation of a four-sided civil war between pagan traditionalists, Muslims, the Wa-Fransa (Catholic supporters of the French missionaries) and the Wa-Ingleza (Protestant supporters of the British). See Thomas Pakenham, *The Scramble for Africa, 1876–1912*, Abacus, London, 1992, p. 301 and p. 415. See also Geoffrey Moorhouse, *The Missionaries*, Eyre Methuen, London, 1973, Chapter 13.

45. Linda Colley, *Britons: Forging the Nation, 1707–1837*, Pimlico, London, 1994, p. 8 (original edition Yale University Press, 1992).

46. James Loughlin, reviewing Colley, *Britons*, in *Fortnight* (July/August, 1993), p. 50.

47. Colley, p. 5. When 'Britishness' is defined as not-Catholic and not-French how then will 'Irishness' be defined?

48. Colley, p. 52.

49. For the 'Wild Geese' see the chapters by McGurk, in *Patterns of Migration*, and by Henry, in *Irish Women and Irish Migration*, Volumes 1 and 4 of *The Irish World Wide*.

50. F. J. McLynn, *France and the Jacobite Rising of 1745*, Edinburgh University Press, Edinburgh, 1981, pp. 82–3. As McLynn records, O'Heguerty tries to separate out specific Irish interests from more general Stuart, Jacobite and 'British' inter-ests: urging a French invasion of Ireland, O'Heguerty can foresee a time when King Louis XV steps forward as the protector of Ireland against a restored, England-oriented Stuart monarchy.

51. As a note to the discussion of the Weber thesis, it was, of course, the entrepre-neurial activity of these migrant Irish Catholics that created the financial base from which they could support the Stuart cause.

52. 'John O'Sullivan, an Irish officer in the French service, bluff and heavily built, an incompetent mediocrity with a convincing line of blarney which made his limited military experience and capabilities seem more impressive than they really were.' Ian and Kathleen Whyte, *On The Trail of the Jacobites*, Routledge, London, 1990, p. 137. O'Sullivan's own account of the expedition and the rescue of Prince Charles has been published as Alistair Tayler and Henrietta Tayler,

1745 and After, Thomas Nelson & Sons, London, 1938.

In 1995, the year of commemoration of 1745 in England and Scotland, this Irish migrant dimension has largely been ignored, no doubt overshadowed in Ireland by commemoration of 1845. 'The fact remains that the Irish on the Continent were not a separate race, but a part of the Irish people and Irish history; they are, to reiterate, the missing dimension in that history.' William D. Griffin, 'The Irish on the Continent in the eighteenth century', *Studies in Eighteenth Century Culture*, Vol. 5 (1976), p. 468.

53. Colley, *Britons*, p. 82.
54. Colley, *Britons*, pp. 84–5. McLynn, p. 11, makes a similar point. Note that O'Heguerty thought that British interference with the Irish wool trade would cause Irish Protestants to make common cause with Irish Catholics, if the French invaded Ireland (McLynn, p. 83).
55. Robert Hughes, *The Fatal Shore: a History of the Transportation of Convicts to Australia, 1787–1868*, Collins Harvill, London, 1987, p. 2, makes the comparison with the prison system of the Soviet Union, and later (p. 181) speaks of Australia as 'the official Siberia for Irish dissidents'.
56. To give a flavour of the conversations that have shaped this series, we can look at the legend that Father Harold sang 'The Exile of Erin' on the beach at Sydney. Many scholars accept the legend: for example, Philip Butterss, ' "Convicted by the laws of England's hostile crown": popular convict verse', in Oliver MacDonagh and W. F. Mandle (eds), *Irish Australian Studies: Papers delivered at the Fifth Irish-Australian Conference*, Australian National University, Canberra, 1989, p. 15, citing Patrick O'Farrell, *The Irish in Australia*, and Bob Reece, 'Introduction', in Bob Reece, *Exiles from Erin: Convict Lives in Ireland and Australia*, Macmillan, London, 1991, p. 8, citing H. Perkins, *The Convict Priests*. The original source for the story is a memoir written for R. R. Madden in the 1840s by Richard Sheil, who had known Harold: Madden was then collecting material for his *The United Irishmen, their Lives and Times*.

The suggestion is that the song Harold sang was 'The Exile of Erin' by the Scottish poet Thomas Campbell. The origins of that song are well known (see Mary Ruth Miller, *Thomas Campbell*, Twayne Publishers, Boston, 1978, p. 111). Campbell wrote the song after meeting the United Irishman refugee, Anthony MacCann, in Germany in 1800: Campbell sent his five stanzas back to England, and the song appeared in the *Morning Chronicle* on 28 January 1801, with a preface urging mercy for such men. The historian of literature must therefore express mild surprise to hear that Harold sang the song in Australia in January 1800.

But this song, by a Scottish poet, is important in the history of Irish migration, for, more than any other single influence, Campbell's song, 'The Exile of Erin', shaped the nineteenth-century Irish discourse of emigration as 'exile'. The United Irishmen refugees were, indeed, political exiles, and the song, the theme of 'exile' and the plea for mercy formed a complete political package. Sheil's recollections of Harold are part of that package, and the first line of the song seems to picture Harold's predicament: 'There came to the beach a poor exile of Erin.' Thereafter the lyric's imprecision allows indefinite expansion of the 'exile' theme. Campbell's song still appears regularly in Irish song anthologies: see, for example, *Walton's New Treasury of Irish Songs and Ballads, Part 2*, Walton's Musical Instrumental Galleries, Dublin, 1966, pp. 104–5.

57. Dennis J. Clark, 'The Irish Catholics: a postponed perspective', in Randall M. Miller and Thomas D. Marzik, *Immigrants and Religion in Urban America*, Temple

University Press, Philadelphia, 1977, p. 49, draws attention to this contrast, as a starting-point for the study of United States Catholic experience.

58. I think, for example, of chapters by Forth in O'Sullivan (ed.), *The Irish in the New Communities*, or the studies of Irish women by Letford and Pooley and by Mary Kells in O'Sullivan (ed.), *Irish Women and Irish Migration*.

59. As McAuley reminds us there is the very readable general introduction in Rory Fitzpatrick, *God's Frontiersmen: the Scots-Irish Epic*, Weidenfeld and Nicolson, London, 1989. See also, Jack White, *Minority Report: the Protestant Community in the Irish Republic*, Gill and Macmillan, Dublin 1975, and Kurt Bowen, *Protestants in a Catholic State: Ireland's Privileged Minority*, McGill-Queen's University Press, Kingston and Montreal, 1983.

60. Fallows, pp. 63–5; Akenson, 'The Irish in the United States', pp. 99–106. For further discussion of the oft-cited figure of 40 million 'Irish–Americans' see Michael Hout and Joshua R. Goldstein, 'How 4.5 million Irish immigrants became 40 million Irish Americans: demographic and subjective aspects of the ethnic composition of white Americans', *American Sociological Review*, Vol. 59, 1994. However, Hout and Goldstein make unwarranted assumptions (Note 4, p. 66) about the routes of the Irish into the United States: see Akenson, *Irish Diaspora*, p. 230.

61. Akenson, *Irish Diaspora*, p. 245; David Noel Doyle, 'Catholicism, politics and Irish America since 1890: some critical considerations', in P. J. Drudy, *The Irish in the United States: Emigration, Assimilation and Impact*, Cambridge University Press, Cambridge, 1985, p. 192.

62. See the discussion of Michael J. O'Brien in Akenson, *Irish Diaspora*, pp. 248–9.

63. The obvious source for Mitchell's title is a line from Stanza 3 of 'Non sum qualis eram bonae sub regno Cynarae', a poem by Ernest Dowson. But that poem, with its confused syntax, lacks the sense of elegaic loss that we read into the phrase, 'gone with the wind'. Versions of the phrase were current, and 'Gone in the Wind' is a poem, on the perennial poetic theme of transience, by the Irish poet James Clarence Mangan. Stanza 7 reads:

> Solomon! where is thy throne? It is gone in the wind.
> Babylon! where is thy might? It is gone in the wind.
> Happy in death are they only whose hearts have consigned
> All Earth's affections and longings and cares to the wind.

The editor of the first American edition of Mangan's poems was John Mitchel, the Young Irelander who was transported for treason-felony in 1848, escaped to America from Van Diemen's Land in 1853 and who supported the southern states and defended slavery as editor of the *Enquirer*, the semi-official voice of President Jefferson Davis. (Irish supporters of the Confederacy used Irish arguments about Irish home rule to defend secession.) Two of Mitchel's sons were killed fighting for the Confederacy. And John Mitchel, more than any one person, is responsible for shaping Irish ways of understanding the Famine (see the chapter by Davis in *The Meaning of the Famine*, Volume 6 of *The Irish World Wide*).

That John Mitchell found the time to publish a volume of poems by his friend Mangan demonstrates the importance he attached to Mangan's poetry and Mangan's vision: see David Lloyd, *Nationalism and Minor Literature: James Clarence Mangan and the Emergence of Irish Cultural Nationalism*, University of California Press, Berkeley, 1987, p. 32.

The 'Irishness' of the novel, *Gone with the Wind*, was strengthened in Margaret Mitchell's second draft, as she incorporated her research. The heroine had been called 'Pansy' in the first draft (unimaginable, isn't it?). 'Scarlett' is an Irish family name, and the Irish tradition of using family names as given names is long established. 'Sophronisba Scarlett' is an aged virago, dead at the beginning of a novel by another Southern woman writer of Irish heritage, Marie Conway Oemler, *A Woman Named Smith*, The Century Company, New York, 1919, p. 3. Margaret Mitchell had certainly read Oemler. And it is in another Oemler novel, the famous *Slippy McGee*, that the link is made between the vanishing of the Confederacy and that phrase from Mangan's poem. The novel begins with a meditation on the statue of the Confederate soldier upon the local monument: 'as a work of art he is almost as bad as the statues cluttering New York City. But in Appleboro folks are not critical; they see him not with the eyes of art but with the deeper vision of the heart. He stands for something that is gone on the wind.' Marie Conway Oemler, *Slippy McGee, Sometimes Known as the Butterfly Man*, The Century Company, New York, 1917, p. 5, and cited in Darden Ashbury Pyron, *Southern Daughter: The Life of Margaret Mitchell*, Oxford University Press, Oxford and New York, 1991, pp. 316–17.

64. The fact that the key figures in the Irish theatre movement were of Protestant background also lent a Protestant/Catholic dimension to the controversy. But the theological conflict is visible in the lives of creative people of Irish heritage throughout the world. See, for example, the discussion of Georgia O'Keeffe in John Dillenberger, *A Theology of Artistic Sensibilities: the Visual Arts and the Church*, SCM Press, London, 1986, pp. 139–42.

65. Akenson, *Irish Diaspora*, p. 214, considering Gerard Connolly, 'Irish and Catholic: myth or reality: Another sort of Irish and the renewal of the clerical profession among Catholics in England, 1791–1918', in Roger Swift and Sheridan Gilley (eds), *The Irish in the Victorian City*, Croom Helm, London, 1985.

66. See, for example Paul Connerton, *How Societies Remember*, Cambridge University Press, Cambridge, 1989, where ceremony and 'bodily practices' are seen as mnemonics, and E. Thomas Lawson and Robert N. McCauley, *Rethinking Religion*, where, with a return of the language metaphor, ritual is seen as language, and, following Chomsky, we all have competence and creativity within our ritual system (p. 175). Thus they report that their students, Protestant and Catholic, have no problems in creating a ritual for divorce.

67. Ingla Clendinnen, 'Franciscan missionaries in sixteenth-century Mexico', in Jim Obelkevich, Lyndal Roper and Raphael Samuel (eds), *Disciplines of Faith: Studies in Religion, Politics and Patriarchy*, Routledge & Kegan Paul, London, 1987, p. 229.

68. Edmund M. Hogan, *The Irish Missionary Movement: a Historical Survey, 1830–1980*, Gill & Macmillan, Dublin, 1990; Norman W. Taggart, *The Irish in World Methodism, 1760—1900*, Epworth Press, London, 1986. This literature fits into the pattern of oppression/compensation/contribution outlined in my General Introduction. For a wider approach to the issues see Julian Pettifer and Richard Bradley, *Missionaries*, BBC, London, 1990, and Geoffrey Moorhouse, *The Missionaries*, Eyre Methuen, London, 1973.

69. John P. Jordan, *Bishop Shanahan of Southern Nigeria*, Clonmore & Reynolds, Dublin, 1949. See also, P. B. Clarke, 'The methods and ideology of the Holy Ghost Fathers in Eastern Nigeria, 1885–1905', in O. U. Kalu, *The History of Christianity in West Africa*, Longman, Harlow, 1980: Clarke offers a critique of Jordan, alerting us to the dangers, in this area of study, of relying on only Irish sources.

70. David W. Miller, reviewing Hogan, *Irish Missionary Movement*, in *Irish Literary*

Supplement, Vol. 10, No. 2 (Fall 1991), p. 8. Miller concludes that Hogan offers disappointing history but up-to-date theology.

71. Place these two chapters about religious orders alongside Gerard Hanlon, 'Graduate emigration: a continuation or a break with the past?', in O'Sullivan (ed.), *Patterns of Migration*. Within the patterns of migration, how precisely does an international religious organization differ from an international financial organization?

72. Akenson, *Irish Diaspora*, p. 142 onwards, where the discussion makes use of Ronald Robinson, 'Non-European foundation of European imperialism: sketch for a theory of collaboration', in Roger Owen and Bob Sutcliffe (eds), *Studies in the Theory of Imperialism*, Longman, London, 1972.

73. I am referring, of course, to the character of 'Jack' in Brian Friel, *Dancing at Lughnasa*, Faber, London, 1990.

74. If you teach on James Joyce, *Portrait of the Artist*, you teach on the Jesuits, and Jesuit presentations of Catholic theology: 'the lessons taught and standards set by the Jesuits of the Irish Province are woven warp and woof through the writings of James Augustine Joyce'. Louis McRedmond, *To the Greater Glory: a History of the Irish Jesuits*, Gill & Macmillan, Dublin, 1991, p. 240. See also the discussion, pp. 204 onwards.

75. Barry Coldrey, *Faith and Fatherland: the Irish Christian Brothers and the Development of Irish Nationalism*, Gill & Macmillan, Dublin, 1988.

76. *Our Boys*, 1981, directed by Cathal Black, written by Dermot Healy and Cathal Black, melds a dramatized narrative with interviews with former pupils of the Christian Brothers, in a disturbing mix of anger and understanding.

77. David Fitzpatrick, 'Review article: women, gender and the writing of Irish history', *Irish Historical Studies*, XXVII, No. 107 (May 1991), p. 270.

78. See Margaret MacCurtain, 'The challenge of researching Nuns' lives', in Suellen Hoy and Margaret MacCurtain (eds), *From Dublin to New Orleans: the Journey of Nora and Alice*, Attic Press, Dublin, 1994. See also Catríona Clear, 'The limits of female autonomy: nuns in nineteenth-century Ireland', in Maria Luddy and Cliona Murphy, *Women Surviving: Studies in Irish Women's History in the Nineteenth and Twentieth Centuries*, Poolbegs, Swords, 1989.

79. Gail Malmgreen, 'Domestic discords: women and the family in East Cheshire Methodism, 1750–1830', in Obelkevich, Roper and Samuel, *Disciplines of Faith*, p. 65.

80. William Breault, SJ, *The Lady from Dublin*, Quinlan Press, Boston, 1988, p. 80. Breault, p. 75, makes clear that McAuley herself was initially ambivalent about the appropriateness of the religious order as a model and structure for her work.

81. The death of Irene McCormack shocked Australia and Ireland, and in both countries there were attempts to understand the revolutionary war logic that dictated her death. David Scott Palmer (ed.), *The Shining Path of Peru*, Hurst & Company, London, 1992, is a good introduction in English to the history and ideologies of Sendero Luminoso. Deborah Poole and Gerardo Renique, 'The new chronicles of Peru: US Scholars and their "Shining Path" of peasant rebellion', *Bulletin of Latin American Research*, Vol. 10, Number 2 (1991), is a critique of the approach of researchers like David Scott Palmer.

1 The convict priests: Irish Catholicism in early colonial New South Wales

Anne-Maree Whitaker

> The number of Catholic convicts is very great in the Settlement, and these in general composed of the lowest class of the Irish nation, who are the most wild, ignorant and savage race that were ever favoured with the light of civilization, men that have been familiar with robberies, murders and every horrid crime from their infancy ... Many of the Irish convicts are well acquainted with the art of war, and all the secret intrigues that can work upon the minds of the ignorant and unwary ... All the Catholics want is some legal sanction to assemble together ... [but] so long as the Catholic religion is not tolerated, they can never meet in sufficient numbers without awakening the jealousy and suspicion of the Government. (Revd. Samuel Marsden, Anglican Chaplain to the Colony of New South Wales, 1807)[1]

Following the loss of the American colonies, the British founded New South Wales in 1788 to provide an alternative place of banishment to clear the overcrowded gaols and hulks (prison ships). Although the first convicts were culled from English gaols, there were Irish amongst them as evidenced by names such as Francis Carty, Patrick Delany, Redmond McGrath and Cornelius Teague. Before the sailing of the First Fleet a petition was sent to the Home Secretary, Viscount Sydney, by Father Thomas Walshe requesting permission for two priests to accompany the convicts to the new settlement.[2] Father Walshe had evidently been attending some of those sentenced to transportation, for he states that 'they earnestly desire some Catholick clergyman may go with them and I trust to the known humanity of Government that a request which seems to promise some hopes of their reformation will not be denied.'[3] The request was not granted but the pressure continued, particularly with the start of transportation direct from Ireland in 1791. The following year a small group of New South Wales Catholics petitioned Governor Arthur Phillip to approach the home government to allow a priest to come to the colony, as 'nothing else could induce us ever to depart from his Majesty's colony here unless the idea of going into eternity without the assistance of a Catholick priest.'[4]

There was an Anglican chaplain, Richard Johnson, on the First Fleet, and he was joined in 1791 by an assistant, Samuel Marsden. The governors insisted on all convicts attending the Sunday church services, a ruling that was unpopular not only with the Catholics. In October 1798 the small wooden church at Sydney Town was burnt down, and it was strongly suspected that convicts were responsible.[5] By 1800, it has been estimated, the Irish made up 20 per cent of the white population of 4500. About half the inhabitants were convicts and the rest were soldiers, marines and their families, along with a handful of free settlers. There were only 550 women, over half of them convicts.[6] In January 1800 the *Minerva* arrived from Ireland carrying 71 political prisoners from the 1798 Rebellion, of whom 56 (79 per cent) were Catholic, and 89 criminals of whom 80 (90 per cent) were Catholic. Among the political prisoners was a priest, Father James Harold, who was the first resident Catholic clergyman in the 12-year-old colony.

Successive governors found the Irish convicts a sinister group. After the arrival of the *Minerva* and the *Friendship* in early 1800, Governor Philip Gidley King wrote: 'the number of seditious people sent from Ireland since the late disturbances in that country is 235, exclusive of the Defenders sent out in 1794, and many other Irish who have been sent out for felonies.'[7] Similar complaints followed the arrival of the next four ships from Ireland.[8] In effect the governor regarded as rebels, or potential rebels, all the 780 Irish arriving between 1800 and 1802. This judgement was not as pusillanimous as some have portrayed it, given the difficulty of obtaining accurate information on convictions, and the fact that many of the criminal convicts supported rebellion, particularly if it held the prospect of escape. The arrival of Father Harold and two other priests (James Dixon in February 1800 and Peter O'Neil in February 1801) added a religious element to the truculence of the Irish, as Governor King explained to London: 'they have frequently felt uneasy at being excluded from exercising their religion, which has been heightened by the idea of having priests among them who are forbid preaching to them.'[9]

Almost nothing is known about the appearance of the convict priests, except that O'Neil was tall and Dixon was short. Their training was typical of the generations before the opening of the first Irish seminary at Maynooth in 1795, in hedge schools and European seminaries — Harold went to Antwerp, Dixon to Salamanca and Louvain, and O'Neil to Paris. James Harold was appointed parish priest of Rathcoole, Co. Dublin, in 1794. During 1798 he reputedly exhorted his flock 'to shun all disorder and discord', but also rebuked the yeomanry and military for their 'reckless barbarity'.[10] He was named by an informer, and it was rumoured that pike heads had been found in or near his house.[11] Father Harold, referred to in New South Wales as 'the old priest', was 55 years old when he disembarked from the *Minerva* on the Octave of the Epiphany, 1800. The next night his first social engagement in the colony was to dine at the home of Thomas Fyshe Palmer, a Unitarian minister and one of the 'Scottish Martyrs' transported in the 1790s for sedition. After dinner Harold was induced to sing 'The Exile of Erin', and was encouraged by the enthusiastic crowd on a nearby beach to deliver it a second time.[12]

None of this would have impressed colonial authorities, who regarded all the Irish as rebels and the arrival of a rebellious Catholic priest as nothing short of disaster. Father Harold's irascible temperament did little to improve the situation. Michael Hayes, a United Irishman who in later years became a pillar of the Catholic Church in New South Wales, had a mixed opinion of Harold. Writing to his brother Richard, a Franciscan priest based in Rome, Michael Hayes said of Father Harold that he was 'a learned man and a great orator. He did not practice all that he preached. He was avaricious and petulant to a degree, for which he has often been rebuked by his friends here.'[13]

The second convict priest, 41-year-old James Dixon, arrived on the *Friendship* one month after Father Harold. In 1798, at the time of his arrest, Dixon was the curate of Crossabeg, Co. Wexford. He was tried in Wexford on 26 May, charged by an informer with commanding a company of rebels at Tubberneering, near Gorey.[14] His cousin was the rebel captain Thomas Dixon, responsible for the summary execution of 100 Loyalists on the bridge at Wexford Town on 20 June 1798.[15] Father Dixon was apparently quite a different character from Harold. The bishop of Ferns, Dr Caulfield, who was with Dixon during the three-week rebel occupation of Wexford town, offered this opinion of him to the archbishop of Dublin:

> The poor man is a real object of pity, for I am convinced, in my conscience, that he was, and is, as innocent of the rebellion, and of everything tending to it, as any man in Ireland ... Father James was of the first who complained to me of his cousin-german [Father Thomas Dixon] on account of his agitating and encouraging the people to unite ... This early step, with his uniform conduct before and during the rebellion, left me not a scruple of doubt of his loyalty and virtue; nor would anyone give stronger or plainer proofs of his abhorrence of the rebellion. I know him intimately these many years, and never heard that he injured, insulted, or offended man or womankind. He ever appeared to me a simple, sober, virtuous, pious priest, so that I cannot but feel for his unmerited sufferings.[16]

Another arrival on the *Minerva* was Henry Fulton, an Established Church minister also transported for alleged rebel activities. Initially Fulton was regarded with equal suspicion, which soon evaporated in view of the chronic shortage of Anglican clergy. Fulton, who had travelled to New South Wales with his wife and children, was granted a conditional pardon on 8 November 1800 and appointed as the chaplain on Norfolk Island, a penal settlement, some 1041 miles east-north-east of Sydney, which was reserved for the most recalcitrant offenders.[17] For the Catholic priests, however, the situation was more difficult, as Father Harold stated in his petition to Governor John Hunter some two and a half months after his arrival:

> I did, indeed, expect some assistance from individuals and from the people; but I am sadly disappointed. The people are so devoted to the gratification of their passions that they do not allow themselves a single moment's rational consideration ... Those with whom I shou'd think proper to associate find it their duty to keep me at a distance, while a few others begin, especially of late, consider it

unsafe to hold communication with me. Thus am I obliged either to spend my time in places of riot and intoxication, or commit myself to the dreary walls of a solitary hutt.[18]

Nevertheless it is clear that, even without authorization, Harold was exercising his ministry in private. An enquiry in September 1800 into a planned rebellion by the Irish prisoners from the *Minerva* centred on gatherings at Father Harold's house, probably private Masses. As a result of what he heard on these occasions Harold had tipped off the surgeon, William Balmain, that something was afoot but refused to name those who had told him. Harold claimed that his response to one plotter was: 'you Damnation Fool had you not better be content with the Government you have than set up one of yourselves which would soon turn out to be one of Tyranny and Oppression.'[19] Later in the hearing Harold was recalled and asked again if he would identify the plotters. In response he:

> preremptorily declared with a confidence highly unbecoming him that he w'd not reveal more than he had done — that he was sorry he had given any information — that his conscience, as a Priest, shielded him from making such disclosure — that he thought himself competent to manage the Revolters himself and that if he was a Turk he should feel himself bound to act in the same manner.[20]

It is unclear whether Harold was claiming benefit of clergy over information gained in the confessional: the claim that his 'conscience, as a Priest' protected his sources would seem to confirm this assumption, but the later assertion that he would act the same way 'if he was a Turk' provides a contradiction. Perhaps he was deliberately trying to confuse the tribunal, or it may simply have been his hotheaded reaction to being pressed for an answer which he regarded as violating his priestly conscience. The enquiry sentenced five men to 500 lashes and another four to 100 lashes. These nine together with Father Harold and Joseph Holt were sent to other settlements 'to prevent the iniquitous tendency of their diabolical Schemes being disseminated amongst other ignorant and deluded Convicts.'[21] All had arrived on the *Minerva* nine months earlier, seven as political prisoners and the others as criminal offenders. As well as exile to Norfolk Island, the committee recommended:

> that the said due Correction and Corporal Punishment be inflicted on a Public Day at the Public Stores, where the said James Harrold be also publickly brought in person as a Culprit and Ordered to Attend and bear Witness of the said several Sentences being severely carried into Execution, as a peculiar Mark of Infamy and Disgrace the said James Harrold has Ignominiously Stamped his Conduct withal.[22]

Holt, also forced to witness the floggings, described the scene thus:

> The place they flogged them — their arms pulled round a large tree and their

breasts squeezed against the tree so the men had no power to cringe or stir. Father Harold was ordered to lay his hand against the tree by the hand of the man that was flogging. There was two floggers ... Rice was a left handed man and Johnson was right handed, so they stood at each side, and I never saw two thrashers in a barn move their strokes more handier than those two man killers did ... I turned once about and as it happened I was to leeward of the floggers and I protest, though I was two perches from them, the flesh and skin blew in my face as they shook off of the cats.[23]

Cardinal Moran hypothesized that forcing Father Harold to place his hand on the flogging tree was meant to convey the impression that he was responsible for the punishment being inflicted, because he had refused to identify the plotters.[24] In fact it may simply have been that the New South Wales Corps officers were reluctant to flog him for fear of the reaction of the Irish convicts, and this was the most unpleasant non-corporal punishment that they could devise.

The third convict priest, 43-year-old Father Peter O'Neil, arrived in New South Wales on 21 February 1801. As parish priest of Ballymacoda, Co. Cork, he was accused of presiding at a meeting of United Irishmen and organizing the murder of an informer. He was stripped and flogged at Youghal before being embarked without trial on the convict ship *Anne* for the long journey to Australia.[25] Having sailed in convoy from Cork on 26 June 1800, the *Anne* travelled alone after leaving the Canary Islands and on 29 July was still three weeks short of Rio. On that day the Captain, mate and gunner were below decks fumigating the prison, when about 30 convicts ambushed them and seized control of the ship. After two hours Father O'Neil persuaded them to surrender, winning praise from the ship's captain and surgeon which later contributed to his lenient treatment on Norfolk Island.[26]

Following the suppression of the mutiny one of the convicts, United Irishman Manus Sheehy, was executed by firing squad. Sheehy has the dubious distinction of being the only convict executed in this manner on board ship during 80 years of transportation to Australia. He was reputedly the nephew of Father Nicholas Sheehy of Shanrahan, Co. Tipperary, who was executed for Whiteboyism in 1766.[27] At Rio, Father O'Neil went ashore to celebrate Mass and obtain a supply of holy oils for administering Extreme Unction. For the remainder of the voyage he was allowed to gather the convicts to sing hymns and recite the rosary, and during one storm in Antarctic waters their prayers for the intercession of the Blessed Virgin were credited with saving the ship from an icy destruction.[28] He was unlucky to be sent to New South Wales at all, as a letter exonerating him arrived in Cork only four days after the ship set sail.[29] During his two months in Sydney and 21 months on Norfolk Island, Father O'Neil also exercised a clandestine ministry, in particular proselytizing the Aboriginal population.[30] O'Neil's pardon followed on another ship, and when the colonial authorities endorsed it in January 1803 he lost no time in returning to Ireland, where he published a 'Remonstrance' to clear his name and then spent a further 43 years as parish priest of Ballymacoda. He died there in 1846 at the venerable age of 88.[31]

With Father Harold on Norfolk Island from late 1800, Father Dixon was the only Catholic priest on the mainland apart from the brief sojourn of Father O'Neil in early 1801. Obviously he also continued his ministry, but less conspicuously than Father Harold. Apparently unconvinced by Marsden's fulminations against Catholic toleration, Governor King decided that such a step would prove a settling influence. In 1802 Lord Hobart wrote, in reply to King's enquiry on the subject:

> The Catholic priests Dixon, O'Neal and Harrold ... have been represented to me as persons who may not be undeserving of the conditional emancipation ... If their conduct should have justified this representation, and you should be of the opinion that the priests may be usefully employed, either as schoolmasters or in the exercise of their clerical functions, you may avail yourself of their services and allow them such moderate compensation as, under the circumstances of their case, you may judge reasonable.[32]

Curiously, Hobart is usually regarded as an opponent of concessions to Irish Catholics. The eldest son of the third Earl of Buckinghamshire, he was aide-de-camp to successive Lord Lieutenants of Ireland from 1784 to 1789, and Chief Secretary of Ireland from 1789 to 1793. His role in the history of New South Wales derives from his position as Secretary of State for War and the Colonies, which he held from March 1801 to May 1804.[33] In May 1803 King informed Hobart that Father O'Neil had returned to Ireland, and assessed the other two priests:

> I am glad to say that the conduct of Dixon ... has been exemplary since he has been here; whilst Harrold's (who is at Norfolk Island) has been the reverse ... Your Lordship's suggestion respecting the exercise of their clerical functions I have most maturely considered, and weighed the certain advantages with the possible disadvantages ... Possessed as I am of your Lordship's liberal sentiments on this head, and not doubting Mr. Dixon's professions ... I have allowed him to exercise his clerical functions ... I am hopeful much good, or at least no harm, will result from it.[34]

In fact the colonial authorities had apparently already permitted some relaxation of the rules. A letter dated 8 January 1803, from Father Harold on Norfolk Island to his nephew, refers to ill-health forcing him to close his school there the previous June.[35] Accordingly, on 12 April 1803, an order was signed requiring every person professing the Roman Catholic religion to attend a muster on Wednesday 20 April at either Sydney, Parramatta (15 miles west), or Hawkesbury (30 miles north-west). The *Sydney Gazette* printed the regulations under which Father Dixon was permitted to operate:

> First: They will observe with all becoming gratitude that this extension of liberal toleration proceeds from the piety and benevolence of our Most Gracious

Sovereign to whom, as well as to our parent country at large, we are, under providence, indebted for the blessings we enjoy.

Second: That the religious exercise of their worship may suffer no hindrance, it is expected that no seditious conversations that can anywise injure His Majesty's Government, or affect the tranquillity of this Colony, will ever happen, either at the place prescribed for their Worship or elsewhere. But that they will individually manifest their gratitude and allegiance by exercising themselves in detecting and reporting any impropriety of that or any other nature, that may fall under their observation.

Third: As Mr. Dixon will be allowed to perform his clerical functions once in three weeks at the settlements at Sydney, Parramatta and Hawkesbury in rotation, the Magistrates are strictly forbid suffering those Catholics who reside at the place where Service is not performing from resorting to the settlement and district at which the Priest officiates for the day.

Fourth: The Catholic Service will be performed on the appointed Sundays at nine o'clock in the morning.

Fifth: No improper behaviour during the time of Service is to be allowed by the Priest, who will be responsible to the Magistrates for his Congregation's going regularly and orderly to their respective homes after the Offices are ended.

Sixth: And to the end that strict decorum may be observed, a certain number of Police will be stationed at or about the places appointed during the Service.

Seventh: Every person throughout the Colony will observe that the law has sufficiently provided for the punishment of those who may disquiet or disturb any assembly or religious worship whatever, or misuse any Priest or teacher of any tolerated sect.[36]

Like every civil and military officer being inducted to a new post, Father Dixon was required to take a series of oaths: the oath of abjuration, the oath of assurance and a declaration 'that I do believe that there is not any Transubstantiation in the Sacrament of the Lord's Supper, or in the Elements of Bread and Wine, at or after the Consecration thereof by any Person whatsoever.'[37] The first public Masses were held at Sydney on 15 May, Parramatta on 22 May and Hawkesbury on 29 May. Weddings and funerals were also permitted. Having received recognition from the civil authorities, Father Dixon sought to regularize his ecclesiastical authority by petitioning the Pope for the faculties commonly accorded to missionaries.[38] Pope Pius VII went further, creating the Apostolic Prefecture of New Holland and appointing Dixon as the first Prefect Apostolic.[39]

There is no contemporary evidence of who comprised his congregation, but most of those identified as active Catholic laity after 1818 were already in New South Wales by 1803. Almost all were United Irishmen who regarded themselves as the élite of the convicts, particularly in religious and moral matters. They included Andrew Byrne, Peter Ivers, John Lacey, John Reddington, Edward Redmond (or Edmond McRedmond) and Martin Short from the *Minerva*, William Davis, Michael Hayes and James Meehan who arrived with Father Dixon on the *Friendship*, John Butler and

James Dempsey of the *Atlas II* in 1802, and Hugh Byrne, Michael Dwyer and James Sheedy who were sent out on the *Tellicherry*, reaching Sydney in 1806. Dempsey and Butler were Carmelite tertiaries,[40] while one of Sheedy's descendants, basing his work on now unavailable family documents, said that he 'lived and died virtually a priest, a man who did not drink, smoke or use bad language ... Although James may have been disappointed originally in not joining the Church, the religious folk agreeing that his transportation to New South Wales was an act of God.'[41]

The handful of non-Irish Catholics included two London-convicted cousins named Joseph Morley, who between them signed all three petitions to the New South Wales authorities for Catholic toleration, the first in 1792 and the last in 1820;[42] and Gabriel Louis Marie Huon de Kérilleau, a Breton who arrived as a soldier in 1794, and 25 years later acted as interpreter for the Catholic chaplain of the visiting French ship *l'Uranie*.[43] Between a quarter and a third of the soldiers were also Catholic, although like the convicts they were obliged to attend Protestant services. Nevertheless some at least maintained their faith, according to later evidence:

> There were several soldiers who went to their weekly Communion in the 17th Regiment, and at least twenty who went once a fortnight. One young man I particularly remember. He was quite a contemplative. He had received the Carmelite Scapular before he entered the Army from the Reverend Father Pope at Congelton, and had persevered in a habit of prayer and fasting ... The incidents of a barrack-room, and the rigours of military discipline, served him as subjects of self-mortification. And he certainly had both a tender conscience and an habitual sense of the presence of God. He kept several of his comrades steady to their religious duties, and from time to time brought others to the Sacraments.[44]

Governor King's 'liberal' experiment seemed to work well, and after six months he reported his satisfaction to London:

> The Irish, of whom we have so great a proportion, in general behave well, which I cannot but attribute to their being indulged with the exercise of their religion, in performing the functions of which Mr. Dixon conducts himself and his congregation so well that I have availed myself of your Lordship's permission in giving him 60 pounds per annum.[45]

A similar report was sent after a further six months, stating that Hobart's 'indulgence has had the most salutary effects on the number of Irish Catholics we have, and since its toleration there has not been the most distant cause for complaint among that description, who regularly attend Divine Service.'[46] That despatch was dated 1 March 1804, but ironically it was only three days later, on the third Sunday in Lent, that the Irish convicts began the Castle Hill Rebellion which came close to overwhelming the colony. In the culminating 'Battle of Vinegar Hill' an estimated 250 convicts were routed by about 70 soldiers and volunteers. Over 20 rebels were killed and another 10 subsequently hanged. Most of this latter group were Irish and recent arrivals: none of the *Friendship* or *Minerva* convicts was involved. The two main leaders were ex-soldiers: William Johnson from Sligo who arrived on the ship *Rolla* in May 1803, and Philip Cunningham, a United Irishman from Kerry, who was allegedly the leader of the shipboard mutiny quelled by Father O'Neil.

The political motivation of the rebellion is confirmed by the fact that two of the leaders were emancipated convicts and two others were overseers with their own houses. This was not the desperate act of the hopeless, but a calculated attempt to take military control of the lightly guarded colony in order to organize a mass escape.[47] Father Dixon's behaviour during the crisis was again exemplary in the eyes of the authorities. He was summoned from his bed at around 4.30 on the Monday morning, and assembled with James Meehan and Joseph Holt.[48] Dixon was taken to the parley between the rebel leaders and the New South Wales Corps officers, where he attempted to persuade the rebels to avoid bloodshed.[49] Despite these endeavours, however, Governor King concluded that the public Masses had provided a gathering place for the Irish which facilitated the planning of the rebellion. The choice of 'Saint Peter' as the rebel password may have fuelled his suspicion. Some months later the governor mentioned in a despatch to London that he had withdrawn the salary from 'the Romish priest Dixon, for very improper conduct, and to prevent the seditious meetings that took place in consequence of the indulgence and protection he received.'[50] It is not clear precisely when Dixon's salary was stopped, as the despatch covers a number of appointments and dismissals as well as other financial matters. Some commentators assume that Dixon was kept on the government payroll for the five months following the rebellion, but the report of his dismissal may have been a belated confirmation to London of a decision taken earlier. By inference the public Masses were terminated at the same time.

Samuel Marsden, the only Anglican clergyman in New South Wales (Fulton was on Norfolk Island) from 1801 to 1807, made a visit to London from 1807 to 1810 during which he wrote a number of reports to the London Missionary Society. One of these, 'A Few Observations on the Toleration of the Catholic Religion in New South Wales', gives his assessment of the government's leniency to Father Dixon and proposes toleration as the direct cause of the Castle Hill Rebellion.[51] Marsden's dual appointment as chaplain and magistrate inevitably gave rise to controversy, and the nickname 'The Flogging Parson'. Curiously his reputation is much higher in New Zealand, to which he made seven missionary visits between 1814 and 1837, and it may be that the Irish convicts contributed to the odium with which he is still regarded in Australia. As a young man Marsden was influenced by Wesley, and remained firmly in the evangelical stream of the Established Church.[52] Nevertheless his criticism of Catholic toleration is based on political rather than theological grounds, apart from the common enough assertion that the Catholics were 'superstitious'.

In a colony characterized by most commentators as rife with drunkenness and prostitution, Marsden describes the Irish as irreligious, depraved and generally beyond redemption even by their own clergy: 'the want of the celebration of the Mass is not the cause of that dissatisfied, turbulent, rebellious spirit, which is so strongly marked in the Irish Catholic convicts, but their natural ferocity which nothing can ever eradicate.'[53] Marsden's harsh judgement of the Catholics was not unnaturally reciprocated. Writing to his family in Dublin in 1812, United Irishman Michael Hayes stated:

> The Protestants of this Colony are disgusted with their Preachers, they are comprised of Tradesmen, such as Smiths, Shoemakers, Masons, &c., &c., that does not know a word of Greek or Latin, nor spake Good English. Their principal who acts as Bishop (Marsden) is a Blacksmith by Trade, well known to Mr. Dixon, to whom I refer you.[54]

Hayes's letter was taken to Ireland by the Irish Protestant rebel leader Joseph Holt, who displayed a more lenient view of Catholicism than Marsden. On the way home he visited Rio de Janeiro:

> It is a great sight to behold the image of the Virgin Mary and Our Saviour in her arms, and many other saints in full figure and size ... I have went to some of their grand processions and I say it took the lead of all I ever seen ... It is past my knowledge to describe the images that is in each church and, all hours of the day and night, you will find some people at their prayers, with their beads in their hands. I have been brought in by some of the padres to view the works of their churches ... and I never will see such again while on this earth ... It would make the most hardened sinner on earth to relent for his sins.[55]

In his 'Observations' Marsden advocated the compulsory attendance of all convicts at his own services, and urged the sending of schoolmasters to the colony to educate the convicts' children in the Established Church. He believed that in a generation the Irish could be converted, a claim which might have been true except for three factors: the clandestine ministry of Fathers Dixon and Harold, the presence of a core of devout Catholics centring on the Irish rebels and the arrival of more convicts from Ireland.

The political situation in New South Wales changed dramatically on 26 January 1808, when the New South Wales Corps staged a military coup and imprisoned Governor William Bligh of 'mutiny on the *Bounty*' fame. The leader of this so-called 'Rum Rebellion' was George Johnston, who had crushed the Castle Hill Rebellion four years earlier. The officers ran the colony until the arrival of the new Governor, Lachlan Macquarie, two years later. Father Dixon, who had received a pardon from London, left for Ireland in October 1809,[56] and with Parson Marsden away and Fulton suspended the colony was left without any clergy at all, 'bar an incensing preacher that neither Roman nor Protestant would go hear.'[57] Joseph Holt's son solved the problem by receiving permission from the Lieutenant-Governor for a military officer to perform a civil marriage, but Holt senior commented that 'there was no clergyman to visit the sick, baptize the infant or church the women, so we were on equal terms with the natives of Botany Bay.'[58] Father Harold, who had been moved from Norfolk Island to Van Diemen's Land (Tasmania) in 1808, was given permission to return to Sydney, although his stay was short as he sailed for Rio in August 1810. After he left a parcel arrived for him, which was found to contain two suits of vestments, breviaries and other religious items, confirming that he had maintained his clandestine ministry to the last.[59] Harold went to Philadelphia where he became embroiled with his nephew's Haroldite Schism, returning to Ireland in 1813. He died in 1830 at the age of 86 and was buried in Dublin.[60]

From this time onward Michael Hayes petitioned for Catholic priests to be sent to the colony, but it was impossible to find any willing to travel the vast distance to the notorious settlement. Finally Father Jeremiah O'Flynn, a close friend of Father Richard Hayes, was appointed Prefect Apostolic of New Holland and arrived in Sydney in November 1817. Unfortunately he had failed to gain approval from the Government in London, and was therefore not recognized by Governor Macquarie and deported after six months. Macquarie, himself a native speaker of Scots Gaelic, criticized O'Flynn's poor English, but another contemporary said the French-trained priest had 'the sweetest and swiftest tongue of Irish I ever heard.'[61] At his departure O'Flynn left behind, whether by accident or design, a conse-crated host. The following months have given rise to one of the enduring legends of Australian Catholicism, as a small but growing group of Catholics centred their priestless devotions on the home where the Blessed Sacrament was kept. The cedar press, pyx and embroidered bag which con-tained the host have been preserved to this day. Earlier historians identi-fied the home as that of Wexford blacksmith-turned-pikemaker William Davis, but it has alternatively been asserted that the custodian was the Carmelite James Dempsey, a stonemason and United Irishman from Tipperary:

> Mr. Dempsey secured the assistance of five or six other religious old men, whose whole duty and pleasure was to watch and pray in that room, in which an altar had been erected and a tabernacle placed to receive the holy pix. This room was converted into a little chapel, and it was no unusual thing on a Sunday, when Catholics could assemble to join the prayers at Mass which were being read in that room, to see many of them kneeling under the verandah, aye even in the street, much to the amusement of the scoffers, who said we ought to be sun-struck.[62]

The gatherings included the singing of Sunday Vespers, consisting of Psalms 109 to 113 and the Magnificat.[63] Psalm 113, on the exile of the Israelites in Egypt, was a powerful image for the Irish convicts. Perhaps not coincidentally this association was repeated in the Australian folk song 'The Convict's Arrival', written by Irish convict Frank MacNamara in the 1830s and sung to the air of 'Boolavogue'.[64] In December 1819 the Irish

were joined in Dempsey's house by officers of the visiting French exploration vessel *l'Uranie*: 'That these officers, who were so polite and who
were on visiting terms at Government House, should kneel down with the
poor Irish ... in that small room, in that obscure house, was to the
Protestants a source of amazement.'[65] Resulting from O'Flynn's deportation there was a debate in the British Parliament in 1819 on the need for
Catholic chaplains in New South Wales. Emotional claims were made during the debate:

> A large proportion of the convicts were Irish Catholics, who had no religious
> instruction whatever, for he did not think they derived any from the order of the
> Governor, who compelled them, by the intervention of a number of constables,
> to attend a place of Protestant worship every Sunday. In the church, where they
> were thus assembled, everything took place except what was most suitable to it.
> He had been also told that the Catholics, rather than submit to have the various
> religious ceremonies performed by Protestant clergymen, lived together unmar-
> ried, that their children were unbaptized, and that, in short, they submitted to
> no ceremony but that of being marched to church by the constables.[66]

In regard to compulsory church attendance it is recorded that William
Davis, among others, had been flogged and locked in the black hole for
refusing to attend the Established Church,[67] but by 1808 the constabulary
was predominantly made up of Irish convicts, many of them ex-rebels, and
the rule was less strictly enforced.[68] The situation changed with Governor
Macquarie's arrival in 1810, for he was a strict Sabbatarian and ordered the
convicts to stop work on Sundays and attend church. The punishment was
a warning on the first offence, and an hour in the stocks for second and
subsequent offences.[69]

From the peak of 1800 to 1803, transportation from Ireland slowed to a
trickle between 1803 and 1813. In the seven years following the arrival of
the *Tellicherry* in 1806, only four ships arrived from Ireland carrying a total
of 405 men and 152 women. In the meantime, 23 males convicted in Ireland
had arrived in ships which sailed from England, most of them British
soldiers convicted by courts-martial.[70] During this period most of the
convicts who had arrived in 1800–3 completed their sentences and set up
businesses or farms. As emancipated convicts they were no longer compelled to attend Sunday church parades, and with relatively few convicts
arriving from Ireland in the period from 1803 to 1813, the number of
Catholic convicts subject to compulsory attendance at Anglican services
decreased substantially.

In any case for most of the decade from 1800 to 1810 there were hardly
any Anglican clergy in the colony. After Marsden's departure for England
in 1806, Fulton was brought back from Norfolk Island to replace him, but
he was suspended in early 1808. Thereafter services were conducted by
Congregationalist missionaries, most of whom had come to New South
Wales after unsuccessful attempts to convert the Tahitians.[71] Nevertheless
some Catholics were married and buried by the available Anglican clergy.
On the eight ships which reached Sydney from Ireland between 1800 and

1806 there were 1023 male convicts. A total of 77 of them are listed in the Church of England burial register in the period 1800 to 1810. Another 14 were married in the Anglican church during the same period, although there was almost always a Catholic priest available.[72] There is evidence of at least two marriages performed by Father Dixon well after his official approval had been withdrawn in 1804, between James Galvin and Jane Morgan,[73] and William Davis and Catherine Miles.[74] Another couple, Martin Burke and Phoebe Tunstall, were married by Father Harold.[75] In a letter to his brother in 1812, Michael Hayes assured him that his three eldest children were baptized by Fathers Dixon and Harold, although the youngest born in 1811 was still unbaptized.[76]

A report of public toleration is found in a complaint from Bligh in Van Diemen's Land that the military regime installed by the Rum Rebellion had once again permitted 'the Romish priest' to minister in public.[77] While there is no confirmatory evidence of public Masses being permitted, it is likely that the absence of any other clergy had given rise to a certain leniency, particularly in the case of weddings. As the Anglican registers after 1810 no longer recorded the convicts' ship of arrival it is virtually impossible to identify the Irish convicts. However in the Catholic baptismal registers of the 1820s, the column reserved for the name of the clergyman who had married the parents includes several references to 'Dominus Marsden' and other Anglican chaplains.[78] Until 1907 Catholic canon law recognized the validity of marriages performed in the Anglican Church, and there is anecdotal evidence to suggest that some of those who preferred what Marsden delighted in calling 'concubinage' had probably left spouses behind in Ireland. On the other hand Michael Hayes was adamant that it was religious scruples which kept Catholics away from the Established Church: 'above eleven hundred children of Catholic parents are not Baptised, some Ten years of age, and many desirous of being married have lived in open violation of the Laws of God.'[79]

There are scattered reports of Catholic religious activity during this time. James Dempsey read prayers with those condemned to the scaffold.[80] A similar occasion was graphically described:

> The Catholics had a practice of sewing, on the front of their caps and on the front of their shirts, large black crosses, in which to appear on the scaffold. These men did so. As soon as they were on the scaffold, to my surprise, they began to say their ejaculation aloud and in a kind of solemn chorus: 'Into Thy hands I commend my spirit. Lord Jesus receive my soul', repeating it until the fall and the ropes stopped their voices forever.[81]

Another lay catechist was the Wicklow rebel leader Michael Dwyer, now a constable at Liverpool (19 miles south-west of Sydney), who is remembered as riding around the countryside to lead the rosary and read aloud works by the popular Catholic devotional writer Bishop Alphonsus Liguori.[82] Despite the brevity of public toleration, both Fathers Dixon and Harold were permitted to run schools during their stay in the colony. In

1806 a prisoner from the *Friendship*, Jeremiah Kavanagh, received a conditional pardon to work as a Catholic teacher.[83] In the 1806 muster he is listed as a self-employed schoolmaster while Father Dixon is described as a self-employed Roman Catholic priest.[84] Women such as Michael Dwyer's wife Mary, who was later housekeeper to the Archpriest Therry for many years, and William Davis's wife Catherine, would also have ensured that some children at least were taught the elements of their religion. When Father Therry arrived in the priestless colony in 1820 he was surprised to find that 12-year-old John Fitzpatrick and his 10-year-old brother Colm had been taught the Latin responses to serve Mass. They had arrived with their parents, Bernard and Catherine, in 1811.[85]

In 1814 transportation from Ireland resumed in earnest, with 25 ships bringing 2954 male and 658 female convicts to the colony over the next five years.[86] This influx, combined with the pressure of Michael Hayes in New South Wales, the former convict priests back in Ireland and priests attending prisoners sentenced to transportation, along with the deportation of Father O'Flynn, were the catalysts which led to the appointment of two Catholic chaplains. The arrival in Sydney of Fathers John Joseph Therry and Philip Conolly on the feast of the Holy Cross, 3 May 1820, marked the official establishment of what is now the largest religious denomination in Australia. By then, Catholics made up between a quarter and a third of the population of 30,000. The convicts were outnumbered by the free inhabitants — emancipated convicts, soldiers, settlers and their families.[87] Thirty-two years had passed since the colony was founded; Catholicism had been officially permitted for only one year, and priests were available on a clandestine basis for a further ten years. A small group centred on the Irish rebels had endeavoured to maintain the faith, and they formed the nucleus of the laity in the 1820s and beyond.

Notes

1. Revd. Samuel Marsden, 'A Few Observations on the Toleration of the Catholic Religion in New South Wales', MLMSS 18, Mitchell Library, Sydney.
2. *Historical Records of New South Wales (HRNSW)*, Government Printer, Sydney, 1898, Vol. 1, part 2, pp. 119–20.
3. *HRNSW*, Vol. 1, part 2, pp. 119–20.
4. *HRNSW*, Vol. 2, pp. 484–5. The petition was dated 30 Nov. 1792, and signed by Thomas Tynan, a marine, three ex-convicts named Simon Burn (Byrne), Joseph Morley and John Brown, and Mary Macdonald (née Butler), a marine's wife.
5. *Historical Records of Australia (HRA)*, Library Committee of the Commonwealth Parliament, Melbourne, 1915: Hunter to Portland, 1 Nov. 1798, Series I, Vol. ii, p. 236, and Hunter to Portland, 1 May 1799, Ser. I, Vol. ii, p. 358.
6. Carol Baxter (ed.), *Musters and Lists, New South Wales and Norfolk Island, 1800–1802*, Australian Biographical and Genealogical Record, Sydney, 1988, p. xix.
7. King to Portland, 28 Sept. 1800, *HRA*, Ser. I, Vol. ii, p. 614.
8. King to Portland, 10 March 1801, *HRA*, Ser. I, Vol. iii, p. 9, and King to Hobart,

9 Nov. 1802, *HRA*, Ser. I, Vol. iii, p. 654.

9. King to Hobart, 9 May 1803, *HRA*, Ser. I, Vol. iv, p. 83.
10. Patrick Francis Moran (Cardinal), *History of the Catholic Church in Australasia*, Oceanic Publishing, Sydney, no date [c. 1895], p. 26.
11. Harold Perkins, *The Convict Priests*, published by author, Melbourne, 1984, pp. 13–18, citing *inter alia* Richard Sheil, 'Memoir of Rev. James Harold sent to Dr. R. Madden', National Library of Ireland, Madden Papers, No. 291; and Sir R. Musgrave, *History of the Civil Wars of Ireland*, Dublin, 1801.
12. Sheil, Madden Papers, No. 291, National Library of Ireland.
13. Michael Hayes to Father Richard Hayes, 25 Nov. 1812, p. 3a, original in Franciscan Archives, Dun Mhuire, Killiney, Dublin, and copy at A3586, Mitchell Library, Sydney.
14. Moran, *Catholic Church*, pp. 34–6.
15. Thomas Pakenham, *The Year of Liberty: the Story of the Great Irish Rebellion of 1798*, Hodder and Stoughton, London, 1969, pp. 254–5, 350.
16. Cited in Moran, *Catholic Church*, pp. 35–6.
17. Douglas Pike (ed.), *Australian Dictionary of Biography* (*ADB*), Melbourne University Press, 1966–7, Vol. 1, pp. 421–2.
18. Harold to Hunter, 23 April 1800, *HRA*, Ser. I, Vol. ii, pp. 503–4.
19. *HRA*, Ser. I, Vol. ii, pp. 575–6.
20. *HRA*, Ser. I, Vol. ii, p. 576.
21. *HRA*, Ser. I, Vol. ii, p. 583.
22. *HRA*, Ser. I, Vol. ii, p. 583.
23. Peter O'Shaughnessy (ed.), *A Rum Story: the Adventures of Joseph Holt, Thirteen years in New South Wales 1800–1812*, Kangaroo Press, Sydney, 1988, pp. 61–2.
24. Moran, *Catholic Church*, p. 30.
25. Moran, *Catholic Church*, p. 45, citing Remonstrance of the Revd. Peter O'Neil, Dublin, 1803.
26. Perkins, *Convict Priests*, p. 78.
27. Sidney Harold Sheedy, 'United Irishmen in New South Wales 1800–1806', MLMSS 1337, p. 130, Mitchell Library, Sydney.
28. Moran, *Catholic Church*, p. 50.
29. Moran, *Catholic Church*, p. 47.
30. Moran, *Catholic Church*, p. 50.
31. Moran, *Catholic Church*, p. 52.
32. Hobart to King, 29 Aug. 1802, *HRA*, Ser. I, Vol. iii, p. 564.
33. *ADB*, Vol. 1, p. 542.
34. King to Hobart, 9 May 1803, *HRA*, Ser. I, Vol. iv, pp. 82–3.
35. Moran, *Catholic Church*, pp. 32–3.
36. *Sydney Gazette*, 24 April 1803.
37. Moran, *Catholic Church*, p. 38, citing the proclamation by Governor King, 19 April 1803.
38. Perkins, *Convict Priests*, p. 59, citing Vatican Archives.
39. Ralph Wiltgen, *Founding of the Catholic Church in Oceania*, Australian National University Press, Canberra, 1979, pp. 182–6, citing Vatican Archives.
40. Paul Chandler (Father), 'Lay Carmelites in Botany Bay, 1802–1838', in *Carmelus*, Rome, Vol. 32, 1985, pp. 107–49.
41. Sheedy, 'United Irishmen', p. 70. For another reference to James Sheedy's intention to join the priesthood, see Sheedy, p. 23.
42. For the 1792 petition see above note 4; 1818 petition, Bonwick Transcripts, 11215, Mitchell Library, Sydney; 1820 petition, Bonwick Transcripts, BT 21, Vol.

127, pp. 3935–43.

43. Chandler, 'Lay Carmelites', p. 126.

44. William Bernard Ullathorne, *From Cabin Boy to Archbishop: the Autobiography of Archbishop Ullathorne*, Burns Oates, Sydney, 1941, pp. 109–10. Ullathorne arrived in Sydney in 1833, and wrote the manuscript in 1868. The 17th Regiment was in New South Wales from 1828 to 1836.

45. King to Hobart, 17 Sept. 1803, *HRA*, Ser. I, Vol. iv, p. 394.

46. King to Hobart, 1 March 1804, *HRA*, Ser. I, Vol. iv, p. 470.

47. For more information on the Castle Hill rebellion see (i) *HRA*, Ser. I, Vol. iv, pp. 563–77; (ii) *HRNSW*, Vol. v, pp. 314–15, 345–58; (iii) Anne-Maree Whitaker, *Unfinished Revolution: United Irishmen in New South Wales 1800–1810*, Crossing Press, Sydney, 1994, pp. 89–115; (iv) James G. Symes, *The Castle Hill Rebellion of 1804*, Hills District Historical Society, Sydney, 1979; (v) R. W. Connell, 'The convict rebellion of 1804', *Melbourne Historical Journal*, Vol. V, 1965, pp. 27–37; (vi) Al Grassby and Marji Hill, *Six Australian Battlefields*, Angus and Robertson, Sydney, 1988; (vii) O'Shaughnessy, *A Rum Story*, pp. 79–87; (viii) Lynette Ramsay Silver, *The Battle of Vinegar Hill: Australia's Irish Rebellion 1804*, Doubleday, Sydney, 1989.

48. G. W. Rusden, *Curiosities of Colonisation*, London, 1874. James Meehan, a United Irishman from Shinrone, Co. Offaly, was by this time the deputy government surveyor in the colony, while Joseph Holt, the Protestant rebel leader from Wicklow, was a farmer.

49. Major George Johnston to Captain John Piper on Norfolk Island, 12 April 1804, Piper Papers, A256, pp. 325–31, Mitchell Library, Sydney.

50. King to Hobart, 14 Aug. 1804, *HRA*, Ser. I, Vol. v, p. 99.

51. Marsden, 'Catholic Religion', *passim*.

52. *ADB*, Vol. 2, pp. 207–12.

53. Marsden, 'Catholic Religion', *passim*.

54. Hayes letters, No. 3, 25 Nov. 1812, p. 3b. Governor Lachlan Macquarie held a similar view of Marsden and his recruits: 'Mr. Marsden and some of the assistant chaplains are originally of low rank, and not qualified by liberal educations in the usual way for the sacred functions entrusted to them, and are also much tinctured by Methodistical and other sectarian principles.' Macquarie to Bathurst, 7 Oct. 1814, *HRA*, Ser. I, Vol. viii, p. 337.

55. O'Shaughnessy, *A Rum Story*, p. 134.

56. *Sydney Gazette*, 8 Oct. 1809, p. 2. Moran, *Catholic Church*, p. 41, records that he returned to the parish of Crossabeg where he died as parish priest in 1840 at the age of 81.

57. O'Shaughnessy, *A Rum Story*, p. 109. The 'incensing preacher' was William Pascoe Crook, a Congregationalist missionary.

58. O'Shaughnessy, *A Rum Story*, p. 109.

59. Hayes letters, 25 Nov. 1812, p. 3a.

60. Moran, *Catholic Church*, p. 33.

61. Ullathorne, *Autobiography*, p. 108.

62. Cornelius James Duffy (Monsignor), *Catholic Religious and Social Life in the Macquarie Era*, Catholic Press Newspaper, Sydney, 1966, p. 12, quoting letters written by Columbus (Colm) Fitzpatrick between 1865 and 1874, and his younger brother Ambrose in 1884.

63. Duffy, *Catholic Religious Life*, pp. 36–7. The Magnificat, or Canticle of the Blessed Virgin Mary, is in St Luke's gospel 1:46–55.

64. John Meredith and Rex Whalan, *Frank the Poet: the Life and Works of Francis*

MacNamara, Red Rooster, Melbourne, 1979, pp. 31–8. The song, better known as 'Moreton Bay', was a favourite of Australian hero Ned Kelly, whose father served time with MacNamara in Van Diemen's Land.

65. Duffy, *Catholic Religious Life*, p. 13. The midshipmen's journals record large numbers of devout Irish attending Masses celebrated by *l'Uranie*'s chaplain on 28 November, 5 and 19 December 1819: Archives Nationales Marines, Paris, 5JJ 63, 5JJ 69C, 5JJ 73, with transcripts respectively at B1293, B1284 and B1285, Mitchell Library, Sydney.
66. Moran, *Catholic Church*, p. 74.
67. Moran, *Catholic Church*, pp. 69–70.
68. Captain Edward Abbott to ex-Governor Philip Gidley King, 13 Feb. 1808, *HRNSW*, Vol. vi, pp. 832–4.
69. Anthony Hewison (ed.), *The Macquarie Decade: Documents Illustrating the History of New South Wales 1810–1821*, Cassell Australia, Melbourne, 1972, p. 75.
70. Charles Bateson, *The Convict Ships 1787–1868*, Library of Australian History, Sydney, 1983 (third edition), pp. 338–43, 381–3.
71. *ADB*, Vol. 1, pp. 521–2.
72. Church of England burial registers, Vol. 2, and marriage registers, Vol. 3, New South Wales Registrar-General's office, Sydney.
73. Copies of baptisms and marriages, Revd. Philip Conolly, 1820–1, St Mary's Cathedral Archives, Sydney. An entry for 18 February 1821 notes that James Galvin and Jane Morgan 'hi conjuncti sunt circ. 14 annos per Dominum Dixon'.
74. *Sydney Gazette*, 29 March 1826, p. 3. Mrs Davis states that she arrived in September 1808 and was married the following January, but the records show that she actually arrived in August 1806.
75. Colonial Secretary's papers, 4/1767, p. 68, Archives Office of New South Wales, Sydney. In a letter dated 21 November 1823, Burke stated that he was married by Harold in Sydney in 1807, but as the priest did not return from Van Diemen's Land until 1809 it is more likely that the wedding took place in that year.
76. Hayes letters, 25 Nov. 1812, p. 3b.
77. Bligh to Castlereagh, 8 July 1809, *HRA*, Ser. I, Vol. vii, p. 163. Bligh, relying on rumours reaching him from Sydney, states that the unnamed priest 'is now wildly following his functions, which were before kept within proper bounds.'
78. Revd. P. Conolly, church registers; see note 73.
79. Hayes letters, Michael to Patrick Hayes, 8 Dec. 1817, pp. 9 and 13.
80. Deposition of Elizabeth McKeon, 4 Aug. 1826, Therry Papers, MLMSS 1810/65, p. 163, Mitchell Library, Sydney.
81. Ullathorne, *Autobiography*, p. 84, describing a mass execution on Norfolk Island in 1835.
82. N. McNally (Father), 'The men of '98', in *Journal of the Australian Catholic Historical Society*, Vol. III, part 1, 1969, pp. 26–46, based on an anecdote told in 1880 by the Very Revd. John Dwyer, grandson of Michael, recorded in the *Advocate* (Melbourne) and the *Irish Press c.* 1941. Liguori, founder of the Redemptorist Order, died in 1786 and was canonized in 1839.
83. 4 June 1806, Register of Conditional Pardons 1791–1825, 4/4430, Archives Office of New South Wales, Sydney. See also note 35.
84. In the muster, held on 12 August 1806, Kavanagh is listed as Joseph Cavenagh. See Carol Baxter (ed.), *Musters of New South Wales and Norfolk Island, 1805–1806*, Australian Biographical and Genealogical Record, Sydney, 1989, pp. 20, 30.
85. Duffy, *Catholic Religious Life*, p. 17.

86. Bateson, *Convict Ships*, pp. 340–5, 381–3.
87. Hewison, *The Macquarie Decade*, p. 9.

Additional select bibliography

Collins, Paul (Father), 'Jeremiah O'Flynn: persecuted hero or vagus?', *Australasian Catholic Record*, Vol. LXIII, Nos. 1 and 2 (1986).

Donohoe, James Hugh, *The Catholics of New South Wales 1788–1820 and their Families*, Archives Authority of New South Wales, Sydney, 1988.

Duffy, Cornelius James (Monsignor), *The Leaving of the Consecrated Host by Father Jeremiah O'Flynn in 1818*, Diocesan Archives, Sydney, 1967.

Hosie, John (Father), 'Davis, Dempsey and the leaving of the Blessed Sacrament – the controversy and a possible solution', *Australasian Catholic Record*, Vol. LXVII, No. 1 (Jan 1990), pp. 81–6.

O'Brien, Eris (Monsignor), *The Dawn of Catholicism in Australia*, Sydney, 1928.

O'Farrell, Patrick, *The Catholic Church and Community in Australia: a History*, Nelson, Melbourne, 1985.

Suttor, Timothy Lachlan Lautour, *Hierarchy and Democracy in Australia, 1788–1870*, Melbourne, 1965.

Waldersee, James, *Catholic Society in New South Wales 1788–1860*, Sydney University Press, Sydney, 1974.

2 Under an Orange banner: reflections on the northern Protestant experiences of emigration

James White McAuley

Protestants saw America as a providential nature in the world, expanding the areas of Protestantism, freedom democracy and the ability of the individual to improve his [sic] own lot.[1]

[I]f we assume the continuation of the present natural increase differential between the two communities and no emigration, Roman Catholics will eventually form the majority of the population.[2]

Because Catholics were forced as a result of various forms of discrimination to emigrate more than Protestants, they were used to this attitude and took it for granted. But it comes as something of a shock to the average loyalist to find that after years of protesting his [sic] Britishness he is treated by the English like just another 'Paddy'.[3]

Introduction

Any close inspection of the Irish community in Britain identifies clearly a series of dominant images of Irish emigrants. They are projected as an almost homogeneous grouping, unified by coherent culture and hegemonic icon. Within such images the culture and politics of the 'Irish nation' is transferred as a whole to an 'imagined community' abroad.[4] This is obviously false. The Irish community abroad is internally demarcated by the social identity of those who comprise it: by life chance; by social class; by occupation; by cultural tradition; sometimes by religion and often by gender. Such social divisions exist even amongst those who would readily call themselves 'Irish', the factor which gives the grouping some social cohesion. There is of course another set of migrants from the island with whom the self-identity of being Irish does not fit comfortably, if at all: that is, those from the northern Protestant and/or Unionist cultural tradition. Their icons and symbolism are very different. They in turn have a stereotypical image, ranks of men wearing orange sashes, marching behind large fluttering banners depicting William crossing the Boyne on his white horse.[5] It is the experiences of this social group with which this chapter is mainly concerned.

Some of course may argue that this focus is misguided, that in some sense there is no 'Protestant' experience of emigration. Some might say that the experience of this grouping can only be understood if we consider Protestant emigration as part of the overall political, social and economic experience of the whole island. In part this is true. However, in important ways the northern Protestant experience is different: in settlement patterns; in self-identity; in terms of motivation and the group identity they have sought to establish abroad. As Hughes has pointed out,

> we need to look not for a single culture of emigration, but, rather, for often con-flicting — now weaker, now stronger — cultures of emigration.[6]

The literature concerning these cultures of emigration is now growing rapidly. One recent bibliography of the experiences of the Irish in Britain contains 713 entries.[7] Two clear gaps, however, appear obvious in the available material. Firstly, the experiences of Irish women are underresearched.[8] Secondly, and perhaps even less researched, are the experiences of Irish Protestants. This chapter makes no claim to fill entirely this latter gap. What it does attempt to do is to lay some markers, to set some parameters and to highlight in broad terms the relationship between social identity, politics and emigration concerning northern Protestants. Finally, the chapter suggests some further areas for research. The chapter has several underlying themes: the sociological experience of northern Protestant migration; the 'politics' of Protestant migration; and the social construction of identity, at home and abroad.

Patterns and processes of 'Protestant' emigration

For anyone researching Protestant migration several key phases and patterns emerge to set the framework. Clear and persistent links are identifiable, particularly between the Protestant community of north-eastern Ireland and Scotland, Canada, the United States and Britain. Each of these routes has its distinct patterns and features, some of which are highlighted in what follows. It is also necessary to consider the broad sweep of each, to outline the experience of 'Protestant' emigration and to give it wider sociological meaning.

Emigration to North America

The history of 'Protestant' emigration begins early. Large-scale migration from Ulster to the Americas has been recorded from around the early 1700s. The ship *Friends Goodwill*, for example, left Larne harbour in April

1717 with the first of 5000 emigrants that year.[9] Indeed, there was then a sizeable movement of population from Ulster to North America, during 1717 and 1718. Most of this wave settled in Pennsylvania. A further large exodus took place from Ulster between 1725 and 1729 and the ranks of emigrants were again swollen in 1740 and 1741. This later bout of emigration was largely precipitated by a period of severely bad weather and subsequent famine in Ulster.

Marshall argues that one clear indicator of the strength of emigration from Ulster at this time can be seen in the names of the settlements which were built. Throughout the United States of America there are, for example, 18 towns called Belfast, 16 named Derry, nine called Antrim and seven Tyrone.[10] By the early 1730s there were around 6000 Ulster emigrants settled in and around Philadelphia, which remained the hub of much of the region's emigration. As Mageean notes,

> a combination of hostility in New England and the economic opportunities and religious freedom offered in Pennsylvania diverted almost all Scottish-Irish Emigration to that state from about 1725.[11]

While Stewart explains the situation as follows,

> [Most] Scotch–Irish (as they were called in America) settled in Pennsylvania, or pushed on into Virginia or North Carolina where they had distinctive settlements, peopled with familes called Dunlop, Crawford, Boyd, Pollock, Jackson and so on — familiar Ulster surnames. Everywhere they formed the cutting edge of the westward movement, settling in the back country, fighting the Indians and bringing land under cultivation.[12]

However, while Pennsylvania remained the base for many, others began to push out towards Kentucky, North Carolina, Tennessee and along the Ohio valley. This set lines of settlement which were solidified throughout the period between 1700 and 1776, when at least 200,000, and perhaps up to a quarter of a million left Ulster for the American colonies.[13] These settlers naturally transplanted much of their culture. One clear example of this was in their music. Traditional Scottish and Irish tunes, and music derived from it, can, for example, still readily be heard in and around the Appalachia mountains.[14] This has led Williams to suggest that,

> Ireland's initial impact upon American music came predominantly from Ulster ... Whatever their influence in terms of cabin and barn styles, field layout, town planning and so on, it seems likely that the greatest and most lasting contribution of the Scotch–Irish was music. And however one may define their particular religious and ethnic identity, musically they should be considered Ulstermen, for they brought with them the mixture of Scottish and Irish tunes which is still characteristic of large parts of northern Ireland.[15]

None the less, the culture of Ulster's emigrants was mediated by their overall experience. By the time of the war against Britain this had become clear.

Again, Stewart provides a useful insight into the politics of many of Ulster's Presbyterians,

> They were anything but loyalist in outlook, their attitude to the Crown reflect-
> ing their attitude in Ulster to the Church of Ireland landlords, the Irish
> Parliament and Dublin Castle, the seat of English authority. They became there-
> fore the most ardent supporters of colonial grievance against the home govern-
> ment, and when the war came Washington paid tribute to their rebel qualities.
> 'If I am defeated everywhere else,' he said, 'I will make my last stand among the
> Scotch-Irish of my native Virginia.'[16]

Religion remained central to the culture of many. By 1760 there were over 300 recorded Presbyterian congregations in the new world. This marked a dramatic increase, over 1705 for example, when there had been just seven. The experience of Ulster Protestant emigration to the new world had, by the early part of the nineteenth century, become both persistent and estab-lished. By the end of the first quarter of the nineteenth century, Ulster still contributed about half of all Ireland's emigrants to North America.[17] Ulster Protestants' links with the new world were already a century old and oper-ating along well-established channels.

The disproportionately high number of Protestants emigrating to North America continued to around the 1830s. From this point, however, although Protestant farmers continued to leave in high numbers from Antrim, Down, Derry and Donegal, there were an increasing number of Ulster Catholics also emigrating. This was especially the case of those from Tyrone, Monaghan and Cavan. By the end of the 1830s Catholic emigrants from Ulster outnumbered Dissenter. Also at this time, although many were still leaving Ulster, the majority emigrating from Ireland were from the south and west of the island. That said, the numbers leaving Ulster were large. Between 1800 and 1840, Ulster supplied at least 40 per cent and pos-sibly even half of all Irish emigrants to North America. In total this was between 400,000 and 500,000 people.[18]

It was, of course, the Famine which marked the watershed in Ireland's demographic history. In the century before 1845 Ireland's population had at least tripled; in the hundred years following the Famine, it halved. In the decade after 1841 there were more than one million deaths over the figure which could normally be expected. On top of this massive loss of life, another 1.2 million emigrated. Ulster, as elsewhere on the island, saw the numbers leaving increase dramatically. The decade beginning 1841 saw Ulster's population fall from 2.4 to 2 million. In particular, great numbers left Fermanagh, Monaghan, Tyrone, Armagh and Cavan. It was only in the easternmost counties of Down and Antrim that emigration rates fell below the national level. Here, perhaps as few as one in ten of the people emi-grated.

In overall terms, Ulster suffered between 200,000 and 250,000 Famine-related deaths.[19] There was some relief provided by the rural textile industry, and Belfast's numbers were swollen greatly by an influx of refugees from the countryside. It was at this time also that the number of Catholics in Belfast grew considerably. Overall, between 1861 and 1901 Ulster's Catholic population fell from 50 to 44 per cent. This suggests a higher migration rate for Ulster Catholics than for Protestants. None the less, Presbyterians and Episcopalians continued to leave in substantial numbers, which has drawn surprisingly little comment. As Campbell notes, the popular belief that northern Protestants have always formed a monolithic bloc, all holding the same political, social and religious views, with a common set of experiences, obscures a complex truth. This is part of a wider phenomenon, whereby the 'dissenting voice' of liberal Protestantism has been gravely neglected in the recording of Irish history.[20]

Ulster did have several distinct demographic features. Between 1821 and 1841 the birth rate in Ulster moved in line with the national average. The death rate, however, was considerably below average. This meant Ulster had a high level of population increase, at least compared with the rest of Ireland. This was offset by an emigration rate of between 8.4 and 9.4 per 1000. This must be compared with 7 per 1000 throughout the rest of the island. The result was, as Clarkson[21] argues, that, when the Famine did strike, Ulster was able to ride out the crisis better than elsewhere.

Mageean[22] has provided an excellent study of the effect on Ulster society of emigration, particularly from the north-west of the province, during the mid-nineteenth century. Using shipping registers for the years 1847 to 1867, she notes that emigration through Derry was strongly established by the eighteenth century. Emigration drew heavily on the immediate hinterland of Donegal, Tyrone, Antrim and Fermanagh. Much of the emigration in the late seventeenth and early eighteenth century had been motivated by fears of religious persecution. Indeed, many Presbyterian ministers led large numbers of their congregations to the New World. It was this which was central in engendering and locating a 'mentality of emigration' in the region. Mageean further points out that by the nineteenth century there had been important changes in the social composition of emigrants. One of the most dramatic responses to the famine was the increasing trend for whole families to leave.

The Canadian experience

Not all emigrants who set sail for North America were bound for the United States. From the early 1800s on, an increasing number of emigrants from Ulster were destined for Canada. Initially at least, many were attracted by the cheaper fares, which were on offer aboard commercial vessels. The principal phase of Irish emigration to Canada was between the years 1815 and 1855.[23] This established a clear and distinct pattern, which was little altered by later smaller waves of migrations. The vast majority of nineteenth-century emigrants came from Ulster, although the northern part of Leinster was also well represented. Populist, large-scale and widespread migration to Canada, from Ireland, was in fact a very short-term phenomenon. It was also restricted to an extremely limited geographical region.

According to Houston and Smyth[24] it was these key features which gave emigration to Canada its particular hue, and which in particular, differentiated it from the pattern in the United States. Thus, when the numbers of Catholic emigrants to Canada rose, during the 1830s and 1840s, they encountered established settlement patterns with a strong Protestant base. Further, many Catholics used Canada only as a stopping point on their way to the United States, where, in many cases, they in turn found strong kinship ties already in place.

In Canada the churches continued to provide an important feature in the formation of the cultural identity of Protestant emigrants. They acted in part as 'forums for ethnic fusion'. Central also was the role of the Orange Order, to the extent that, by the end of the nineteenth century, about one-third of all English-speaking Canadians were members.[25] With this of course went a particular political world view,

> In creating the rules for life in the new environment the tried and proven Old World models of behaviour and organisation were the prime points of reference, the main source of inspiration — loyalty, Protestantism, and conservatism. Orangemen found on the new frontier reasons to continue and deploy their colonial Irish ideals. They were not there to create or allow a republic. In their view, Canada would be Protestant and British, would fear God, and would Honour the King (or Queen).[26]

For many Protestants another core feature of their social identity was to see themselves in the role of 'defenders' of British Canada. Initially, the perceived threats were from the republic of the United States. There was also a perceived internal threat, in the shape of political agitation from French Canadians and Nationalists. The situation, however, became more confrontational following the large influx of Irish Catholics over the Famine period. There was a growing concern for the increasing organization of the Fenian Brotherhood. The Orange Order in response functioned to strengthen social solidarity and provided a direct link with social and political values of the 'homeland'. While no doubt some of the motivation was overtly sectarian, the social role and support functions of the Order should not be underestimated. Orange Lodges provided a well-established network into which new emigrants could quickly be slotted. They also provided welfare support, helping to take care of the sick and elderly, and quickly established a widows' pension and insurance scheme. For many, the Orange Lodges provided the only source of organized social welfare, and served to ease the burden of emigration and social hardship. Again, as in Ireland itself, Orange membership was, in many cases, a necessary prerequisite for finding work opportunities and employment.

Another reason the Orange Order assumed the importance it did in Canadian society was that, at the height of mass emigration, so many people who left Ireland for Canada had been members. Canada had its own folklore and traditions, and its own 'Orange martyrs', but most of its symbolism was quickly recognizable to those recently arrived from Ireland. Canadian Orange culture drew on a common set of values and styles of life. For the emigrants, the Canadian Orange Order represented the embodiment of this distinct culture, even several thousand miles from home. By 1900, there were more Orange Lodges in Canada than in Ireland. The Orange Order in Canada was well organized and structured, especially in Ontario. Toronto, for example, quickly earned the nickname 'Little Belfast'. As Fitzpatrick puts it, Toronto

> until the middle of the twentieth century was controlled, though by no means exclusively populated, by the Scots-Irish.[27]

Local politics bore a strong resemblance to those of the later Stormont Parliament. City Officials were almost always Orange members, and the Orange 'slate' nearly always proved crucial in election results. The values and culture of Orangeism were to prove extremely long lasting in the history of Protestant Canada.

Although it no longer has such political influence, the cultural values of Orangeism remain to be seen in Canadian society. Glenn Patterson, the Northern Irish writer,[28] describes one summer of his youth spent in Canada as follows,

> I followed one band I knew as it made its way between skyscrapers and shopping malls to a pedestrian precinct in downtown Toronto. I attended socials in a Rangers' Club-cum-bandhall west of Toronto and heard the 'Protestant Boys' sung in the bug-crackling darkness of late night poolside parties.[29]

The *Orange Standard*, the official newspaper of the Orange Order in Ireland, was recently able to report that,

> The Canadian 'Twelfth' was held on Saturday, July 13 with 40–50 bands and lodges taking part. The parade assembled at Queen's Park, Toronto, and after two hours on the march it arrived at St. James Park.[30]

It was the continuance and strength of emigration, compounded with a long history of Presbyterian emigration from Scotland to Ulster, which gave many Ulster Protestants their initial identity upon reaching Canada. This wide-scale experience provided the base for the social construction of the 'Scots-Irish' community in America.[31] The Scots–Irish were those who sought to distinguish themselves from other Irish who emigrated, whom many at best regarded as socially different, at worst, inferior. Socially and culturally different, it may even be that the Scots–Irish considered themselves a distinct 'race'. Subsequent waves helped reinforce this identity.[32] Such notions have been resurrected by some in recent years.[33] This is a point to which we shall return in the context of the contemporary politics of emigration in Northern Ireland.

In the United States the experience differed. Ulster Protestants more quickly became 'Americans'. Any residual antagonisms between Orange and Green were quickly institutionalized, and at a different level, that of formal politics. This can be clearly seen in the history of political identification with the Republican and Democratic parties by Protestants and Catholics respectively. In Canada the experience of 'Orangeism' remained more relevant. As one commentator puts it,

> Orange is more the colour of choice in Canada ... Orange lodges run the parades. When the Irish gather north of the [USA/Canada] border to establish a common identity it is more often around the standard of the Ulster Defence Association. Although transplanted Protestants have been more likely than Catholics to assimilate fully, lately there has been a corresponding cultural movement amongst Protestants in America, giving them a new ethnic distinctiveness.[34]

Scotland and the links with Ulster

One does not have to cross the Atlantic, however, to find Orangeism as a focus for Protestant emigration. The mass movement of people from Ireland to Britain is, of course, a long-standing phenomenon. It is important to highlight several patterns to that migration. As Davis has pointed out, such population movements have tended to follow three clear arterial routes: a southern pathway from South Leinster and Munster, often through South Wales or Bristol to London; a midland route from Connaught and Leinster to the north and Midlands of England; and a northern path, from North Connaught and Ulster to Scotland.[35] Holmes has recently confirmed that by the 1930s a clear overall pattern had emerged across the British Isles.

> In England and Wales the majority of the Irish came from the Irish Free State; in Scotland by contrast, the larger number of a smaller global total had birthplaces in Northern Ireland.[36]

Migration between Ulster and Scotland can be traced back to prehistory.[37] In the contemporary period, there has been a constant flow of people and workers to Scotland from the eighteenth century onwards. Such migrant workers have proved of no little consequence to Scotland's economic development. The movement of population increased noticeably in the early nineteenth century, with the introduction of the commercial ferry services between the north of Ireland and the Clyde. There were also overt attempts by employers in Scotland to recruit from Ireland. Irish labour was cheaper, and low-paid Irish workers were a much-sought-after economic resource. They quickly found themselves in direct competition with Highland labour. As Gallagher suggests, both 'Highlanders and Irish were locked in competition for unskilled jobs.'[38]

By the 1860s, there was a substantial Ulster Protestant community living in Glasgow. Indeed, they may have comprised up to one in four of the Irish in the city. The real history of Scottish Orangeism begins at this time.

Throughout the period from 1876 to 1910 there continued to be heavy emigration from Ulster to Scotland. The six counties which now comprise Northern Ireland regularly provided three-quarters of the emigrants. Large numbers were labourers. However, there was also an important exchange of skilled labour between the shipyards of Belfast and Clydeside. In Belfast, Orangeism and the opportunity to work in skilled labour were intertwined. By the late 1870s this was also entrenched in the Glasgow shipyards. The importance of this should not be underestimated. The ability to hire, fire and allocate work was very often carried out in an authoritarian manner, either by employers, or by proxy. As Foster and Woolfson explain,

> Most yards pursued a policy of retaining a core of loyal and highly skilled workers, experts in fairing, plating and riveting, usually Masonic, sometimes Orange and often occupying tied shipyard housing. These men would lead teams that secured the most favourable and lucrative areas of work (and in riveting this could make up to 34 per cent difference in earnings). In addition, at least some yards cultivated a policy of ethnic discrimination that utilised the divisions within a population that was split, roughly, 20 per cent Irish, 20 per cent Highlander and 60 per cent Lowland Scot.[39]

Orangeism thus became deeply rooted in the industrialized Lowlands of Scotland. Its primary task was one of social closure, excluding Irish Catholics on the grounds of religion and ethnicity, and allowing the protection of economic privilege by excluding less skilled workers. The existence of Freemasonry, Orangeism and craft unions all ensured that the bulk of Scottish craft work was protected from the infiltration of unskilled Irish workers.[40]

Politics in Ireland often had a direct relevance to, and influence upon, politics in Scotland. At times, as for example, during the Home Rule crisis of the 1880s, sectarian tensions rose dramatically. They did so again during the Easter Rising of 1916. However, as Bruce suggests, after partition, the 'Irish Question' increasingly fell from the political agenda. Given the very high rates of 'intermarriage between Protestant and Catholic, sectarian conflict and ethnic discrimination became difficult to sustain and gradually the numbers who wanted to maintain it declined.'[41] Scotland, like Canada, however, remains one of the few places in the world where Ulster Loyalists can find vocal, political and practical support.[42]

'Orange' and 'Green' in Liverpool

While Glasgow was a focal point for emigration, Liverpool attracted even larger numbers of people leaving Ireland. Once again, a substantial proportion of these were Ulster Protestants. Liverpool formed the third point in the great industrial triangle, along with Belfast and Glasgow, upon which the British Empire's industrial strength rested. Here too, there was a substantial movement of skilled and craft workers between the city and the

Belfast shipyards and engineering works. The sectarian experience in Liverpool was not as intense as in Glasgow. None the less, such social divisions were more clear-cut than in any other English city. This was reflected in the strength of Orangeism in the region. From 1800 onwards, Orange Lodges began to be formed in Britain. They eventually combined to make the English Orange Institution in 1807. Neal[43] has suggested that much of the momentum for an amalgamation came from a violent confrontation at that year's 'Twelfth' demonstration, which precipitated the first major clash recorded between 'Orange' and 'Green' in England. This established a pattern; certainly there were a continuous series of street skirmishes recorded from the early part of the decade onwards.

Outside London, Liverpool remained a prime target for emigrants. Sectarian opposition to large-scale Irish immigration quickly established itself as an everyday feature of political life in the city. Further, from around 1835 on, sectarian affiliation played an increasingly dominant role in party politics in that city. Hence, when in 1841 the Liberals lost control of the local council, direct Tory appeals to put 'Protestantism' before class position proved remarkably successful. The situation, already serious, was made worse by mass emigration during the Famine years and further tensions created by a poor relief system totally unable to cope. Much of the coverage of the time was typical of Victorian middle-class views on the new urban poor.[44] What was different in Liverpool was the strength of anti-Catholic feeling.[45] In the 1880s, Home Rule for Ireland dictated Liverpool politics. The Catholic Irish population of the city mobilized, forming the Nationalist Party.

It was this strength of Irish Nationalist feeling, and the response of an Orange-Tory populist alliance which gave Liverpool politics its particular direction and momentum. The city itself was physically segregated along religious and political lines. Catholic Nationalism drew most of its support from the Scotland Road, North Docks and City Centre areas. Militant Protestants occupied the east of the city, particularly the Netherfield and St Domingo Road areas.

Relations between the two communities were far from easy. Take this description of the aftermath of one confrontation in May 1909, which bears a remarkable resemblance to events in Belfast, during the earliest phase of the contemporary conflict:

> The city was torn by sectarian violence. Priests at St. Anthony's [the church was on Scotland Road, but the parish extended into Protestant Netherfield Road] knew of 157 families (833 individuals) who fled from Protestant streets. There were Protestant victims too. The parish of St. Martins-in-the-fields, which included Scotland and Vauxhall Roads, was four-fifths Catholic, but here the Church School was stormed and 110 Protestant families left the neighbourhood, houses were marked to denote the creed of their inhabitants; beatings and looting were common as partisans aimed to enforce a monopoly of faith in their area.[46]

This may well have been one of the more serious series of incidents. While not all divisions manifested themselves in violence, the city certainly remained politically segregated. The 'Protestant Party' was founded in 1922, and although it never had more than six city councillors in its history, it was always an important ideological focus for militant Protestantism.

Perhaps even more importantly, the city remained divided socially. Both Protestant and Catholic working classes had developed their own mutually exclusive subcultures. Neal explains this in the case of the Protestant working class as follows,

> Over a hundred years of Orangeism in Liverpool had, by 1919, produced a strong working class culture with its own music, songs, traditions and social organisation of benefit clubs, burial societies and quasi-religious ceremonies.[47]

It was not until the late 1930s that any real signs of the erosion of sectarian politics could be seen in Liverpool. By 1936, the Working Men's Conservative Association, which at the century's turn had numbered 8000 could boast only a few hundred members. The strength and significance of the Labour Party grew as it recruited from both the Catholic and Protestant working class. Liverpool politics began to reflect much more directly the patterns of direct class alignment found in the rest of Britain. Post-war affluence, and the claim of growing *embourgeoisement*, undermined any economic validity which remained in Orangeism. At a more fundamental level, the huge programmes of physical redevelopment meant the break-up of traditional working-class communities and the patterns of sectarian socialization which were integral to such communities.

'Protestant' emigration: a social and cultural framework

The previous sections have sought to establish some of the key patterns and features of 'Protestant' emigration up to the partition of Ireland. It is important to try and place these experiences in the context of two wider sets of social relationships. First, there is the relationship with the society which has failed to hold the emigrant. Secondly, there is the relationship with the society which the emigrant has moved to. Clearly these relationships are no less relevant to Irish Protestants than to other social groups. Emigration is a form of social behaviour which often conforms to group norms and the parameters set by the wider social structure. However, emigration must also involve personal strategies of choice and timing to put it into practice.

There are three major reasons often given as to why people may be motivated to emigrate. The first of these is economic, with a real or perceived lack of opportunities at home. The second major reason is aspirational, the desire to seek an alternative, often 'better' life. The third main reason is that of dislocation, that is, a strong feeling of detachment from one's own society. Emigration may also be located in temporal terms. So, for example, the initial waves of Protestant emigration to the north Americas were motivated by both economic and aspirational factors. Not only was there the search for a better lifestyle, but also the strong desire for, and motivation of, possible religious freedom. With later emigration it is more likely that the prime motive was economic. For this reason Miller[48] has claimed that Protestant emigrants saw their experience in essentially 'positive' terms.

Like all emigrants, Protestants have sought to establish their own social and political links with the 'homeland' and to establish or re-establish some sense of their own community. Following Cohen[49] it is possible to begin to define a community, at its most basic level, as a group whose members have something in common with each other. They also, however, are a group within which members can be distinguished, in significant ways, from other groups. Community thus implies the construction of an identity, which at the same time stresses both similarity and difference. Many emigrants from a Protestant background merely sought to integrate themselves into their new societies as rapidly as possible. For others, especially the earliest emigrants, the sense of community they desired was best expressed through an overt re-expression of their traditions, including Orangeism.

The situation may not have been that different from that in many rural areas of Northern Ireland today.[50] Here, the Orange Order continues to play a major role in expressing community identity, much more so than in the city. In rural areas, Larsen suggests,[51] the symbolic significance of the `Twelfth' is primary. This can be seen as twofold: as a message from the Protestant community as a whole, mediated through `official' spokespersons in the Orange Order; and as a medium through which `ordinary' participants can discern and communicate values by which they perceive their identity. The Orange Order provided many emigrants with political continuity. No less important was the social support the Order provided against the hardships of emigration. In some cases the Order was able to determine job opportunities and provide access to employment. Protestant emigration has its own patterns and trends, some of which have been identified. These patterns were established quickly, and it is important to identify them, because it was upon these foundations that subsequent experiences rested.

Post-partition Ireland and the 'politics of emigration'

Partition institutionalized many of the political and sectarian relationships in Ireland. It also institutionalized many of the social divisions in Irish society. One of the main considerations in determining the physical boundary of Northern Ireland was that it included those areas with a Protestant majority. The new Northern Irish state, however, also contained a substantial Catholic minority within its boundaries. Its religious composition was approximately 33.5 per cent Catholic, 31.3 per cent Presbyterian, 27 per cent Church of Ireland, 3.9 per cent Methodist and 4.3 per cent of other religions.[52] There were fears expressed from the beginning, from within sections of the Protestant community, that Catholics might one day constitute a majority. There appeared, initially at least, to have been little real evidence to support these Unionist fears. By 1961, for example, Northern Ireland's Catholic population stood at 34.9 per cent, only slightly higher than at partition. One key reason for this was the high rate of Catholic emigration.

It is also useful to highlight briefly the main differences in emigration patterns between Northern Ireland and the Irish Free State Republic after partition. Like the Free State Republic, Northern Ireland had experienced overall net emigration for most of the period from the Famine. Between 1921 and 1981 this amounted to around 440,000 people (about 7000 per year on average). Although it remained high, both in relative and absolute terms, emigration from Northern Ireland was considerably less than that from the Free State Republic for the fifty years following partition. During the decade of the 1970s, however, the rate for Northern Ireland was actually higher than the Republic. In fact, Northern Ireland experienced a fall in its population for the first time since the creation of the state. This trend was short lived. Today, large-scale emigration continues to occupy a central position in the social structure of Northern Ireland.

The Irish Free State Republic also experienced its own distinct pattern of emigration. In terms of this chapter, perhaps the most noteworthy feature of the southern state was the disproportionately high numbers of Protestants leaving the 26 counties in the immediate post-partition period. Here a number of pressures combined to make the general atmosphere uncongenial for many.[53] More generally, however, between 1945 and 1951, 24,000 people left the Irish Republic each year. For the period between 1956 to 1961, there were 42,000 permanent emigrants annually. It was not until the 1960s that there was a reduction in emigration rates. This process continued, so that between 1971 and 1979, the Irish Republic actually experienced a net inflow of people. This trend, however, was a short-lived phase. The general pattern quickly returned to its previous form, so that in 1985–6, for example, 31,000 emigrated from the Irish Republic, and on average 40,000 left each year throughout the 1980s.[54] The most recent evidence suggests that levels of emigration have again slowed.[55]

There are then significant differences between the emigration patterns of the two states. More important perhaps, are the clear differences in trends by religion within Northern Ireland. Until recently, the rate for Catholics was consistently more than twice that for Protestants. One major reason for this has been different access to labour markets. The 'politics of emigration' has, first and foremost, to be considered against the economic background of Northern Ireland.

A constant feature of Northern Ireland, since the formation of the state, has been its low socio-economic status. At partition, the economy rested on an outmoded agricultural sector. Shipbuilding and linen, both of which were desperately vulnerable to the fluctuations of the world capitalist economy, provided the other foundations of its industrial base.

Furthermore, shipbuilding, its related engineering works and the linen industry were extremely geographically concentrated, in and around Belfast. The narrowness of Northern Ireland's industrial base meant it suffered badly in the post-war economic restructuring. By the mid-1950s it was clear to the Unionist leadership that shipbuilding, textiles and engineering did not make for a viable economic future. Rowthorn and Wayne describe some of the consequences:

> Despite the new jobs in manufacturing, construction and services, *total* employment was hardly affected — the gains were virtually cancelled out by an equally large decline in the old manufacturing and in agriculture. Given Northern Ireland's traditionally high birth rate, this failure to increase total employment would have led to a huge surplus of labour, were it not for an enormous exodus of people from the province. During the 1950s a third of all school leavers were forced to emigrate in search of work. Many were Protestants, but a majority were Catholic.[56]

Attempts to attract external capital in the form of multinational companies proved reasonably successful, but only in the short term. In more recent years, this economic base was subsequently undermined, particularly as recession caused transnational companies to relocate physically. From 1979 on, Northern Ireland found itself subject to the overall process of de-industrialization common to the UK economy.[57] The decline in manufacturing was partly offset by a rise in service industries, which rose by two-thirds between 1958 and 1980.[58] There was also a growth in work related to 'security'. Nevertheless, Northern Ireland's regional economy remained extremely weak.

One vital feature of the Northern Irish economy has been the different employment patterns of Protestant and Catholic workers.[59] One example of this can be seen in comparative unemployment figures.[60] Unemployment rates in Northern Ireland have always been much higher than in the rest of the UK. In the 1920s, for example, the figure was close to 20 per cent, and in the 1930s it averaged 27 per cent. Even with the onset of the economic 'boom', and a commitment to full employment, as part of the post-war consensus, the unemployment rate in Northern Ireland stood at three times the UK average. By the mid-1980s, the unemployment rate stood at 21 per cent compared with a Uk average of just over 13 per cent.

Overall unemployment rates have disguised markedly different historical employment patterns, between Protestants and Catholics.[61] The simplest explanation for the weaker occupational position of Catholic workers is discrimination, shown in favour of Protestants, at both an institutional and local level. As the north of Ireland industrialized heavily in the late nineteenth century, Belfast attracted large numbers of migrants from rural areas, many of whom were Catholic. They found employment largely in the unskilled sector of the labour market. Skilled work, particularly in shipbuilding and engineering, was mainly occupied by Protestant men. Local hiring and firing practices, similar to those in the Scottish shipyards described earlier, ensured that the social divisions between Protestant and Catholic workers were maintained. The core notion remains that of Protestant workers having formed an 'aristocracy of labour' to protect economic privilege.

These social divisions of labour remain apparent today, although in a considerably diluted form. While the notion of a labour aristocracy rests on incontrovertible differences between the two communities,[62] the attempt to transpose the social relations of the 1890s on to contemporary Belfast does not make for a direct, or easy, fit. There have, for example, always been a considerable number of unskilled Protestant workers and a growing Catholic middle class. As Hout explains,

> Protestants might be alone at the top of the status hierarchy in Northern Ireland but Catholics are not alone at the bottom.[63]

So while many Catholics were less well-off in material terms than Protestants, the weaker economic position of Catholics cannot, alone, fully explain the numbers of Catholics who emigrated. Poverty and poor housing are now common experiences of large sections of both communities.[64] What is being questioned here is not the notion that in broad terms Protestant workers were, and in many cases remain, better-off than Catholic workers. Rather, it is whether such differences can be used to explain the historically different emigration rates between Catholics and Protestants. To explain these differences fully it is necessary to widen the issues beyond the simple economic position, to consider other social attitudes, such as those towards the legitimacy of the Northern Irish state itself.

Protestant identity and the 'emigration of politics'

Initially, the lack of commitment many Catholics felt towards the new Northern Irish state may have manifested itself in a greater willingness of Catholics to leave than Protestants. Buckland has suggested, for example, that many Catholics avoided any direct engagement with the state, because, they feared participation would somehow bestow legitimacy.[65] The state itself, in turn, did little to encourage full participation from the Catholic community. Burton sets the context well,

> The history of plantation and division between Catholic and Protestant, and its viscous manifestations through the industrialization of the North became epitomized in the creation of a separate Northern Ireland. Partition was hardly conducive to easing the *laager* mentality of the Protestant people. The border came to symbolize all the real and supposed peculiarities of the two religious groups. The polarization of political allegiance along religious lines, and the Orange, and now Unionist, hegemony was reflected in the State's intransigence.[66]

Emigration from Northern Ireland has, therefore, to be set against the dominant ideological position being reproduced by the Unionist state. This rested on the core idea that Northern Ireland was an integral part of the United Kingdom, and further, that any differences between Northern Ireland and Britain were minimal. Part of this Unionist ideology was certainly élitist and triumphalist. Indeed, it is possible to suggest that substantial Catholic emigration was an overt policy goal of the Unionist administration; a tactic, used in order to limit the numbers of nationalists within the Northern Irish state.

There was, however, another side to fifty years of Unionist government. Certainly in the post-war period, there was a commitment, albeit a limited one, to the social democratic philosophy of the British state. This may have moved slightly against emigration, especially as it involved the provision of advanced welfare services. In part, this must be seen in the context of ensuring the continued allegiance of the Protestant working class. It was also, in part, an attempt to seduce political allegiance to the state from the Catholic working class, a propaganda weapon, to be used in comparisons with the situation in the Irish Republic. None the less, the provision of welfare benefit, for whatever reason, may for some have tipped the scale against the insecurities of emigration. The culture of emigration, however, was deeply instilled in the Catholic population of Northern Ireland. They tended to migrate in large numbers. Between 1951 and 1961, for example, Catholic males were twice as likely to migrate as their Protestant counterparts. For females, the Catholic rate was three times greater than for Protestants.[67]

Another central feature of demographic change in Northern Ireland has been the 'politics of numbers'. Given that it is possible for a majority living in Northern Ireland to opt out of the United Kingdom, the actual numbers of Protestants and Catholics living within Northern Ireland have always been of more than academic interest. Tomlinson puts it in straightforward terms when he says that Unionists have always been haunted 'by the spectre of being outbred by nationalists.'[68] Traditionally, it was the high level of Catholic emigration which offset their higher rate of population increase. Protestants in Northern Ireland, by contrast, had a lower birth rate and a lower rate of emigration.

Overall, the differences between the two net population rates show a small, but steady, growth in the Catholic population. Since partition, Catholics have persistently increased their proportion of the population, to the point that today they constitute about 40 per cent of the overall population. The 'bottom line' for many Unionists is, of course, that if the present natural increase between the two communities and emigration rates are held constant, then Roman Catholics will eventually form a majority of the population. The essential question then becomes 'when', rather than if, this is likely to happen.

There are several variables to the equation. The most important are the rates of natural increase, within the respective denominations, and the comparative rates of emigration. Within Northern Ireland, during the 1960s and 1970s, the Protestant birth rate was low, in line with the general pattern in western Europe. In direct contrast, for the same period, the Catholic birth rate, although it too declined in the 1970s, remained high, well above the European average. Compton[69] writing on data available up to the mid-1970s suggested that using estimates based on fertility and mortality rates, and assuming no emigration, it would be possible to predict a simple Catholic majority could be achieved by around 2020. This would be reflected in voting behaviour sometime between the years 2025–35. Using later figures, based on the 1981 census, Compton again estimated that, with current birth and death rates and no emigration, Catholics would achieve a majority by 2026. He recognizes that emigration rates have kept down the Catholic percentage of the population, and that Catholic birth rates are falling with increased contraceptive use. Taking these factors into account Compton suggested that the Catholic share of Northern Ireland's population would rise more slowly in the future, stabilizing at around 44 per cent.

Recent reports have suggested that the above is an underestimate, that Catholics will be in a majority in Northern Ireland, sooner, rather than later.[70] These latest projections, based on the 1991 census, have, however, again been open to extremely conflicting interpretations. Partly this is due to the very incomplete returns concerning religious affiliation for the previous 1981 census. The extent of this only really became apparent with initial analysis of the 1991 census. Changes in overall demographic trends are therefore somewhat difficult to assess. The returns do seem to suggest that Catholics now make up about 43 per cent of the population. Crucial is the accuracy of any predictions in the pattern of growth of the Catholic population. Compton has recently suggested that the rate has slowed down, stabilized at around 1.5 per cent per decade.[71] This being the case, it would be another 60 to 70 years before a simple Catholic majority was in place in Northern Ireland.

What is certain is that demography has a real, everyday effect on politics in Northern Ireland. Eleven of Northern Ireland's 26 district councils now have a Catholic majority. The long-standing geographical division across Northern Ireland, between a Catholic west and Protestant east, has become more pronounced. Belfast is a city now not only clearly demarcated along lines of sectarian division, but also social class. In overall terms, it is clear that the traditional patterns of migration, with larger numbers of Catholics leaving, has been severely disrupted. Throughout the best part of the 1960s, for example, around 60 per cent of those emigrating were Catholic. In recent years, however, with rapidly contracting labour markets abroad, Catholic emigration has fallen dramatically. The departure rate for Protestants has, however, increased over the same period. Even these stark differences obscure important details.

Young, gifted and 'gone'

One group of interest are those leaving Northern Ireland to undertake higher education at British universities. In 1984/5, 2043 students registered

at institutions outside Northern Ireland. This represented some 32 per cent
of those going into higher education from Northern Ireland. By 1987/8 this
had risen to 2872 students, 40 per cent of all those progressing to higher
education. Furthermore, in the same year over 17 per cent of those gradu-
ating at both of Northern Ireland's universities found work outside the
province.[72] Such trends have serious implications for the future of
Northern Irish society. Jefferson puts this in the wider economic context:

> On average, migrants tend to be from among the younger, more active and more
> skilled members of the labour force so that the regional economy is losing above
> average workers and is left with a higher ratio of dependants to workers.[73]

The continued outflow of Northern Ireland's students, has been described
as 'the biggest Irish exodus since the famine'.[74] At a popular level, it certainly represents a 'sizeable brain drain'.[75] Northern Ireland is continuing
to lose considerable numbers of young, well-educated people. For the
majority of these people, the move is permanent. Almost 40 per cent of
Northern Ireland's university entrants attend British institutions. Two out
of three of these are Protestant. Furthermore, it is not too great a stretch of
the imagination to suggest that this emigrant group may well contain the
more liberal elements, both socially and politically, of those from a
Protestant Unionist background.

One obvious reason for the migration of large numbers of Northern Irish
youth is the 'troubles', and the continued levels of political violence and
social conflict. As Cairns explains,

> one cannot be surprised that young people are not simply expressing a rejection
> of the violence that surrounds them ... but indeed are literally voting with their
> feet against the type of society Northern Ireland has become.[76]

However, while important, a fear of violence is not necessarily central to
the motivation to leave. In one recent sample, for example, 43 per cent of
those interviewed claimed that even if the violence were to end they would
have no desire to return to Northern Ireland.[77] Other common features
appear to be a disillusionment with local politicians and politics and the
extremely conservative nature of Northern Irish society.

There is, however, little empirical material available to confirm much of
the above. The processes involved in these young people's decision to emigrate needs much further research. Is the decision that the majority seem to
take, not to return to Northern Ireland, based on economic considerations?
Or is it, as much anecdotal evidence seems to suggest, that many young
people leaving Northern Ireland reject the thought of return, because the
distance reveals to them just how conservative and socially restricted the
society is that they have left?

Questions such as those above are not merely of academic interest.
Underlying much contemporary government policy is the notion that
improving economic conditions in Northern Ireland will not only reduce

community conflict, but will eventually draw back many of those who have left. This appears to be more asserted than shown. It leans heavily on the idea that the prime motivator, in the decision to emigrate, is economic, rather than social. This is a key area demanding further research. It is vital to try to identify what, in the contemporary period, actually does initiate the choice to emigrate.

Protestant identity at home and abroad

Parallel to the above is another important area for further research. Little work has been carried out on changing political and social identification amongst emigrants. Which views are held constant, which views are allowed to change? Such considerations are particularly relevant to those from a Protestant-Unionist background. Todd[78] has distinguished two key locations for the identity of northern Protestants. She distinguishes between 'Ulster Loyalist' and 'Ulster British' as political ideologies. The core characteristic of 'Ulster Loyalist' ideology is a primary identification as Northern Protestant, while any identification with Britain is a secondary loyalty. Within the 'Ulster British' ideology the imagined community is Greater Britain, although there is a distinct secondary regional identification with Northern Ireland. Those who subscribe to such an ideology identify strongly with British parliamentary traditions and largely disapprove of sectarianism and overt anti-Catholicism. For others, the attempt may be made to transpose social and political relations to a new location. Loyalist paramilitaries, for example, claim branches in Scotland, England and Wales, while outside the United Kingdom, Canada and South Africa have provided important, if somewhat insubstantial, pockets of support for the loyalist cause.[79]

'Double migrants' — contradictions of Unionist emigrant identity

A more common experience, for those who carry with them either Unionist or Loyalist ideological baggage, is that emigration brings into sharp relief the contradictions of their identity. The experience of emigration to Britain can prove particularly shattering in these terms. As one leading Loyalist explained, when talking to an American writer,

> If, for instance, I was to take you to Bradford, or Birmingham, or London, or somewhere in England at the present time, you would be accepted as an American. But they hear my accent and say, 'Oh he is Irish.' They don't treat me as British. I am one of the black Irish.[80]

In this sense, the experience of northern Protestant emigrants, especially those who seek to construct their identity as 'Loyalist or Unionist', or who have done so in the past, is particularly alienating. They can best be understood as 'double migrants'. On the one hand, they do not regard themselves either symbolically, socially or politically as part of the mainstream 'imagined community' of the Irish overseas. On the other hand, their own self-construction of identity alienates them from the very society to which many claim such strong allegiance.

One variable is social class. Those from working-class backgrounds are more likely to identify themselves as loyalist, and to experience fully the feelings of alienation outlined above. Those Unionists from a middle-class, higher educational background, with the resultant better-life opportunities, however, may find it easier to integrate themselves more quickly into British society. One other consideration, and another area certainly worthy of further research, is whether there is an adjustment in cultural identity amongst northern Protestants who emigrate, towards an identity which is best described as 'Northern Irish'. Certainly evidence exists, again, albeit largely at a folklore level, of northern Protestants and Catholics in exile finding more in common with each other, than with those from either the Irish Republic or Britain. This is certainly an area which deserves fuller research. Why and how are previously deeply held political ideologies altered? Gallagher's work on Scotland, for example, indicates how, in relatively recent times, a growing Scottish identity weaned people away from a direct identification with the Ulster crisis. One result was a rejection of the more overt and political forms of sectarianism. In a similar vein, Neal has argued that growing working-class affluence in Liverpool in the 1960s lessened sectarianism.

A common thread to both these studies is how sectarianism, where it does still exist in a contemporary form, in both Glasgow or Liverpool, does so largely as a form of cultural expression. It is sectarianism, in its institutionalized and politicized form, in Northern Ireland, which has made the problem so intractable. Clearly, social and political thought is not open-ended. It remains restricted by the cultural world in which people exist. Everyone constructs his or her own particular world view out of the range of ideas to which they are exposed and which are projected to them as meaningful. Put simply, the range of reference points by which Protestants construct their social world in Northern Ireland may well become increasingly distant, and in many cases increasingly meaningless, after migration. In Britain, for example, the core values by which many Ulster Protestant emigrants have made sense of their everyday world are increasingly challenged. These views are altered by the rejection by British society that many northern Unionists feel, once they have moved to Britain. This does not mean, however, that they readily adopt an 'Irish' identity. There remains for many an inability to affiliate with the imagined community of the majority of Irish emigrants.

Some conclusions

This chapter has been painted with an extremely broad brush, and does little for the details of history, or the craft of the historian. It has presented an extremely condensed and selective view of Protestant emigration. However, because of the lack of material available on the subject, hopefully this approach is understandable. It is crucial to lay out some markers. One of the key problems of trying to study 'Protestant' migration has been that the label 'Irish', meaning 'Catholic Irish', has been almost universally and stereo-typically applied to all those from the island of Ireland. Partly, of course, this reflects the fact that the bulk of emigrants were Catholic. The Catholic Church was highly visible in providing a vital role in the transmission of culture and in the provision of welfare. As such, this was part of the central experience and tradition of emigration for many. These traditions, which have been invented for the Irish emigrant, directly reflects this commonality of experience.[81] However, it has also resulted in the Protestant experience of emigration being subsumed under the weight of the more general one.[82] The experience of Protestant emigration is a hidden history.

In particular, there were, and remain, for many Protestant emigrants, severe problems finding any affinity with the ways in which many Irish emigrants expressed their politics. This is part of a much wider social and political phenomenon. Archard, discussing traditional identities in Northern Ireland, puts it like this,

> When Irish nationalists assert a claim to the unification of Ireland, they appeal to a notion of Ireland and Irishness which explicitly excludes northern protestants. Or, which may be worse, they paternalistically ascribe this group's lack of a felt Irish identity to an externally induced false consciousness.[83]

This position should be challenged.[84] The experience of Ireland's peoples, and its emigrants, is far from homogeneous. Northern Irish 'Protestant' emigration deserves to be considered in its own right. It directly reflects the experience of one tradition and culture on the island. Central to this experience, but certainly not exclusive to it, is sectarianism and social division. In-depth study may well reveal why, and in what circumstances, such issues have dropped off, or been forced off, the political agenda. The experiences of Protestant emigrants, past and present, must be made more directly relevant to contemporary Irish politics and society. This is required, if only to confirm what has been suggested throughout this chapter, that the social and political identity of those from the Unionist tradition may not be as fixed as some would suggest. If this is true, the experience of Protestant emigrants may well be at least as relevant to Ireland's future as the experiences of those who remain. If the social and political conditions can be created abroad which make sectarianism increasingly less relevant, surely this may also be done at home.

Notes

1. Bernard Aspinwall, 'Irish Americans and American nationality, 1848–66', in

T. Gallagher and J. O'Connell, *Contemporary Irish Studies*, Manchester University Press, Manchester, 1983, p. 112.

2. Paul Compton, 'The demographic background', in D. Watt (ed.), *The Constitution of Northern Ireland: Problems and Prospects*, Heinemann, London, 1981, p. 88.

3. J. Holland, *Too Long a Sacrifice: Life and Death in Northern Ireland since 1969*, Penguin, New York, 1982.

4. I am of course using the term here in the way described by B. Anderson, *Imagined Communities: Reflections on the Origin and Spread of Nationalism*, Verso, London, 1991. Here Anderson traces in detail the creation and global spread of the 'imagined communities' of nationality. There are necessary pre-conditions, partly material and partly psychic, for the emergence of nationalism. The principal material condition for nationalism is 'print-capitalism' (wide-scale commercial printing which spreads the ideology of nationalism). Anderson also points to the mental processes involved — members of the smallest nation can never know all their fellow nationals, 'yet in the minds of each lives the image of their communion.' A nation is an 'imagined political community — and imagined as both inherently limited and sovereign' (p. 15).

5. For the internal significance of such symbols it may be useful to refer to M. W. Dewar, J. Brown and S. E. Long, *Orangeism: a New Historical Appreciation*, Grand Orange Lodge of Ireland, Belfast, 1967.

6. Eamonn Hughes, 'Art, exiles, Ireland and icons', in D. Smyth, (ed.), *Voyages of Discovery, Supplement to Fortnight*, No. 295, 1991.

7. M. J. Hickman (ed.), *The History of the Irish in Britain*, Irish in Britain History Centre, London, 1986.

8. This is not to deny of course that some excellent material has been produced in this area. See for example, Ann Rossiter, 'Bringing the margins into the centre: a review of aspects of Irish women's emigration', in S. Hutton and P. Stewart (eds), *Ireland's Histories*, Routledge, London, 1991; Monica McWilliams, 'Women in Northern Ireland' and Hazel Morrisey, 'Economic change and the position of women in Northern Ireland', in E. Hughes, *Culture and Politics in Northern Ireland*, Open University Press, Milton Keynes, 1991. See also M. Lennon, M. McAdam and J. O'Brien, *Across the Water — Irish Women's Lives in Britain*, Virago Press, London, 1988, and P. O'Sullivan (ed.) *Irish Women and Irish Migration*, Leicester University Press, London, 1995.

9. Ronnie Hanna, 'By the Dawn's Early Light: Ulster emigration to freedom and the New World in the eighteenth century', in *New Ulster—The Journal of the Ulster Society*, No. 16 (Spring 1992).

10. W. F. Marshall, *Ulster Sails West*, Genealogical Publishing, Baltimore, 1979.

11. Deirdre M. Mageean, 'From Irish countryside to American city', in Colin G. Pooley and Ian D. Whyte (eds), *Migrants, Emigrants and Immigrants: a Social History of Migration*, Routledge, London, 1991, p. 44.

12. A. T. Q. Stewart, 'The mind of Protestant Ulster', in David Watt (ed.), *The Constitution of Northern Ireland: Problems and Prospects*, Heinemann, London, 1981, p. 38.

13. By far the most detailed account of the period remains R. J. Dickson, *Ulster Emigration to Colonial America, 1718–1775*, Graham Omagh & Sons, 1988. It was first published in 1966. See also E. R. R. Green (ed.), *Essays in Scotch–Irish History*, Ulster Historical Foundation, Belfast, 1992. It was originally published in 1969 but the new edition contains an excellent new 'Introduction' by Steve Ickringill of the University of Ulster.

14. This point is widely developed in M. O'Connor, *Bringing It All Back Home*, BBC Books, London, 1991.
15. W. H. A. Williams, 'Irish traditional music in the United States', *America and Ireland: 1776–1976*, Greenwood Press, USA, cited in M. Hall, *Ulster's Scottish Connection*, Island Publications, Newtownabbey, 1993.
16. A. T. Q. Stewart, 'The mind of Protestant Ulster', p. 38.
17. K. Miller, *Emigrants and Exiles: Ireland and the Irish Exodus to North America*, Oxford University Press, New York, 1988, p. 197.
18. S. Clark and J. R. Donnelly, 'Introduction to Part II, Land and Religion in Ulster', in Samuel Clark and James Donnelly, Jr, *Irish Peasants: Violence and Political Unrest, 1780–1914*, Manchester University Press, Manchester, 1983, p. 150.
19. T. Wilson, *Ulster: Conflict and Consent*, Basil Blackwell, Oxford, 1989, p. 27.
20. See Flann Campbell, *The Dissenting Voice: Protestant Democracy in Ulster from Plantation to Partition*, Blackstaff, Dundonald, p. 190.
21. L. A. Clarkson, 'Population change and urbanisation, 1821–1914', in Liam Kennedy and Philip Ollerenshaw (eds), *An Economic History of Ulster, 1820–1939*, Manchester University Press, Manchester, 1985, p. 142.
22. Deidre M. Mageean, 'From Irish countryside to American City'.
23. For a highly readable account of Irish emigration to Canada see D. McKay, *Flight From Famine. The Coming of the Irish to Canada*, McClelland and Stewart, Toronto, 1990. For a more general account see G. Woodcock, *A Social History of Canada*, Penguin Books, Toronto, 1989.
24. C. J. Houston and W. J. Smyth, *Irish Emigration and Canadian Settlement: Patterns, Links and Letters*, University of Toronto Press, Toronto, 1990.
25. Houston and Smyth, *Irish Emigration and Canadian Settlement*, p. 169.
26. Houston and Smyth, *Irish Emigration and Canadian Settlement*, p. 181.
27. R. Fitzpatrick, *God's Frontiersmen. The Scots–Irish Epic*, Weidenfeld and Nicolson, London, p. 218.
28. His own excellent novels give a clear understanding of the background to everyday life in contemporary loyalist Northern Ireland. See G. Patterson, *Burning Your Own*, Chatto and Windus, London, 1988; *Fat Lad*, Chatto and Windus, London, 1992.
29. *Fortnight*, No. 286 (1990).
30. *Orange Standard*, November 1991, p. 6.
31. By the time America declared for Independence, around 250,000 people had emigrated from Ulster. This grouping made up some 15 per cent of the overall population. Because of the Lowland Scots ancestry of many, these Ulster settlers became known as the 'Scotch–Irish', and more recently as the 'Scots–Irish'.
32. See, for example, J. G. Leyburn, *The Scotch–Irish: a Social History*, University of North Carolina Press, Carolina, 1962.
33. I am thinking here in particular of the work of several groupings who in recent years have sought to 'rewrite' and reconstruct the history of Ulster Protestants so as to strengthen links with Canada and the United States of America. The Ulster Society, for example, exists to promote Ulster's 'contribution to the growth and development of other countries [which] is reflected in the presence of members in the USA, Canada, Australia and South Africa'. See, for example, R. Hanna, *Land of the Free: Ulster and the American Revolution*, Ulster Society, Lurgan, 1992; R. Hanna, *The Highest Call: Ulster and the American Presidency*, Ulster Society, Lurgan, n.d.
34. Claudia Harris, 'America's part in the greening of Ireland', *Fortnight*, No. 274

(June 1989), p. 13.

35. Graham Davis, 'Little Irelands', in Roger Swift and Sheridan Gilley (eds), *The Irish in Britain*, Pinter, London, 1989, p. 129.

36. C. Holmes, *John Bull's Island. Immigration and British Society, 1871–1971*, Macmillan, Basingstoke, 1988, p. 120. See also Colin Holmes, *A Tolerant Country? Immigrants, Refugees and Minorities in Britain*, Faber and Faber, London, 1991.

37. For a recent work emphasizing this, see M. Hall, *Ulster's Scottish Connection*, See also F. J. Bigger, 'From Uladh to Galloway and from Galloway to Uladh', *Red Hand Magazine*, Vol. 1, No. 3 (November 1920).

38. T. Gallagher, *Glasgow — the Uneasy Peace*, Manchester University Press, Manchester, 1987, p. 347.

39. J. Foster and C. Woolfson, *The Politics of the UCS Work-In*, Lawrence and Wishart, London, 1986, pp. 144–5.

40. This phenomenon of social closure by a 'labour aristocracy' was far from unique at this time. For more general discussions see E. J. Hobsbawm, 'The labour aristocracy in nineteenth-century Britain', in E. J. Hobsbawm, *Labouring Men: Studies in the History of Labour*, Weidenfeld and Nicolson, London, 1964; *Worlds of Labour*, Weidenfeld and Nicolson, London, 1984; G. Stedman Jones, 'Class struggle and the Industrial Revolution', *New Left Review*, 90 (1975); H. F. Moorhouse, 'The Marxist theory of the labour aristocracy', *Social History*, 3/1 (1978); A. Reid, 'Politics and economics in the formation of the British working class: a response to H. F. Moorhouse', *Social History*, 3/3 (1978); T. Matsumura, *The Labour Aristocracy Revisited*, Manchester University Press, Manchester, 1983; C. More, *Skill and the English Working Class, 1870–1914*, Croom Helm, London, 1980; J. Walvin, *Victorian Values*, Cardinal, London, 1988; J. Foster, *Class Struggle and the Industrial Revolution*, Weidenfeld and Nicolson, London, 1974; R. Gray, *The Aristocracy of Labour in Nineteenth-Century Britain c. 1850–1914*, Macmillan, London, 1981.

41. S. Bruce, *The Red Hand: Protestant Paramilitaries in Northern Ireland*, Oxford University Press, Oxford, 1992, p. 157.

42. Loyalist paramilitary organizations, such as the Ulster Defence Association, have for example consistently claimed to have groupings in Scotland which they have been able to draw on for support. The monthly magazine of the UDA regularly carries a 'Scottish Page' or news from the 'Scottish Brigade'.

43. F. Neal, *Sectarian Violence. The Liverpool Experience 1819–1914*, Manchester University Press, Manchester, 1988.

44. This period saw the construction of a particular view of poverty, which distinguished between the 'deserving' and 'undeserving' poor, often on overtly moralistic grounds. Within this context social work developed as an expression of middle-class fears about the urban working class and saw largely middle-class women promoting the development of 'casework' as a means of personal betterment through the supposedly 'universal' institution of the family. See, for example, G. Stedman Jones, *Outcast London*, Oxford University Press, Oxford, 1971; M. Hewitt, *Wives and Mothers in Victorian Industry*, Barrie and Rockcliffe, London, 1958; K. Woodroffe, *From Charity Work to Social Work*, Routledge & Kegan Paul, London, 1962; A. F. Young, and E. T. Ashton, *British Social Work in the Nineteenth Century*, Routledge & Kegan Paul, London, 1956.

45. G. Davis, *The Irish in Britain, 1815–1914*, Gill and Macmillan, Dublin, 1991.

46. P. J. Waller, *Democracy and Sectarianism: Liverpool 1868–1939*, p. 238, cited in Harry Law, 'Labour in Liverpool', *Campaign for Labour Representation in*

Northern Ireland, Belfast, 1992.

47. F. Neal, *Sectarian Violence. The Liverpool Experience 1819–1914*, p. 244.
48. K. Miller, *'Emigrants and Exiles'*, pp. 132–4, 157–8, 174–5, 227–8.
49. A. P. Cohen, *The Symbolic Construction of Community*, Tavistock, London, 1985.
50. For more general discussions of the relationships between Protestants and Catholics in a rural setting, see R. Harris, *Prejudice and Tolerance in Ulster*, Manchester University Press, Manchester, 1972; H. Donnan and G. McFarlane, ' "You get on better with your own": social continuity and change in rural Northern Ireland', in P. Clancy, S. Drury, K. Lynch and L. O'Dowd (eds) *Ireland: a Sociological Profile*, Institute of Public Administration, Dublin, 1986; H. Donnan and G. McFarlane, 'Informal social organisation', in J. Darby (ed.), *Northern Ireland: The Background to the Conflict*, Appletree, Belfast, 1983.
51. S. Larsen, 'The Glorious Twelfth: the politics of legitimation in Kilbroney', in A. P. Cohen, *Belonging: Identity and Social Organisation in British Rural Culture*, Manchester University Press, Manchester, 1982, pp. 278–91.
52. S. Wichert, *Northern Ireland Since 1945*, Longman, London, 1991, p. 27.
53. K. Bowen, *Protestants in a Catholic State: Ireland's Privileged Minority*, McGill/Queen's University Press, Montreal, 1983. For an excellent review of the social, economic and political position of Protestants in the Irish Republic see J. Whyte, *Interpreting Northern Ireland*, Clarendon, Oxford, 1991, pp. 151–9, 181–2.
54. 'Job seekers should stay put in Ireland', *Irish Post*, 17 October 1992, p. 7.
55. The London-based *Irish Post*, for example, recently reported the main findings of a GMB report that the number of Irish people working in Britain had fallen by nearly 100,000 (26 June 1993).
56. B. Rowthorn and N. Wayne, *Northern Ireland. The Political Economy of Conflict*, Polity Press, Oxford, 1988, p. 73.
57. For an excellent review of this period see F. Gaffikin and M. Morrissey, *Northern Ireland: The Thatcher Years*, Zed Press, London, 1990.
58. K. A. Kennedy, T. Giblin and D. McHugh, *The Economic Development of Ireland in the Twentieth Century*, Routledge, London, 1988, p. 98.
59. There is now a considerable literature in existence, both historical and contemporary, addressing such issues. See for example, P. Teague, 'Discrimination and fair employment in Northern Ireland', in Paul Teague (ed.), *The Economy of Northern Ireland. Perspectives for Structural Change*, Lawrence and Wishart, London, 1993; R. Munck, *The Irish Economy. Results and Prospects*, Pluto Press, London, 1993; A. M. Gallagher, *The Majority Minority review, No. 2, Employment, Unemployment and Religion in Northern Ireland*. Centre for the Study of Conflict, University of Ulster, 1991; Fair Employment Commission for Northern Ireland, *First Annual Report*, HMSO HC 630, London; J. Knox and J. O'Hara, 'Fair employment legislation in Northern Ireland', in B. Hepple, B. and E. M. Szyszchzak, (eds), *Discrimination: The Limits of the Law*, Mansell Publishing, London, 1992.
60. See for example David McKittrick, 'Catholics remain Ulster's poor relations', *Independent*, 5 July 1993.
61. See the Fair Employment Commission, *A Profile of the Workforce in Northern Ireland: a Summary of the 1990 Monitoring Returns*, FEC, Belfast, 1991.
62. Catholic men are still more than twice as likely to be unemployed as their Protestant counterparts. In the mid-1980s Catholic men were 2.6 times more likely to be unemployed. By 1991 this ratio had fallen to 2.2; *Guardian*, 26 June 1993.

63. M. Hout, *Following in Father's Footsteps: Social Mobility in Ireland*, Harvard University Press, Harvard, 1989, p. 155.
64. See, for example, R. Wilson and D. Wylie, *The Dispossessed*, Pan Books, London, 1992, pp. 105–82; S. Stitt and M. McWilliams, *A Life of Poverty: Northern Ireland*, Social Policy Society, University of Ulster, 1986; E. Evason, *On the Edge: a Study of Poverty and Long Term Unemployment in Northern Ireland*, CPAG, London, 1985; E. Evason, L. Allamby and R. Woods, *The Deserving and Undeserving Poor — the Social Fund in Northern Ireland*, CPAG, Derry, 1989; N. Gillespie, T. Lovett and S. Garner, *Youth Work and Working Class Youth Culture — Rules and Resistance in Northern Ireland*, Open University Press, Milton Keynes, 1992; P. McNamee and T. Lovett, *Working Class Community in Northern Ireland*, Ulster People's College, Belfast, 1989.
65. See for example P. Buckland, *A History of Northern Ireland*, Gill and Macmillan, Dublin, 1981.
66. F. Burton, *The Politics of Legitimacy — Struggles in a Belfast Community*, Routledge and Kegan Paul, London, 1978.
67. C. Curtin, R. O'Dwyer and G. Ó Tuathaigh, 'Emigration and exile', in Thomas Barlett, Chris Curtin, Riana O'Dwyer and Gearóid Ó Tuathaigh (eds), *Irish Studies: a General Introduction*, Gill and Macmillan, Dublin, 1989, p. 79.
68. See M. W. Tomlinson, 'Outbreeding the Unionists? Emigration and the Northern Ireland State', *Irish Reporter*, No. 1 (Spring 1991), pp. 21–5.
69. P. Compton, 'The demographic background'.
70. This point has been under much discussion lately following the release of the 1991 census figures, especially the immediate political issue of 'when this is likely to take place' and the likely unionist reaction. See the *Independent on Sunday*, 1 November 1992, for example, which led with 'Catholics to be majority in Ulster'.
71. Compton has in turn challenged the argument in the *Independent on Sunday*. He claims that the overall rise in the Catholic population is not as sharp as it may appear. This is largely due to the large number of Catholics who did not complete the 1981 census because of a boycott organized in many areas throughout Northern Ireland in support of the Republican Hunger Strikes. See *Sunday Life*, 8 November 1992.
72. P. McDonagh, 'Where have all the students gone?', *Fortnight*, No. 227 (October 1989), pp. 12–13.
73. C. W. Jefferson, 'The labour market', in R. Harris, C. Jefferson and J. Spencer, *The Northern Ireland Economy: a Comparative Study in the Economic Development of a Peripheral Region*, Longman, London, 1990, p. 154.
74. F. Donnelly, 'The biggest Irish exodus since the potato famine', *The Listener*, 25 November 1982.
75. A. Williamson, A. Reid, K. Cormack and R. Osborne, 'The characteristics of Ulster's students', *THES*, 10–11 January 1982.
76. E. Cairns, 'The political socialisation of tomorrow's parents: violence, politics and the media', in Joan Harbinson (ed.), *Children of the Troubles: Children in Northern Ireland*, Strandmillis College, Belfast, 1983, p. 126.
77. F. Donnelly, 'The biggest Irish exodus since the potato famine'.
78. Jennifer Todd, 'Two traditions in Unionist political culture', in *Irish Political Studies*, 2 (1987), pp. 1–26.
79. See A. Guelke, *Northern Ireland: the International Perspective*, Gill and Macmillan, Dublin, 1988.
80. Andy Tyrie, cited in Jack Holland, *Too Long a Sacrifice*.

81. The point that many 'ancient' traditions are in fact recent 'inventions' is well made in several articles in E. Hobsbawn and T. Ranger (eds), *The Invention of Tradition*, Cambridge University Press, Cambridge, 1984, and R. Samuel and P. Thompson (eds) *The Myths We Live By*, Routledge, London, 1990.
82. At the anecdotal level I was reminded of this recently when talking to one of my students, Noel Gilzean, who is President of the University of Huddersfield Irish Society. He confirmed that, despite the efforts of the Irish Society, there was little, if any, participation from northern Protestants attending the university. He suggested that preconceived notions of what 'Irishness' is had meant they had not even approached the society.
83. D. Archard, 'Appraising allegiances: how the liberal democratic state can cope with traditional identities and communities', in Damian Smyth (ed.), 'Conflict and community', *Supplement to Fortnight*, No. 311.
84. I am aware of the magnitude of the argument being addressed here. Indeed, the discussion concerning the 'false consciousness' of Protestant workers has structured much of the debate within the Irish Left for several decades at least. There are two readily identifiable 'schools' of thought. The first, drawing on traditional Irish Marxist discourse, suggests that Protestant workers have suffered from a 'false ideology' which has been implanted by the dominant class. This perspective can be read in works such as G. Bell, *The Protestants of Ulster*, Pluto, London, 1976; M. Farrell, *The Orange State*, Pluto, London, 1976; D. Reed, *Ireland: the Key to the British Revolution*, Larkin, London, 1984. The second, counter-body of 'revisionist' literature, is best represented by P. Bew, P. Gibbon and H. Patterson, *The State in Northern Ireland, 1921–1972*, MUP, Manchester, 1980; P. Bew and H. Patterson, *The British State and the Ulster Crisis*, Verso, London, 1985; P. Bew, E. Hazelcorn and H. Patterson, *The Dynamics of Irish Politics*, Lawrence and Wishart, London, 1989. I have expanded my own thoughts on the matter in J. W. McAuley, *The Politics of Identity: A Loyalist Community in Belfast*, Avebury Press, Aldershot, 1994.

3 The psychology of song; the theology of hymn: songs and hymns of the Irish migration

Leon B. Litvack

> I have an aunt Biddy ... and herself and Mary-in-Jacks, a Callaghan girl, went to work in a big house in Wilmington [Delaware, USA] ... They were sitting at the fire one night talking about old times when they heard a noise at one of the windows. They were frightened, for they knew it was a burglar and, as the house was off by itself, they could get no help. Then my aunt said to Mary, 'Do you know what we'll do? We'll sing a song, and let on to him that we are not a bit frightened.'
>
> At that both of them started, and though Mary-in-Jacks could not sing a note, she kept chiming in ... Suddenly the noise at the window stopped and they could hear a man going back down the ladder.
>
> A few days after that they got a postcard delivered to the house. It was from the burglar, who said that the song they were singing was the song his mother had sung to him back home in Ireland ... When he heard the song he could not go on with it.[1]

Communal singing is invoked on many important occasions during the course of human life (marriage and death are the two central ones) and provides a stylized interpretation of events. Songs can reveal the utmost depth of feeling, and can document reactions to circumstances and their causes which might not otherwise be evoked, because of an inability to find appropriate words. The accompanying music provides a mnemonic which helps songs to be remembered in a way which other works of literature can only envy. Their power is not fully understood by musicologists, sociologists or psychologists. They have the ability, as in the above instance, to move in ways which are not wholly rational.[2] A critical examination of them can, in the best instances, provide insight into the very core of human existence.

When individuals or communities are faced with an ongoing crisis, they tend to formulate, over time, certain rituals, which reflect unique patterns of understanding and coping with what is transpiring. Ireland was a particularly appropriate setting for the development of such ceremonials, because of its Celtic heritage, and its predominantly rural population. Some pagan practices and beliefs had survived the advent of Christianity (traditionally marked by the arrival of St Patrick in 432), while others were blended with Christian observances. Among the latter were the celebration of St John's Eve, festive wakes for the dead, observances at holy wells and the endowment of Christian (particularly Roman Catholic) emblems with sacramental powers; all of these practices, notes David Miller, gave the rural population a sense of identity and stability.[3] The Irish migrations — particularly those to the United States — engendered certain other rituals, which became the stylized expressions of joy, sorrow, hope and fear associated with this momentous trend. One custom concerned 'frog bread', prepared by roasting and pulverizing a frog, mixing the ashes with oatmeal and giving the resultant loaf of bread to the emigrant to be used as part of his provisions on the voyage to America. It was believed that frog bread would keep the traveller immune from fever. Other charms included the provision of the migrant with a caul (the inner membrane enclosing the foetus before birth) to prevent drowning; and the presentation of a cutting of pubic hair to an emigrant by a lover left behind, as an assurance of certain return and continuing love.[4]

By far the most widespread custom — and one which had strong religious overtones — was what has been termed the 'American wake'. This communal event engendered an atmosphere of understandably mixed emotion: marking as it did a departure from family and community life, it evoked, especially in the early years of the migrations when travel was slow and the fate of individuals uncertain, a sense of irrevocable loss, and therefore seemed as final as the physical loss of life. It occasioned such remarks from participants as 'People made very little difference between going to America and going to the grave.'[5] Later on, however, with improvements in transportation and the increasing frequency of 'American letters' from emigrants who had achieved varying degrees of success (and who often sent home passage tickets for relatives and money), the wakes acquired a more festive mood, and became occasions of jollity and excitement.

The diminishing — though not complete disappearance — of the melancholy ambience allowed for the institution of dancing, drinking and, most importantly, ballad singing. These songs, which were among the most immediate and candid reactions to the migration experience, embodied the thoughts and feelings of those leaving and those left behind. They told of the difficulty of parting, the loneliness and heartbreak of parents and the hardships of emigrant life. The ballads represented the emotional climax of the American wake and prompted, as Schrier notes, 'a general outburst of weeping and lamentation'.[6]

It is characteristic of moments of supreme emotion to lose the ability to express in words what the heart feels. The final departure, accompanied by the wringing of hands, clasping and kissing and keening over the 'dead' one, in shrill, piercing tones, was an occasion when ballads answered supremely to the calls by the Irish for the words they wished to hear to describe their experiences. It is interesting to note, as Theodore Hoppen does, the contrast between the ballads of the pre-Famine period, which were created at a genuinely popular level and as characterized by a 'savage imagery and muscular tones', with the more numerous and decorous productions of the 1850s and after, by which time the wakes and scenes of departure had shed their melancholy aura, thus fostering a situation in which language and sentiments were 'neutered' so as to make them acceptable to a 'culturally laundered' society.[7] Thus, as the stark memory of the Famine faded, the ballads increasingly reflected the literary conventions of an emerging bourgeois nationalism, rather than the authentic mentality of emigrants themselves. In assessing the validity of this view, it must be remembered that the ballads were, unlike more traditional Irish folk songs, tailor-made compositions — hastily written, often by professional ballad-makers, crudely printed, and sold or peddled throughout the country for a penny a sheet. Though not works of great literary merit, the songs nevertheless fulfilled an important cathartic role, reflecting desired and cultivated feelings and attitudes of the Irish towards migration. Their abundance and popularity attest to the depth of their penetration into the popular psyche.

On the causes of emigration the songs had common themes. Some, like 'Evictions in Ireland! or, Why Did I Leave my Country' spoke of the oppression of tenants by landlords:

> Why did I leave my country? why did I leave my home?
> Why did I leave the Emerald Isle across the sea to roam?
> Because I was evicted, and my rent I could not pay,
> But my heart is with old Ireland tho' I am far away.[8]

Others, including 'the Song of the Black Potatoes', shift the blame to the land itself, which yielded poor crops:

> The potatoes that failed, brought the nation to agony,
>   The poor house bare, and the dreadful coffin-ship.
> And in mountain graves do they in hundreds lie,
>   By hunger taken to their beds of clay.[9]

Many spoke of Ireland as the land of slaves, who worked to the death under impossible conditions, to supply English tables with bountiful produce:

> I would not live in Ireland now, for she's a fallen land,
> And the tyrant's heels is on her neck, with her reeking bloodstained hand.
> There's not a foot of Irish ground, but's trodden down by slaves,
> Who die unwept, and then are flung, like dogs, into their graves.[10]

The songs reflect the desire of many emigrants to reach America. While it was difficult to leave home, America was perceived as a land of plenty, which was not bound by the chains of the class system, and where everyone could rise in status and enjoy the wealth, if he or she was willing to work:

> I'm bidding farewell to the land of my youth
> And the homes I love so well,
> And the mountains so grand, in my own native land,
> I'm bidding them all farewell.
> With an aching heart I'll bid them adieu
> For tomorrow I sail far away,
> O'er the raging foam, for to seek a home
> On the shores of Amerikay.[11]

There was also a sense of gratitude for the opportunity offered by America to make a new start:

> America dear Eden land
> We fondly turn to thee
> Where still the homes and altars stand
> Of sacred Liberty.
>
> Faithful to thee may every deed
> Of Erin ever prove
> For friendship in the hour of need
> Demands returning love.[12]

While the excitement communicated in many of the ballads clearly reflected the experience of many migrants, they also acknowledged the hazards of the crossing. The songs emphasize that although the transatlantic journey is the appropriate one to undertake, travellers should be aware of the dangers. In 'Burning of an Emigrant Ship', the implication is that the disaster is due to divine judgement, which has been actuated by a wrathful God. The distraught mothers raise their voices in prayer for divine mercy:

> O God, the cries of children dear!
>   The blazing, pitchy seams:
> The mother's bitter tears could not
>   Subdue the cruel flames!

Two stanzas later, they appear again:

> The mothers to their children clung.
>   'O, we may rue the day
> We left our poor old Ireland,
>   For countries far away!'

The idea here, with the display of maternal tenderness and affection, is that remaining in Ireland would have been better than the cruel death at sea; at the same time there is the suggestion that God was moved to anger by the Irish migration. This sentiment is reinforced at the end of the song, where there is an appeal for prayer to end the persecution at home, so that migration would become unnecessary:

> O, neighbours dear, O, Irishmen,
>   Let every Christian pray,
> That God will rid our native land
>   Of racking landlord sway;
> And as these banish'd people did,
>   In awful sufferings, die, —
> God grant them sweet salvation
>   With his dear son on high![13]

This pattern of a call to all 'good', 'faithful' or 'tender' Christians to give ear, the brief relation of events, the focus on a mother and child, whose deaths are described in a heart-wrenching manner, followed by a final doxology in which all good Christians are invited to pray together, is repeated many times in the migration ballad tradition. It creates a fellow-feeling with those who have suffered, and calls for a communal display of Christian faith as an aid to salvation of both the living and the dead.

The hazards of the voyage only compounded the problem of separation from loved ones — a heavy burden for the migrants to bear. This note of sadness concerning those left behind pervades most of the migration ballads. The weight of tradition attached to the cohesive family and community prompted ballad-writers to picture the departure in lines filled with pathos and guilt. Sometimes those left behind are parents:

> Oh, mother, the dreary winter night is passing fast away —
> The Eastern sky has a gleam of light 'neath its gloomy veil of grey,
> And ever the light is growing more bright — I may no longer stay,
> The lark is winging his morning flight, 'tis the dawn of our parting day
>
> 'Oh, the blackest night I would sooner see, with never a hope of dawn
> Than the morning that takes you away from me, my darling, my Carroll *ban*!
> 'Tis lonely and dark my home will be when the light of your smile is gone —
> When your clear voice ringing so true and free is heard in my heart alone![14]

On other occasions they are lovers:

> Come change your mind, love, and you will find
> That we'll have better times yet on Erin's shore,
> And I'll endeavour to work and labour,
> For to maintain you a week ashore.
> I love you dearly, true and sincerely,
> But if you leave me and go away,
> My heart will break, love, all for your sake,
> While you are placed in America.[15]

The songs, however, carry the implication that departure does not mean severing one's ties with Ireland completely. The weight of history is recalled by looking back to the migrant's forebears, as in 'The Emigrant':

> Oh, land of my forefathers, sea girded Erin!
>   My heart throbs aloud as thy hills disappear.[16]

or in 'The Emigrant's Farewell to Ireland':

> Farewell to old Ireland, the land of my fathers,
>   Which now I'm going for ever to leave.[17]

Likewise, it is impossible to shake off one's Irishness — an essential component of the migrant's cultural baggage:

> Though fondest hopes here hold me, there's part of me that lies,
> Midst the ruins of that homestead beneath blue Irish skies,
> Where roses bloom by the window and around the faded door,
> Of the cot which save in memory I never shall see more.[18]

The dream of a return was strong in the minds of those still at home, who elicited a promise from the migrant to do so — particularly in the love songs, like 'The Flow'ry Shannon Side':

> When seven long years were past and gone, this young man cross'd the ocean,
> He being blessed with riches, to his love returned again,
> 'Now since you've proved so faithful, I will make you my fair bride,
> And we will roll in splendour, down by the Shannon side.[19]

and also in a whole series of songs devoted exclusively to nostalgia for Ireland. Among these was 'the Old Bog Road':

> My feet are here on Broadway, this blessed harvest morn,
> But O the ache that's in them for the spot where I was born,
> My weary hands are blistered from work in cold and heat,
> And O to swing a scythe today thro' fields of Irish wheat.
> Had I the chance to wander back, or own a king's abode,
> 'Tis soon I'd see the hawthorn tree by the Old Bog Road.[20]

The few songs which treat returned migrants are mixed in tone. 'The Emigrant's Return' (which was appropriately set to the tune 'Auld Lang Syne') was published in the United States, and is unhesitatingly exultant:

> I'm home again! I'm home again!
>   Nor will I leave it more!
> I'll spend my days in love with you,
>   Dear friends, till life is o'er.
> We never love our home so well
>   Till far from it we roam;
> For, other lands can ne'er bestow
>   The sweets of Childhood's Home.[21]

The most famous return of all — and, significantly, the most tragic — was that of 'Noreen Bawn', a widow's daughter whose passage to America was paid by a relative. After a long sojourn she lands in Ireland:

Weary years that mother waited
Till one evening, at her door,
Stood a gorgeous looking lady,
Awful grand the clothes she wore,
Whispering, 'Mother, don't you know me?
Now I've only got the cold.'
Yet those purple spots upon her cheeks
The tragic story's told.

In this case the experience of leaving home produced fatal results: despite the veneer of prosperity, the girl is deathly ill. The mother surmises while weeping over the grave:

'Twas the shame of emigration
Laid you low, my Noreen Bawn.[22]

According to this ballad, migration does not produce the expected result. The participants must overcome the seemingly insurmountable forces of tradition, memory, culture, family and, in some cases, an indisposed God, to face hardship, disease and potential death, all of which seemed preferable to the life of affliction in Ireland. Yet they cannot break completely, as these lines make clear:

They'll be like troubled spirits,
    Who can find no rest on earth,
'Til they die, worn out with longing,
    For the green land of their birth.[23]

The fact that the ballads concerned with migration were, for the most part, produced in Ireland rather than America (which was the primary focus) helps to explain the predominant mood. 'American letters' conveyed a general impression of happiness and satisfaction with the New World and the opportunities it offered. Songs of migration, on the other hand, painted a darker picture: there the pervasive mood was one of melancholy, evoking the imagined distress and grief felt by those left behind (especially parents), an awareness of the difficulties that lay ahead and the hope of a return one day to Ireland. The migrant, a casualty of conflicting emotions, was characterized as lonely, homesick and, though motivated by necessity, remorseful for ever having left. The verses did not distort the facts of migration, but rather reinforced the attachment of the Irish, whether at home or abroad, to the land of their birth, and thus strengthening Hoppen's point about the reinforcing of sanitized nationalism, particularly in the post-Famine period, through the singing of these songs.

Hymns were the other musical medium through which thoughts and feelings concerning the migrations were expressed. They differ from ballads and songs in certain respects. On the most fundamental level, a hymn is a metrical composition adapted to be sung, in praise to God, at a religious service. This definition is, however, deficient, for it does not take into account the meaningful reality beyond mere words or music to which such compositions aspire. Like ballads and songs, they are used on many important occasions during an individual's life, and tend to express feelings for which individuals and congregations cannot themselves find appropriate words. They are sometimes joyful, at other times plaintive, contemplative or consolatory; hymns can, as I have said of song, provide insight into the very core of human existence. Yet hymns are different, for they are specifically associated with a religious tradition, and hence must be sung by individuals whose minds are directed not primarily to poetic or musical but to religious values; this means that the poetry and music must be perfectly compatible with certain religious values to which whole Christian communions are expected to subscribe. They must, in Erik Routley's words, 'fit into the ancient scheme that prevailed in the Middle Ages when there was no difference between goodness and piety in art'.[24] Also, their range of subject matter is necessarily limited to encompass established theological canons, creeds and doctrines. By singing about them in simple words, and with a musical mnemonic which makes them easily called to mind, an individual or congregation reinforces these tenets of faith, and accepts the hymn in which they are enclosed as their peculiar cultural heritage. This enforces a certain discipline or limitation on hymn-writing and hymn-singing to which songs and ballads are not subjected: while songs may depict individual, sometimes idiosyncratic migrants as protagonists, the hymns cannot do so. Unlike the songs, they were never intended to give the impression of real migrants relating their experiences. More often than not they were written by clergymen who had the formal training believed necessary to evoke orthodox theological views, and who, in the comfort of their studies or organ lofts, were far removed from situations which they were describing. Yet because a hymn must be accepted musically, theologically and personally by the singers in order to thrive and become popular, it is an acceptable mechanism for the expression of what people want to say, in both worship and ordinary speech, about themselves, and their relationship with God and the community.

Hymns particularly associated with the migrations are, because of restrictions inherent in the medium, relatively few in number. Significantly, they are closely associated with the Roman Catholic, rather than the Protestant, tradition. Part of the reason for this dichotomy stems from the peculiar development of Irish church history. The plantation of English and Scottish settlers in the seventeenth century espoused a system whereby these communities looked to their bases across the Irish Sea for their religious sustenance. With the advent of vernacular hymnody, this meant that the hymns used by the Church of Ireland, Methodists, Congregationalists and Baptists came, from the most part, from their sister churches in England. The Presbyterians traditionally used the Scottish

Psalter and, while individual congregations produced hymn-books to suit their particular needs, the Presbyterian Church at large only accepted the singing of original compositions with the appearance of the *Church Hymnary* in 1898. Even when native Protestant hymn-writers did appear, such as Cecil Frances Alexander, Thomas Kelly and Emma Toke, almost none of their original compositions — as opposed to their translations — used references to Ireland to communicate their various messages.

An indigenous Irish hymnological tradition did, however, exist, and was the almost exclusive possession of the Roman Catholic Church. These compositions developed according to a Catholic-Celtic pattern, which was, according to tradition, established by St Patrick with the introduction of Christianity to Ireland. This great Christian missionary encountered a powerful Celtic culture, with its peculiar agrarian rituals (some of which found their way, in an adapted form, into Christian observances), and its attachment to nature and the spiritual world. The clearest lyrical expression of this tradition may be found in Patrick's own hymn 'Breastplate' (*Atomriug indiu niurt tren*), which is an example of a *lorica*, a typically Celtic outpouring of prayer and hymn, where echoing lines invoke the power of God to ward off all the possible evils of life. It was composed, according to tradition, shortly after Patrick's landing in Ireland in 432 to spread the Christian faith there. The *lorica* is a supreme expression of the wholeness and holiness of nature in Celtic Christianity, and is beautifully captured by Robert Macalister, in his translation for the *Church Hymnary* (1927):

> To-day I arise
> by splendour of sun and flaming brand,
> by rushing wind, by lightning grand,
> by depth of sea, by strength of land.[25]

In combining incantation, war-song and credal statement, the verses recreate a peculiarly Irish atmosphere, in which the life and work of St Patrick are almost mystically invoked. The hymn represents, in many ways, feelings for the apostle of Ireland which permeated the lives of Irish people — particularly Roman Catholics. He has continually been a clear focus for belief, in pilgrimage, invocation, prayer and song. The history and legend which surround this saint have transformed him into a symbol or icon for Irish Catholics, embodying their country, their faith and their destiny.

Heroic figures, like St Patrick or William of Orange, or legendary events, such as the victory of Patrick over Laoghaire at Tara, or the Battle of the Boyne, have always been important and useful to both Catholics and Protestants in Ireland. To each communion history is not simply an agglomeration of facts, but a living set of symbols with direct relevance to the present; past events become, through immediate links in the genealogical chain, events in the present. This transformation may clearly be seen in the reminiscences of Michael MacGowan (1865–1948) from Co. Donegal, who describes how he spent St Patrick's Day in the 1890s in the Klondike. Early in the morning he heard a piper in the distance, playing 'St

Patrick's Day'. His initial reaction was this:

> There, then, was I, three thousand miles from home but, in the time it would take you to clap your hands, I fancied I was back again among my own people in Cloghaneely. My heart leaped up with so much joy that I was sure it was going to jump out of my breast altogether.

As the piper reaches the camp, the Catholic migrants join him in a march to celebrate 'our very own day — the blessed feast-day of St Patrick'. As the march proceeds the piper is confronted by a disgruntled Orangeman, who attempts to tear the green ribbons from his pipes. MacGowan overpowers him, but the man recovers and, joined by some like-minded associates, mounts a second attack; this too is put down by angered celebrants. MacGowan surmises:

> We were incensed ... by that time that every man of us would have died for the cause for which we had fought. Indeed, I think St. Patrick would have pardoned such an uproar being created for the sake of his name. But we showed to the people from all those countries that were there that we were faithful to him and that we wouldn't allow anybody, that hated the things we loved, to fling them in our teeth.[26]

The perpetuation of sectarianism, in this highly symbolic form, so far from home reinforces Akenson's view that the Protestant and Catholic Irish are 'among the most historically aware of European peoples.'[27] Yet in considering their reactions to the Famine and migrations in particular, there is a clear divide: while both groups were profoundly affected by the event, only the Catholics incorporated it into their own mythology and cosmology. Their folkloristic and religious interpretation of the Famine was in terms of supernatural judgement. Akenson confirms that studies of Irish folk tradition point to popular interpretation of the Famine as some form of divine punishment by the Christian God for the people's sins or as the action of non-Christian spirits who had been vexed into attacking the Irish people. This national folk memory was eventually combined with (and later superseded by) a rationale — disseminated through John Mitchel's book of 1860, *The Last Conquest of Ireland (Perhaps)* — which was, in its domestic form, anti-Protestant, and in its external visage, anti-British. It claimed that the tragedy was a British conspiracy to exterminate the Roman Catholics.[28]

In Irish Roman Catholic hymnody of the migration, the writers' thoughts on supernatural judgement and anti-Protestantism often came together in focusing on St Patrick. In addition to being the supreme Irish example of sustained faith in his God, it was he who gradually overcame the heathen, protected new converts and ultimately Christianized Ireland. Patrick, a clear symbol of stability and confidence, served as the receptacle for polemical outpourings which could, at best, serve as the Irish Catholic expression of feelings about their situation, which was often uncertain, and their future. The opportunities for singing these 'Patrick-hymns' were many: although vernacular compositions were not used in the course of the Mass, they did permeate into Vespers, Benediction, the Rosary, non-liturgical congregational meetings and private devotions at home. There arose multiple opportunities, in a variety of settings, for reinforcement of the newly-created Patrician image of Irish Roman Catholic reaction to the Famine and migrations. One of the earliest and most popular pieces was a plaintive, nostalgic, somewhat melancholy hymn, attributed to Sister Agnes, of the Convent of Charleville, Co. Cork, which appeared in *Easy Hymns*, a collection of 1853:

Hail, glorious St Patrick, dear Saint of our isle!
On us, thy poor children, bestow a sweet smile;
And now thou art high in thy mansions above,
On Erin's green valleys look down in thy love.

Hail, glorious St Patrick! Thy words were once strong
Against Satan's wiles and a heretic throng:
Not less is thy might where in Heaven thou art;
Oh, come to our aid, in our battle take part.

In the war against sin, in the fight for the faith,
Dear Saint, may thy children resist to the death;
May their strength be in meekness, in penance and prayer,
Their banner the Cross, which they glory to bear.

Thy people, now exiles on many a shore,
Shall love and revere thee till time be no more;
And the fire thou hast kindled shall ever burn bright,
Its warmth undiminished, undying its light.

Ever bless and defend the sweet land of our birth,
Where the shamrock still blooms as when thou wert on earth;[29]
And our hearts shall yet burn, wheresoever we roam,
For God and St Patrick and our native home.[30]

This hymn reflects a heartfelt attachment to 'the sweet land of our birth'; yet there is also a note of sadness evoked in such expressions as 'thy poor children', who are 'now exiles on many a shore'. All the while we must recall that the writer probably had little direct experience of the famine and its associated migration to other lands. The hymn, like many of the songs considered above, is a sanitized, distanced and probably second-hand account of the experiences it attempts to describe. It embodies the literary conventions of a bourgeois Irish nationalism, and evokes a stereotype that associates the production of music and heightened religious fervour with poverty and persecution. Here St Patrick's aid is invoked to save this powerless population, who have brought these troubles upon themselves through sin, and must now be regenerated through 'meekness', 'penance' and 'prayer'. Also noteworthy is the war-cry, uttered in 'the fight for the faith' which, while primarily directed against Satan and sin, is also carried, by implication, to those whom the Irish immigrants meet 'wheresoever we roam'; thus all may aspire to the achievements of St Patrick in converting the 'heretic throng'.

The militancy — spiritual or otherwise — which is advocated to preserve and promulgate the Catholic faith is again found in the *Crown of Jesus Hymn Book* (1862) which was published simultaneously in Dublin and London. While this book was heavily influenced by Ushaw College, a training centre for Roman priests in northern England, the very masculine, confident, almost courageous stance which some of the hymns take is significant when applied to an Irish situation. Hymn No. 62, though it has no geographical frame of reference, is significant when one remembers that it was intended for Irish congregations. While there is little of literary merit in the lines, there is a certain kind of brutish strength which recommends it for use in spiritual meetings and missions:

> I am a faithful Catholic,
>   I love my holy Faith,
> I will be true to Holy Church,
>   And steadfast until death.
>
> I shun the haunts of those who seek
>   To ensnare poor Catholic youth;
> No Church I own, no schools I know,
>   But those that teach the Truth.
>
> *If base it is to yield before*
>   *The Persecutor's Rod;*
> *Then baser far to side with those,*
>   *Who insult the Church of God.*
>
> *Oh! far from me such wickedness!*
>   *One treasure I hold dear*
> MY HOLY FAITH. *I fear not men,*
>   *'Tis God alone I fear.*[31]

If one can disregard the Marian elements and the other peculiarly Catholic references, then this hymn bears a striking resemblance to the Protestant missionary battle-hymns found elsewhere in the religious spectrum. These Protestant compositions were occasioned in Ireland by the so-called 'Second Reformation', which began in the 1820s and reached fruition at the time of the Famine. A consequence of the growth of evangelicalism in the various Protestant communions was a pronounced interest in missionary work, which was directed not only against the 'heathen' overseas, but also at the Catholic populations of England and Ireland.[32]

When they appear in Roman Catholic hymns, the Protestants in Ireland are consistently seen as the aggressors or intruders, who bring with them a false faith.[33] As well as being an instinctive reaction to the disruptive proselytism of the Second Reformation, the sentiments expressed are a reflection of an international trend in nineteenth-century Catholicism to combat the increasingly pluralist and rationalist society by a vigorous assertion of its exclusive claims to truth and authority. In Ireland the mood was personified by Paul Cullen (1803–78) consecutively Archbishop of Armagh and Dublin, who dominated Catholic affairs in the country from about 1850 onwards, and is credited with the boast that he had never dined with a Protestant, and commended an Archaic ecclesiastical regulation which forbade any priest from doing so.[34] The religious apartheid and Catholic ascendancy which such views excited are captured in the following hymn from the *Crown of Jesus* for St Patrick's Day, in which there is a clear identification of the Roman Catholics as the only true people of Ireland, for it is they who genuinely revere their apostle, who has served as a symbol of light and life in the face of the darkness and death that is Protestantism:

> Then what shall we do for thee, heaven-sent father?
>   What shall the proof of our loyalty be?
> By all that is dear to our hearts, we would rather
>   Be martyred, sweet Saint! than bring shame upon thee!
> But oh! he will take the promise we make
>   So to live that our lives by God's help may display
> The light that he bore to Erin's shore—
>   Yes! Father of Ireland, no child wilt thou own,
> Whose life is not lighted by grace on its way;
>   For they are true Irish, O yes, they alone,
> Whose hearts are all true on St Patrick's Day.[35]

A hymn which evokes a similar aggressive Catholicism comes from *The Holy Family Hymns* of 1860. Written by an individual identified only as 'W.H.L.',[36] this Patrick-hymn is equally condemnatory of the 'heresy' that is Protestantism, but less sentimental in its praise of Patrick. The writer compares and contrasts the pre-Patrician pagans of Ireland with the Protestants who are agents of the 'devil's tyranny', and have 'struck her sons with Satan's darts':

> On the wings of holy charity
>   To Erin's coast St Patrick came,
> To curb the devil's tyranny
>   And spread the love of Jesu's name.
>
> CHORUS
>
> The Faith is firm in Erin's land,
>   And Patrick dear to Irish hearts;
> Though heresy has raised her brand;
>   And struck her sons with Satan's darts.[37]

The sheer number of hymns which recall St Patrick point to an extraordinary feeling on the part of Irish Roman Catholics for their patron saint, and the debt owed to him for the part he played in their past, and continues to play in their present. John Healy, Archbishop of Tuam in 1905, manages to summarize the perceived virtues of Patrick, and the valuable lessons which may be learned from a consideration of them, in his *Life and Writings of St Patrick*. In addition to humility and unceasing communion with God, Healy numbers among St Patrick's qualities his power of conversion and his attachment to the Irish people. He summarizes:

> Is it any wonder that the people of Ireland, with the knowledge of these facts in their minds from the beginning, should love their great Apostle with a deep and passionate love which is certainly not excelled in the case of any other saint in the Calendar except the Blessed Virgin Mary ...

> No other man before or since ever travelled so far or accomplished so much for God and for Ireland, in the face of so many difficulties and dangers, as was accomplished by St Patrick.[38]

In his analysis Healy wished to follow the authority of the ancient biographers (rather than the medieval sources), for the early writers, he claims in the preface, 'had no motive but to write the truth, so far as it was known to them, for the instruction and edification of posterity.' He continues:

> There was then only one Church and they could have no motive in representing St Patrick to be anything else that what he was known to them — a great and successful Christian missionary of the Catholic Church.[39]

There is a somewhat uneasy feeling about this statement, which confirms the emotion captured in the 'All praise to St Patrick' hymn: while the sentence can be read in two ways, the one that Healy presses more strongly is that the saint is the exclusive property of the Catholic — that is, *Roman* Catholic, rather than universal — Church.

While most Irish Catholic hymns concentrated on militancy and resistance as ways to reconcile the differences between Catholics and Protestants, there were among English Catholic hymn-writers those who attempted to heal the rift between the two communions through a spirit of gentle persuasion and fervent faith and prayer. Francis Stanfield's 'Hymn for Ireland' (1860) is of this type, and communicates its soothing, conciliatory message through a series of long four-line stanzas, and an almost mesmerizing repetition of the phrase 'O Sacred Heart':

O Sacred Heart, Our home lies deep in Thee,
  On earth Thou art an exile's rest,
In heaven the glory of the best.
  O Sacred Heart. O Sacred Heart.

O Sacred Heart, Bless our dear Fatherland,
  May Erin's sons to truth e'er stand,
With faith's bright banner still in hand,
  O Sacred Heart. O Sacred Heart.

O Sacred Heart, Watch o'er our sister isle
 Till faith e'er long return once more
And find a home on England's shore,
  O Sacred Heart. O Sacred Heart.

O Sacred Heart, Lead exiled children home,
  Where we may ever rest near Thee,
In peace and joy eternally,
  O Sacred Heart. O Sacred Heart. Amen.[40]

Stanfield's role as a conductor of Roman Catholic missions and retreats in Hertfordshire might explain the gentle, reflective tone of this hymn, which does not condemn Protestantism, but rather concentrates on a popular devotion. The 'exile' referred to in stanza 1 is, on one level, this earthly life, with the physical and spiritual hardships it entails; but it is also applicable to those who are outside the Catholic fold. Unlike most of the other hymns considered, this one does not display an overpowering sense of a history which places an unshakeable sense of responsibility upon the shoulders of the singer. What comes across most strongly is the devotion to a particular set of rituals (highly significant, as already noted, in a Catholic-Celtic setting) and a sense of nurturing the Catholic faith, so that it will gradually and naturally be accepted by 'our sister isle'.

Another sympathetic English Catholic was Frederick William Faber (1814–63), a disciple of John Henry Newman and a convert. The author of such fine hymns as 'My God! how wonderful Thou art' and 'O come and mourn with me awhile', he made it his goal to do for Catholics what other hymn-writers (Anglicans and Methodists foremost among them) had done for their communions: to produce simple, intense, high-quality vernacular verses for use as an integral part of public worship. His hymns were particularly suited to the period of the Irish migration: those who left after the Famine were mostly the young, unmarried rural poor who, when resident in Ireland, did not meet even the minimum obligatory levels of religious practice laid down by the Church, but rather found spiritual fulfilment in the non-canonical religious practices which had survived from pre-Christian Celtic religion, and were an integral part of pre-Famine culture.[41] In the New World, where these rituals were strangely absent, the emigrants lost their religious bearings. What they required in their exile, on a spiritual level, was a focal point for worship, and on a psychological level, a sense of stability, identity and purpose. To the question of a focus they found an answer, in the new-found religious freedom of the diaspora, in the Eucharist, that central act of Christian devotion in which faith is reaffirmed and the spirit renewed. As for a sense of purpose, they found a positive attraction in a quest or mission to convert others to the Catholic faith.[42] Faber, who was strongly influenced in his Anglican years by Evangelicalism, sounds both these notes in his hymns.

While many of Faber's hymns had an Irish or Irish immigrant audience in mind, the composition with the greatest relevance is 'Faith of our

Fathers! living still', which first appeared in his *Jesus and Mary* collection of 1849. He published two versions of the hymn: one, of four stanzas, headed 'for England' and another, in seven, marked 'for Ireland'. The most significant stanzas from the latter run as follows:

> Faith of our Fathers! living still,
> In spite of dungeon, fire and sword:
> Oh! Ireland's hearts beat high with joy
> Whene'er they hear that glorious word,
>   Faith of our Fathers! Holy Faith!
>   We will be true to thee till death!
>
> Faith of our fathers! guile and force
> To do thee bitter wrong unite;
> But Erin's Saints shall fight for us,
> And keep undimmed thy blessed light.
>   Faith of our Fathers! Holy Faith!
>   We will be true to thee till death!
>
> Faith of our Fathers! distant shores
> Their happy faith to Ireland owe;
> Then in our home, oh, shall we not
> Break the dark plots against thee now?
>   Faith of our Fathers! Holy Faith!
>   We will be true to thee till death![43]

This richly sentimental hymn, which was particularly well suited for missions and schools, was the single most popular one amongst Roman Catholics in the nineteenth century;[44] it is highly significant for its dual purpose: Faber wished it to be the simple expression of history, aspiration and conflict for both the English Catholics (who had recently experienced emancipation and restoration of the Roman hierarchy) and Irish Catholics of his day. For the Irish who emigrated, the message was the continued adherence, while abroad, to the Catholic faith,[45] and for those who remained at home, the protection of their religion against Protestant intruders. The stanzas added to the Irish version have a wider historical framework, which harks back (inevitably) to the time of Patrick, Columba and the other Irish saints who effected the spread of Christianity throughout the British Isles. We find the same appeal to the saints as is found in the Patrick-hymns, for aid in foiling the 'dark plots', which rely on 'guile and force' to achieve their sinister objective.[46]

The title of Faber's hymn sums up much of what the Irish were meant to have felt — and did feel — for their homeland. Both the songs and the hymns emphasize the long history and tradition, both secular and religious, which Ireland retains. Both modes of singing are communal, nationalistic and are concerned with the implications of leaving home for the migrants. While the atmosphere conducive to the writing of these verses probably bears no resemblance to the events or emotions described, the songs and hymns themselves transcended these circumstances, and answered the needs and longings of the inner life, comforting, challenging or raising the spirit. When singers or listeners are truly touched by songs and hymns they become part of their make-up — an aspect of identity. For some, the reminiscences will centre on history, religion and how one can maintain the link with these in spite of having left the epicentre, where the attraction (and pressure) are strongest. For others, the crucial memory will concern loved ones, and the affairs of the heart which the various relationships involve. For all, however, it is clear that the ties that bind them to their country are indissoluble, so that, no matter where they roam, the Irish identity, and culture, will always cling to them. In MacGowan's words, though many of the migrants would never see Erin again, they would spend 'two-thirds of the day nostalgically recalling to themselves the places where they first saw the light.'[47]

Notes

1. Dept. of Irish Folklore, University College Dublin, MS 1411, pp. 251–2. This material is in the form of notebooks, the contents of which were based on questionnaires serviced by the Irish Folklore Commission through its country-wide network of professional interviewers in 1955. In 16 counties of above average emigration, 26 100-page notebooks, more or less completely filled, were returned.
2. Some people who have fallen into comas, for example, are known to have been revived through the stimulus of a familiar hymn or song; see Susan S. Tamke, *Make a Joyful Noise Unto the Lord: Hymns as a Reflection of Victorian Social Attitudes*, Ohio University Press, Athens, 1978, p. 3.
3. David W. Miller, 'Irish Catholicism and the Great Famine', *Journal of Social History*, 9,1 (Fall 1975), p. 91.
4. Arnold Schrier, *Ireland and the American Emigration, 1850–1900*, Russell & Russell, New York, 1970, p. 85. For a detailed contemporary account of both Protestant and Roman Catholic Irish folk rituals see Charles McGlinchey, *The Last of the Name*, ed. Brian Friel, Blackstaff Press, Belfast, 1986.
5. MS notebook III of Conall O'Byrne, Dept. of Irish Folklore, University College Dublin.
6. Schrier, *Ireland and the American Emigration*, p. 89.
7. K. Theodore Hoppen, *Elections, Politics and Society in Ireland 1832–1885*, Clarendon Press, Oxford, 1984, p. 427.
8. Robert L. Wright (ed.), *Irish Emigrant Ballads and Songs*, Bowling Green University Popular Press, Bowling Green, 1975, p. 50.
9. Quoted in Wright, p. 91.
10. 'The Emigrant's Farewell'; quoted in Wright, p. 129.
11. 'Shores of Amerikay', *The Guinness Book of Irish Ballads*, Dublin, n.d., p. 5.
12. 'Voice of Erin'; quoted in Wright, p. 200.
13. *The Universal Irish Song Book: a Complete Collection of the Songs and Ballads of Ireland*, P. J. Kennedy, New York, 1884, pp. 298–9.
14. 'The Dawn of the Parting Day', Edward Hayes (ed.), *The Ballads of Ireland*, James Duffy, Dublin, 1905, 1, pp. 302–3.
15. 'The Emigrant's Farewell to Ireland'; quoted in Wright, pp. 350–1.

16. Patrick A. Walsh (ed.), *Songs of the Gael*, Browne & Nolan, Dublin, 1922, p. 46.
17. Quoted in Wright, p. 138.
18. 'The Call of Home', Sam Henry Ballad Collection 2, No. 658, Irish Department, Central Library, Belfast.
19. Quoted in Wright, p. 387.
20. Quoted in Wright, pp. 610–11.
21. Quoted in Wright, p. 627.
22. *Walton's 132 Best Irish Songs and Ballads*, Walton's Musical Instrument Galleries, Dublin, 1955, p. 107.
23. 'The Emigrant's Farewell, for 1865', *The New Emigrant Songster*, John F. Nugent, Dublin, n.d., p. 5.
24. Erik Routley, *Hymns and Human Life*, John Murray, London, 1952, p. 3.
25. 'St Patrick's Breastplate'; quoted in Erik Routley, *A Panorama of Christian Hymnody*, GIA Publications, Chicago, 1979, p. 133. Mrs Alexander also produced a version of this hymn, 'I bind unto myself to-day/The strong name of the Trinity', which was based on English prose translations given to her by H. H. Dickinson. It too has a sense of primeval nature mysticism about it.
26. Michael McGowan, *The Hard Road to Klondike*, ed. Proinnsias O Conluain, trans. Valentin Iremonger, Routledge & Kegan Paul, London, 1962, p. 129.
27. Donald Harman Akenson, *Small Differences: Irish Catholics and Irish Protestants, 1815–1922, An International Perspective*, McGill-Queen's University Press, Kingston and Montreal, 1988, p. 144.
28. Akenson, *Small Differences*, p. 145.
29. According to tradition, St Patrick illustrated the concept of the Trinity to the unconverted by the aid of the shamrock.
30. H. A. Rawes, *Hymns Selected from Various Sources, by the Rev. Father Rawes, of the Congregation of the Oblates of St Charles*, W. Knowles, J. Duffy, London and Dublin, 1865, hymn no. 135. For an account of the hymn's authorship, see John Julian (ed.), *A Dictionary of Hymnology*, John Murray, London, 1907, p. 1644.
31. *Crown of Jesus Music*, Thomas Richardson, London, Dublin and Derby, 1862, hymn no. 62, stanzas 1–4. The hymn-book was designed to complement a Catholic manual of devotion, doctrine and instruction which bore the same title, and was published the same year.
32. See Desmond Bowen, *The Protestant Crusade in Ireland, 1800–1870*, Gill and Macmillan, Dublin, 1978.
33. Norman notes that in the mid-nineteenth century, the Irish language had only one word to denote both 'Protestant' and 'intruder' (E. R. Norman, *The Catholic Church and Ireland in the Age of Rebellion, 1859–1873*, Cornell University Press, Ithaca, 1965, p. 1).
34. Sean Connolly, *Religion and Society in Nineteenth-Century Ireland*, Dundalgan Press, Dundalk, 1985, pp. 26–7. The increased assertiveness in defence of Catholic interests, and the refusal to submit blindly to the will of the political establishment, may also be seen in the refusal by Archbishop Daniel Murray (Cullen's predecessor) in 1846 to accept a place on the Irish Privy Council. Such actions were, in Connolly's estimation, 'the most eloquent testimony to the status which the Catholic Church had achieved by mid-century' (p. 35).
35. *Crown of Jesus Music*, Thomas Richardson, London, Dublin and Derby, 1862, hymn no. 154. (To be sung to a very jaunty Irish air, the rhythm of which is a jig.)
36. 'W.H.L.' is also the author of 'The Cross! The Cross! ye young men all!' 'All things on earth are vain' and 'Joy, joy to the choir celestial', all of which are

included in *The Holy Family Hymns.*
37. *The Holy Family Hymns,* Richardson and Son, London, 1860, hymn no. 65.
38. John Healy, *The Life and Writings of St Patrick,* M. H. Gill & Son, Dublin, 1905, pp. 544–5, 551.
39. *Life and Writings of St Patrick,* p. iv.
40. *Crown of Jesus Music,* hymn no. 180, stanzas 1, 3, 4, 7. The hymnal also prints a general version of this hymn, which simply omits the third and fourth verses.
41. Miller, 'Irish Catholicism and the Great Famine', pp. 89–91.
42. While Irish emigrants — particularly to Britain and the United States — tended to cluster in urban districts, they did not (contrary to the myth) congregate in Irish 'ghettos' to the exclusion of other ethnic groups. Therefore, even in such great 'Irish' cities abroad as Liverpool, Manchester, Glasgow, London, New York, Philadelphia, Boston and Chicago, the opportunities for meeting potential converts were ubiquitous.
43. Rawes, *Hymns Selected from Various Sources,* hymn no. 155.
44. The popularity of 'Faith of our Fathers' was not restricted to a religious environment: it was sung at hurling matches in Ireland right up until the 1960s.
45. The genuine concern on the part of the Catholic hierarchy for the spiritual welfare of Irish emigrants prompted the establishment in 1842 of All Hallows Seminary in Dublin, specifically designed to train Irish priests as missionaries for America and other English-speaking countries. An example of a hymnal used by such missionary priests is the Redemptorist *St Cecilia's Hymn Book,* which carried the following message in its preface: 'Ireland is essentially a believing and singing land; and her prayer will easily voice itself in song. Such an alliance will do much for sacred art; while it will at the same time give her faithful children a powerful instrument for their fuller expression of their love for Him for whose greater glory this work has been undertaken' (Arthur de Meulemeester (ed.), *St Cecilia's Hymn Book,* Cahill & Co., Dublin, 1911).
46. 'Faith of our Fathers' received, in a somewhat altered version, a wider exposure than Faber ever intended. By 1853 (four years after its original appearance) it was adopted by Hedge and Huntington for their Unitarian *Hymns for the Church of Christ.* For Faber's original

Faith of our Fathers! Mary's prayers
Shall win our country back to thee

they substituted

Faith of our Fathers! *Good men's* prayers
Shall win our country *all* to thee.

With this alteration it has passed into several Nonconformist collections in Britain and America, so that Roman Catholics and Unitarians were singing the same words about their history (Julian, *Dictionary of Hymnology,* p. 363).
47. MacGowan, *The Hard Road to Klondike,* p. 138.

Acknowledgements

I gratefully acknowledge the assistance of the following in gathering research materials for this chapter: Dr S. Gilley, Dept. of Theology, University of Durham;

Ms A. Germaine, Dept. of Irish Folklore, University College Dublin; Central Library, Belfast.

4 Secularization of Irishness in the American South: a reading of the Novels of Ellen Glasgow and Margaret Mitchell

James P. Cantrell

Ireland and the American South

There has been relatively little scholarship examining the Irish in the American South, and on the surface this lack of attention seems quite understandable. After all, when we think of Irish migrants in the United States, we tend to envision Irish Catholics in the metropolitan areas of the north-east and Midwest. What could be further removed from the expected Irish migrant experience than the South, a rural land overwhelmingly dominated by fundamentalist Protestants? Gavin Stevens, the most often used character of the pre-eminent Southern novelist, William Faulkner, says of the European settlement of his northern Mississippi,

> Then the roadless, almost pathless perpendicular hill-country of McCallum and Gowrie and Frazier and Muir translated intact with their pot stills and speaking only the old Gaelic and not much of that, from Culloden to Carolina, then from Carolina to Yoknapatawpha still intact and not speaking much of anything except that they now called the pots 'kettles' though the drink (even I can remember this) was still usquebaugh.[1]

Stevens acknowledges that Gaelic culture is integral to his South's folk culture and its settlement, but his vision is of Scottish Gaelic rather than Irish, which coalesces with the fiery Protestantism endemic to the South.

A recent work of literary scholarship reveals the extent of the acceptance of the stereotype that the Irish must have had little or no impact on the South. Charles Fanning's *The Irish Voice in America: Irish-American Fiction From the 1760s to the 1980s* is exhaustively true to its title except in one area: the South. Fanning opts to write on but a single unequivocally Southern novel: John Kennedy Toole's *A Confederacy of Dunces*, which he dismisses as a work in which 'the dialogue is hilarious but hollow.'[2] Fanning reveals his stumbling-block to recognizing the importance of the Irish to the South in the opening chapter: 'as the focus will be the fictional self-image of the

American-Irish, writers of Irish background who have chosen not to consider Irish ethnic themes — Flannery O'Connor, for example — will not appear.'[3] Though O'Connor's fiction explores themes I consider inherent in Irish-American writing (religion and family especially), Fanning does not accept O'Connor as a writer concerned with Irish ethnicity because, true to the Southern setting, her characters tend to be Protestants, and most of the Catholics bear surnames less than obviously Irish. The problem for Fanning is that he too easily equates Irish-Catholic with Irish, thereby excluding the Irish-Protestant experience from being truly Irish.

While most scholars have ignored not only the Irish in the South but the Scottish as well in favour of imagining the white South as all but the quintessence of Anglo-Saxon blood and culture,[4] a few have demurred and discovered the prominent presence of Irish migrants and their descendants in the South, long before the Great Famine of the 1840s. Dennis Clark, for example, notes that Irish-born John Daly Burke, a Virginian by adoption, was a popular patriotic poet.[5] Clark also recognizes that Catholic and Protestant Irish in the South congregated first in the Appalachian mountains and foothills where 'their hardy individualist lifestyle, their racy Irish music, and their suspicious secretiveness were already a tradition in the Southern mountains from the Smokies of Virginia to the Ozarks before the Civil War.'[6]

Though in comparison with Clark's study it is limited in time and geography, David Noel Doyle's *Ireland, Irishmen and Revolutionary America, 1760–1820* is a more challenging work of scholarship, especially concerning the Irish and Southern culture. Doyle makes the connection between Irish migrant and quintessential Southerner in his introduction:

> Andrew Jackson, with piercing blue eyes, face as long as a Lurgan spade, high shock of red hair, and lonely resolution, would embark on the career of frontier soldier, land-speculator, professional English-hater, Southern politician, and national hero that would lead him to the Presidency in 1828, and make of him a symbol of the political reconciliation of the older Ulster Irish stock in American and the incoming thousands of Catholic Irish.[7]

Doyle makes two points here that should not be overlooked. First, he suggests that there is sufficient cultural connection between Irish Catholics and Protestants as to require only a symbol of unification to begin the process of mutual acceptance. Second, in acknowledging that man to be Jackson, a fairly typical Southerner though certainly larger than life, Doyle inadvertently links the South to Irish culture. Like Clark, he sees Irish music, especially Ulster forms, as the matrix of white Southern folk music, but he goes a step further. Of the mountain and hill areas of the eighteenth-century South he writes, 'that . . . the native Irish took up land in the same counties as the Ulster Scots raises the issue of their mutual acceptance which the interpenetration of their folk-music in these regions does.'[8]

Doyle's work examines the presence and contributions of the Irish to all of America in the revolutionary age, but his most original scholarship lies in his work on the South. If Doyle were the only historian to suggest the importance of the Irish to white Southern culture through a synthesis of Irish Catholic and Protestant, he could be dismissed more readily. Grady McWhiney and Forrest McDonald, however, go beyond even Doyle in their assertions. In brief, their thesis is that peoples from Celtic lands (Ireland, Scotland and Wales) and from the English areas bordering Scotland and Wales formed the preponderance of European migrants to the South during its formative period. Just as Doyle sees Irish Catholic and Protestant differences almost vanishing when they are together in the Southern backwoods, McWhiney and McDonald argue that primary 'Celtic' folk culture characteristics were shared by migrants from Ireland, Scotland and Wales, and that the similarities were more important than the local, tribal differences when, for instance, a group of Irish Catholics settled near a group of Scottish Presbyterians. In other words, when faced with a hostile new geography and the presence of American Indians and Africans, as well as the hostility of the English on the coast, Celtic migrants and their descendants banded together to form a new culture in the South, in fact the majority Southern culture: Cracker Culture, to use McWhiney's term.

The first example of the scholarship advocating the Celtic-Southern thesis the intrigued reader should examine is 'The Ethnic Origins of the American People, 1790', by Forrest McDonald and Ellen Shapiro McDonald. The article is a critique of the American Council of Learned Societies' study of the national origins of white Americans as revealed by the 1790 census. Published in the 1931 *Annual Report of the American Historical Association*, the work was primarily done by Howard F. Barker and Marcus L. Hansen, with Barker devising a method to calculate the numbers of migrants from the Germanic-speaking lands and the British Isles. It lies beyond the scope of this chapter to assess the mathematical calculations made by the McDonalds; however, their work suggests that Barker's highly flawed system grossly underestimated the number of Americans of Celtic ancestry in 1790, the height of the formative period of the various American regional identities. The McDonalds' analyses indicate that while the American North, especially New England, was overwhelmingly Anglo-Saxon in settlement, and therefore heritage, the area south and west of Philadelphia consisted of settlers primarily of Celtic background.

In order to reveal the nature of the bigotries the McDonalds found underlying Barker's methodology, it is necessary to include this lengthy quotation:

> Among the first kind of errors, he made clear that his interest was not in culture but in 'blood', or supposed genetic strains in the population. That approach obscures the centuries of wars, conquests, and other forms of interactions that altered the 'blood' of both Celtic and Anglo-Saxon peoples but left cultures intact and even hardened them. Consequently, Barker was led into making some strange classifications. For instance, he distinguished between 'Celtic Irish' and 'Ulster Irish', as if the latter, though most were of Scottish origins, were some-

how not Celtic. On the other hand, he treated the Welsh as if they were 'Cambrian' English; indeed, of the twenty-two names he selected as distinctively English, no fewer than twelve were distinctively Welsh.[9]

There are two essential points here that must be addressed. First, the proponents of the Celtic-Southern thesis are not interested in race *per se* but in the folk cultural characteristics of people. Second, though the McDonalds are loath to proclaim it, the primary bigotry underlying Barker's distinctions that led to his underestimating the number of Celtic migrants to America by 1790, and thereby undervaluing Celtic contributions to the early development of the United States, appears to be religious. The only possible explanation for labelling not only Irish Presbyterians but also the Welsh as non-Celtic, leaving their numbers and cultural contributions to be usurped under the heading English, is that both are Protestant. Apparently, Barker equated Celtic culture with Irish Catholicism and Protestantism inextricably with Anglo-Saxon culture.[10]

The first book-length study to be published promoting the Celtic-Southern thesis was *Attack and Die: Civil War Tactics and the Southern Heritage* by Grady McWhiney and Perry D. Jamieson. Their thesis is that the strategies and fighting styles of the Union and Confederate armies reveal a significant cultural difference between the North and the South: the North fought a characteristically English war while the South fought Celtic-Style campaigns. Though I find this the least persuasive component of the Celtic-Southern thesis, I must acknowledge that sections of the book are challenging. This is especially true of the last chapter, in which the authors move beyond military tactics to a larger comparison of folk cultures.[11]

Thus far, the major contribution to the thesis is Grady McWhiney's *Cracker Culture*. While *Attack and Die* restricted itself to military tactics, thereby leaving itself too thin to be fully persuasive in its larger cultural arguments, *Cracker Culture* approaches the thesis from myriad subjects. The work's 'Prologue', written by Forrest McDonald, provides a brief introduction to Celtic history and the distinguishing characteristics of Celtic folk culture. McDonald then summarizes the migration of Celtic peoples in the seventeenth and eighteenth centuries to the American South, noting that the overwhelming majority were Irish Protestants.[12]

McWhiney's study is one in which he makes a comparative examination of folkways. He does this through travel accounts. In short, McWhiney presents innumerable examples from the *ante bellum* period of both foreigners comparing Southern folkways to those of Celts and Northern folkways to those of the English and of Northerners responding to and condemning Southerners much as Englishmen of the age responded to and condemned Celts. McWhiney divides his comparisons into ten areas of life: Settlement, Heritage, Herding, Hospitality, Pleasures, Violence, Morals, Education, Progress and Worth. While the McDonalds' critique of Barker's population study indicated that large numbers of Celts migrated to the South by 1790, becoming a majority throughout the frontier areas, McWhiney's book demonstrates that within two generations of the first US Census the folk culture characteristics of those Celtic migrants had come to dominate most of the South.

This lengthy review of historical scholarship has been a necessary preparation for my reading of Southern literature. Without it, my essay would seem to suggest merely that Southern writers have utilized Irish characters. What I am arguing here is that my reading of Southern literature supports the McWhiney-McDonald Celtic–Southern thesis. What is left largely unstated in McWhiney's work, and may lead to unwarranted attacks, is that though Cracker Culture had come to dominate the majority of the South by the *ante bellum* period, the original coastal South had remained culturally Anglo-Norman. The tension between those two distinct transplanted European cultures lies behind much of Southern literature.

Though *Cracker Culture* is intriguing, if not exhaustively persuasive, it is flawed by its strength: the exclusive use of travel accounts to argue its case. McWhiney ignores *ante bellum* Southern literature because he believes that its authors, 'the most cosmopolitan and learned of Southerners, were not representative of Cracker culture; indeed, many of them were not Crackers at all.' McWhiney notes, and I believe correctly at least for the *ante bellum* age, 'Crackers infrequently took pen in hand, and the resulting documents seldom survived to be examined by scholars.'[13] Acceptance of this view, however, creates a problem for the reader knowledgeable of Southern culture. Vann Woodward, perhaps the pre-eminent historian of the South, says of Southern novelists, 'they have given history meaning and value and significance as events never do merely because they happen', and Frank Owsley, Jr, affirms, 'perceptions and ideals are difficult to capture in historical narrative, and thus we rely on the novelist to deal with these issues.'[14] This symbiosis between Southern fiction and Southern history suggests that if the Celtic-Southern thesis is valid, Southern novelists will have revealed in their works the importance of Celtic migrants and their descendants, especially the Irish, to the development, expansion and perpetuation of Southern culture. Nor does this present the kind of problem McWhiney feared. Not only are a large number of Southern novelists, especially in the twentieth century, of Irish and Scottish heritage, but Southern literature is primarily one predicated on folklore. It is created 'out of the rag-tag and bob-ends of old tales and talking',[15] and if the folk culture is primarily transplanted Celtic, then the novels will reveal it to be so.

Of particular interest to me is the synthesis of various Irish, Scottish and Welsh local cultures into Southern folk culture. In this essay, I will examine the fictional use of characters of Irish background. Any such sympathetic or thematic portrayal of Irish Catholics is significant because of the South's traditional fundamentalist Protestant hegemony. That positive Irish Catholic characters would be not merely composed but accepted by Southern audiences suggests that a synthesis of the folk cultures of Irish Catholics and Protestants did indeed occur in the Southern backcountry, and that synthesis undergirds Southern culture.

Ellen Glasgow

Virginian Ellen Glasgow (1873–1945) is the novelist who best bridges the Reconstruction period with the Southern Renaissance. Her first novel was published in 1897, 30 years before the flowering of the 1920s, and the last published during her life, for which she won her only Pulitzer Prize, appeared in 1941.[16] Her parents represent the two primary, always contrasting and often conflicting, white cultural groups in the South: Crackers and Anglo-Normans. 'Thomas Francis Glasgow, born in west Virginia,' notes Anne Goodwyn Jones, 'came from Scottish and Irish ancestors.' While the paternal heritage was Gaelic, 'Glasgow's mother . . . came from Tidewater aristocrats who thought Richmond far enough west to settle.'[17]

Life and Gabriella (1916) is, as its subtitle indicates, 'The Story of a Woman's Courage'. As the novel opens, Gabriella Carr is a young woman in late nineteenth-century Virginia. Her sister Jane is married to a man who lives the role of Anglo-Norman gentleman, albeit a drunken, abusive cavalier. Jane, unquestioningly accepting of the mores of her age, flees to her mother during her husband Charley's excesses, only to return home to her proper place once the storm has subsided. While Jane can mutter only a feeble 'It wasn't my fault,' 'one can always do something if it's only to scream,' rejoins Gabriella.[18]

The allotted place for women in this society is one roughly equivalent to that of children. Mrs Carr, a widow, tells Jane of her desire to have Cousin Jimmy Wrenn decide what to do; 'men know so much more than women about such matters.' Somewhat later, Uncle Meriwether wants Gabriella, a maiden, to leave the room while the men discuss Jane's options because 'the less women and girls know about such matters, the better.'[19] Gabriella's fiancée of two years, Arthur Peyton, reveals the social norm regarding women in his explanation to Gabriella of his opposition to her plan to work outside the home: 'You're so sacred to me . . . I always think of you as apart from the workaday world. I always think of you as a star shining serenely above the sordid struggle.'[20] The Richmond men, and they are symbolic of the Anglo-Norman South, require their women to be secular madonnas on a pedestal rather than flesh-and-blood human beings.

The novel traces Gabriella's development from a young woman who understands instinctively that the chivalric view of women is not merely condescending but impoverishing as well ('I'm tired of being on charity just because we are women')[21] to a mature woman who creates her own life. What is most important about Gabriella's development to me is the ethnic-cultural slant taken by Glasgow. Though Gabriella is native to an eastern Virginia city synonymous with the descendants of the Anglo-Norman First Families of Virginia, her background is Irish. Glasgow provides no history of the Carr family that demonstrates conclusively its cultural ancestry, but the Southern Carrs I have known have all claimed either Scottish or Irish Protestant antecedents. Added to this, the fact that Gabriel Carr's reckless passion appears to have set him apart from most of Richmond society suggests that he is one of McWhiney's Crackers. This, however, is not the extent of Gabriella's Irish ancestry. While waiting for Arthur to arrive to escort her to a party, and mulling over the sexism and hypocrisy endemic to Richmond society, Gabriella 'told herself with grim determination that she would never go to a party again. The Berkeley conscience, that *vein of iron* [emphasis mine] which lay beneath the outward softness and incompetence of her mother and sister, held her, in spite of her tempting youth, to the resolution she had made.'[22]

As we shall see more explicitly in the novel bearing it as a title, 'vein of iron' is the central phrase in Glasgow's work, and it inevitably refers to the inner strength of character inherent in Southerners of Gaelic cultural heritage. What initially may seem somewhat odd here is that Gabriella's 'vein of iron' derives from the distaff Berkeley family. Not only does Berkeley not sound particularly Irish, but both Gabriella's mother and sister appear to be culturally at one with Richmond society. The use of the name Berkeley is intriguing, especially when we recall Church of Ireland theologian and philosopher George Berkeley (1685–1753). His biographer declares, 'Berkeley was an Irishman of English descent', that 'born, bred, and educated an Irishman in Ireland', Berkeley not only wrote his greatest works in Ireland, but he also referred to himself as Irish.[23]

Because there is no reason to suspect that in *Life and Gabriella* Glasgow intends 'vein of iron' to mean something other than what she spells out more specifically in subsequent novels, we are safe to assume that the Berkeley family is Irish. If so, Glasgow's use of the name is subtly suggestive on two levels. First, there is the above noted recognition that Episcopalians may be culturally and nationally Irish. Second, in having an Irish family possessing the 'vein of iron' become weakened after it has embraced Anglo-Norman society of the Virginia Tidewater, Glasgow reviews critically not only the mandarin minority Southern culture but the genteel Episcopalianism that accompanies it. As has already been demonstrated, Glasgow equates the Southern chivalric subjugation of women to Anglo-Norman culture, and as Gabriella frees herself of that culture's tentacles, she will rediscover fully her Irish 'vein of iron'.

The seductive sway of the society's beliefs is revealed when Gabriella meets George Fowler. She is enthralled by this paragon of gallantry: 'In his eyes, which said enchanting things, she could not read the trivial and commonplace quality of his soul — for he was not only a man, he was romance, he was adventure, he was the radiant miracle of youth!'[24] True to his culture, George 'abhorred independence in a wife', declaring that a knowledge of and interest in business made her 'a mannish woman'.[25] Seduced by what she should recognize to be frippery, Gabriella will be forced to locate and embrace the 'vein of iron' in order to make her life fulfilling.

Gabriella's marriage to George is an abysmal failure. Raised primarily in New York, George has had no direct access to the Virginian 'Scotch-Irish inheritance' that has made his father such a good man.[26] George drinks, squanders money and attempts to hide his actions from both his wife and his family. Not only does he have an affair, but George eventually leaves his wife and children, forcing Gabriella to assume the full responsibility for not only her life but those of her children as well.

At each crisis in her life, the 'vein of iron' saves Gabriella. Before her marriage when George refuses to allow her mother to live with them, Gabriella finds the strength to defy the man she sees as a romantic knight in a story-book: 'Something stronger than herself — that vein of iron in her soul — would not bend, would not break though every fibre of her being struggled against it . . . The vein of iron held her firm in spite of herself.'[27] When her mother writes and asks for $400 to go to Florida for her health, Gabriella must face the consequences of having lied to protect her worthless husband because

> custom exacted that a wife should be willing to lie in defense of her husband. Some obscure strain of dogmatic piety struggled in the convulsed depths of her being, as if she had been suddenly brought up against the vein of iron in her soul — against the moral law, stripped bare of clustering delusions, which her ancestors had known and fought for as 'the Berkeley conscience'. The Berkeley conscience, bred for centuries on a militant faith, told her now that she was punished because she had lied to her mother.[28]

George's affair with Florrie prompts Gabriella to look inward for strength in order to avoid becoming a lifetime martyr like her sister: 'Thanks to the vein of iron in her soul she would never — no, not if she died fighting — become one of the victims of life.'[29] Glasgow does not use the phrase 'vein of iron' when Gabriella is faced with George's leaving her, but she has her heroine turn immediately to Madame Dinard, 'who had been born an O'Grady', for employment.[30]

Though Gabriella is a successful worker and single mother, she realizes 'Yes, I've missed life.' Then she notices a red-haired man who 'was doubtless devoid of those noble traditions by and through which, her mother always told her, a gentleman was made out of a man — the traditions which had created Arthur and Cousin Jimmy as surely as they had created George and Charley.'[31] Archibald, Gabriella's son, is immediately drawn to Ben O'Hara, but Gabriella's initial assessments of O'Hara are predicated upon the Tidewater views of her upbringing and therefore hostile. 'I dare say he has a great deal of force,' she tells her maid, 'but you must admit that blood tells, Miss Polly.'[32] The remainder of the novel reinforces this truth but not as Gabriella believes, for she has confused 'blood', the heritage of culture, the vein of iron in her soul, with the veneer of Anglo-Norman civility that coats both the violence of Charley and George and the ineffectiveness of Arthur.

Gabriella develops a grudging respect for O'Hara through her talks with him, discovering that he was born into the direst poverty and despises sanctimonious hypocrisy above all else, but

> never for an instant would it have occurred to the granddaughter of that sanctified snob, Bartholomew Berkeley, who despised the lower orders and fraternized with the Deity in his pulpit every Sabbath, that the red-blooded and

boisterous O'Hara — the man of force and slang — could by any accident usurp
the sacred shrine where the consecrated relics of her first love reposed.[33]

Gabriella begins to overcome her social prejudices when George arrives
'home' to die from his acute alcoholism. O'Hara steps in to handle the DT
fits, and Gabriella realizes, 'even Arthur would have appeared at a disad-
vantage beside O'Hara at that moment.'[34] After observing O'Hara's
strength of character, Gabriella feels 'suddenly humbled'. Eventually, the
combination of Archibald's adoration, Polly's admiration, O'Hara's em-
pathetic handling of George and his stories of his childhood and his wife's
morphine addiction all contribute to Gabriella's realization that O'Hara
'had never lost a natural chivalry of mind beside which the cultivated
chivalry of manner appeared as exotic as an orchid in a hothouse.'[35]

The novel concludes with Gabriella's proclamation to O'Hara, 'I'll come
with you now — anywhere — toward the future.'[36] This has been the purpose of the novel. Glasgow's heroine is a representative Southern woman
of the age who searches for a worthwhile future. The men of her Tidewater
South, aping a chivalry that denigrates woman, are all failures. 'Glasgow
does not find in the South,' writes Anne Goodwyn Jones, 'an image of man-
hood that can heal by unifying energy and virtue, physical potency and
intelligence, nature and culture.'[37] What is significant is that the man who
qualifies as the soul mate to Gabriella's vein of iron is the child of Irish
migrants to New York City. Through this union Glasgow suggests the
importance of cultural similarities. Gabriella, whose vein of iron marks the
pre-eminence of the Irish in her, finds the culturally Anglo-Norman men of
her native Richmond to be at best ineffectual. The Irish–American born in
New York, however, is the man with whom she can build a future. Note
especially that religious differences carry no weight here. Gabriella's background is Irish Protestant and O'Hara's is Irish Catholic, but the difference
is so meaningless as to be unworthy of any discussion. The suggested
cultural similarity overrules differences of religion and social status.

Linda Wagner views *Life and Gabriella* and *Virginia* (1913) as novels
telling a similar story about native Southern women facing problems
created by sexism. She further argues that through the novel's title, the
heroine of *Virginia* should be seen as widely symbolic.[38] If this is so, then
Gabriella must also be a symbol of Southern womanhood. Read this way,
Life and Gabriella suggests that Southern men, opting to live by the culturally false dictates of the Anglo-Norman Tidewater, have failed Southern
women, at least those who have maintained the Irish vein of iron in the
soul, and those are the Southern women in Glasgow's works with the
greatest strength of character. The result is that the female symbol of the
South must, in order to have a future, mate herself with the child of Irish
migrants.

'Her eighteenth novel is in some ways her richest', Wagner writes of *Vein
of Iron* (1935).[39] The novel's protagonist is Ada Fincastle, the daughter of a
former Presbyterian minister who has lost two congregations due to his
philosophical writings. The family is from Ironside village in Shut In

Valley at the foot of the Appalachians. As Donald Akenson could point out, the family name would be considered English by many, but the Fincastles are of Irish Presbyterian ancestry: 'Scotch–Irish, people called the pioneers, though after they were driven out of Strathcylde they had stayed to themselves in Ulster, and had seldom or never crossed blood with the Irish.'[40] This segregation of Gaelic tribes, perceived or actual, will be important in the novel's resolution.

The Fincastles reinforce their emphasis on the family's Scottish heritage, both Highland and Lowland, at every opportunity. John, Ada's father, tells his sister Meggie, who is writing a letter to a distant relative in Scotland, to declare that Ada 'has eyes like the Hebrides'.[41] John regularly reads chapters of *Old Mortality* aloud to the family, and Ada wants to name her doll Flora, the 'prettiest name in the world'.[42] Other than the Fincastle line, the family stress the Graham heritage most. Margaret Graham Fincastle, John's grandmother, 'infused a romantic legend, as well as an aristocratic strain, into the Fincastle stock. There was a cherished tradition that the Graham ancestor who had fled from Scotland to Ireland in 1650 was a near kinsman of the great Montrose.'[43]

The novel traces Ada Fincastle's search for meaning and happiness in life. It opens in her childhood and closes as she faces middle age, finally at peace with herself, her past and her future. The love of Ada's life is Ralph McBride, who has 'an Irish strain in his blood. Mother said this gave him his charm and his amused, friendly manner.'[44] Not only is the McBride family presumably of Irish Catholic heritage, even though the family members have been Presbyterian for some time, but Ralph's paternal grandmother, Molly O'Boyle, 'had come from Ireland when she was a child.' Barney McBride, Ralph's father, dead before the birth of his son, had married 'Rebecca Murihead, of a dour Scottish family'.[45] This mixing of Gaelic cultures often divided by religion both explains Ralph's character and furthers the fictional exploration of the Gaelic basis for Southern society Glasgow had begun in *Life and Gabriella*.

Ada's world begins to collapse when Ralph is forced to marry Janet Rowan, the daughter of the wealthiest family in the village. At a party, Ada began to fight with Ralph over his drinking moonshine, spurred on by Janet among others. Ada's anger pushes her to leave, and when she takes the firm stand not to allow the men in her life to act inappropriately towards or with her, Ada, like Gabriella, senses the 'vein of iron far down in her inmost being, in her secret self, could not yield, could not bend, could not be broken.'[46] The next morning Ada discovers that Janet, pregnant by someone she cannot or will not name, had invited Ralph into her room, after which she screamed because she allegedly had seen a mouse. The Rowans and Mr Black, the minister, have convinced Ralph he must marry Janet. Ralph 'had sacrificed himself, and her also, to a last rag of chivalry, to a tradition in which he did not even believe.'[47]

Like Gabriella, Ada finds the Anglo-Norman chivalric codes to be destructive. *Vein of Iron*, however, features fewer critiques of Tidewater culture and mores than *Life and Gabriella* and focuses more on critically reviewing Southern Calvinism, which derives from Ireland and Scotland, not from English Puritans. After Janet has 'lost' the baby and had an affair, Ralph comes home and he and Ada spend two days together in a cabin before he reports for military service in the First World War. They find that their love is stronger than ever, even though Ralph has become cynical. A conversation between them provides a key to the novel:

> 'I'm always waiting for punishment. I suppose I'm still incurably Presbyterian.'
> 'Or Irish?' she laughed. 'Perhaps an Irishman makes a bad Presbyterian.'
> 'Or a Presbyterian a bad Irishman.'[48]

The significance of this playful exchange is revealed later when Ada visits Mrs McBride with the hope of discovering whether Janet's divorce has been granted and Ralph has been shipped overseas. During her conversation with the woman who had become increasingly puritanical since her husband's death, Ada realizes, 'religion could be a bitter and a terrible thing!' Mrs McBride, she senses, finds 'a thrill of cruelty in the Christian symbols of crucifixion and atonement.'[49] Gaelic Calvinism, Presbyterianism, is seen in this novel as primarily negative, but the reader should be careful not to confuse the organized religion with its practitioners. These Southern descendants of Irish and Scottish migrants may all have the vein of iron, but if so it is due to the maintenance of family tradition not specific theology. Ada is faced with recreating that family tradition in the modern world: 'Was the past broken off from the present? she mused, or did that vein of iron hold all the generations together?'[50]

The answer that Ada will eventually discover is yes, the vein of iron will hold all the generations together if the individual works to maintain it. Before Ada can marry Ralph, however, the family must face a crisis: Ada is pregnant. The family has already become pariah due to her father's opposition to the war, and illegitimacy further isolates them. In addition, Ada is isolated within the family as her grandmother understands neither her willingness to sleep with Ralph nor her lack of shame in bearing his child before they are married. The family's financial misfortunes (John no longer has students to teach) and its new status contribute to a move to Queensborough, a city in eastern Virginia. Though the move offers the prospect of a better future once Ralph returns, Ada realizes, 'in Ironside, poor as they were, they had built upon rock. Now in Queensborough, it seemed to her, life was an air plant, springing up out of emptiness. Vapor it was yesterday, and vapor it would be again tomorrow.'[51]

Though Ada hopes she and Ralph can 'build a home in the wilderness of the machines as their forefathers had cleared the ground and built a home in the wilderness of trees',[52] and during the boom of the 1920s the family prospers financially, her dream cannot be realized in Queensborough, a world away from the family's roots, roots necessary to the vein of iron. Ada appears to understand this when she hopes they can save enough money to repurchase the manse, the Fincastle family home in Ironside, 'for this had been her secret dream ever since she had lived in the city. To go back, not now, but some day when they had prospered and saved.'[53]

Linda Wagner believes 'one must, at some point, connect the character of Ralph McBride — impractical, volatile, "Irish," — with the men in Glasgow's own life.'[54] Her assessment is not only that Ada has been failed miserably by Ralph but that somehow Ralph's Irishness explains his lack of character. As already noted, Ralph begins to turn cynical after the community treats him unjustly concerning Janet Rowan. This cynicism grows as a result of his service in the war: 'I'm not so sure civilization is worth saving,' he quips.[55] Furthermore, Ralph is unfaithful to Ada, and he does fail to honour fully his obligations to his family in other areas.

That, however, is only half the picture, and failure to understand that Ralph is Ada's proper mate can lead to confusion about the novel's conclusion. For instance, the one act of Ralph's impracticality that is directly linked to Irishness is positive. Unwilling to ask for charity, the Hamblens, an elderly couple, kill themselves during the Great Depression. They do not leave sufficient funds for burial, and Ralph offers half of his weekly salary to defray the costs. John Fincastle is glad Ralph 'was still capable of a magnificent folly. It was the Irish in him.'[56] This unsolicited willingness to aid the less fortunate is more characteristic of Ralph than his failures, and it is why Ada loves him.

John Fincastle's own magnificent folly paves the way for the family's restoration. He had turned from organized Christianity to philosophical writing 'that owed nothing to the dynamo' because he could not affirm unswerving belief in all Presbyterian tenets. 'Perhaps in some distant future,' he muses, 'man might turn away, disillusioned, from the inventive mind, and human consciousness might stumble back again along the forgotten paths of blessedness and mystic vision.'[57] Considering his emphasis on family heritage, Fincastle's 'inventive mind' refers to the scientific, empirical, dogmatic and his 'forgotten paths of blessedness and mystic vision' suggests the religious heritage of the Celtic Church, which may well be imbedded in his vein of iron. As he meditates on this, he acknowledges the blessedness in nature, 'not only in beauty; it is in the little things also.'[58]

After he realizes that death is near, Fincastle wonders whether he has been failed by philosophical speculation: 'He was more at home nowadays with the humblefolk ... who spoke neither the hollow idiom of facts nor the dead tongues of the schools, but the natural speech of the heart.' 'Pure philosophy,' he acknowledges, 'is a wordless thing', and if wordless, it must also lack something essentially human.[59] This revelation that much of his life and most of his intellect had almost wasted, forces him to conclude that he must return home to the manse to die because 'only in Ironside could he find the freedom to sink back into changeless beatitude, into nothing and everything.'[60] Fincastle returns to Ironside and enters the ruined gate leading to the now dilapidated manse, but like Moses he will be denied the promised land. The first death blow 'stripped him of all that he had once thought of as his immortal part, as his inviolable personality. Nothing remained but a blind faith in some end that he could not see, in some motive he could not understand.'[61]

That 'end' is the salvation of his family. The city was monster machine enough, but the Depression had further dehumanized it. Ada senses in the fall of 1932, 'distraught, chaotic, grotesque, it was an age ... of cruelty without moral indignation, of catastrophe without courage.'[62] Her grandmother had told Ada, 'even in the wilderness Scotch-Irish housekeepers seldom became slatterns. If you have the proper pride, you may keep nice among savages.'[63] Indeed, when the esteemed German philosopher Hardenburg comes 'to pay homage to one of the greatest among living philosophers', Fincastle observes of his sister Meggie, serving as hostess, 'never had she appeared so natural, and yet so dignified. The mountain poise had not deserted her. His mother had never lost it, and beyond his mother — how far beyond! — he remembered the noble bearing of that grandmother who had been Margaret Graham, walking on her bare feet through the drenched grass.'[64]

The family may have maintained its pride, but it had lost its bearings. Fincastle's trip home to die not only forced his family members to return, but it allowed them the time to step back from the lifeless life of the city to reflect on what they really want and need. Looking at the manse, Ralph initiates the possibility of staying there, and Ada adds that her father's insurance money could purchase the place. When she oversimplifies the work required to repair the manse and have enough to eat by suggesting they would have it easier than their pioneer ancestors, Ralph injects his comical Irish cynicism to bring Ada back to reality: 'it takes conviction to set out to despoil the wilderness, defraud Indians of their hunting-grounds, and start to build a new Jerusalem for predestinarians.'[65] When the decision to return is made, Ada has

> a sense, more a feeling than a vision, of the dead generations behind her. They had come to life there in the past; they were lending her their fortitude; they were reaching out to her in adversity. This was the heritage they had left. She could lean back on their strength; she could recover that lost certainty of a continuing tradition.[66]

Having Ada rediscover the strength of her heritage in the midst of the Depression suggests that *Vein of Iron* should be seen as a novel of encouragement for the South in the midst of its greatest crisis since the time of the War Between the States and Reconstruction. The symbolic family representing the strength of Southern character required to survive the Depression and to begin the process of rebuilding is of Gaelic heritage. At the novel's conclusion, the marriage of Ralph and Ada also assumes symbolic significance. As noted, Glasgow suggests that the Scotch-Irish had mixed little with the Irish before migrating to the South, leaving them the weakened descendants portrayed in the novel: the Calvinist fanatic Mrs McBride, the social-worshipping Rowans, the ineffectual philosopher Fincastle, whose brilliance cannot be tolerated by Presbyterianism. Ralph brings to this dour Scottish breed, as Glasgow sees them, the other half of Gaelic culture that they have suppressed: ecstatic joy, wild, satirical humour and impracticality, especially when someone is in need. Ranny, the son of Ralph and Ada, who vows he will do something about all the hungry people when he grows up, is the fruit of this mating of Irish and Scotch–Irish. He is the Southerner of secularized Irish ancestry Glasgow portrays as the hope for the future. And the novel closes on an optimistic note with Ralph and Ada silently viewing the manse: 'he reached out his arm, and while she leaned against him, she felt the steady beating of his heart as she had felt it — how long ago? — when they were lovers. Never, not even when we were young, she thought with a sudden glow of surprise, was it so perfect as this.'[67]

Margaret Mitchell

In her analysis of Glasgow's 'revision of her 1928 Harper's article, "The Novel in the South," which she published in *A Certain Measure* as the preface to *The Miller of Old Church*,' Anne Goodwyn Jones writes, 'Glasgow interestingly includes Margaret Mitchell among the novelists of protest against the mediocrity of Americanism.'[68] That Jones, whose book contains chapters on both Glasgow and Mitchell, should find it interesting rather than obvious that Glasgow would recognize Mitchell as a fellow Southern woman novelist with similar views is a condemnation of the shoddy, sparse scholarship on *Gone With the Wind* and its author. Like the Glasgow novels discussed in this chapter, Mitchell's fictional world centres on a strong woman attempting to define herself in a sexist world. Also like Glasgow, Mitchell is a Southern realist, by which I mean her realism is undergirded primarily by Southern traditions and codes rather than Freud and twentieth-century science. Neither can be labelled a modernist in technique, and both are writers keenly aware of the importance of familial and cultural heritage to the individuality of their characters.

The cover of the Avon paper edition of *Gone With the Wind* advertises it as 'The Epic Novel of Our Time'. The blurb writer was probably referring to its sales, but I accept the novel as 'The Southern Epic'. *The Reader's Companion to World Literature* defines an epic as 'a long narrative poem in which the characters and the action are of heroic proportions.' The standard attributes for epics in the West were laid down by first Homer and then his Roman imitator Virgil: 'the underlying theme concerns basic and eternal human problems; the narrative is a complex synthesis of experiences from a whole epoch of man's history or civilization; the hero embodies national, cultural, or religious ideals; the style is earnest and dignified; the poem plunges . . . *in medias res*.'[69] With the exception of beginning *in medias res* and requiring the work to be a poem, *Gone With the Wind* meets the epic criteria. Its theme of struggling through the adversities created by war is universal, and its historic period is the focal point of Southern history.[70] In avoiding modernist techniques, which the author might have considered fashionable when she began her novel, Mitchell could be seen as maintaining a dignified, traditional narrative style.

Cultural myopia causes us to exclude prose from epics. Because the Greeks, Romans and Germans all wrote their epics in poetry, most scholars have erroneously concluded that all epics must be in verse. Most pertinent to students of Irish culture is that the Irish epic, *Tain Bo Cuailgne*, is prose with lyrics scattered intermittently. The modern epic language, like that of ancient Ireland, is prose rather than poetry, as James Joyce understood.

This definition of epic, however, remains incomplete. Many works of literature from a given culture could meet most, if not all, of the epic characteristics, but I know of no culture with more than two epics. This is not to say that there are not several surviving attempts at epics. The *Argonautica* is one, but no one considers it 'The Greek Epic', a title rightfully accorded to both the *Iliad* and the *Odyssey*. The reason is that the complete definition of epic is a work of literature containing most of the characteristics listed above and accepted by its audience as the work best exemplifying the unique traits of the group in question. In short, the *Iliad* and the *Odyssey* are not epics because scholars pronounced them to be so; they are epics because both Greeks and non-Greeks recognized that they defined Greek culture and character better than any other works of literature. Similarly, *Gone With the Wind* is accepted by both Southerners and non-Southerners as the work of literature that best defines Southern culture.

Mitchell's epic protagonist, who embodies the South much as Achilles and Odysseus combine to personify Greece, is Scarlett O'Hara. Though it is all but inconceivable to think of Scarlett as bearing any surname other than that with which she is born, not the Scottish Lowland Hamilton, nor the Highland or Irish Kennedy, nor the Hiberno-Norman Butler, and certainly not the English Wilkes, the novel focuses on Scarlett's struggle to define herself. Her father Gerald is a quintessential Celt: loquacious, shrewd, forthright, contentious, determined, Gerald loves his land above everything else, for 'to anyone with a drop of Irish blood in them the land they live on is like their mother'. Scarlett 'found it comforting to be in his presence. There was something vital and earthy and coarse about him that appealed to her'.[71] On the other hand, Scarlett's mother Ellen is a 'Coast aristocrat of French descent'. In opposition to Gerald's concrete, practical life on the land, Ellen is abstract and intangible, so much so that Scarlett confuses her with the Virgin Mary. The O'Hara parents represent two basic white cultures in the South: Gerald, the Celtic, and Ellen, the Norman, which is usually thought of in terms of the Virginia Tidewater cavalier. *Gone With the Wind* is not merely a novel about fighting and rebuilding from a losing war; it is an epic in which the protagonist ultimately has the tragic perception that her life has been false in cultural terms. The conflict in *Gone With the Wind* concerns which of the two different cultures should be pre-eminent in the South, a conflict Mitchell embodies in Scarlett's love for Ashley Wilkes.

Though Scarlett loves her mother to the point of idolatry, she is Gerald's child. Ellen is able to train Carreen and Suellen, Scarlett's younger sisters, to be demure Anglo-Norman ladies, 'but Scarlett, child of Gerald, found the road to ladyhood hard.'[72] In the library at Twelve Oaks, Scarlett attempts to play the role but fails when Ashley says that he will marry Melanie: 'then her rage broke, the same rage that drove Gerald to murder and other Irish ancestors to misdeeds that cost them their necks.'[73] When Rhett Butler sarcastically praises her courage for donating her wedding ring to the Cause, 'all that was Irish in her rose to the challenge of his black eyes.'[74] In fact, it is Scarlett's untameable Irishness that attracts Rhett. He tells her of the Twelve Oaks barbecue, 'it is one of my priceless memories — a delicately nurtured Southern belle with her Irish up — You are very Irish, you know.'[75] Nor is Rhett the only person to recognize Scarlett's Irishness. Mammy, the character most in the know throughout the novel, thinks in the midst of her argument over Ellen's drapes, 'Lordy, 'twas right funny how de older Miss Scarlett git de mo she look lak Mist' Gerald and de less lak Miss Ellen.'[76]

The importance of Scarlett's Irishness is manifested after the burning of Atlanta when she arrives home. She understands why Gerald stood on the porch and refused to allow the Yankees to burn his home: 'There were too many Irish ancestors crowding behind Gerald's shoulders, men who had died on scant acres, fighting to the end rather than leave the homes where they had lived, plowed, loved, begotten sons.'[77] When she is exhausted to the point of resignation in her attempt to provide for everyone at Tara, Scarlett recalls family stories of survival against all odds in the face of unspeakable horrors. Her Irish ancestors may have lost physically, but they were never beaten spiritually: 'They had not whined, they had fought. And when they died, they died spent but unquenched. All of those shadowy folks whose blood flowed in her veins seemed to move quietly in the moonlit room. And Scarlett was not surprised to see them, these kinsmen who had taken the worst that fate could send and hammered it into the best.'[78] Scarlett's vision includes the French Robillards and Prudhommes on her mother's side, but the vision itself is Irish. It marks Scarlett as Irish in clan, for the Celtic sense of family considers both ancestors and descendants as important as the living.

While Scarlett is culturally Celtic, Ashley is an Anglo-Norman gentleman. Upon being told by his favourite child that she wants to marry Ashley, Gerald blusters, 'Our people and the Wilkes are different ... The Wilkes are different from any of our neighbors — different from any family I ever knew. They are queer folk, and it's best that they marry their cousins and keep their queerness to themselves.'[79] The reason for the differences of the Wilkes family is revealed in the novel's opening chapter. Brent Tarleton tells his brother Stuart in reference to Ashley's love of Europe, 'you know how the Wilkes are. They are kind of queer about music and books and scenery. Mother says it's because their grandfather came from Virginia. She says Virginians set quite a store by such things.'[80] Unlike the rest of their neighbours who are living a culture that Grady McWhiney would label as essentially transplanted Celtic transformed into Southern, the Wilkeses are culturally Anglo-Norman cavaliers. In the Tidewater or in Charleston or Savannah, the Wilkeses would be in the majority culture and the O'Haras,

MacIntoshes and Tarletons would be crackers, hillbillies or peckerwoods. But in the rest of the South the Wilkeses are 'queer'.

Scarlett's tragedy is that she refuses to listen to her father and throws her life away thinking she loves Ashley. In the midst of the war, she considers him 'still a young girl's dream of the perfect knight', an early hint that deep-down Scarlett knows Ashley is false.[81] In the midst of attempting to keep the family together in the War's last days, Scarlett realizes, 'everything her mother had told her about life was wrong', yet she persists in her dream of Ashley much as her mother had done with her memory of Philippe Robillard.[82] Though Scarlett's intensity to have Ashley wanes — after being kissed by Rhett 'the quiet face of Ashley Wilkes was blurred and drowned to nothingness'[83] — she does not realize fully the mistakes she has made until after Melanie's death, when Ashley admits to her that his wife was his life. Scarlett then understands that Ashley 'never really existed at all, except in my imagination . . . I loved something I made up, something that's just as dead as Melly is. I made a pretty suit of clothes and fell in love with it . . . I kept on loving the pretty clothes — and not him at all.'[84]

At this point we must recall that as an epic protagonist, Scarlett O'Hara is, to some degree, a symbol of the South. Nor should a female Southern personification be startling. In opposition to the English John Bull and the American Uncle Sam, the South, like Ireland, is always seen as female. Scarlett's story then is not merely a personal love tragedy; it reflects a larger cultural tragedy. On her way home to try to explain her realization to Rhett, Scarlett says to herself, 'I've never been able to see the world at all, because Ashley stood in the way.'[85] She tells Rhett of her mistakenly believing she had loved Ashley, 'It was — well, a sort of habit I hung on to from when I was a little girl.'[86] Scarlett and Ashley are representative of the two primary cultures of the South: respectively, Celtic and Anglo-Norman cavalier. Scarlett, Mitchell's embodiment of the South tragically rejects what she truly is, and her Irish culture, in an attempt to become what she is not. Rhett sums up the issue in his attack on Scarlett for believing that Ashley could manage Tara, 'You'll never make a farm hand out of a Wilkes — or anything else that's useful. The breed is purely ornamental.' He concludes, 'Strange how these illusions will persist even in women as hard headed as you are.'[87] If the basis of the majority Southern culture is Celtic, then attempting to play the role of 'ornamental' cavalier is false, as is the South's desire to be that Norman gentleman. The South's tragedy then is that its Celtic hardheadedness did not prevent it from choosing the pretty illusions of cavalier gentility, which include a cavalier defence of chattel slavery and the caste system that goes with it. The South, like Scarlett, blinded itself to reality, and thereby lost what was most precious to it.

Mitchell's epic is one in which her Irish symbol of the South almost destroys herself by refusing to be what she is, Celtic, and in chasing a false culture that appears to be more refined. But Mitchell ends the novel on a note of optimism. Scarlett will return to Tara to recoup herself before attempting to win back Rhett. After her miscarriage, she had gone to stay at Tara and had returned reinvigorated, 'the unhealthy pallor had gone from her face and her cheeks were rounded and faintly pink'.[88] The symbolic importance is apparent: Tara, which is located in Gerald's native County Meath, is the traditional capital of ancient Ireland; it is the spiritual centre of Irish culture. To atone for her mistakes and prepare for her future, Mitchell's symbol of the South must return to the roots of her Irish culture.

'It is the novel's social and intellectual insights,' writes Frank Owsley, Jr, 'that make it most useful to historians.'[89] The chief social insight to be found in *Life and Gabriella*, *Vein of Iron*, and *Gone With the Wind* is that the Irish have been instrumental in the development of Southern culture. Each novel closes optimistically: Gabriella has found her mate in an Irish migrant, Ada and Ralph have rediscovered the vein of iron, and Scarlett turns to Tara for spiritual and emotional strength. *Life and Gabriella* makes no claims concerning the predominance of Irish culture in the South, but in having its symbolic heroine be a Southern woman of Irish heritage who turns away from her generation's Ashley Wilkeses to Ben O'Hara, Glasgow acknowledges a connection between the best of Southern culture and Ireland. *Vein of Iron* reveals the strength of character Glasgow sees as inherent in the Southern descendants of Irish Protestant migrants, but suggests that the best of Southern character is formed when Irish Protestant is mated with Irish Catholic. *Gone With the Wind* is the most important, for it reveals that Irish Catholics, not merely Irish Protestants, were important to the development and expansion of Southern culture. Speaking of the nineteenth-century Savannah area, the coastal South and therefore more Anglo than Celtic, Mitchell writes, 'America, in the early years of the century, had been kind to the Irish.'[90] What is more amazing is that not only would the symbolic heroine of the Southern epic be Irish Catholic but that it would seem so natural as to require no explanation in the Protestant South. Clearly, the many descendants of those Irish Protestant migrants instinctively understand that the Southern vein of iron is Gaelic, and the religion is irrelevant. They respond to Scarlett not as Catholic, but as a fellow descendant of Irish migrants, as not only one of their own, but as their cultural epitome.

Notes

1. William Faulkner, *The Town*, Random House, New York, 1957, pp. 316–17.
2. Charles Fanning, *The Irish Voice in Fiction: Irish–American Fiction From the 1760s to the 1980s*, University of Kentucky Press, Lexington and London, 1990, p. 344.
3. Fanning, *The Irish Voice*, p. 4.
4. For a quick overview, see Grady McWhiney, *Cracker Culture: Celtic Ways in the Old South*, University of Alabama Press, Tuscaloosa and London, 1988, pp. 2–4. The word 'Cracker' is apparently of Scottish origin, and means 'Boaster' — it has become a pejorative term for White Southerners (McWhiney, p. xiv).
5. Dennis Clark, *Hibernia America: the Irish and Regional Cultures*, Greenwood Press, Westport, Connecticut and London, 1986, p. 94.
6. Clark, *Hibernia America*, p. 96. Though I unequivocally accept Clark's con-

tention here, I must note that the part of the Appalachian chain most commonly called the Smokies lies on the Tennessee-North Carolina border. The mountains in Virginia are usually referred to as the Blue Ridge.

7. David Noel Doyle, *Ireland, Irishmen, and Revolutionary America, 1760–1820*, Mercier Press, Dublin and Cork, 1981, p. xvii.

8. Doyle, *Ireland*, p. 104.

9. Forrest McDonald and Ellen Shapiro McDonald, 'The ethnic origins of the American people, 1790', *William and Mary Quarterly*, Third Series, Vol. XXXVII, No. 2 (April 1980), p. 184.

10. The reader interested in this scholarship should also see the *William and Mary Quarterly*, Third Series, Vol. XLI, No. 1; articles by Thomas L. Purvis and Donald H. Akenson and responses by them and the McDonalds further highlight this important article.

11. The reader interested in military tactics should examine not only *Attack and Die*, University of Alabama Press, Tuscaloosa and London, 1988, but also James Michael Hill's *Celtic Warfare, 1595–1763*, John Donald Publishers, Edinburgh, 1986.

12. Forrest McDonald, 'Prologue', *Cracker Culture*, pp. xxi–xliii.

13. McWhiney, *Cracker Culture*, p. xviii.

14. C. Vann Woodward, *The Burden of Southern History*, Louisiana State University Press, Baton Rouge, 1960 and 1968, p. 39, and Frank L. Owsley, Jr, 'Introduction', *The Long Night*, by Andrew Lytle, University of Alabama Press, 1988, p. 5.

15. William Faulkner, *Absalom, Absalom*, Random House, New York, 1936, p. 303.

16. For a brief sketch, the reader should see 'Ellen Glasgow', by Tonette Bond Inge, in *Encyclopedia of Southern Culture*, eds, Charles Reagan Wilson and William Ferris, University of North Carolina Press, Chapel Hill and London, 1989, pp. 883–4.

17. Anne Goodwyn Jones, *Tomorrow is Another Day: the Woman Writer in the South, 1859–1936*, Louisiana State University Press, Baton Rouge and London, 1981, pp. 226–7.

18. Ellen Glasgow, *Life and Gabriella*, Doubleday, Page and Company, New York, 1916, p. 4.

19. Glasgow, *Gabriella*, pp. 7, 21.

20. Glasgow, *Gabriella*, p. 36.

21. Glasgow, *Gabriella*, p. 27.

22. Glasgow, *Gabriella*, p. 30.

23. A. A. Luce, *The Life of George Berkeley, Bishop of Cloyne*, Thomas Nelson and Sons, Ltd., London and New York, 1949, pp. 25–6. Luce succinctly summarizes the process by which non-Irish settlers became Hibernicized: Berkeley's 'family came originally from England, no doubt; but Irish air acts quickly; one generation can alter the outlook, and Berkeley's father was settled in Ireland, if not born there' (p. 25).

24. Glasgow, *Gabriella*, p. 87.

25. Glasgow, *Gabriella*, pp. 99, 102.

26. Glasgow, *Gabriella*, p. 153.

27. Glasgow, *Gabriella*, p. 112.

28. Glasgow, *Gabriella*, pp. 187–8.

29. Glasgow, *Gabriella*, p. 242.

30. Glasgow, *Gabriella*, pp. 212, 253.

31. Glasgow, *Gabriella*, pp. 367–8.

32. Glasgow, *Gabriella*, p. 391.
33. Glasgow, *Gabriella*, p. 437.
34. Glasgow, *Gabriella*, p. 445.
35. Glasgow, *Gabriella*, p. 480.
36. Glasgow, *Gabriella*, p. 529.
37. Jones, *Tomorrow is Another Day*, p. 262.
38. Linda H. Wagner, *Ellen Glasgow: Beyond Convention*, University of Texas Press, Austin, 1982, pp. 8, 41.
39. Wagner, *Ellen Glasgow*, p. 94.
40. Ellen Glasgow, *Vein of Iron*, Harcourt, Brace and Company, New York, 1935, p. 19.
41. Glasgow, *Vein of Iron*, p. 7.
42. Glasgow, *Vein of Iron*, pp. 23, 30.
43. Glasgow, *Vein of Iron*, p. 39.
44. Glasgow, *Vein of Iron*, p. 71.
45. Glasgow, *Vein of Iron*, p. 113.
46. Glasgow, *Vein of Iron*, p. 135.
47. Glasgow, *Vein of Iron*, p. 166.
48. Glasgow, *Vein of Iron*, p. 220.
49. Glasgow, *Vein of Iron*, p. 239.
50. Glasgow, *Vein of Iron*, p. 248.
51. Glasgow, *Vein of Iron*, p. 277.
52. Glasgow, *Vein of Iron*, p. 278.
53. Glasgow, *Vein of Iron*, p. 290.
54. Wagner, *Ellen Glasgow*, p. 99.
55. Glasgow, *Vein of Iron*, p. 287.
56. Glasgow, *Vein of Iron*, p. 416.
57. Glasgow, *Vein of Iron*, pp. 110, 111.
58. For a discussion of the Celtic Church and nature, see Christopher Bamford, 'The heritage of Celtic Christianity', in *The Celtic Consciousness*, ed. Robert O'Driscoll, George Braziller, New York, 1982.
59. Glasgow, *Vein of Iron*, pp. 426, 427.
60. Glasgow, *Vein of Iron*, p. 452.
61. Glasgow, *Vein of Iron*, p. 454.
62. Glasgow, *Vein of Iron*, p. 373.
63. Glasgow, *Vein of Iron*, p. 138.
64. Glasgow, *Vein of Iron*, pp. 424–5.
65. Glasgow, *Vein of Iron*, p. 460.
66. Glasgow, *Vein of Iron*, p. 461.
67. Glasgow, *Vein of Iron*, p. 462.
68. Jones, *Tomorrow is Another Day*, pp. 229–30.
69. Lillian Herlands Hornstein, Leon Edel and Horse Frenz (eds), *The Reader's Companion to World Literature*, Second Edition, Mentor Books, 1973, pp. 176–7.
70. In a discussion at the University of Arkansas in October 1990, Peggy Whitman Prenshaw revealed that on her recent tour of the Soviet Union to speak on Southern women writers the book that the audience at every location wanted to focus on was *Gone With the Wind*.
71. Margaret Mitchell, *Gone with the Wind*, Macmillan, New York, 1936, pp. 34, 31.
72. Mitchell, *Gone with the Wind*, p. 58.
73. Mitchell, *Gone with the Wind*, p. 117.
74. Mitchell, *Gone with the Wind*, p. 186.

75. Mitchell, *Gone with the Wind*, p. 195.
76. Mitchell, *Gone with the Wind*, p. 546.
77. Mitchell, *Gone with the Wind*, p. 411.
78. Mitchell, *Gone with the Wind*, p. 421.
79. Mitchell, *Gone with the Wind*, p. 34.
80. Mitchell, *Gone with the Wind*, p. 16.
81. Mitchell, *Gone with the Wind*, p. 214.
82. Mitchell, *Gone with the Wind*, p. 434.
83. Mitchell, *Gone with the Wind*, p. 835.
84. Mitchell, *Gone with the Wind*, p. 1016.
85. Mitchell, *Gone with the Wind*, p. 1022.
86. Mitchell, *Gone with the Wind*, p. 1028.
87. Mitchell, *Gone with the Wind*, p. 628.
88. Mitchell, *Gone with the Wind*, p. 972.
89. Owsley, 'Introduction', *The Long Night*, p. 5.
90. Mitchell, *Gone with the Wind*, p. 44.

5 'Staging a Lie': Boston Catholics and the New Irish Drama

Paula M. Kane

The reception of Synge in Dublin and Boston

When the Abbey Players of Dublin brought John Synge's *Playboy of the Western World* to Boston in 1911, they opened in a new theatre near the city's thriving entertainment district. The Abbey production was competing with dozens of entertainment choices which that week included Houdini's straitjacket escape act and a Japanese soprano from Tokyo's Imperial Opera House. Considering the variety and 'exotic' content of popular and high culture available in Boston, it is perhaps surprising that anyone took the trouble to single out Synge's play as offensive to a specific ethnic and religious group. None the less, well before the play opened, local Irish societies had petitioned City Hall to prevent its appearance on the grounds of obscenity.

The charge of obscenity, and additional allegations of blasphemy and heresy, levelled against Synge reprised the outrage that had surrounded the play's première in Dublin in 1907. The charges suggest profound cultural conflicts between sexual license and restraint, artistic freedom and religious oppression, and traditional identities and modernization. These tensions have been addressed in an extensive scholarship about how literature and drama defined an Irish cultural identity and catalysed a nationalist movement in Ireland in the early twentieth century. This chapter builds upon that history of cultural nationalism to explore how religious ideology affected the formation of nationalism among a diaspora population. Below I examine what serious religious doctrines Irish Catholics thought that Synge was blaspheming or dismissing, in order to suggest how the Catholic Church was inseparably linked to the creation of Irish Ireland and of Irish Americanism.

At the close of the nineteenth century Irish nationalism entered its cultural phase, wherein writers, poets and playwrights aligned with the leading figure in the so-called Irish Revival, William Butler Yeats, who looked to culture to guide and dominate political praxis. In Yeats's view, a representative genius such as himself would become the new spiritual leader who incarnated Irish nationalism. This cultural revival, often termed Anglo-Irish, spawned a variety of frequently self-contradictory and esoteric strategies, including groups advocating a return to Gaelic, a revival of Celtic and pre-Christian arts and legends, a flight from reality into mysticism and occultism and a nationalist drama centred on the playwrights and productions of the Abbey Theatre. One cultural critic has summarized the Anglo-Irish revival as 'an attempt to regain leadership (intellectual and cultural where moral and social leadership had faltered) by concealing new symbols of power in cabalistic language and gesture.'[1] The attempts the cultural nationalists made to recover their lost authority would precipitate numerous crises within the Irish nationalist movement.

Cultural nationalism supported the general nationalist project of ending Ireland's colonized status under the control of Great Britain. The choice of method, whether through a moderate parliamentary solution of Home Rule or through revolutionary separation from England, was still undetermined. The frictions between cultural nationalism, led by a Protestant Anglo-Irish élite, and a century-old tradition of Irish nationalism that was overwhelmingly Catholic, led to a leadership crisis within nationalism that had three results: it brought Protestant-Catholic religious tensions to the foreground in the debates over cultural nationalism; it placed control of cultural production at the centre of the question of Irish identity; and it exposed the class tensions between a dying landlord-gentry and a bourgeoisie.

These three factors coalesced at the Dublin première of Synge's *Playboy of the Western World* at the Abbey Theatre in 1907. The play caused boisterous riots because it was perceived as obscene, anti-Catholic and anti-Irish. On opening night, the unfolding of Christy Mahon's humorous adventures in the first and second acts was well received. The action occurs mostly in a shebeen in County Mayo on the west coast of Ireland, following the arrival of young Mahon, a stranger who claims to have murdered his father by striking him with a spade. He is soon treated as a bold hero by the villagers, welcomed to their games and festivals and sought after by young women and elderly widows alike. Although Christy surmises that his defiant act of patricide will make him the subject of heroic ballads and gallous stories in the western world, the Mayo villagers turn against him when they witness the sudden arrival of Old Mahon, very much alive, and hear Christy vow to murder his father a second time. Pegeen Mike, the young woman who is largely responsible for inventing Christy's heroism, ultimately comes to lament the gap between his alleged 'dirty deed' and his 'gallous story' about it.[2] In its most universal sense, the playboy's false tale of parricide dramatizes Synge's theme of the conflict between reality and romance.[3]

Christy Mahon's deed did not itself provoke the audience, which began to whistle and shout upon hearing the word 'shifts', referring to women's petticoats, in the middle of the third act. Christy utters the word while defending the sincerity of his love for Pegeen, a shebeen owner's daughter, against the offer of 'a drift of chosen females standing in their shifts' lining the width of the country. This kind of pornographic fantasy did not sit well in Ireland, perhaps even more so because, only 15 years earlier, a woman's shift had been waved by the enemies of Charles Parnell to symbolize his adultery. Parnell's sexual indiscretion cost him the support of the majority of the Catholic clergy for the Home Rule movement.[4] Unfortunately for Synge, not only did the word 'shift' have volatile sexual and political over-tones, but the actor also garbled the offensive line of dialogue at the pre-mière, inserting 'Mayo girls' for 'chosen females.'[5] As if slaying his father was not villainous enough, Christy Mahon now seemed to be revelling in a lecherous fantasy about the women of the heart of rural Ireland — the Gaelic, lawless western world. By this stroke, Synge transgressed tradi-tional gender images and violated barriers in the social geography of Ireland that associated Catholics and Protestants with distinct and differ-ent regions and landscapes.

Noise drowned out the rest of the première, and spontaneous riots con-tinued to disrupt the remaining week of performances in Dublin, despite the presence of policemen who were stationed in the theatre at the request of Yeats, a co-founder of the Abbey. Some catcallers were arrested and fined on the third and fourth nights, and much of the play's dialogue went unheard until the fifth performance because of the hissing, singing and shouting from the patrons.[6] By the fourth night, police in the theatre were 'as thick as blackberries in September', although the actual total was prob-ably no more than 50. Unwilling to sacrifice the remaining performances, Yeats planted Trinity College students in the audience to applaud Synge's play. Some saw his gesture as a blow for free speech; others branded Yeats a traitor who revealed his true loyalties to the British police and to the Anglo-Protestant collegians.

The role of Yeats in the reception of *Playboy of the Western World* would remain a contested yet integral one because he defended the autonomy of the Abbey writers against narrow-minded nationalists and offered himself as the genuine model of a nationalist hero.[7] As the leading defender of Synge, Yeats shaped the critical reception of *Playboy of the Western World* in 1907 by portraying the conflict over the play as one between the autonomy of art and the philistinism of Irish nationalism.[8] However, as George Watson has suggested, Yeats contrived a false contrast between aesthetics and popular consciousness, between a 'a free and somehow "neutral" art, represented by the Abbey Theatre, and a narrow and aesthetically abused nationalism.' Rather than a contest between creativity and nationalism, Watson maintains that the conflict involved 'a clash between two different kinds of cultural and political consciousnesses.' Watson concludes, as have many others, that the Irish public could not accept even sympathetic Protestant writers like Synge and Yeats simply because they were outsiders to Catholic Ireland.[9]

Because politics and theatre in Ireland were so closely linked between 1900 to 1922, or roughly between the collapse of Parnell's Home Rule coali-tion and the formation of the Irish Free State, the language and characters of playwrights were carefully scrutinized by the spectrum of nationalists — conservatives, home-rulers, militants and their transatlantic fellow-trav-ellers. Internal opposition to the Irish literary renaissance was sharpest in the decade prior to 1916 when the various factions of Irish nationalists questioned whether the use of folk idioms and the aesthetic exploitation of peasant life by Protestant 'outsiders' such as Synge, Gregory and Yeats, who wrote in English, was appropriate to an anticipated independent national drama.

Because Yeats set the parameters for the reception of Synge's play in Dublin, and because Synge died in 1909, Yeats continued to occupy the centre of the controversy. Like Synge, Yeats embodied the split character of cultural nationalism. As described by Seamus Deane, this schizophrenic Irish consciousness was 'dominated by two versions of the self — the Protestant or Ascendancy self, characterised by solitude, and the Catholic or peasant self, characterised by its collective (folk) nature.'[10] Although Yeats came from the Protestant bourgeoisie, he identified himself with the Protestant aristocracy, or Ascendancy class. Yeats was an unlikely hero for the Catholic masses because he was doubly alienated from them by his false attachment to the Ascendancy self and by his disgust for his own middle-class origins.[11] None the less, Yeats's objective was to capture the loyalty of Catholic people and to fashion himself into the voice of a reformed nationalist movement by renewing the Irish people's links to their Celtic myths and legends.

Because of his class and religious background, Irish Catholics accused Yeats of subverting cultural nationalism by introducing elements that were foreign and even unassimilable to a Catholic communal-folk ideology. The accusations against Yeats are essential to our discussion of Synge because they defined one of three recurring types of attacks on *Playboy of the Western Word*, which I will label the 'pagan conspiracy theory'. Opponents of the new drama represented by Yeats, Synge and the Abbey Theatre frequently called it inauthentic because it was non-Catholic, non-Christian and even irreligious. We shall return to the pagan conspiracy approach later. Here we only note that it became a favourite tactic used by the Catholic Church against the Anglo-Irish promoters of cultural nationalism.

Yeats transmitted his support for Synge directly to American audiences when he accompanied the Abbey troupe to Boston, where the furore over *Playboy of the Western World* was repeated during the Abbey Theatre's 1911–12 tour of the United States. Because of Synge's untimely death, it fell to the Theatre's directors, Yeats and Lady Gregory, to defend his American première. Though Lady Gregory and the actors had softened the play's language after the Dublin riots, like Yeats they saw the brewing controversy in America as another chance to strike a blow against censorship.

In the United States, and particularly in New England, Irish-Americans were struggling with a different kind of divided identity. Were their loyalties to Ireland or to America? In cities with concentrated Irish populations, including Boston, Providence, Philadelphia, New York City, New Haven and Chicago, Ireland seemed victorious. Synge's play was met with hisses, and showers of hurled vegetables, eggs and asafoetida, often coordinated by Irish-American fraternal and ethnic associations who pressured theatre managers to cancel the production.[12] When the *Playboy* finished its

American première in Boston, audiences in New York City protested about the play by slinging rotting garbage, cigar tins, cigarette boxes and even their rosaries on-stage.[13] In Philadelphia, the entire Abbey company was arrested for immorality.[14] Chicago's performances were relatively peaceful, despite an anonymous death threat sent to Abbey co-founder, Lady Augusta Gregory.[15]

In contrast to the unplanned outbursts against Synge in Dublin, these American protests against the Abbey players were orchestrated in advance by Irish-American societies that targeted local theatre owners and city censorship agencies. Some groups seem to have been incited directly by agitators in Ireland. Only in Washington, DC, did it appear that the Catholic Church played an overt part in organizing opposition to Synge.[16] None the less, the Church's impact in cities such as Boston was considerable simply because Catholicism was becoming inseparable from Irish-American identity.

In September, 1911, the Abbey Players prepared to open a five-week run at Boston's new Plymouth Theatre, which had been hailed as the ideal intimate setting for modern drama. For the ceremony welcoming Gregory and Yeats to Boston, Mayor John Fitzgerald appealed to his listeners to regard the new Irish dramas as 'only one phase of the many-sided renaissance in Ireland.'[17] Fitzgerald's hopes exceeded the tolerance of his constituency, who expected him to invoke the city's obscenity regulation to bar production of the play. In compliance with recently revised municipal regulations of 1908, that placed joint authority for determining obscenity in the hands of the mayor and police commissioner, Mayor Fitzgerald dispatched his private secretary, William Leahy, an Irishman educated at Harvard University, to watch the first performance with a censor authorized by Commissioner Stephen O'Meara.[18]

The Plymouth Theatre was not crowded on opening night. Scattered boos and hisses from the Irish-Americans were offset by cheers from a bloc of Harvard men invited by Lady Gregory and by the applause of Brahmin cultural leaders like Isabella Stewart Gardner. Yeats watched the play from the rear of the orchestra, while Lady Gregory stood in the foyer. Contrary to the expectations of the Irish community, the censor reported to Mayor Fitzgerald that there was no reason to prohibit the play because nothing in it justified charges of obscenity or immorality. Fitzgerald's secretary concurred with the censor's lenience:

> They (the Mayor and Commissioner) are not called on, as I take it, to approve or disapprove a particular school or writing. Now the language in this play, wisely softened from the original by the players themselves, is still rather coarse in parts, and the incident of the biting of Shawn's leg by the playboy is monstrous and disgusting. But a stick of moral dynamite is the last thing to look for here. If obscenity is to be found on the stage in Boston, it must be sought elsewhere, and not at the Plymouth Theatre.[19]

Mayor Fitzgerald agreed. This in itself raised eyebrows among Irish Catholics. As a resident of nearby Watertown observed wryly in a letter to the *Boston Globe*: 'Mayor Fitzgerald and O'Meara have agreed on something for once, even if it is on a subject that neither of them knows much about.'[20] It was not that Mayor Fitzgerald was averse to theatre censorship: he had recently invoked the obscenity charge to yank the character of a corrupt mayor from a recent production of *Get Rich Quick Wallingford*, claiming that the play impugned the integrity of mayors. Rather, it was unusual for Fitzgerald, as a Democratic mayor, to support O'Meara, a Republican Party member close to the city's Yankee élite. Commissioner O'Meara may have been influenced in his support for Synge by his numerous Brahmin friends, including Philip Hale, art critic for the Boston *Herald*.[21] In supporting the play, O'Meara acquitted himself better than the police chief in New Haven, Connecticut, who demanded certain cuts in the *Playboy*, only to learn later that the matinée he had attended was George Bernard Shaw's *Blanco Posnet*.[22]

No doubt to demonstrate her intellectual broadmindedness, the Mayor's 21-year-old daughter attended the play's première fully aware of the impending controversy. Rose Fitzgerald's ambivalent emotional and intellectual responses were perhaps shared by many Irish Catholics. She recorded her initial embarrassment at seeing on stage 'just those qualities of poverty, dirt and sloth which the Yankees had always accused (the Irish) of having and there they were, depicted as characters of the old country — unvarnished and naked to the eye.'[23] Rose observed also that the Brahmins' barometer of gentility, Isabella Stewart Gardner, was enjoying the play. Still, while Mrs Gardner reported to the theatre manager and the newspapers that she had 'loved every minute', only in private did Rose Fitzgerald admit that the performance was entertaining, while complaining that Synge distorted the Irish by portraying them as unsophisticated rustics.[24] A fellow Bostonian suggested that local Yankee–Irish tensions contributed to Irish unease, and imagined that if Irish-Americans could 'see the play among themselves, with no strangers present, they would see the farce in it and enjoy it.'[25] He and Rose Fitzgerald struck at the heart of the matter: the Boston Irish resented the Protestant intelligentsia of the Abbey theatre currying favour from the Brahmin élite for an Irish play that seemingly degraded the Irish.

Despite its high concentration of Irish residents, Boston's reaction to the *Playboy* was surprisingly mild. Elsewhere in America, the anti-Synge protests were more excessive than in Dublin.[26] There was no cathartic climax of a Yankee–Irish brawl on opening night, although it is easy to imagine Harvard students, guests of Lady Gregory, being tackled by their Catholic rivals from the Jesuit Boston College, urged on by the shouts of the fraternal members of the Ancient Order of Hibernians. A starting-point for examining the relatively puny anti-Synge demonstrations lies with the class, ethnic and religious identifications of Irish-Americans.

In Boston, Irish Catholics faced a formidable rival that was tantamount to their British colonizers in Ireland: the Yankee Protestant, who for nearly three centuries had controlled the social, economic and cultural life of Massachusetts. In the mid-nineteenth century, Boston, as home to the novelists, poets, Utopians and eccentrics of the American literary renaissance, had enjoyed a reputation as the 'Athens of America'. Between 1880 and 1920, however, this white, Anglo-Saxon Protestant élite, known as the Boston Brahmins, was facing the loss of its once formidable hegemony over New England. To compensate for a loss of political power especially to Irish immigrants, the Brahmins began to reassert their cultural superiority through a variety of means.

In the 1880s Irishman Oscar Wilde dubbed Boston a 'paradise of prigs', and American philosophers began to mourn the death of a genteel tradition long associated with the city's pre-eminence in cultural production. Yankee patricians traced this decline to the waning of Puritanism and the loss of a Calvinist ethos where 'the Cabots speak only to God', an assertion which had a basis in demographic and economic, if not aesthetic and spiritual reality. Between 1850 and 1900, immigration dramatically shifted the ethnic composition of New England away from its English Protestant roots, though not necessarily from its Calvinist moralism. By 1905 Irish Catholics composed Boston's largest single religious and ethnic group. These descendants of Irish Famine immigrants who had begun to arrive after 1846 were viewed as morally lax, anti-democratic and intemperate by the ruling Protestant élites. Subsequently, the Irish became a convenient target of blame for Boston's cultural malaise as well as for all forms of social deviance.

Yankees contrasted their own cultural achievements with the degeneracy of the Irish, whom they blamed for the spread of immorality, juvenile delinquency and political corruption in Boston. Traditionally, the Brahmins had used their authority to inhibit Irish assimilation and mobility in three ways. First, they established educational quotas, practised employment discrimination and proposed immigration restriction legislation. Their scapegoating efforts were so successful that unlike the rest of the nation, Massachusetts retained an oversized Irish underclass that undercut national patterns of Irish–American assimilation well into the twentieth century.

Second, after the 1890s, the fading WASP élites hoped to re-establish their control of Boston's cultural reputation through invoking non-partisan, 'good government' tactics that had been used by retreating patricians in New York and Philadelphia hoping to destabilize the Irish political machines.[27] Brahmins strove to accomplish this goal in Boston in part by revising municipal censorship and licensing regulations. As the Irish began to secure and consolidate their political power at the local level through the ward bosses of the Democratic Party, WASP Republicans responded by revising civil codes to restrict the power of the mayor by tying licensing of theatres and censorship of plays to the office of the police commissioner. The commissioner of police, who was appointed by the governor rather than elected, would presumably continue to reflect the views of the largely WASP-controlled state house rather than answering to the Irish monopoly at City Hall. Between 1900 and 1920, Republicans continued to dominate and dictate state politics, while 'Green Power' ruled

Boston from the election of John Fitzgerald in 1907 through to the 1960s.

Finally, while Yankee politicians worked to limit the power of the Irish machines over cultural matters by complicating regulatory practices and by reforming the civil service system, the Yankee–Irish split in Boston was enlarged by a division between the aims of Yankee social reformers, known as Progressives, and the objects of their reforms, namely foreign immigrants. Irish Catholic theatre-goers of 1911, together with other ethnic groups, were the targets of a national movement by Progressive reformers to control the urban masses. Linked to both Good Government movements before World War I and to the drive for '100 per cent Americanism' after the war, the forces of order and culture were growing 'locked together in harmonious union', leading Brahmins and Progressives to propose comprehensive plans for disciplining immigrants and for moulding them into civilized Americans.[28]

The *Playboy* episode reminds us that the Americanizers' plans to instill and to enforce personal and social hygiene were sometimes resisted by assimilating groups in the form of direct action such as confrontations in theatres. While the Catholic Church provided immigrants with its own 'shalt nots' for bodily discipline, reinforced by the regimen of its parochial schools and religious orders, Catholic notions of propriety apparently did not satisfy the definitions of Protestant social workers and Americanizers. At a moment when American audiences were otherwise becoming noticeably quiescent, Boston's Irish protesters seemed an unwanted throw-back to the 'raucous, independent audiences of the nineteenth century' and thus an irritant to the Yankee highbrows hoping to civilize immigrants and especially the 'savage' Irish.[29] In Ireland too, the Protestant élite had associated the Catholic masses with uneducated mobs and mobocracy, frustrating Ascendancy supporters like Yeats, who quoted Victor Hugo to the effect that a people should be enthralled by its own national spectacle and be moved to decorously observe 'the sacred drama of its own history'.[30] The call for more passive, reverential audiences served parallel functions in Ireland and the United States, as part of the anxious response of a fading Protestant élite to maintain cultural leadership. In Ireland, the savages were the natives; in Boston, they were thought of as immigrant intruders. Irish–Americans were therefore obliged to defend themselves on three fronts: from Yankee nativism, from the patrician élitism of the Brahmins and allied Progressive reformers and from their own potentially divisive class conflicts.

At the same time that Irish-Americans faced Yankee Protestant resistance to their assimilation in America, the future of their ethnic unity appeared to be threatened by stratification within their own community. Now several generations removed from immigration, a minute percentage of Irish Bostonians entered the upper middle class, seeking to make a dent in the hegemony of the Brahmins without endangering their own new respectability. A small Irish professional class of lawyers and physicians was also emerging. Together, these prosperous 'lace-curtain' Irish, quipped local comedian Fred Allen, were envied for having fruit in the house when no one was sick. As the Catholic bourgeoisie expanded, it purchased homes and moved to nearby suburbs, thereby breaking its former organic ties to the Irish neighbourhoods. The lace-curtain Irish demonstrated their racial solidarity by opposing the Abbey productions, but they also demonstrated a bourgeois concern for appearances by avoiding physical violence that risked fulfilling Brahmin stereotypes of Irish hooliganism. To the poorer 'shanty' Irish, who earned their livings as shopkeepers, factory workers, day labourers and domestics, middle-class airs and house-pride became sources of both ridicule and imitation.

One strategy for overcoming class divisions among the Irish in a diaspora setting was to cultivate a myth of Irish origins that helped to propagate and nurture an exile mentality which cut across classes. Since the Famine departures of the 1840s, images of being unwilling participants and, in fact, victims of the migration process had filled the thoughts and writings of Irish-Americans. The usefulness of this tactic was fading, however, and according to Kerby Miller, the few years before the Easter Rising of 1916 represented 'the "last hurrah" for this image of the Irish emigrant as "exile".' Thereafter, Irish-Americans quickly lost interest in Ireland following the Anglo-Irish treaty and the embarrassment of the subsequent Irish civil war of 1921–2.[31] While their dual sense of alienation from Protestant England and from Mother Ireland did not disappear immediately after 1921, Irish-Americans made a difficult transformation to represent themselves as model Americans committed to democratic government and the pursuit of economic security.

Both lace-curtain and shanty Irish were able to maintain, however, a paradoxical relationship with a rustic peasant mentality that had come to symbolize their origins and that was perhaps a more durable unifying factor than their exiled pose. Although Irish Boston responded meekly to the Abbey players, it shared with other Irish-American enclaves the certainty that Synge's play defamed Irish peasants. The fact that this stance lacked a solid basis in reality for middle-class and working-class Irish alike bears examining. For their part, bourgeois Irish-Americans were torn between loyalty to a nostalgic maternal Ireland promoted by Irish nationalism and to the prospect of social mobility into the world of affluence and genteel taste epitomized by the Brahmins. Working-class Irish-Americans also continued to call themselves peasants, although they had no connection with the land or agricultural pursuits. In fact, during this era 'Irish-Americans' became nearly synonymous with urban settings and municipal jobs.

Boston therefore lacked a discernible rural Irish peasantry whose reputation was allegedly being tarnished. Irish immigrants who were ghettoized in the Atlantic seaboard cities never became tenant farmers or freeholders in America. Nor had they ever been part of a working rural economy in the United States. Furthermore, although they claimed solidarity with the Irish peasantry, the Boston Irish seemed unsympathetic to a timely theme in Synge's play relating to land inheritance practices in Ireland, personalized in a son's demand for fair treatment from a tyrannical father. Without some overwhelming injustice to incite him, why else would a son try to kill his father? But the Boston Irish did not support Christy Mahon's rebellion against Old Mahon as the just demand of a son for his inheritance, nor did they see it as a call to support the overthrow of the Ascendancy landlords in Ireland. Perhaps for lace-curtain families in their suburban homes one step removed from the ethnic ghetto, rebellion against their new Yankee 'fathers' seemed too dangerous. Perhaps for the Irish poor, America's golden opportunities still seemed within reach. Moreover, as American citizens, the Boston Irish had no urgent need to certify the nationalist credentials of Ireland's Abbey Theatre. But since the creation of an independent Ireland was a political concern to many second- and third-generation Irish-Americans, then two questions concern us. First, why did the Boston Irish feel compelled to defend the image of the virtuous Irish peasant? Second, what relationship existed between the Catholic Church and the peasant image in defining an Irish-American identity?

It is likely that rumour and hearsay were far more responsible for the negative reaction to Synge than familiarity with the text of *Playboy of the Western World*. The play was familiar to Harvard University students in the English courses of Professor George Pierce Baker but was unknown to most Bostonians. Given the shouting that plagued the performances and the actors' deletions from Synge's original text, it is unlikely that Bostonians even heard the notorious word 'shifts'. Instead, an emotional animus against the play seems to have been built in in advance from Dublin and spread by ardent Irish nationalists to Irish-Americans. Rather than acknowledging any truth in Synge's portrayal of the lawlessness of western rural life and the plight of landless sons, the Irish could only respond by condemning Christy as an outlaw and by condemning the play as obscene.

Not surprisingly, certain Irish-Americans in Boston were predisposed against Synge's work due to reports from Dublin that described his attacks on the peasant as libellous. Days after Synge's première in Boston the Central Council of the Irish County Associations, representing all the counties of Ireland, unanimously voted to condemn the play 'as bearing false witness and the foulest level that has ever been perpetrated on the Irish character', and demanded its withdrawal.[32] The manager of the Plymouth Theatre countered the Council's demand by inviting professional actors from Boston to express solidarity with the Abbey troupe by attending its matinée performance of three one-act plays. In the following week the outraged Central Council, claiming that 150 of its 160 delegates were peasants or sons of peasants, held a special meeting to form a permanent drama committee to observe 'plays where Irish characters are in the cast and report to them so they can take any necessary action.'[33] Interviewed shortly thereafter in New York City, George Bernard Shaw observed that while the Central Council of Boston claimed to know Ireland as children know their mother, the simile was poorly chosen 'because children never do know their mothers; they may idolize or fear them, as the case may be, but they don't know them.'[34]

The ultimatum by Boston's self-styled 'children of Ireland' gave momentum to a national campaign against the new Irish drama in America. In 1912, the Ancient Order of Hibernians passed a resolution condemning the works of Synge, Yeats and others, and organized theatre boycotts in major American cities. Since about 1909 the Hibernians had led a crusade to rid theatre of the older damaging stereotypes of the 'stage Irishman', a stock character dating from the Elizabethan stage who had devolved since the eighteenth century into a swearing, swaggering and belligerent tippler of ruddy hair and face, named Pat, Paddy or Teague.[35] But since the *Playboy* invoked these offensive peasant behaviours only as a subplot in a scene involving the attendance of Michael Flaherty at a funeral wake, the Hibernians did not have much of a case against Synge in this respect. None the less, the AOH was able to prolong the Synge controversy by associating him with the propagation of images of the Irish that were obnoxious residues from the English stage.

In addition to Irish societies and fraternal organizations, Irish radicals in America helped to heat up the conflict over Synge. In September, Irishman John Devoy, head of the Clan na Gael and an advocate of physical force against Great Britain, contributed an inflammatory article to his magazine, the *Gaelic American* of New York City, giving a lurid impression of Synge's play. An added spark came from a similar letter to the *Boston Post* in October concerning another play in the Abbey repertoire. The author of the letter, Dr J. T. Gallagher of Boston, called T. C. Murray's *Birthright* a 'vulgar, vile, beastly, and unnatural' play, 'calculated to calumniate, degrade, and defame a people and all they hold sacred and dear.'[36] Together, these two protests suggest that radicals emphasizing political goals above economic ones, and bourgeois conservatives advocating economic assimilation in America above Irish independence, joined efforts to turn popular sentiment in Boston against the Abbey Theatre for producing plays that defamed Ireland and retarded its freedom.[37]

In contrast to Devoy's rebellious radicalism and the single-minded Clan na Gael, the sympathies of moderate Irish-Americans from the middle and working classes were forged from a more diverse combination of goals and allegiances. Most Irish-Americans preferred 'only plays about lovable mothers, virtuous daughters, and manly young men, all behaving themselves in accord with sentimental tradition.'[38] Understandably, to Irish-Americans raised on the idyllic Ireland of Charles Kickham's Fenian novel *Knockagnow* (1867), the *Playboy* would seem depraved for its disturbing view of Irish life.[39] Although the aesthetic standards of many Irish-Americans seemed indistinguishable from the sentimental codes of bourgeois Victorianism, their protests against Synge harkened back to a purified peasant past. Their identification with 'the peasant' was enhanced by the existence of Irish cultural clubs, such as the Knights of St Brendan, and professional societies, such as the Knights of Columbus, which often combined working-class and middle-class memberships, obscuring their class differences with the rhetoric of medieval feudalism: the camaraderie of a loyal peasantry and chivalrous knights. In Boston moreover, the

Catholic Church held up the communalism of peasant life as a symbol of Irish-American resistance to decadent materialist influences associated with Yankee Protestants and with American city life. Catholic charities were non-discriminatory, the Church was fond of pointing out; the Puritan helped only his own kind. Irish Catholics of differing degrees of assimilation were thereby apt to affirm their Irish identity as rooted in the image of the peasant. Whether the oppressor was England or New England, Catholicism, ethnic communalism and rural virtue were conjoined in the minds of the Boston Irish.

The Boston press played its part in the Synge episode by providing coverage that generally played down the theatre protests. This was to be expected from newspapers controlled by Brahmin or Yankee traditionalists, such as the stodgy *Boston Evening Transcript* and the *Boston Herald*, who took the occasion to congratulate themselves for defending artistic freedom. The *Boston Herald*'s review was written by Philip Hale, a prominent Brahmin painter and art teacher. The day before the play opened in Boston, Hale previewed it in a lengthy column; the morning after, it was Hale who, in a departure from his often caustic comments, reviewed the performance favourably and who tried to defuse opposition by describing the hissing as 'ludicrously weak'. The *Herald* had prepared its readers to like the *Playboy* a full five weeks before its opening. Its Dublin correspondent had interviewed Lady Gregory about her impending visit to Boston and the play's Irish reception. Gregory positioned herself as an even-handed observer who was compelled to support its 'honest objectors' and condemn its churlish protesters, 'armed with tin trumpets, who prevent other members of the audience from hearing it at all.'[40] To round out the local coverage, the *Christian Science Monitor*, founded by the Christian Science Church in 1908 and offering a hybrid of sectarian and secular opinion, gave a sensitive positive review of the play with the aside that one could not overlook its 'spiritual squalor'. The *Monitor* ended with a commonsensical reminder that taste was a subjective matter in stating that some will like strong drama, and some will not.[41]

Those papers identified with Irish editorial staffs and reporters, however, took a different tack. The *Boston Globe* and *Boston Post* represent a cross-section of the daily press with a notable percentage of Irish employees. The morning edition of the widely circulated *Globe* featured a lengthy discussion of the play by a five-person 'committee of representative Bostonians': James Connolly, a local author of adventure novels about Gloucester fishermen; Michael J. Jordan, a lawyer and member of the United Irish League; P. O'Neil Larkin, an Irish nationalist writer; Thomas A. Mullen, lawyer; and A. J. Philpott, the *Globe*'s art critic. The men shared similar levels of education, professionalism and a political bias toward a free Ireland. Connolly, a native of South Boston, gave the only dissenting and positive assessment of the play; Philpott was tepidly appreciative, though critical of the play's 'low' level of farce. Jordan had 'no hesitation in saying that a coarser, more vulgar, more brutalizing exhibition has never been offered to the public under the name of drama.' Larkin characterized the *Playboy* as 'the meanest and most despicable' of any play that has tended to lower the Irish character. Where the Irish nationalists and the lawyer strongly condemned Synge on moral, religious and ethnic grounds, Connolly retorted that such niggling was pointless: 'Synge and Yeats have written of what they know; and if their minds seem to be attracted to the gloomy, the sordid, that merely means that the dark, the unpleasant themes best suit their genius. And isn't it foolish to be quarreling with the color of a man's genius? We might as well blame him for having black hair or red.'[42] Popular response to the *Globe* seemed to run against Connolly, however. His review was swiftly criticized by one respondent who told him to stick to writing 'fish stories'.[43]

The *Boston Post*, New England's independent Democratic paper, gave a general summation of Synge's play as 'a fantastic praise of courage and bitter descriptions of humdrum life.' Edward Crosby, the *Post*'s journalist who wrote its 'Under the Spotlight' column, was less effusive, although he noted that since the actors had censored themselves to meet Boston's standards, the performance could hardly offend. 'At all events,' wrote Crosby, 'it is tiresome and dull, lacking in brilliancy or wit or dialogue and the plot is dragged through three acts which finally become very wearisome.' His verdict on Synge: tiresome but inoffensive. The *Post*'s coverage also focused on the voluntary and forced departures from the audience on opening night. Whereas Philip Hale had dismissed the disturbances as coming from the negligible cheap gallery seats, the *Post* identified those removed from the theatre as 'prominent' citizens, in addition to two young men from the balcony.[44]

The weekly Catholic newspapers, meanwhile, addressed the specific religious offences in Synge's play. In 1907, the new Irish-American archbishop of Boston had taken over the lay-run *Pilot* newspaper and turned it into the official diocesan organ. The *Pilot* became the conservative mouthpiece of the Archbishop, who wrote many of its editorials. The *Sacred Heart Review* of Cambridge, its only significant rival for Catholic readers, was staffed by both clergy and laity who were nearly all of Irish descent, under the editorship of a diocesan priest who happened to be a long-standing opponent of the archbishop. The fact that the *Pilot* published few comments on the Abbey tour of 1911 is explicable in light of its preoccupation with the imminent naming of the archbishop to the Cardinalate in October. The relative silence of the *Pilot* opened the door for the *Sacred Heart Review* to assume leadership in refuting the Irish players and their 'horrible satires on Ireland's people and its priests.'[45] But despite the *Review*'s antagonistic relationship to the *Pilot*, it reinforced the hierarchy's traditional monitory role by criticizing the failure of Boston's Catholic politicians (such as Mayor Fitzgerald?) 'to warn the Catholic people of Boston' against the new Irish drama.[46]

By contrast, reviews of *Playboy of the Western World* from assimilated, educated Irish Catholics were generally favourable, unlike the defensive hostility of recent immigrants self-identified as peasants, physical force nationalists, or of clergy who used the occasion to disguise their anxiety about their own status as moral indignation about modern decadence. Among the clerical élite, however, Father John Talbot Smith of New York was one iconoclast who approved of the Abbey playwrights. Smith was a priest and seminary reformer with a lifelong interest in theatre. He would found the Catholic Actors' Guild in 1914, and was known to Bostonians through his frequent theatre articles in the Knights of Columbus monthly magazine. He praised the virtuous aims of the Irish Revival playwrights and congratulated them for surpassing the 'decadent offspring' of the previous generation of Irish dramatists, by which he meant the lightweight works of Dion Boucicault that had been popular in Dublin and America.[47] Smith's own passage here into a middle-class élite is evidenced by his distancing himself from Boucicault's taint of the 'popular'.

Three prominent lay Catholics of Boston echoed Smith's enthusiasm for Synge. Mary Boyle O'Reilly, daughter of heroic Fenian exile and former editor of the *Pilot*, John Boyle O'Reilly, reported favourably on the Abbey productions for the *Boston Sunday Post*. She thanked the troupe for destroying the stock image of the Irish buffoon, and offered them, on behalf of Boston, 'a very humble apology'.[48] Author James Connolly, whose comments had appeared with the *Globe*'s group of representative Irishmen, confided from his own experience as a writer that 'your great artist is not necessarily a moralist; that is, a moralist of the kind who plainly labels all his characters and fails not to reward his heroes and punish his villains in exact proportion to their desserts while they are here on earth.'[49] Even poet Denis McCarthy, who was offended by Yeats's paganism, admired the Abbey plays for providing full-length productions 'to remind us that we are Irish.' He found the plays to be an improvement over the cultural desert of his childhood in Ireland, where the Christy minstrel shows and wandering actors fell far short of a representative Irish drama.[50]

Smith, O'Reilly, Connolly and McCarthy praised Synge for escaping shallow and clownish stereotyping of the Irish. The quartet's appreciation of the farcical humour and tragic sensibility of the play extended also to their acceptance of Synge's device of self-parody. From Boston's Catholics comes further evidence to suggest that exposure to higher education increased the potential for Irish-American tolerance of Synge. For example, William Leahy, the mayor's secretary who judged the play not obscene, was a Harvard alumnus. Catholic schools tried to be moderate in their views as well. An undergraduate at Holy Cross College, a Jesuit institution in Worcester, Massachusetts, offered his own theories to explain why Synge wrote the *Playboy*. One possibility, he speculated, echoed a standard complaint made against the Abbey writers, that they were driven by commercial greed; the other was Synge's noble hope of arousing 'some dormant Irish genius'. Using an 'end justifies means' approach often attributed to his Jesuit mentors, the student excused Synge's flaws by viewing the play as a catalyst for racial unity.[51]

The Catholic Church and antimodernism

Despite its strength in Ireland, the Catholic Church was responding to centuries of declining status in Europe. Its medieval hegemony had been challenged in the sixteenth century by the Protestant Reformation, and in the eighteenth by the Enlightenment rationalism and the anticlerical excesses of the French Revolution. In the late nineteenth century the Church had shored up its defences at Vatican I (1869–70) against new forms of political liberalism, nationalism and radicalism. The Council's declarations of papal infallibility and papal jurisdiction recalled the triumphalism of the Counter-Reformation era while reasserting clerical and papal power. Neo-Scholastic philosophy and theology, regularized by a papal decree of 1878, preserved Catholic dogma and theological methods as codified by Thomas Aquinas in the Middle Ages, and rejected modern culture as deficient according to the Church's eternal truths. The most reactionary tenets of Catholic antimodernism had been enumerated by the 80 theses anathematized in the Syllabus of Errors of 1864, which had been reiterated in 1907 in the encyclical condemning the heresy of modernism.

While these documents primarily represent anti-liberal responses of the papacy to European political revolutions and to the emergence of both democratic and communist mass politics, avant-garde aesthetic movements were always considered an important aspect of the challenges posed by 'modernity'. At least since the mid-1800s Catholic doctrine had taught that art, including drama, must always recapitulate the social order: the omnipotence of God over humankind, the authority of priests over laymen and the dominance of parents over children.[52]

Throughout the stages of Irish nationalism the antimodernism of the Catholic Church remained an important factor in the definition of Irishness, as seen in this Dubliner's criticism of Synge: 'In any representation, therefore, of Irish life, the element of religion can not be omitted or neglected: for by it that whole life is colored. A complete and satisfactory representation must deal with this strong religious element from a sympathetic standpoint; otherwise the artist will be approaching the life of the Irish peasant from the outside, and will misinterpret half his actions and misjudge half his motives.'[53] Clearly, popular support existed in Ireland for the notion that the Catholic religion provided a key to the peasant mentality because of the Church's solidarity with peasants. This view was not wholly accurate, as the Church had recently opposed plans for land redistribution to benefit peasants in the west of Ireland, and had rejected cooperative dairy schemes that would seem to have benefited the poor. During the Land League agitations and agrarian violence of the 1880s, the Church had again sided with the landlords, not with peasant proprietors. In fact, since the Famine, the Church's devotional core in Ireland had been strongest among the prosperous tenant farmers, not among the peasantry.[54]

When Synge's play appeared, the Church was advocating a moderate political viewpoint favouring legislative tactics to create Home Rule for Ireland without disrupting middle-class property claims. Yet despite its recent record of allegiance to the interests of the middle class, the Church could also legitimately continue to claim to be the mouthpiece of the peasants, in so far as it remained a cultural symbol of organic, anti-English feeling that cut across class divisions and honoured the virtues of poverty and the simple rural life. When Synge's play was travelling to Boston, about 30 per cent of Ireland's farmers still lived on holdings of two or less acres, suggesting that a small-holding peasantry survived even after the massive emigration of the poorest during the nineteenth century. Boston's peasants, as we have found, were largely an emotional invention.

In Ireland as well as throughout the Christian world, the Catholic Church was historically accustomed to viewing itself as the voice of the oppressed, sanctioned by its control of supernatural power through the sacraments, and its social and political authority against non-Catholics. It was not used to being part of a group conversation with multiple sources of power in competition with its own, particularly the secular philosophies and subjectivist principles embodied by nineteenth-century Romanticism or by twentieth-century modernist drama. On the whole the Catholic Church had bred audiences that did not expect art to claim to be a unique invention of human subjectivity and agency. Rather, Catholics were supposed to view art as the expression of an eternal divinely ordained morality. As Paul Giles has observed, this aesthetic served as a foil to the Romantic temper and to Protestant individualism because Catholicism maintained a 'skeptical attitude toward the whole idea of lyrical or subjective intuition: the emphasis within traditional Catholic thought on a pre-existent, objective world has ensured a profound incompatibility between Catholic aesthetics and the romantic view that art might involve some new type of knowledge.'[55]

From an idealist position that art should elevate the soul by representing heroic characters and situations, Church spokesmen interpreted Synge's work as a rival to its belief that culture should be led by the Catholic Church and processed through its filters. Without priests, who filled the leadership role played by the bourgeoisie in other European nations, the Church implied that Ireland's social order, moral values and aesthetic unity would be lost. In this regard, Synge's image of Catholic beliefs in Ireland as just one more coating of superstitions encrusted on the consciousness of the people, was worrisome to the Church. So was his populist attack on the middle-class that recalled Yeats's élitist attack on middle-class philistinism. Yeats was dismissible by the Catholic Church because his Romantic anti-democratic outlook was unlikely to threaten Catholic communalist ideology. Synge, who came from a privileged Anglo-Irish background, adopted peasant credentials and even learned Gaelic, but his attack on the middle-class from below shared Yeats's aristocratic distaste for the vulgar bourgeoisie who were now the Catholic Church's mainstay in Ireland.

Religious assaults on Synge were defended by sources that transcended the localism of Irish politics and class conflicts. They mirrored the aesthetic judgements of the Catholic Church in the early twentieth century, which were a blend of anti-modernism and Thomist theology. The popularity of so-called neo-Scholasticism joined philosophic idealism and Aristotelianism to insist that all art was an expression of the divine. The neo-Thomists believed further that art's sole purpose was to serve truth, which was objective and eternal, by offering only beautiful objects for human contemplation. Catholic theology was hampered by its profound suspicion that the imagination was a mental faculty easily confused without the stern guidance of the rational intellect. Consequently, arguments against Synge's drama were identical to Church attacks on other dangerous modernisms: against the moral relativism of non-Thomist philosophy, the environmentalism of naturalist fiction and even against the sensationalism of popular culture represented by vaudeville, nickelodeons, dime novels and their transient urban consumers. In the following decades, the Church's reactionary standards would be extended to justify Catholic censorship of motion pictures as well.

As perhaps the only institution capable of organizing social solidarity of the Irish against an external oppressor, the Catholic Church performed comparative cross-class functions in Ireland and America. In Ireland, it crystallized anti-British feeling among peasants and prosperous farmers and merchants, while stopping short of endorsing revolution or anti-landlord violence. As we turn from Ireland to America, the Catholic Church continued to represent a key institution in the Irish community of Boston. In Boston the Church had overseen immigrant survival by providing basic social services since the 1850s, and in return had prospered from the overwhelming numbers of Irish men and women who joined its religious orders as well as from the laity who financed and built its parishes and schools. The Church coped with the uneven integration of its many ethnic communities in the United States by representing Catholic values as timeless, continuous, communal and superior to the materialist individualism of a Protestant, capitalist America. This polarization drew further energy from a rural versus urban paradigm familiar to Irish immigrants, as the Catholic Church added its voice to polemics against the evils of city living. Its idolization of rural virtues, in part an evasion of the growing presence of Catholics in American cities, helped structure the Irish-American response to exploitation at the hands of the entrenched Yankees, although it could not satisfy the 'land hunger' of a premigration Irish sensibility.

In Boston, the flavour of Roman Catholicism was Irish and conservative. The Church's antimoderism was exhibited in the Jansenist morality, clericalism and loyalty to Roman discipline that had stemmed from Ireland's nineteenth-century devotional revolution.[56] But the Church's relationship to the precapitalist and anti-acquisitive norms of Irish Catholics were becoming problematic in an American society driven by the mythology of the ambitious self-made man. The competition between individualism and communalism placed the Catholic middle class at a turning-point in the creation of an Irish-American ideology. The Church viewed its task as preventing the leakage of newly prospering Catholics into Protestant or secular allegiances.

While the Church was not necessarily the leading voice to protest about Synge in 1911, it was a significant contributor. Sometimes intersecting, sometimes diverging from those who branded the Irish Revival writers as false nationalists, the Catholic Church made particular objections to Synge that can be classified as a trinity of interrelated 'conspiracies': a pagan conspiracy, a social chaos conspiracy and an anti-Ireland conspiracy. All three suggest why the Church feared a secular cultural nationalism that sought to displace its authority over the Irish people, and why the Church wanted to maintain the alliance with the middle class that it had achieved in Ireland.

As briefly defined earlier, the pagan conspiracy view held that the Irish Revival was promoted by non-Catholics or even non-Christians, whose goal was to defame the Catholic Church and destroy the popular basis of its power. One of the Church's strongest weapons in crushing the 'pagan conspiracy' was its priests, who served as opinion-makers for the Irish community. For example, among the Irish-American publications that opposed Synge's play, the *National Hibernian* took its views not from American sources, but from the pages of the *Irish Ecclesiastical Record* of Dublin, which had accused the Irish playwrights of selling themselves to 'financial backers who only wish to disseminate the noxious doctrine inculcated in the plays.' The *Record* decried the new Irish drama as part of a 'pagan renaissance', 'encouraged by those who seek to destroy the religion and morality of Ireland and misrepresent its people.'[57] In America, Father Smith, here in solidarity with his fellow clergy, stated that Synge's 'inability to understand the Catholic spirit made him indifferent to the spiritual feelings of his characters.' Synge's irreligion and his implication that Catholicism was merely a thin veneer laid over an innately pagan Irish sensibility further alienated his Catholic critics.[58] Synge never professed to be Catholic, nor had he embraced the rigid evangelical Protestantism of his mother. Rather, Synge's abandonment of Christianity led him to a Bergsonian vitalism that was manifest in his use of exaggerated grammatical constructions and in his quest for unusual phrases and cadences. Vitality, or wildness intended to express the 'Gaelic spirit' thus appears as a virtue in all of Synge's plays and notably in the gallous stories of Christy Mahon, to the incomprehension of the Church.

Among the Irish laity, too, fear of a pagan conspiracy struck a chord. Yeats himself had recently become suspect among the Irish nationalists for even permitting the production of Synge's play. In Boston, Yeats's paganism drew a similar negative reaction from prominent laymen such as Denis McCarthy, an Irish-born poet, who stated, 'I don't understand many of the things that Yeats says, and there are many things in his school of playwrighting that I cannot stand for ... The pagan poses that most of these people assume in the plays gets on my nerves.'[59] This first portion of the pagan conspiracy argument thus challenged the religious credentials and mercenary motives of the Irish writers; another opposed the contents of their plays.

Both Smith and Synge saw themselves as protectors of 'the Gaelic spirit', but this was understood by the Church to mean a Catholic spirit. Hence the Church objected to elements in the new Irish drama that subverted Catholic doctrine. Primarily, the Church condemned Synge's characters for not displaying orthodox moral priorities and proper filial deference. In traditional Catholic teaching, seeking God's grace and showing respect for elders should precede any quest for self-fulfilment and self-assertion. Christy, therefore, was guilty of failing to observe the first and fifth commandments. If there is a triumph at the end of the play, it is the playboy's new vision of himself, which can only emerge through the slaying of his father and the poetic embroidery of the tale.[60] But it was precisely this triumph of the autonomous self that the Church found unacceptable.

Secondarily, the Church condemned Synge's use of 'obscene' words such as 'shifts', and his staging of certain violent acts, which offended the repressed sexuality of Irish Catholicism and its familial values. Catholic critics particularly disliked the episode in which the playboy bites his rival's leg, and the scene in which Pegeen tortures Christy for lying about killing his father, by tying him to a table and scorching his leg with a chunk of burning sod. This latter gesture, however, is the only on-stage violence; Christy's two attacks on Old Mahon with a spade are never represented. The violence, like the drift of Irish women arrayed in their shifts and the sex between Pegeen and Christy, must be imagined. By withholding the enactment of aggressive and libidinal desires from the characters and the audience, Synge cleverly exposed the ambivalent attitude of the Irish towards violence, who lauded the audacity of a son who would kill his da, but recoiled from the possibility of having to witness a real murder after the appearance of Old Mahon in his bloodied bandage. Similarly, by having the young lovers only imagine the exquisite beauty of their future passion, Synge comments on the way in which poetic talk replaces action.

By accenting the gap between Christy's extravagant language and the sordid premises for his heroism, and between Pegeen's adoration and its fulfilment, the contents of Synge's play drew a second parallel to the frustrated desires of his audience. Irish spectators were led to confront the contrast between the imaginary world on-stage and the helplessness of their colonized condition. Thus, Christy's gallous tale also exposes a glaring contrast between the flattering self-image of rural Ireland and its impoverished dependency. Synge achieves a dramatic doubling effect because the enchantment of Christy's story-telling operates upon the audience as well as upon the characters in the play. Both groups are led to wonder if mere fantasy can become reality. His dark picture of Irish life was not uncommon in contemporary Irish literature, but neither was it wholly welcome. While Synge himself may have imagined Christy striking a blow against inertia and economic dependency by seeking an identity apart from his domineering father, the gap between the romance of Irish independence and the reality of life under British domination may have proved too much for Irish audiences. They projected their anger on to Synge for daring to show a son's intention to kill his father rather than turning the mirror towards themselves. For its part, the Church could only condemn the gap between fantasy and reality as the source of dangerous anti-Christian and anti-authority sentiments that might topple its own receding power and reduce Ireland to barbaric paganism. Because churchmen refused to relinquish their place as the *vox populi*, they were unwilling to concede the humour and appeal of Synge's innovative use of folk idioms. Most literary critics concede that Synge's fanciful talk was excessive in the *Playboy*, but are far less harsh than Catholic opponents. One Catholic newspaper severely judged the play's colourful language 'rotten enough to taint entirely the entire programme of the Irish players and to condemn the whole movement that they represent.'[61]

The Catholic Church's suspicion of Synge's moral relativism and linguistic hyperbole related to its second conspiracy theory, one that accused Synge's play of fomenting social chaos by undermining the Church's paternal authority over the masses. In Synge's play, the themes of oedipal conflict and of fantasy clearly disturbed Catholic commentators. When Christy, claiming to have split 'his da with a blow of a loy', becomes a hero in a Mayo village and wins the heart of Pegeen Mike, Synge fully exploits the absurd possibilities of the situation. Clerical critics of Synge, seemingly immune to Christy's story-telling magic, demanded that art should uphold Biblical laws supporting familial and social hierarchies, which Synge had violated by invoking a non-Christian myth and by inverting the proper relationship of father and son.

But just as the play's exploration of Oedipal tensions was not considered on its own terms by the Church, neither was Synge's portrayal of the transformative and redemptive potential of story-telling that brought a murdering rogue to be sheltered and even rewarded by the love of an honest woman. Where Synge devised the play to produce a calculated social and sexual imbalance — there are no married couples in the cast, for example, only widows and singles — Catholic purists demanded a didactic parable. But no marriage occurs at the end of the play, and the audience is left wondering what to make of Pegeen's loss of the playboy and his departure with his miraculously revived father to tell stories of the fools in Mayo. Not only did Synge frustrate conventional theatre critics by rupturing the dramatic conventions of comedy, but he also violated Catholic aesthetic principles by denying the audience a conclusion that confirmed the values shared by many of them: filial deference, clerical respect, conjugal union and fecundity. From the Church's standpoint, Synge was a heretic because he refused to treat art as a precise mirror of divine truth and because he failed to name God as the ultimate source of all creativity and all morality.

Church officials exposed their own Oedipal fears in the sweeping assertion that the lack of filial respect shown by Christy Mahon, and the degrading representation of the Irish generally, devalued the Catholic clergy and would end in a denouncement of the Church itself. No doubt, Synge's jibes directed at Pegeen's abandoned suitor, Shawn Keogh, caricaturing him as a hapless priest-ridden peasant contributed to the general impression that priests and religion were for the weak-minded. In social environments like Dublin and Boston that were experiencing class conflict stemming from ethno-religious exploitation, the fears of religious and ethnic propagandists mutually reinforced each other, as indicated in the 1911 resolution against Synge by the United Irish-American Societies of New York to 'drive the vile thing from the stage, as we drove "McFadden's Row of Flats" and the abomination produced by the Russell Brothers.'[62] The Irish societies asked for the aid of 'every decent Irish man and woman, and of the Catholic Church, whose doctrines and devotional practices are held up to scorn and ridicule in Synge's monstrosity.'[63]

The Church's use of a 'social chaos conspiracy' theory, although couched in positive terms that defended Irishness, parental authority and female purity, was also motivated by the fear that the new Irish drama undermined two kinds of standards: respect for clerical leadership and habits of family solidarity. The principles of social harmony and familial order esteemed by the Church had been challenged by nineteenth-century artists and writers, as well as its political revolutionaries. An article published in an American Catholic devotional magazine at the time of the *Playboy*'s Boston showing summarized the Church's concern that drama preserve 'natural' social hierarchies:

> Among productions objectionable in spite of their goodness, the foremost place belongs to those which destroy reverence for authority or which present examples of pious untruthfulness and religious posing . . . For example, the stupid, foolish, ignorant, and unjustly tyrannical parent, priest or teacher is a bad character for a child to contemplate; so is the priest presented so familiarly that his sacerdotal qualities are obscured by the prominence of his purely human side.[64]

Even priests who appreciated Synge, such as Father Smith, agreed with the opinion above that overfamiliarity with priests breeds contempt for their Christ-like qualities. Ultimately, Smith described Synge's characters as 'out of proportion' because Synge 'seems never to have taken into account their own knowledge of their proper relations to the hierarchies of heaven and earth.'[65] Irish-American priests desired to maintain the high status of the clergy in Ireland, who in the absence of an aristocracy or a sizeable bourgeoisie had assumed leadership roles in the nationalist struggle.[66] It therefore seemed imperative in Boston, where the archbishop and nearly every priest was of Irish descent, that the Catholic Church present a united front of hierarchy, clergy and laity to the Protestant American public, as seen in this overplayed *Pilot* editorial of 1911: 'The loyalty of the Catholics of Boston has been proverbial. There is, and always has been a perfect understanding between the laity and the clergy, between the clergy and the hierarchy. There are no cases of dispute between the Most Reverend Archbishop and his priests; the harmony between both is excellent and indicative of the best order.'[67]

The Church's desire to portray Catholics as 'one big happy family' points to a second reason why educated priests and lay intellectuals wanted art to avoid and forestall social crisis. By articulating the values of sacerdotal authority and family unity, cultural productions would create a bond between the ecclesiastical and social orders, between the values of religious élites and those of the Irish-American middle class.[68] Synge's drama, however, threatened the symbiosis between priests and bourgeoisie. This alliance between Catholic morality and bourgeois culture was problematized in the character of Christy Mahon. Although Christy was technically a peasant and the son of a farmer, the peasantry rejected him for attempting to kill his father. The bourgeoisie had certain affinities to Christy because he trades upon his personal achievements to resolve conflict without the interference of the traditional authorities of king, landlord or Church. Christy's hard-won independence from ancient authority symbolized Synge's theory of an independent people and an autonomous drama, which together would reconstitute Irish nationalism without a Catholic or sectarian base. In America, moreover, Christy's situation may have corresponded to the emergent desires of the Irish middle class for autonomy from institutional repression. Yet in Boston, this middle class could not admit such nakedly self-serving aims because horizontal loyalties of cross-class ethnic and religious unity were required to defend the Irish Catholic community against Yankee Protestant power.

Religion was deeply embedded in the Church's first two conspiracy images, which suggest the Church's desire to maintain its status as protector of the individual and corporate bodies of Ireland, and depended upon its delicate balancing act as guide for the middle class and peasantry. A final religious critique of Synge may be characterized as an anti-Irish conspiracy, which presented Synge as mocking the virtue and patriotism of the entire Irish people. In this third strategy, the Church absorbed power from the national movement by overlapping with Irish Ireland's assaults on Synge. After all, anyone who exposed the hypocrisy of Irish attitudes about Catholic morality or female purity as he had done, also challenged the independence movement and its myth of 'holy Ireland'. Irish nationalists active in America and the Irish-American clergy used the same tactics as their Irish counterparts in describing Synge's anti-Irishness. They mobilized Catholicism and bourgeois nationalism to oppose threats to individuals (moral or sexual violations) and to condemn social forms of oppression (political and economic constraints).

The representation of womanhood in Synge's play became a site of Church resistance because, since the emergence of the novel and a realist tradition in literature, the body, and especially the female body, reflected the very project of modernist art to reveal 'external' reality as a whole.[69] In the case of Ireland, the Church 'increasingly came to identify Ireland as a virginal Motherland which could be best served by safeguarding our native purity of "faith and morals" against the evil influence of alien cultures.'[70] It was bad enough that Synge depicted an Irish peasant as a boastful tramp lionized for killing his father. It was worse that he portrayed a woman as a foolish romantic who scorned decent local boys in favour of a fugitive murderer. Thus, in addition to the controversy generated by Christy, the character of Margaret Flaherty, the publican's daughter, became suspect because her sex and virginity raised audience expectations that she would serve as the vehicle for nationalist propaganda. As Richard Kearney has stated succinctly, 'Woman became as sexually intangible as the ideal of national independence became politically intangible.'[71]

The connection between the desexualization of women and the idealization of the Irish independence cause was a motif familiar to European romantic nationalism and to Catholic spirituality. Instead of embodying an inviolate Ireland, however, Pegeen Mike falls under the spell of the playboy's gallous tales and spends a night with him unchaperoned in her father's house while the father attends a funeral.[72] Pegeen's irresponsibility provided yet another spark to ignite the crowds already aghast at Christy's attempted parricide. In the heated climate of the 1910s, Ireland had to be represented on stage as the virginal love object (or as the 'son-obsessed mother') while her sons must be portrayed as sanctified self-sacrificing knights. Synge's anti-heroic parodies of these mythical types naturally aggravated his Catholic opponents, who stood for Mother Church and Mother Ireland. Perhaps even more significantly, Synge had stolen the 'myths of renovation' that formerly were the property of Catholic Ireland, to serve the 'spiritual heroics' of the dying Ascendancy class engaged in fashioning its own colonial mythology.[73]

While the Ascendancy writers appropriated the cult of virginity and other Catholic symbols to cast blame upon Catholics for the sorry state of Ireland, the Church, like other opponents of the Irish Revival, attacked Synge with hysterical accounts of immorality (drunkenness, immoral love and patricide) in his plays that by extension degraded all Irish, peasant as well as bourgeoisie. In this way, the Church reinforced the view that all loyal Irish men and women (and the Catholic Church) must be united and respected as symbols of Ireland's inviolability. In the anti-Irish conspiracy, therefore, Irish Ireland's complaints coincided with the objections of Catholic critics that the Ireland pictured in the *Playboy* was 'not queenly and inspiring, but low, bestial, and repulsive, a people who naturally make a hero of patricide.'[74] Irish patriots wanted more evidence in Synge's play of the 'spirit of self-sacrifice' that they deemed the moving force behind the Irish character.[75]

Synge derided these reactions in a famous stinging letter to a friend that uncovered his contempt for the middle class:

> the scurrility, and ignorance and treachery of some of the attacks upon me have rather disgusted me with the middle class Irish Catholic. As you know I have the wildest admiration for the Irish Peasant, and for Irish men of known or unknown genius . . . but between the two there's an ungodly ruck of fat faced, sweaty headed swine. They are in Dublin and in Kingstown, and also in all the country towns.[76]

Synge's romance with the peasant and the genius offended the swinish bourgeoisie of Ireland. His play provoked its fears of losing ground, and its insecurities about its cultural pretensions. Irish-Americans likewise balked at Synge's anti-bourgeois attitude, but they masked their unease by attacking his deficient view of the peasant, because it remained at the core of their diaspora identity. Beneath the surface, however, it seems that Irish-Americans were similarly unnerved by Synge's attacks on the middle class because it implicated their own self-serving interests.

The Irish diaspora and the impeccable peasantry

Historians, folklorists and literary critics who have debated the demotic claims of the Irish Revival concede that it was mainly the product of Anglo-Irish, non-resident, non-Dublin and non-Catholic writers who wrote in English. Synge, Yeats and Gregory fit this description, as did Douglas Hyde, the driving force behind the movement to preserve Gaelic. Synge had been criticized by Irishmen for living abroad for five of his 32 years, although his efforts to 'impatriate' himself among the Aran Islanders showed that he at least recognized the chasm between himself and them, 'unlike his fellow Ascendancy men.'[77] Yeats and Lady Gregory had no intimate relationship with the peasant agrarian classes or with rural deprivation, despite Yeats's earthy motto for the Abbey Theatre that all productions 'must come from contact with the soil.'[78] Unlike Hyde and Synge, Yeats and Lady Gregory had only second-hand familiarity with peasant idioms, acquired by studying the speech of servants, or by listening to actors hired expressly for their regional accents. Although their Abbey troupe had evolved from its original self-definition as a poetic theatre to one supporting 'p.q.' (peasant quality), its plays were not authentically folkloric so much as influenced by Irish folklore. Even in America it was apparent that Yeats and Augusta Gregory looked not to the poor peasant, but to the established Protestant intelligentsia for patronage of their plays. Although in Boston Lady Gregory visited 'many old friends ... settled in their own homes', including some former tenants, she confided to her memoirs that she valued the approval of the Harvard faculty and students more than the acclaim of Irish–Americans.[79] Moreover, her public appearances accompanying the Abbey tour in Boston were held in such places as Fenway Court, the Isabella Gardner mansion, and at the WASP-led Twentieth Century Club, not in the Irish wards, at Knights of Columbus dinners or in the Catholic literary unions.[80] The Brahmins' warm reception of the Anglo-Irish literati probably irritated the Irish middle class, who saw these occasions as further evidence of an Anglo-Protestant alliance against Catholics based on a class superiority defined by religious difference. The negative reaction to the *Playboy* from the religious and ethnic associations of Boston suggests, further, that nationalist hopes remained alive in America before 1916 among the native-born Irish and among recent immigrants. While advocacy of parricidal violence against England remained a minority view, the ethnic prejudices of the Boston Irish against their own local Protestant rivals threatened to drown out defences of Synge's artistic freedom. This is precisely what had happened in Dublin.

Because the Catholic Irish and the Protestant Anglo-Irish were equally determined to valorize the peasant, Synge's portrayal of peasant life in *Playboy of the Western World* was scrutinized across the span of Irish religious and nationalist factions. Hugh Kenner brushes aside claims that the Irish objected to the play's themes of the seduction of Irish womanhood and of parricide, and concludes that the real cause of antagonism was Synge's failure to provide the 'impeccable peasantry' essential to nationalist propaganda.[81] In Kenner's view, Synge ironically brought hostility on himself by not airing his indisputable patriotism widely enough. George Watson's dissection of the *Playboy* episode argues differently that because Synge was Anglo-Irish and therefore a Protestant, religious affiliation was uppermost in the minds of Synge's Irish opponents.[82] Kenner and Watson are both correct in so far as Irish Ireland and Catholicism made common cause in Ireland and America against the attempt of Anglo-Protestants to revive their economic domination of Ireland in the form of cultural capital. But both critics ignore the crucial role of the Irish and Irish-American middle class in the Synge affair. Seamus Deane suggests, contra Kenner, that the Irish bourgeoisie posed a threat to the aristocratic élitism of the Ascendancy writers because the nationalist middle class, as the backbone of the Catholic Church and its ideal of a monolithic Catholic Ireland, proved to be a significant barrier to Protestant renovation of Gaelic Ireland.

Despite the powerful art produced by the linguistic and cultural strands of nationalism born in the 1890s that highlighted Ireland's Celtic heritage, cultural nationalism ultimately succumbed to a Catholic definition of Irish identity, both in Ireland and in Boston. The Catholic Church was willing to make allies among the linguistic nationalists, endorsing the aims of Douglas Hyde's Gaelic League because of its moderate politics and because Gaelic nationalism shared a cluster of Catholic values, even though Hyde was somewhat cerebral for the average Irish Catholic.[83] Clerical leaders and Gaelic advocates also shared a common marginality: celibacy, like Gaelic, was respected but not in wide demand. By 1900, Gaelic too was confined to a minority of the population.[84]

In Ireland the philo-Celtic societies and the Ascendancy poets and playwrights proved to be unequal to the power of the Catholic Church, and cultural nationalism failed in its attempt to reconstitute Irish nationalism without a religious base. This is somewhat remarkable given that the Catholic laity or intelligentsia produced no body of writers for Catholic Ireland to rival Yeats and Synge. The Catholic Church itself played the role of helping the middle class 'broaden its ideological appeal' to those not yet converted to nationalism.[85] While the evolution of Irish nationalism from its linguistic and cultural phases to political and revolutionary strategies has been extensively described elsewhere, and although few would deny the importance of the Catholic Church as a monitor of taste and of moral judgement in Irish culture, the Synge episode is an important reminder of how 'Irish Ireland began as a Gaelic alternative to Catholic nationalism, but ended up as its captive.'[86]

Ironically, Synge's reputation became more palatable to Catholics because of the Easter Rising of 1916. Formerly, Catholic priests represent-ing rural communalism had vilified Synge as a symbol of the corruption of the cities, joining those secular critics in the countryside who likewise questioned Synge's loyalty to the Irish people. One such negative voice, revolutionary Padraic Pearse, revised his initial harsh interpretation of *Playboy of the Western World* as early as 1913. Pearse, as a result of contact with James Larkin and James Connolly, began to associate the Irish martyrs of the insurrection with the sacrifical death and resurrection of Christ, enabling nationalists to reclaim Christy's unsuccessful murder of his father as a kind of prophecy of the Rising against Great Britain.[87] Moreover, the Rising itself shared more qualities with theatre and religion than with pol-itics. As Sheridan Gilley has noted, it came to symbolize a kind of holy folly, 'a theatrical gesture, an act of imagination, rather than a serious military affair.'[88] Pearse, Yeats, Douglas Hyde, Larkin, Connolly and others in the odd alliance formed in 1916 between Protestants, Catholics, Celtophiles and socialists, converted the metaphor of patriotic blood sacri-fice for Ireland's independence into a unifying discourse to overcome the religious divisions among the nationalists.[89] The recuperation of Synge's reputation after 1916 supports the observation that 'each rebel generation, the danger that they presented having dissipated itself, was absorbed into what was by his [Yeats's] day a century-old tradition of nationalism. It was a nationalism thick-textured and thick-skilled . . . and it was overwhelm-ingly Catholic, both as a political movement and as a fabric of sentiments, aspirations, and familial alliances.'[90] As the image of the Rising of 1916 passed from a dirty deed into heroic grandeur, so Synge's non-Catholic outlook could be absorbed into a new nationalist sensibility indebted to Catholic devotionalism, sacrificial imagery and other religious symbology. As described by Sheridan Gilley, 'the fires of 1916 burnt out the foreign matter in Catholic nationalism.'[91] Thus after 1916 even the Church, never an advocate of revolutionary violence, was able to extend its retrospective blessing to the mythologized Rising, and to embrace diverse cultural ele-ments that included even its former rivals.

There are obvious parallels between the moribund condition of the Ascendancy in Ireland, and the waning Brahmin in Boston. The latter WASP élites were losing their control of New England after nearly three centuries of hegemony. In response to their diminishing power, Brahmins made cultural supremacy the proving ground to establish their own pre-eminence in good taste and cultural production against the Irish Catholic philistines, the only significant rival to their political unity. In Boston the Irish Catholic community was torn between its nostalgia for the Old Sod, a (largely imaginary) place of carefree youths and self-sufficient families on their own farms, and the pragmatic recognition that survival in urban America took them far from their rural homesteading fantasies. A long heritage of Yankee nativism in Boston had fed Irish Catholic images of themselves as victims of a Protestant conspiracy and as exiles in a strange land. However, this poor-mouthing from the diaspora Irish grew less plausible in so far as it was no longer a powerless outsider in 1911. By then,

Irish employees and elected officials virtually controlled Boston's City Hall, the Massachusetts lower court system, public school teaching, school administration, the police and the civil service. It became commonplace to summarize Irish male career opportunities as the three Ps: priest, politician, police. Residual anti-democratic tendencies of the Irish, namely their ethnic nepotism, ward bosses and political machines, had also left their mark on Boston life, as indelibly as the Irish nuns, sisters, priests and brothers who directed and staffed the city's hospitals, convents, orphan asylums and parish schools.

Still, despite evidence of these contradictory assimilative and separatist strategies among themselves, and proof of their political success against the Yankees, the New England Irish perpetuated the myth of their own impotence. Father Smith contextualized this exile mentality by tracing it to the continuing Irish experience of Anglo-Protestant oppression. In Massachusetts as in Ireland, he wrote, Protestantism had advanced the Anglo population, while 'the Catholic faith for centuries held the Irish people to a bare living of potatoes and buttermilk, because Protestant England would have it so.'[92] Even after Irish families had put down roots in the United States for three generations and had benefited from the freedom of religious practice guaranteed by church-state separation, the diaspora Irish could interpret their socio-economic inequality as the direct result of religious oppression. In Boston, because of the incomplete integration of Irish-Americans and the city's history of exaggerated ethno-religious tensions, this claim contained more than a kernel of truth. The result was that the Boston Irish remained uneasy about the divisive effects of economic success enjoyed by only a few of them, but sentimental about the village or farm life of their real or imagined ancestors. Synge's stage peasants, therefore, revealed Irish-American ambivalence towards the future as much as its misty romanticization of the past.

The decade following Synge's *Playboy of the Western World* found many Boston Irish identifying themselves intensely with ruralist anti-British feeling in Ireland and immersed in debates over the choice between Home Rule or complete independence from England. Irish-Americans gave money and moral support to Ireland, and the majority supported the moderate strategy of John Redmond's Home Rule Parliamentary Party through the United Irish League that functioned as its political machine. In 1914 however, Redmond's unpopular decision to support England in World War I allowed militant independence advocates such as the Friends of Irish Freedom to supplant the UIL. Irish-Americans kept informed of political developments in Ireland after 1916 through networks of personal contacts, fraternal and benevolent societies, religious organizations and the Irish county associations. The bourgeoisie of Ireland, meanwhile, courted and needed support from the emigrated Irish to support its nationalist counter-hegemonic strategy against the British.[93] It was therefore good policy for Irish nationalists to generate unrest over Synge's play in America in order to rally Boston's Irish to the defence of Ireland.

Working sometimes against these secular agencies, sometimes in close accord, the Catholic Church, symbolizing Irish identity in Ireland, jockeyed to remain the moral centre for American Catholics as well, led by a clerical élite allied with the emergent middle class. In Boston, Catholicism was able to gain the upper hand in forging an Irish identity centred upon the Catholic Church as old links between the Gaelic tongue, Celtic myths and Hibernian identity began to dissolve. By around 1909, Gaelic columns in the Catholic press began to disappear. Hints of the growing interchange-ability of peoplehood and religion surfaced in the comments of the laity defending the Church against the Abbey Theatre: 'Nothing but hell-inspired ingenuity and a satanic hatred of the Irish people and their religion could suggest, construct, and influence the production of such plays,' wrote one Boston physician.[94] As the Catholic Church built up a symbiotic relation with the new Irish-American middle class, in return it expected the laity to defend Catholic moral principles, particularly when Church leaders declared that a playwright had committed heresy by attacking the authority of priests, the modesty of women and the sanctity of marriage. While a few lay Catholics announced their support for Synge, the Church condemned their opinions as regrettable mistakes.

Moreover, the Catholic Church's integration of its authority over competing forms of nationalism gave evidence of the power of the Church's appeal to the image of an innocent past, evidence in its opposition to modernist drama. Irish Catholic objections to Synge were consistent with the Church's global campaign against modernism (in both its highbrow and lowbrow forms) at the opening of the twentieth century. The Church feared Synge's liberation of the artist from the past and his attempt to use art to explore the recognition that 'Nature is cruel to living things.' In contrast to Synge's credo, the Catholic Church became one of the loudest voices raised against the pessimism, irrationalism and subjectivism of literary modernism and against the new permissiveness of popular entertainments.[95]

Neither the Irish nor many of their American descendants properly appreciated the innovations of the drama born in the Abbey Theatre of Dublin. In Boston, the Irish Catholic community may have been divided in its opinion of Synge, but it united in its determination to defend itself against Yankee Protestant domination. Ironically, the Church's communal-demotic ideology was employed to help Irish-Americans survive in a socio-economic system driven by competitive individualism. Irish Catholics were subject to the Catholic Church's role as an intermediary between classes, and although the Church may have hurt the poor and working classes by obscuring class differences, the Church was successful in mobilizing the middle class by relying upon the moral and nearly sacred appeal of the peasant image. To rationalize the success achieved by some of the faithful, without sanctioning violence from the have nots, the Church mystified social inequality by preaching 'the twin gospels of respectability and resignation.'[96] In Boston the Church therefore occupied the conflicting position of espousing Irish ruralism and Catholic nationalism, at the same time as it tentatively promoted American acculturation. It suggested resignation towards the *status quo* for the poor and competitive shrewdness (coupled with generosity towards the Church) for the upwardly mobile. Despite its warnings about the evils of Yankee materialism, the clergy supported an ethos of sobriety and hard work for Catholics that served as useful sectarian contrasts to Protestant acquisitiveness, but which also fostered the emergence of an Irish Catholic middle class that would finance the Church. For the Irish poor, the Church delivered material assistance to neighbourhoods and families in the form of charities, schools, hospitals and asylums.

Within twenty years of the anti-Synge protests in Boston, disapproval of the *Playboy* had dissipated in the United States for reasons related in part to the upward mobility of Irish-Americans. As early as 1913, the Abbey troupe returned to Boston. Plagued by shaky finances, the Irish players looked upon their American and English tours as money-makers, yet this did not prove to be the case. There were no riots in 1913, but neither were there full houses. Changes in popular taste had made the sentimental tradition of Dion Boucicault unfashionable, and the buffoonish stage Irishman had died with vaudeville. In this context, Synge's dramatic innovations no longer seemed shocking.[97] After the establishment of the Irish Free State in 1921, safeguarding the state image of the Irishman became even less necessary in Ireland and America. When Synge's play returned to America in the late 1930s, therefore, its warm reception on New England stages reflected not only growing acceptance of modern drama, but also the sharp decline in Irish immigration after 1930, and the increased Americanization of Irish Catholics.

In the *Playboy* protests, Irish-Americans and the Catholic Church tried to police the boundaries of their heritage by opposing a play and its author who threatened the traditional components of an ethnic identity shared by people and priests. Because of their uneven social and economic integration, Irish-Americans were led to define themselves against the hegemonic claims of a regional Anglo-Protestant culture, even though they had begun to share many of its economic assumptions. Their construction of Irishness appealed largely to an 'imagined community', a peasant Utopia that had little reality in America. The sense of being excluded from mainstream America and being unfit for citizenship was expressed by Irish-Americans as ambivalence towards its urban, acquisitive values. It led the diaspora Irish to valorize peasant lifestyles and to profess a communal identity centred upon Catholicism. The Church was able to offer a still-compelling vision of itself as defender of the Irish community against the combined forces of Brahmin snobs and Yankee capitalists. Likewise in Ireland, the Church was able to overcome competing secular nationalisms and even to absorb them into its vision. None the less, in the case of *Playboy of the Western World*, it may have been Synge's disgust with the self-righteousness and social hypocrisy of the Irish middle class more than his alleged slights upon the Irish peasantry that secretly made his play unacceptable to Irish-American viewers. By exposing the self-serving fictions of his bourgeois audiences and critics, was Synge 'staging a lie', as critics claimed, or revealing an inadmissible 'naked truth' about the middle classes of Ireland and Irish America?

Notes

1. John Wilson Foster, *Colonial Consequences: Essays in Irish Literature and Culture*, Lilliput Press, Dublin, 1991, p. 54.
2. The word 'gallous' describes something wild, mischievous or fit for the gallows. Gallous stories are a durable theme in Irish legend and song that, in retrospect, reveal the ambivalence of the Irish towards individual and mob violence. In the west of Ireland especially, rebels were admired because they struck back against the law, which had been the tool of the hated landlords.
3. See C. L. Innes, 'Naked truth, fine clothes and fine phrases in Synge's Playboy of the Western World', in Joseph Ronsely (ed.), *Myth and Reality in Irish Literature*, Wilfrid Laurier Press, Waterloo, Ont., 1977, pp. 63–75.
4. Donna Gerstenberger, *John Millington Synge* (rev. edn.), G. K. Hall, Boston, 1990, p. 83.
5. Ann Saddlemeyer, 'Introduction' to *J. M. Synge, Plays II*, Oxford University Press, London, 1968, p. xxi.
6. Christopher Fitz-Simon, *The Irish Theatre*, Thames & Hudson, London, 1983, p. 156; Lady Augusta Gregory, *New York Times*, 3, 5, 28 November 1911. Gregory discussed public reaction to the play in her history of the Abbey players, *Our Irish Theatre*, Putnam, New York, 1913. The riots are also detailed in James Kilroy, *The 'Playboy' Riots*, Dolmen Press, Dublin, 1971; Robin Skelton, *J. M. Synge and His World*, Thames & Hudson, London, pp. 110–16. Scattered references appear in Hugh Hunt, *The Abbey: Ireland's National Theatre 1904–1979*, Columbia University, New York, 1979. Excerpts from many contemporary Irish sources are collected in E. H. Mikhail (ed.), *The Abbey Theatre: Interviews and Recollections*, Barnes & Noble, Totowa, NJ, 1988.
7. Revisionist historians and critics have refused to see the failure of Anglo-Irish attempts to secure a Catholic following in Ireland as a tragedy, and have been especially harsh in their criticisms of Yeats, whose mystical, élitist and authoritarian views nurtured his later fascism. Yeats's dawning support for a society run by educated despots and his growing contempt for the Catholic masses spawned censorship and mob politics, rehearsed in the riots against Synge, rather than the transformed Irish community he envisioned would be forged from nationalist art and theatre.
8. In contrast to Yeats's aestheticist polarization of the Synge conflict (and his possibly fatal influence on Irish nationalism), the readings of the play's meaning and context throughout the past eight decades encompass a wide range of viewpoints. The *Playboy* has been described as a tragedy, a comedy, a fantasy, a parable of the making of a poet and a study of the power of language itself. A helpful summary of the range of critical reception and of the unsatisfactory quality of much of it appears in Heidi Holder, 'Between fiction and reality: Synge's "Playboy" and its audience', *Journal of Modern Literature*, 14 (Spring 1988), pp. 527–42. Representative criticism from the 1980s has reflected the contributions of psychoanalytic and post-structuralist theory, generating readings of the play as an expression of anthropological liminality, as an example of Bahktin's 'carnivalesque', as Synge's personal defence of virtuosic imagination against the constraints of the socialist realism endorsed by Maud Gonne, as a

prophetic vision of the failed parricide of the Easter Rising and even as a harbinger of post-modern indeterminacy. These five positions appear, respectively, in Peter Costello, *The Heart Grown Brutal: the Irish Revolution in Literature, from Parnell to the Death of Yeats, 1891–1939*, Rowman & Littlefield, Totowa, NJ, 1978, p. 32; George Bretherton, 'A carnival Christy and a Playboy for all ages', *Twentieth Century Literature*, 37 (Fall, 1991), pp. 322–34; Randolph Parker, 'Gaming in the gap: language and liminality in "Playboy of the Western World" ', *Theatre Journal* (March 1985), pp. 65–85; Ruth Fleischmann offers one attempt to understand the historical context for the play in 'Fathers vanquished and victorious — a historical reading of Synge's Playboy', in Michael Allen and Angela Wilcox (eds), *Critical Approaches to Anglo-Irish Literature*, Barnes & Noble, Totowa, NJ, 1988, pp. 63–74; Stephen Tifft, 'The parricidal phantasm: Irish nationalism and the Playboy riots', in Andrew Parker *et al.* (eds), *Nationalisms and Sexualities*, Routledge, New York, pp. 313–32. Tifft's chapter is an excellent nuanced discussion of the Synge riots in terms of Freud's theory of Oedipal conflict.

9. George J. Watson, *Irish Identity and the Literary Revival*, Croom Helm, London, 1979, p. 64.
10. Seamus Deane, 'National character and national audience: races, crowds and readers', in Michael Allen and Angela Wilcox (eds), *Critical Approaches to Anglo-Irish Literature*, Barnes & Noble, Totowa, NJ, 1988, p. 48.
11. As noted by Terry Eagleton, *Criticism and Ideology: a Study in Marxist Literary Theory*, Verso, London, New York, 1990/1978, p. 152.
12. *New York Times*, 1:5, 28 November 1911; 2:5, 29 November 1911. American reactions to Synge are mentioned in Elizabeth Herlihy (ed.), *Fifty Years of Boston, 1880–1930*, Tercentenary Committee, Boston, 1932, p. 734, and in Peter Kavanaugh, *The Story of the Abbey Theatre*, Devin-Adair, New York, 1950, pp. 93–5.
13. Kavanaugh, *Abbey Theatre*, p. 95; Hunt, *The Abbey*, p. 94.
14. Gregory, *Our Irish Theatre*, p. 225.
15. Daniel J. Murphy, 'The reception of Synge's "Playboy" in Ireland and America: 1907–1912', *Bulletin of the New York Public Library*, 64 (October 1960), p. 533; Hunt, *The Abbey*, pp. 95–6.
16. Murphy, 'Reception,' p. 529.
17. 'The Irish literary revival', *Boston Globe*, 25 September 1911.
18. William Leahy, born in Boston in 1867, was a schoolteacher at Milton Academy, editor of the Boston *Traveler*, and author of several books (*American Catholic Who's Who 1934–1935*, p. 242). Stephen O'Meara, born on Prince Edward Island in 1854, migrated to Boston and climbed up through the ranks of journalism until he owned the *Boston Journal*. Shortly after selling the paper in 1902, he was appointed Police Commissioner by Republican Governors of Massachusetts from 1906 until his death in 1918.
19. *Boston Evening Globe*, 17 October 1911.
20. *Boston Globe*, 24 October 1911.
21. Philip Hale, 'Double bill at the Plymouth: scattered hissing at "Playboy of the Western World" resented by the audience' *Herald*, 17 October 1911. Hale reportedly disliked his journalism job, and frequently gave scathing reviews of mediocre performances: *Dictionary of National Biography*, Vol. 8, Scribner's, New York, 1937, p. 110.
22. Kavanaugh, *Story of the Abbey*, p. 94.
23. Rose Fitzgerald quoted in Doris Goodwin, *The Fitzgeralds and the Kennedys*, St

Martin's, New York, 1987, p. 241. Rose became the mother of future President John Fitzgerald Kennedy.

24. Gardner's remark is reported in the Boston *Post*, 17 October 1911.
25. P. J. O'Neil Larkin, *Boston Globe*, 17 October 1911.
26. D. Murphy, 'Reception', p. 527.
27. On the tactics of the Brahmins, see Geoffrey Blodgett, 'Yankee leadership in a divided city: Boston, 1860–1910', in Ronald P. Formisano and Constance K. Burns (eds), *Boston 1700–1980: the Evolution of Urban Politics*, Greenwood Press, Westport, Conn., 1984, p. 89.
28. Lawrence W. Levine, *Highbrow/Lowbrow: the Emergence of Cultural Hierarchy in America*, Harvard University Press, Cambridge, Mass., 1988, p. 200.
29. Levine, *Highbrow/Lowbrow*, p. 198.
30. Deane, 'National character', p. 50.
31. Kerby A. Miller, *Emigrants and Exiles: Ireland and the Irish Exodus to America*, Oxford University Press, New York, 1985, p. 555.
32. *Boston Globe*, 18 October 1911.
33. *Boston Globe*, 23 October 1911.
34. Shaw, quoted in Kavanaugh, *Story of the Abbey*, p. 96. Shaw, incidentally, scarcely knew *his* mother, and was raised by a pub-going nanny.
35. Maurice Bourgeois, *John Millington Synge and the Irish Theatre*, Constable, London, 1913.
36. Quoted in Hunt, *The Abbey*, p. 93. A few days later Gallagher was one of those asked to leave the theatre during the Synge première in Boston.
37. Not all exiled Irishmen saw the matter in the same way. George Bernard Shaw ridiculed the heated American response to Synge's play and to the Abbey troupe by denying the very existence of an Irish-American: 'There are not half a dozen real Irishmen in America outside that company of actors! . . . You don't suppose that all these Murphys and Doolans and Donovans and Farrells and Caseys and O'Connells who call themselves by romantic names like the Clanna-Gael and the like are Irishmen!' (Shaw, quoted in Gregory, *Our Irish Theatre*, p. 299).
38. William Shannon, *The American Irish: a Political and Social Portrait*, Macmillan, New York, 1963, p. 264.
39. In *Knocknagow*, peasant virtues remained intact despite the vicious depredations of the landlords. Fleischmann, 'Fathers vanquished', p. 66.
40. *Boston Herald*, 10 September 1911.
41. *Christian Science Monitor*, 16 October 1911. The religion of Christian Science was founded in Massachusetts in 1878 by Mary Baker Eddy, who began the newspaper in part to overcome press bias against her church.
42. *Boston Globe*, 17 October 1911.
43. M. J. Cunniff, *Boston Globe*, 24 October 1911.
44. The *Post*'s list of those expelled from the theatre included John O'Hara, a candidate for the state senate; Dr J. H. Gallagher, whose letter started criticism of the play; Dr O'Brien of Charlestown; James Kelley of Roxbury; and P. A. Murray of Waltham, (17 October 1911).
45. *Sacred Heart Review*, 14 October 1911.
46. *Sacred Heart Review*, 7 October 1911.
47. Smith, 'The new Irish drama', *Columbiad*, (10 March 1916). Dion Boucicault (1820–90) was a prolific Irish playwright whose dramas included *The Colleen Bawn* (1860), which had over 3000 performances, and *The Lily of Killarney*, a three-act 'grand romantic opera' (1867). With 124 plays to his credit, Boucicault

freely adapted others' plays and copyrighted them as his own, and is generally considered to have upgraded the image of the stage Irishman, despite the falsified, stereotyped image of Ireland he propagated. He toured the United States in 1853. See Carl Wittke, 'Immigrant theme on the American stage', *Mississippi Valley Historical Review*, 39 (September 1952), p. 217; Maureen Murphy, 'Irish-American theatre', in Maxine Seller (ed.), *Ethnic Theatre in the United States*, Greenwood Press, Westport, Conn., 1983, pp. 224–6; and Heinz Kosok, 'The image of Ireland in nineteenth-century drama', in Jacqueline Genet and Richard Allen Cave (eds), *Perspectives of Irish Drama and Theatre*, Barnes & Noble, Savage, Md., 1991, pp. 50–67.

48. Gregory, *Our Irish Theatre*, p. 317. An excerpt of O'Reilly's review appears in M. Murphy, 'Irish–American theatre', p. 229.
49. *Boston Globe*, 17 October 1911.
50. *Boston Sunday Post*, 8 October 1911.
51. John McCoy Slattery, *The Purple*, Worcester, Mass. (November 1911), pp. 129–30.
52. This summation is derived from Vicenzo Gioberti's 'Essay on the beautiful' of 1864, a major source of Catholic aesthetic commentary. Catholic aesthetics also reflects its much older roots in Platonic idealism.
53. Charles Bewley, 'The Irish national theatre', excerpted in the *Sacred Heart Review*, 1 March 1913, from the *Dublin Review*, January 1913. By contrast, modern critics generally admire Synge for his ability to create an illusion of fidelity to peasant life, according to Maurice Harmon, 'Cobwebs before the wind: aspects of the peasantry in Irish literature from 1800 to 1916', in Daniel J. Casey and Robert E. Rhodes (eds), *Views of the Irish Peasantry 1800–1916*, Archon Books, Hamden, Conn., 1977, p. 157.
54. Emmett Larkin, 'Church state, and nation in modern Ireland', *American Historical Review*, 80 (1975), pp. 1253–4.
55. Paul Giles, *American Catholic Arts and Fictions: Culture, Ideology, Aesthetics*, Cambridge University Press, New York, 1992, p. 51.
56. On the moulding of religious practices in mid-nineteenth-century Ireland that rendered Irish and Catholic identities virtually synonymous, see Emmett Larkin, 'The devotional revolution in Ireland', *American Historical Review*, 77 (1972), pp. 625–52.
57. 'The vicious Irish players', *National Hibernian* (Washington, DC), 15 January 1912.
58. Watson, *Irish Identity*, p. 46.
59. *Boston Sunday Post*, 8 October 1911.
60. See Ann Saddlemeyer, J. M. *Synge and Modern Comedy*, Dolmen Press, Dublin, 1968.
61. *Sacred Heart Review*, 14 October 1911.
62. The Russell brothers based their comedy routines upon impersonating Irish servant girls. Some Irish critics were unnerved by the ambiguity at the heart of gender switching, where identity is not what it seems, and chastised the actors for not representing reality as it is.
63. The 1911 resolution was passed two days before the *Playboy* opened in Boston. M. Murphy, 'Irish-American theatre', p. 229.
64. *Ave Maria* (Notre Dame, Ind.), 11 November 1911, pp. 612–13.
65. Smith, 'The new Irish drama', p. 10.
66. R. V. Comerford, 'Nation, nationalism, and the Irish language', in Thomas Hachey and Lawrence McCaffrey (eds), *Perspectives on Irish Nationalism*,

144   *Paula M. Kane*

University of Kentucky Press, Lexington, Ky., 1989, pp. 36–7.
67. *Pilot*, 20 May 1911.
68. See Kerby Miller, 'Class, culture, and immigrant group identity in the United States: the case of Irish-American ethnicity', in Virginia Yans-McLaughlin (ed.), *Immigration Reconsidered: History, Sociology, and Politcs*, Oxford University Press, New York, 1990, p. 99.
69. Recent feminist readings of Synge's *Playboy* have focused not upon Christy and his father, but upon Pegeen, the village girls and Widow Quin. Once seen as merely reinforcing the youthful romanticism and poetical character embodied by Christy, or as accenting the theme of generational conflict between the elders and the playboy, Synge's female characters are read as victims of a patriarchal society whose repressive dimensions were unfortunately recapitulated by literary nationalists and bourgeois Catholics. Despite their avowed project of using Ireland's literary heritage for radical political ends, nationalists sanitized the sexuality of the powerful women in the ancient Gaelic legends for the consumption of Irish Ireland. Patriarchy and Victorian prudery thereby undercut the authenticity of the nationalist recovery of the Gaelic past. See Elin Ap Hywel, 'Elise and the great queens of Ireland: "Femininity" as constructed by Sinn Fein and the Abbey Theatre, 1901–1907', in Toni O'Brien Johnson and David Cairns (eds), *Gender in Irish Writing*, Open University Press/Milton Keynes, Philadelphia, 1991, pp. 23–39. On the construction of Irish womanhood by the Gaelic League see Elin Ap Hywel, ' "Naughty, Vulgar, Low": Irishwomen and the home language 1899–1901', in Joseph McMinn (ed.) *The Internationalism of Irish Literature and Drama*, Barnes & Noble, Savage, Md., 1992, pp. 279–83.
70. Richard Kearney, 'Myth and motherland', in Field Day Theatre Company, *Ireland's Field Day*, University of Notre Dame, Notre Dame, 1986, p. 76.
71. Kearney, 'Myth and motherland,' p. 76.
72. However, Sara Allgood, one of the Abbey cast in the Dublin première, suggested that Dubliners were more outraged that Pegeen did not immediately deliver Christy to the authorities than by her nocturnal impropriety.
73. Seamus Deane, 'Heroic styles: the tradition of an idea', in Field Day Theatre Company, *Ireland's Field Day*, University of Notre Dame, Notre Dame, 1986, pp. 47–8.
74. Slattery, *The Purple*, 24 (November 1911), p. 129.
75. See for example, A. J. Philpott, *Boston Globe*, 17 October 1911.
76. Skelton, *J. M. Synge and His World*, p. 117. A slightly variant version of the letter appears in Costello, *Heart Grown Brutal*, p. 33.
77. This was the opinion of Catholic Daniel Corkery, in *Synge and Anglo-Irish Literature*, Mercier Press, Cork, 1931/1966, p. 56. Corkery was well aware of the impact of colonization on the Irish, having served for 20 years as an elementary schoolteacher in Cork under the British system. He became a leading (but not necessarily representative) Catholic novelist and Gaelic enthusiast in the decades after Irish independence.
78. It was Yeats who had encouraged Synge to leave Paris for the Aran Islands off the west coast of Ireland where he could live among the people he wrote about. There Synge caught the colourful expressions, eavesdropped on servants' conversations and heard the folktale which formed the kernel of *Playboy of the Western World*. The story had been recorded at least 20 years before Synge's first visit to Aran according to Richard Bauman, 'John Millington Synge and Irish folklore', *Southern Folklore Quarterly*, 27 (1963), pp. 267, 273. By his own account,

Synge also added elements to the tale from west Kerry and elsewhere.

79. Gregory, *Our Irish Theatre*, p. 175.
80. From reports in the Boston *Herald*, 20 October 1911, and *Sunday Post*, 8 October 1911.
81. Hugh Kenner, *A Colder Eye: the Modern Irish Writers*, Knopf, New York, 1983, p. 24.
82. Watson, *Irish Identity*, p. 24.
83. For this assessment of the Gaelic League, see Tom Garvin, *The Evolution of Irish Nationalist Politics*, Gill and Macmillan, Dublin, 1981, p. 104. For an interpretation of the Irish Revival as a series of unfortunate deflections see Frank Kinahan, 'Douglas Hyde and the king of the chimps: some notes on the de-Anglicization of Ireland', in T. J. Edelstein (ed.), *Imagining an Irish Past: the Celtic Revival 1840–1940*, University of Chicago, David and Alfred Smart Museum of Art, Chicago, 1992, pp. 65–79.
84. K. Theodore Hoppen reports that only one in seven persons spoke Irish in 1901, whereas only one in two hundred did not speak English, see *Ireland Since 1800: Conflict and Conformity*, Longman, London, 1989, p. 131.
85. Miller, 'Irish-American ethnicity', pp. 102–5.
86. Lawrence McCaffrey, 'Components of Irish nationalism', in *Perspectives on Irish Nationalism*, p. 15.
87. Fleischmann, 'Fathers vanquished', pp. 73–4.
88. Sheridan Gilley, 'Pearse's sacrifice: Christ and Cuchulain crucified and risen in the Easter Rising, 1916', in Jim Obelkevich, Lyndal Roper and Raphael Samuel, *Disciplines of Faith*, Routledge & Kegan Paul, London, 1987, p. 490.
89. Gilley, 'Pearse's sacrifice', pp. 479, 481. Feminist critiques of nationalism suggest alternatively that Irish womanhood represented a healthy contrast to the 'death-cult' of male-led nationalism.
90. Thomas Flanagan, 'Nationalism: the literary tradition', in Hachey and McCaffrey, *Perspectives on Irish Nationalism*, pp. 61–78, esp. 73.
91. Gilley, 'Pearse's sacrifice', p. 481.
92. Smith, 'The Irish drama', *Columbiad*, 10 May 1916.
93. Miller, 'Irish-American ethnicity', p. 103.
94. Hunt, *The Abbey*, pp. 94–5.
95. As detailed for American Catholics in general in William Halsey, *Survival of American Innocence: Catholicism and Postwar Dissillusionment, 1920–1940*, University of Notre Dame, Notre Dame, 1980. For the case of Boston in particular, see Paula Kane, *Separatism and Subculture: Boston Catholicism, 1900–1920*, University of North Carolina Press, Chapel Hill, 1994, Chapter 7.
96. I share this assessment of class formation by Kerby Miller, 'Irish-American ethnicity', especially the summary on pp. 114–15.
97. Ida G. Everson, 'Lennox Robinson and Synge's Playboy', *New England Quarterly*, 44 (1971), p. 6.

6 A long journey: the Irish in Scotland

Bernard Aspinwall

The great trek to Scotland is a national problem and a national evil of the first importance. There has been much desultory and some serious writing on the subject. No book which pretends to deal with the running sores from which Scotland suffers, can be absolved from giving some independent view of the matter.[1]

Traditional views

Scottish concern at Irish migration peaked in the interwar years. The Report to the General Assembly of the Church of Scotland on the Irish Problem, 1923, viciously assailed the Catholic Irish.[2] Even in 1968, a writer lamented 'an unusually homogeneous country should be split into two nations': the Irish and Catholicism proved scapegoats for those disturbed by change and 'modernity'.[3] The Irish have been central if neglected in Scottish life. Fewer than in England during the nineteenth century, they were a larger proportion of the total Scottish population throughout the nineteenth century (see Table 6.1).[4] Much of the historical writing on their fortunes, coloured by religious, ethnic or political assumptions, is somewhat simplistic: they are unimaginatively seen as passive, poor, philistine and permanently the same solid group coming in along the same well-worn routes to Scotland. Their contribution is at best grudgingly recognized. As alleged outsiders to the perceived Scottish experience, the Irish have only recently been recognized by historians: the formidable exception, James E. Handley, remains indispensable after almost fifty years.[5] But ironically, the migrants, according to his interpretation, had succeeded through self-help, the classic host value, and solidarity: the cleric celebrates the cohesion, loyalty and achievements of the Irish Catholic community as it was changing beyond recognition. The mentality which evolved was shaped by their efforts at urban adjustment in the nineteenth century.

Table 6.1 Irish-born residents of Scotland and England and Wales as a percentage of the total population (1871–1911)

	England and Wales	Scotland
1871	2.49	6.18
1881	2.17	5.86
1891	1.58	4.84
1901	1.31	4.59
1911	1.04	3.67
1921	0.96	3.26

Note: these figures are taken from David Fitzpatrick, 'A curious middle place ...,' p. 11

The community framework

The Irish community in Scotland had an essentially religious framework. That expressed their 'religious' culture; their voluntary educational, religious and mutual aid; their limited, if growing enfranchisement before 1918; their failed revolutions, failed agitations and failed parliamentary efforts; their weak economic base blocked by social and structural discrimination. For the Church, a permanent, abiding presence, mobilized folk memories, offered solace and security here and in the hereafter to mobile migrants, frequent casualties in a fluctuating economy. Weak within the larger hostile community, their satisfactions were found within themselves and within their group: the priest, the teacher, publican and pawnbroker, their 'independent' men, served their own cohesive community. It had three formative stages: a 'democratic' phase, 1815–46; the Famine and adjustment, 1848–67; and a social evolutionary phase from about 1868 which coincided with pervasive Ultramontanism. Foundation, formation and consolidation.

Each coincided with new waves of arrivals and with significant Catholic religious developments. A religious framework meant few revolutionaries. With moderate social and nationalist views, the Irish enjoyed modest upward mobility and group satisfaction. Like migrants elsewhere they discovered a stronger sense of identity than at home. Irish and Scottish clergy curbed wilder nationalism, preserved loyalty to national and religious identity and introduced their large fluid flock into a larger, growing yet unformed, urban industrial community.

Like England, the Catholic community in Scotland developed in new areas, but even more remote from old Scottish recusant areas. Irish, Highlander and new convert had few roots in the urban industrial order. More united than in England, Catholicism, traditionally centred in the rural North-East, the Highlands and Islands, had to begin afresh as the faithful gravitated to industrial cities and towns.[6] That community of hardship, adjustment and survival slowly became a diversified group, with considerable remigration and mobility: constant migration within the Atlantic world strengthened group identity. Class, politics and economic condition varied. Protestant Irish, though fewer, followed a similar path. Religious loyalties therefore provided the stable focal point of Irish community. Religious voluntarism formed the basic 'democratic' communal structure, sustaining group loyalty of Catholic and Protestant alike.

Reason and religion set the agenda for Irish acceptance, respectability and improvement.[7] Employers and evangelical clergy in the early nineteenth century demanded a disciplined, sober and industrious citizenry. The Irish were to be modernized like the Highlanders and Islanders of Scotland. Folk culture, such as the wakes and celebrations, was to be rationalized and normalized. Reason would eliminate slavery of ignorance, war, popery and drink in a reconstructed culture. To a degree that applied equally to Irish Orangemen, who at times were too vulgar for many Scottish tastes. Transformed by the Scottish élite, migrants would become ideal citizens in an ideal state. Setting ethical norms through social pressures, the élite determined the 'thinkable', acceptable, tasteful. Through law, medicine, art and education, private Irish persuasions were to be transformed. Community, neighbourhood and family, as defined by an essentially Protestant élite, would take precedence over class or ethnicity.

Identity

In the process these champions of individualism and democracy would bring greater state intrusion into private life. Pressured migrants threw themselves back upon their own resources, their old loyalties and identities. Migrants, Catholic, Protestant and indifferent, accommodated themselves to the new life while continuing to hold fast to their peculiar and revitalized traditions.

Their nationalism was clear as Scotland fumbled for a role: a few industrialized counties in an overwhelmingly agrarian country presented considerable difficulties to the tribe. Scottish nationalism remained invisible, inarticulate and inchoate. Scottish migrants, joining English and Irish in new industrial towns, felt the passing of the old order, the demise of older skills and the migration of many to America and elsewhere. Displaced, distressed or disoriented, with their 'improved' lot, they were part of a slowly opening society still attempting to define itself. They found a fractured Scottish culture, as highlighted in the Disruption (1843): Scottish science even questioned the base of creation. In this climate, Scotland like America, significantly, nourished millenarian visions: Edward Irving, Robert Owen, Fanny Wright, 'Shepherd' Smith, the first Mormon missionaries in Britain, Scottish Chartists and later militant socialists, among others, found receptive audiences. In cultural shock, others adopted more traditional, even reactionary nostrums.[8] Competing cultures abounded.

The Irish were the precursors of modernity. They threatened the alleged monoculture of Scotland. Their mainly Catholic culture, ethnicity and class aroused transatlantic nativism. The Irish, respectable or otherwise, represented the challenge of repressed sex, alcohol and gambling. But, as Tom Gallagher has suggested, in the earlier period Irish migrants met greater hostility in the smaller communities and only later enmity in the cities of Glasgow and Edinburgh. But that was not confined to the Irish. It was true of other groups, such as Quakers and Mormons at an earlier and at later stages.[9] But these were the declining, fading forces, uncertain and unwilling to adjust to modernity, to a multicultural society.

Perceptions

The Irish were allegedly peripheral to the Scottish experience. In fact they were *essential* to the nineteenth-century 'Scottish' experience. Antipathy intensified in the wake of the Famine migrants, increased with Home Rule, and the post-war decline from 1919 as some 300,000 people left the country between 1919 and 1926. The Church and Nation Committee of the Church of Scotland annually assailed the Irish through the 1920s. Professor Andrew Dewar Gibb, Professor of Scots Law, Glasgow University, vehemently argued even in 1930 that clerically inspired Irish fecundity was an unwelcome burden upon Scotland as 'the presence of a like number of Hottentots converted to Roman Catholicism. The finest manure makes no impression on concrete.'[10] Working-class Glaswegians were equally comparable to African bushmen: anyone falling asleep in the Bridgegate had as much chance of surviving until dawn as beneath a tree in the Congo. The Glasgow Medical Officer of Health would have agreed with the Webbs' comments on Ireland in 1892: 'The populace are charming but we detest them as should the Hottentots — for their very natures. Home Rule is an absolute necessity *in order to depopulate the country of this detestable race.*'[11] The notions of John and Robert Knox, the theologian and the anatomist, were pervasive: religion, bigotry, eugenics and racial superiority abounded. Even puritan socialists dealt in stereotypes:

> They live in a very Protestant community and remain devoted and sometimes aggressive Roman Catholics who are below the standard of their Scottish neighbours but have a quick wit and a marked fondness for public affairs.[12]

Historians have differed over the Irish impact upon Scotland: they are stereotyped either as a radical injection or as brakes upon progress.[13] L. C. Wright saw the Irish as devoid of radicalism while the clerical James E. Handley worried about earlier lay radicalism.[14] The Irish and their Catholic descendants are invariably portrayed in recent left-wing writings (comparable to that of 1920s eugenicists, not a few of them Scots) as the unthinking conservative cannon fodder of the Labour Party. Some Scottish, unlike American, historians of migration have yet to appreciate the migrants in their own terms, in depth and subtlety. Recent writings such as William Donaldson's *Popular Literature in Victorian Scotland: Language, Fiction and the Press* (Aberdeen University Press, Aberdeen, 1986), have opened up an appreciation of vibrant subcultures. The Scottish Catholic culture and historiography in turn has moved on from the diverting antics of Bruce Marshall's *Fr Malachy's Miracle* (1931) and *All Glorious Within* (1944). More confident, less defensive, less sectarian historians and the *Innes Review* have contributed. The result is an increasingly more balanced view of the complex social experience of migrants in Scottish development.[15]

Recent developments

Equally, more conciliatory ecumenical gestures, the virtual end of Irish migration as the Scottish economy declined, the end of recruitment of Irish Catholic clergy, the recent abandonment of an overt sectarian Protestant policy at Rangers football club, were further relevant developments. By 1951, the migrant Irish community was under 50,000 and comprised but a tiny proportion of the total Scottish population, or about one-seventh of the Irish community in England and Wales. The end of the British Empire in which Glasgow starred as the Second City, the parallel loss of the Scottish role in the English-speaking transatlantic world and the greater emphasis on Europe, turned attention inwards to the roots of Scottish identity. As with American migration, the focus shifted to the skills and values of migrants. Overall Scottish indifference to, if not revulsion at, Ulster savagery and sectarianism since 1969, has helped to push Scotland in a more constructive direction. The Irish dimension might be incorporated into the larger Scottish and European entity. The Thatcher years, marked by the emasculation of Scottish industry, encouraged the rethinking of Scottishness: predictable but also surprising groups produced Scottish solutions to insensitive Westminster rule, from devolution, home rule, federalism, independence, to independence in Europe. A new Scottish identity was forming: the Irish and their descendants were now counted in.

The Scottish nativist challenge

The Irish Catholic migrant was not always welcomed. Native tradition and Ulster Protestant Irish notions coalesced. Religion, poverty, job competition exacerbated Scottish feelings. From Catholic emancipation, to the declaration of Papal Infallibility, to Irish Home Rule, many issues intensified latent hostility. Orange Lodges first appeared in Scotland in 1808 and soon spread through Ayrshire with strong Scottish membership which was largely Ulster Irish in the west of Scotland.[16] The first 12th of July procession was in Glasgow in 1821. Others soon followed. Disturbances invariably followed in their wake. The worst occurred in Airdrie in 1835 when a Catholic chapel, school and houses were destroyed.[17] But native Scots, outraged by such excesses, worked effectively to contain it. Only increasing Irish Protestant migration, enfranchisement and Tory political need gave the Order a significance far beyond its limited membership from the late nineteenth century. The Protestant Association (1835) tried to halt popery. Its popular lecturers, including former Maynooth priest, William Crotty, the first assigned to Scotland, toured the country. In 1837, the Protestant Operatives Association emerged to play a militant role in the Conservative interest, an alliance which persisted throughout the century and beyond.[18]

After 1848, anti-Catholic feeling intensified. The repression of the 1848 revolutions, increased job competition in the wake of the massive Famine migration and the illiberal regimes in Catholic states reinforced social and religious prejudices. Virulent anti-Catholics, like Revd. John Begg and Revd. Alexander Duff, who both preached in America, capitalized on the sentiment. In 1851 only the St Vincent de Paul Society in Glasgow prevented violent Catholic reaction to Orange provocations.[19] Faced with J. S. 'Angel Gabriel' Orr and his violent Orange shipwright supporters, Revd. James Danaher of Greenock misguidedly lectured on debauched Reformation characters in 1852: a week of disturbances ensued. Other anti-Catholic and anti-Irish characters appeared in Scotland. The ex-priest, Alessandro Gavazzi, the Italian nationalist, made two tours in the 1850s; the tours of Louis Kossuth and numerous minor characters added to the tensions. Not a few proved to be scandalous impostors, posing as renegade nuns or priests. Equally one immoral Catholic cleric was exposed and fled to America. Local preachers aided by papers like the *Scottish Protestant* (1851–2) or later the *Bulwark* reinforced existing cultural bias against the Catholic Irish.[20]

Even so in 1868 the Orange Order only mustered around 600 members in Scotland. But as Irish issues dominated British politics so Orange strength developed. In the wake of the International Orange meeting in Glasgow in 1873, some 3000 new members joined. That year some 18 lodges were established in the Partick area, dominated by shipworkers. Soon after, the area had a three-day riot. Three years later a crowd of 100,000 was to attend the 12th of July walk in Glasgow. Another outrage followed at St Mary's in 1879, as migration grew in the economic depression (Table 6.2).[21] Increased Ulster migration and the rise of Irish Home Rule was to exacerbate further Orange and Green relations.

Even so, Daniel O'Connell was rapturously received by Scottish Liberals on his visit in 1835: following his success in Edinburgh, 200,000 allegedly welcomed him on Glasgow Green.[22] Irish political activism was considerable in the 1840s. Glasgow supporters of Repeal allegedly gave as much as £100 on occasions as well as running a political reading room. Revd. Hugh Quigley, a Repealer, was removed to Campbeltown and eventually left for America, where he wrote several Irish novels; he built many churches in his tempestuous career. In the 1848 'bread riots' in Chartist Glasgow, 64 arrests were made: the majority were employed; some 36 were Irish, 26 of whom claimed to be Roman Catholics. More violent Glasgow men were associated that year with Thomas D'Arcy McGee's abortive attempt to aid the anticipated Irish rising: one fled to America. The Fenian campaign in Britain in 1867 attracted little support in Scotland — although claiming some 3000 members there — except for the later amnesty campaign: local

Table 6.2 Irish-born residents of Scotland (1861–1951)

Census	1861	1871	1881	1891	1901	1911	1921	1931	1951
Total	204,083	207,770	218,745	194,807	205,064	174,715	159,020	124,296	89,007
Northern District	152	162	174	118	164				
North-West	455	470	499	405	481				
North-East	1713	1443	1420	1245	1203				
East Midland	20,734	19,302	16,292	12,465	9,604				
West Midland	13,069	12,389	14,955	15,409	15,883				
South-West	137,694	148,519	159,599	143,605	157,166				
South-East	19,698	19,986	20,772	18,232	18,092				
Southern	10,568	5499	5034	3328	2471				
Intercensal percentage increase or decline									
	+1.81	+5.28	−10.94	+5.27	−14.80	−8.98	−21.84	−28.39	

Source: Census of Scotland, 1861, 1871, 1881, 1891, 1901, 1911 and 1961 vol 5 p. xviii table.

Protestant feelings, church antipathy and, as in Pittsburgh, the conservative character of Irish migrants contributed.[23]

However, the unfortunate Catholic Ulsterman Michael Barrett arrested in Glasgow over the Clerkenwell bomb affair, was tried and found guilty on doubtful evidence. His final articulate speech from the dock was a remarkable performance, suggesting he shared a high degree of intelligence and self-education with his Glasgow confrères. He was the last man to be publicly executed in England. The editor of the *Glasgow Free Press*, Peter McCorry, organizer of meetings for the Manchester Martyrs, sustained Barrett's alibi: that he had been in Glasgow at the time of the explosion. His paper, denounced in all Scottish Catholic churches in February 1868, did not help: the *Glasgow Herald*, however, gave far more measured comment on the case than the virulent London *Times*. To the end McCorry vainly bombarded the Home Secretary with telegrams about new evidence. After his new *Glasgow Irish Banner* (1868) collapsed, he went to New York to edit the *Irish People* (1868–) and later the *Catholic Herald*. Like the later misguided bombing campaign of 1883, such endeavours found little support among the migrant community.[24]

Accommodation

Clergy and laity worked together if their interests coincided but in politics independent lay views invariably prevailed. Their visions parted particularly in the later nineteenth century as more educated, independent and enfranchised individuals asserted themselves. In general they were united against external threat. At the Revd. Michael Condon's soirées in Greenock, St Patrick's Day, 1873, were played Scottish and Welsh songs before any Irish melodies. He delighted in Scotland and its history, combining progressivism, Home Rule and social amelioration within his parish.[25] The regeneration of a broken community through a sense of tradition, roots and self-confidence was in train. In the same way, the Scottish crofters' leader, John Murdoch, with the help of Irish nationalists, tried to reinvigorate the Scottish Highlanders with Irish–American support.[26] Security and service were practicable but the realization of the Irish dream proved elusive. But it was vital: as Moleskin Joe, a character of Patrick Macgill said, 'there's a good time acoming if we do but live to see it.'[27] In this climate such ideals were marketed to receptive audiences.

The transatlantic dimension

Scotland loomed large in the transatlantic world, with her economic, intellectual and migrant links to North America.[28] Irish experience in Scotland had a peculiar flavour from the context within which it was formed. It differed somewhat from most parts of Britain in encountering less communal violence, if greater antipathy. In a transatlantic Protestant world that antipathy to Catholic Irish was exported to Canada and the United States, New Zealand and Australia. Preachers, migrants and visitors shuttled back and forth, reinforcing stereotypes in books and periodicals. The sense of being part of a larger Scottish and Irish world coloured thinking however transient its members might be in Scotland. Textile workers, bricklayers and miners shifted back and forth across the Atlantic. Patrick McGowan, the Irish Catholic leader of the Glasgow Short Time movement, had many friends in the textiles centres of America and many who had returned.[29] Many Irish clergy in Scotland crossed back and forth to America.[30] The Irish were a voluntary group on pilgrimage in a transatlantic vale of tears.

Catholic Irish community growth

Irish weavers moved into Scotland from the late eighteenth century. Many Irish students trained in Scottish universities. Irish and Scottish radicals in the 1790s and later greatly concerned the government of the day. Conservatives used sectarianism to divide and contain such radical challenges in the 1830s and later. The Glasgow Hibernian Society was founded in 1792: with Scots who had resided in Ireland for a year admitted, it flourished until at least 1824.[31] Many were in Paisley by 1808. Sir John Joseph Dillon, an Irish barrister, defended both textile workers' and Catholic rights in Scotland.[32] On the British Catholic Committee, he worked independently for Catholic emancipation. With leading Church of Scotland ministers, he attended both the Glasgow Presbytery (1812–13) and the General Assembly (1813): 'It is impossible for me to do justice to their personal kindness to myself, and if I had favourable ideas of their body and of Scotch liberality before, they have been confirmed by what I have witnessed.'[33] There he orchestrated and won a sympathetic Presbyterian opinion on Catholic claims in the unsuccessful parliamentary petition for relief.

The Irish-born population greatly increased from 1800 but especially after 1830. Population pressures at home and better wages and opportunities in Scotland encouraged migration. As early as 1831, about a hundred Irish were found in every parish in Wigtonshire.[34] *The Statistical Account* had found groups of migrants in many districts, often living mobile lives apart from the locals. Irish harvesters gradually became permanent residents in Scotland. By 1838 they were the majority in some small Ayrshire towns like Crosshill and St Quivox.[35] Others came as handloom weavers or to new mills like those in Blantyre and Pollokshaws. In 1820 about two-fifths of the weavers were Irish and an estimated one-quarter Catholic. Although not necessarily Irish, 8245 Catholics were recorded in Glasgow as very heavily concentrated in the poorer working class areas. In 1833, the Paisley priest told the Factory Commission he had some 1000 Irish parishioners. With canal and railway development labouring jobs were abundant: in Dumfriesshire alone, 2000 migrants worked on the Caledonian Railway in 1847. In the wake of the Famine the estimated 30,000 Catholics in Scotland in 1800 mushroomed. As early as 1837, they numbered some 50,000 within the Glasgow-Lanark area; 332,000 by the restoration of the Scottish hierarchy in 1878; 433,000 in 1901; 750,000 in 1951 and around 830,000 today (Tables 6.3, 6.4).[36] Comprising 6.7 per cent of the total Scottish population as against around 3 per cent in England in 1861, they were a far higher proportion of Scotland than their co-religionists in England. But it was a predominantly young, mobile, frequently changing, often returning population. Ethnicity and religion were their communal certainties.[37]

They met a strong pre-existing traditional Presbyterian Protestant culture in the main counties of settlement. Within those areas, small-town mentalities suspected anything alien. Nativism was a transatlantic phenomenon. In 1779, a riot in Edinburgh destroyed native Catholic property. The minister of Saltcoats in 1797 worried at 'the constant influx of unknown persons from distant parishes, less under the restraints either of religion or character than the native inhabitants.'[38] An American Quaker, Thomas Wilkinson, was attacked following a visit to Kilmaurs, Ayrshire.[39] Other meetings had large peaceful crowds. Mormon missionaries might also meet violence. Not surprisingly then Irish Catholic migrants were unwelcome. The Famine migration only exacerbated feelings. Often the migrants were merely transients, in seasonal farmwork or later on railway and other construction sites. Sometimes they were in transit to North America.

Around 80,000 seasonal workers a year worked in Britain in the 1840s but only about half that came some forty years later. By that time about 3–4000 from Ulster annually headed for Scotland but numbers halved over the next generation. Increasingly harvesters were either men who were in the process of becoming permanent industrial workers or Irish migrant wives supplementing family income. But young migrant workers continued in agricultural work through the twentieth century. Theirs was a life of movement and change.

Table 6.3 Highest proportion of Irish-born in Scotland by county (percentage)

	1871	1881	1991	1931
Lanarkshire	14.5	12.2	6.93	3.85
Renfrew	14.7	13.4	6.86	4.62
Dumbarton	11.9	11.02	7.2	5.03
Linlithgow	8.0	7.6	4.89	-
Ayrshire	7.8	6.4	3.13	1.45

Source Census 1871, 1881, 1891, 1931.

Table 6.4 Population of Glasgow (including Irish-born) according to birthplace (1831–1911)

	Population–Irish-born Glasgow			Glasgow		Rest of Scotland		England & Wales		Foreign & Coloial	
1831	202,426	35,544	(17.5%)	-		-		-		-	
1841	274,324	44,345	(16.2%)	143,874	(52.4%)	78,185	(28.5%)	6,472	(2.4%)	1,448	(-)
1851	329,097	59,081	(18.22%)	145,022	(44.1%)	184,075	(34.7%)	8,283	(2.5%)	1,846	(0.6%)
1861	395,503	62,084	(15.7%)	201,555	(50.2%)	118,822	(30%)	10,540	(2.7%)	2,502	(0.6%)
1871	477,156	68,330	(14.3%)	226,115	(47.4%)	164,733	(34.5%)	14,364	(3.1%)	3,344	(0.7%)
1881	511,415	67,109	(13.1%)	262,146	(51.3%)	161,452	(31.6%)	16,026	(3.1%)	4,482	(0.8%)
1891	658,198	66,071	(10%)	349,597	(53.1%)	211,477	(32.1%)	24,092	(3.7%)	6,950	(1.1%)
1901	761,709	67,712	(8.9%)	468,542	(61.5%)	184,391	(24.2%)	28,104	(3.7%)	13,060	(1.7%)
1911	784,496	52,828	(6.7%)	482,455	(61.5%)	205,402	(26.2%)	29,724	(3.8%)	14,051	(1.6%)

Conditions

Migrants were frequently found in the poorest and most squalid areas of Scottish cities. But in 1844 in Edinburgh allegedly they were less likely than Scots to be among the lowest classes. That altered with the Famine: Scottish authorities shipped back some 47,000 paupers between 1845–54.[41] They highlighted poverty and Scottish shortcomings amid social and economic change. As the chief police superintendent in Glasgow said of the area around the Catholic cathedral:

> there is concentrated everything that is wretched, dissolute, loathsome and pestilentious. These places are filled by a population of many thousands of miserable creatures. The homes in which they live are unfit even for sties and every apartment is filled with a promiscuous crowd of men, women and children, all in the most revolting state of filth and squalor.[42]

That cathedral parish had almost 18,000 souls while an adjoining parish, St Mary's, comprised 13,400. Not all Irish were poor even in those areas. But in Greenock, reputedly the dirtiest town in Scotland, the Irish were the poorest. Even in the country districts, like 'Dublin' near Kirkfieldbank, Lanark, they were found in the worst houses.[43]

Not surprisingly the end of a project, resulting in a local recession, found the Irish destitute. Lack of three-year residence, bureaucracy and bigotry often meant little or no relief or denial even of a priest in hospitals and relief institutions. As pointed out above, sometimes the migrants were sent back to Ireland. The Irish were not the only poor. Nor were all Irish poor. But they were more likely as a group to suffer from the uncertainties of economic development. In 1830, less than half of those receiving relief in Glasgow were Irish. Seven years later, the Irish only accounted for a third of the total. In 1843 only Dundee and Paisley had more than 100 Irish on their rolls.

Even so not all Irish paupers were Roman Catholic. A witness before the Select Committee on the Poor Law (Scotland), maintained that only half were Roman Catholic.[44] In Glasgow, the City Poor Board in 1870 dealt with some 3159 cases: 1080 were Irish-born; 1187 were Catholics but only 774 were Irish-born Catholics.[45] That proportion declined through the century.

Mobility

The diversity, geographic and social, of migrant experience can be seen in poor relief records. Many Irish had travelled extensively before arriving in Scotland. An analysis of those seeking relief from the Govan Parochial Board highlights some important points. In November–December 1879 for example, the Govan Board dealt with around 55 Irish-born Catholics and 23 Irish-born Protestants.[46] Some had arrived in the country late in life: William Coyle, 67, from Donegal had only arrived in his sixtieth year two years after the death of his wife: his sons were in Brooklyn and Philadelphia. The disabled Patrick Durnan, 30, a Protestant, arrived in 1876. John Miller, a Protestant labourer, had only arrived two months earlier. Others like William Freebairn, a Protestant labourer, spent much time on both sides of the Irish Sea or like James Bryce wandered for work through Britain for eight years. Joseph McKie, 40, a Catholic weaver, migrated seven years before. Some had served in the British army: John Clements, 60, a Dublin Catholic, was 23 years in the 71st regiment; James McLachlan, 42, a Catholic Mayo labourer, spent 12 years in the army before settling in Glasgow in the 1870s; James Scanlan, a Protestant, had served almost 11 years in the 41st regiment; Patrick Larkin, a 60-year-old Catholic ex-soldier, was the son of an Irish soldier. Some had English or Scottish wives. John B. Donnelly, 60, Scottish-born son of Irish parents, had returned in 1873 after spending 20 years in America. His wife had died in New Jersey in 1858. His American-born children thrived in Massachusetts and New Orleans.[47] Some women had been deserted by America-bound Irish-born men, up to 12 years before (see Table 6.5).[48]

Table 6.5a Percentage of Irish-born applicants for relief in Glasgow (1850s to 1890s)

	1850s	1860s	1870s	1880s	1890s
District 1	39	42	40	35	32
District 2	31	33	34	32	32
District 3	38	37	31	27	20
District 4	34	34	34	29	29
District 5	36	40	38	31	31
District 6	28	30	28	38	33
All Districts	36	36	31	31	30

Table 6.5b Total number of relief applicants in Glasgow 1870 by district with Irish-born totals and percentages

District	Total applicants	Irish-born numbers	Irish-born percentage
1	740	300	41
2	471	175	37
3	436	136	31
4	634	203	32
5	398	141	35
6	420	122	28
All Districts	3099	1077	35
All Catholics	1187	-	38
Irish-born Catholics	774	-	24 or 65 of all Irish-born

Note: I am grateful to Dr Andrew Jackson, Strathclyde Regional Archives for these figures.

A similar view emerges from the Glasgow Barony Parochial Board records in 1881. John McBride of Antrim, 46, served almost 20 years in the army before returning to settle in Glasgow. John Irvine, 43, an Antrim labourer, had worked in Belfast, spent ten years in the Royal Artillery, 12 in Quebec, before he came to Glasgow with his three American-born children. Thomas McGovern, 73, a Cavan labourer, had arrived in his fortieth year and after the birth of his fourth child.[49] Equally, any healthy recent Irish arrival in Scotland whatever age and from whatever direction, though sleeping rough in barns, fields or model lodgings, was denied any support: application did not automatically mean aid. Such figures must be used with caution.

Not all Irish paupers in Scotland then were Catholic: neither were all paupers Irish. They comprised on average 10 per cent of the total Scottish paupers.[50] Some were criminals. The most notorious were William Burke and William Hare, who murdered and sold their victims' bodies for anatomical dissection in 1828. Burke was to hang for his crimes in 1829. But in some cases perhaps ethnicity increased the prospect of a guilty verdict.[51]

Settlement and employment patterns

The majority of the migrants worked on canals, docks, mines and in railway construction. A few provided services as shopkeepers, pawnbrokers
and publicans. Irish employees in the Blantyre mills led to a new village
development. Truck payments, bad housing and ethnic rivalry produced
clashes. Other outbreaks occurred on rail construction sites. In 1841, almost
2000 troops were on hand for the execution of two Irishmen for the murder
of a brutal English ganger before some 50,000 spectators: the Irish in
Glasgow, advised by their priests, remained quietly at home.[52] But already
in 1841, the 126,321 migrants formed almost 5 per cent of the total Scottish
population. The community was at its largest in the 1880s and 1890s and
thereafter declined increasingly.[53] They settled overwhelmingly in the
urban and industrial west central belt of Scotland or in the small towns of
Ayrshire and Wigton in the south-west. Greenock's Irish population
peaked in the late 1880s. Lanarkshire, including Glasgow, housed almost
half the Irish-born in Scotland. The largest and most generous Home Rule
organization in Britain was found in Coatbridge amid better-off, securely
employed migrants.[54]

Close to Ireland, geographically, and politically, they supported whatever party showed sympathy with Ireland. Few were found in distant
Aberdeen or the far north: fewer opportunities, a more abundant local
labour supply from the Highlands and few early arrivals failed to attract
later additions. By 1881 the Irish-born population of the burghs of
Dumbarton (18.6 per cent) and Partick (18.29 per cent) paled into insignif-
icance beside Port Glasgow (30.09 per cent). About four-fifths of the 94,000
migrants to Scotland between 1890 and 1910 came from Ulster. By 1911
migrants in Scotland were 30,000 fewer or almost 15 per cent less: in
Glasgow they were down by almost 15,000 or 21 per cent over the decade
(see Table 6.6).[55]

Shuttling back and forth from Ulster and the west, migrants developed
a sense of community; through their churches, their associational activities,
Orange or Green, absorbing the factory disciplines and evangelical values
which provided means of rising above or adjusting to the new social order.
Supply and demand met: neither Catholic nor Protestant, clergy nor laity
were involved in manipulation.[56] Each felt fulfilled with like-minded
brethren. Larkhall, Lanarkshire, for example at an early stage was an
'Orange' centre. Small towns like Airdrie, Coatbridge and Motherwell
attracted considerable Protestant migrants in the later nineteenth century.
Robert Smillie, Keir Hardie's trade unionist friend, migrated from Belfast
to the Lanarkshire coalfields. By the same token, throughout the century
the admittedly small proportion of Scots-born in Ireland consistently
increased. By the turn of the century, County Antrim had 2.4 per cent and
Londonderry 1.2 per cent Scots-born populations, reinforcing the impression of periodic commuting.[57] Between 1841 and 1901, the Scots-born
population had consistently risen from 0.11 to 0.68 per cent.

Table 6.6 Catholic churches opened in the west of Scotland pre-1829 and by decade to 1990

Decade	Glasgow City	Suburbs	Motherwell	Paisley	Total
pre-1829	1	1	0	2	4
1831–40	0	1	1	0	2
1841–50	7	1	3	3	14
1851–60	5	1	7	3	16
1861–70	3	2	3	2	10
1871–80	3	1	11	3	18
1881–90	2	2	2	0	6
1891–1900	5	1	7	3	16
1901–10	5	2	2	0	9
1911–20	0	0	1	0	1
1921–30	3	1	1	1	6
1931–40	3	0	2	1	6
1941–50	10	6	11	7	34
1951–60	18	5	14	5	42
1961–70	13	4	6	5	28
1971–80	2	8	7	2	19
1981–90	0	0	2	1	3

Source: Scottish Catholic Directories. The figures list new permanent churches. They do not show the considerable extensions to existing churches. Nor do they indicate the full extent of churches, chapels mission stations or temporary Mass centres. In the Glasgow archdiocese their numbers grew from 78 in 1880 to 101 in 1890 and to 149 in 1930.

Clergy, parish and school formed the basic communal structure, attracting and sustaining group loyalty. That was true for both Catholic and Protestant communities, although the latter were more readily accepted. They gave continuity, identity, news, social and political networks. Many journals quickly faded but with the *Free Press* (1851–68) and later, after the *Exile* (1884–5), the *Glasgow Observer* (1885–), a more settled course followed.[58] In 1894, Charles Diamond from Derry acquired the paper. He was briefly an Irish MP and later unsuccessful Labour candidate. After 1916, his *Observer* supported Sinn Fein. In 1919 he got six months imprisonment for an editorial, 'Killing No Murder'. Thereafter the paper tended to be more commercial, less Irish and piously parochial. As Owen Dudley Edwards has suggested, he reinforced the worst Scottish notions of the Irish.[59] Such attitudes had contributed to communal conflict, especially in the 1880s as elsewhere in Britain. Such loyalties found later outlet in Glasgow's Celtic–Rangers soccer rivalry.

Not everyone welcomed the alleged importation of poverty and popery.[60] The few who were shopkeepers, dealers or licensees showed immense financial commitment to their church.[61] If not practising Catholics, they were 'Catholic' in culture. To Banffshire-born clergy, to men like Bishop Scott and later, Bishop Murdoch, the Irish were not altogether welcome. Like English bishops, they resented assertive laity signing petitions regarding religion.[62] They were embarrassed, financially and socially by, and unsympathetic at times towards, the Irish: Bishop Murdoch felt the 1848 nationalists should have 'a skinful of bullets'. They posed considerable cultural and financial problems for the Church.[63]

The economic religious challenge

The Second Report of the Commissioners of Religious Instruction (1837) found some 50,000 Catholics within a 20-mile radius of Glasgow. A quarter, 12,500, were in Glasgow, of whom 5000 were communicants including some 300–400 military men. Some 13,000 at three Sunday Masses suggests accommodation — and finances — were inadequate. The cathedral cost some £17,000 in 1816 compared to £509 for the second church in 1824. In spite of massive collections, the debt stood at £9000 in 1837. In Paisley, Revd. H. John Bremner ministered to 8000 Irish, half in the town and half in nearby weaving villages. If overwhelmingly poor, his parish included a couple of manufacturers and some small shopkeepers. His church, built for £4000 in 1807, still carried a debt of £850 in 1838. In Dumbarton, the congregation of some 400 built a church in 1831 for £1400 and within seven years had only £60 debt. Debt however remained a major problem.[64] Bishop Murdoch, almost 20 years later, had little optimism: he believed only 40,000 of more than 100,000 Catholics could afford to pay towards church debt and even then only a shilling a year. By 1858–9, the debt of the Western District was £39,000–£40,000.[65]

Community development

The growth of the ecclesiastical parish, its cultural framework and its political dimension, were vital, related components. Poverty and Scottish misgiving were only to be overcome by the exuberant Anglicized wealthy converts, assiduous Irish clergy and the pennies of the poor. Equally important, a largely Irish laity made generous loans at low rates from six months to over 20 years. Sums ranged from £10 to £2000, which suggests that many migrants either migrated with capital or quickly acquired wealth. It suggests a need for rethinking notions of the absolute poverty of *all* Irish in *all* British cities.[66]

'Catholic' culture

The Irish were not necessarily permanent residents nor permanently in the Church: mission churches might appear and disappear with economic cycles. They were mobile folk within a shifting Irish Catholic community. Neither was static. William McNamee, Irish stepfather of J. Dawson Burn, the nineteenth-century temperance advocate, is a case in point. A veteran, he remained a dogmatic Catholic, a drinker, in and out of jail, who laboured under 'a painful sense of their [Irish] unmerited wrongs.'[67] His real father was an anti-popery weaver. Yet 'he never forgot to pray, morning or evening: ... whether in prosperity of adversity, he never let any of us forget the duty we owed to God and our dependence on his Divine Will.'[68] Some 70 years later, Patrick Macgill followed a similar trail across the land. A. J. Cronin in his early Scottish novels betrays the ambivalent Catholic culture before an alien host: 'I was a Catholic who strayed occasionally into the less dark areas of scepticism but who still at heart clung to his first belief.'[69] The love-hate relationship with Catholicism remained.

Migrant mill girls resisted employer pressures in various ways. Some served their time before further migrating to the United States: Catholic Irish were among those recruited in the 1860s. Many worked in the Dundee mills. At the Catrine mills during their 12-hour day in 1852, they refused their employers' Protestant Bible and read simple Catholic manuals and the Catholic catechism.[70] Ethnic, cultural, class and gender issues were involved.

Finance hampered self-help. The poor and often unemployed were unlikely to be able to transform themselves. Their patron, the Church, was similarly constrained. Hard times hit collections, exacerbated by remigration. Bishop Murdoch told a priest on a collecting mission to America: 'the best of our people continue to cross the Atlantic and ... we will be left a congregation of beggars'.[71]

Churches were heavily in debt. In 1858–9, the Western District was some £40,000 in debt: the previous year it had been reduced by less than 0.037 per cent. Intolerable burdens hit an ill-prepared, uncomprehending church.[72] To service such debts, pew rents were relatively high, 12 shillings for the best. Yet the economic priorities or thrift of the labouring class congregation were such that 3201 of the 4136 places were let. In Glasgow at St Mary's the 600–700 who enjoyed standing room were expected to contribute a penny apart from one free service. Income was rising. In 1835 seat rents and special collections produced almost £1500. Average attendance at Mass of between 8000 and 9000 yielded around 1.7 pence per head (see Table 6.6).[73]

The sums suggest greater organization, financial discipline and voluntary commitment than usually attributed to the stereotyped Irish in Scotland. That contributed to tensions between Irish laity and clergy and their Scottish co-religionists: 'Paddy pays and Sandy owns and that's the way the money goes.'[74]

Migrants gradually developed their own mutual aid and welfare institutions. From 1792 the limited funds of Glasgow Hibernian Society had assisted unfortunates.[75] As early as 1832 the Catholics established an orphanage in Glasgow. However poor, as in Greenock, they were devoted to their religious duties and 'contribute more than the higher class to Christian charities.'[76] By 1841, Glasgow Catholics had begun a house of refuge.[77] In 1869, the government inspector described the Glasgow Catholic Industrial School and Orphanage (1862) as 'one of the most thoroughly industrial schools in Scotland.' In 1879, 142 children were admitted, half were illiterate, 133 had never been to confession and 115 had never been to communion. By 1897, it was dealing with some 600 youths. That fact highlighted other problems.[78]

Considerable Sunday schools and evening classes tried to remedy inadequate schooling and child labour.[79] Priests like the Revd. James Danaher, a Limerick priest at St Mary's, Greenock, established 'ragged schools' for children, a library for adults, new devotions and raised more than £800 for a new church in seven years.[80] But sometimes other immediate challenges diverted attention from long-term objectives.

Education

Education was perhaps a greater priority to clergy and laity alike. Catholic spending on schools, predictably, trailed other Scottish denominations. In 1817 Glasgow merchants founded a Catholic Schools Society, aided by Revd. Thomas Chalmers' charity sermons. Anti-Catholicism created difficulties between 1828 and 1836 but support continued. By 1838 some 20,000 pupils had attended the schools. But ever-increasing numbers characterized the post-Famine age. Migrants who arrived in the 1830s were predominantly Gaelic speakers, with limited English: English language schools had not been established in their home area. That lack of education was reflected in the marriage records between 1861–70: 46.06 per cent of Catholic males and 61.72 per cent of Catholic females could only make their mark on the register.[81] Yet these figures should not be exaggerated: after all, as suggested above, the migrants supported the lively *Glasgow Free Press* (1851–68), other ephemeral journals and lively pamphlet wars.

Later migrants spoke and read English: those who arrived as children had an increasingly better Catholic education available, especially after the Scottish Education Act (1872); the advent of religious orders of teachers, the greater professional training of lay teachers and improved facilities helped. The English-speaking adults faced one less hurdle. They found a community under the restored hierarchy more sure of itself in institutional and building achievements. Institutional structures, physical and emotional networks greatly expanded with the more settled character of the migrant community. But endemic poverty inhibited development. In 1868 the average Catholic school income, 15 shillings and two pence halfpenny, lagged behind the Free Church £1 4s 10d and the Church of Scotland £1 8s 6¾d. A few Irish migrants who persisted from an early stage had acquired some capital, small businesses and begun to enter the professions to service the community. By 1931, 64 per cent of the Irish born in Scotland had been 20 years or more in the country: only 8.6 per cent had been resident less than five years.[82]

Migrants found a more sophisticated, cultivated lifestyle and tone developing in a more settled and ageing community. In 1868, with members of the Italian Opera Company, the Jesuit church, St Joseph's Woodside, Glasgow, put on a concert of Haydn, Rossini and solos by Mr Santley, a well-known Liverpool Irish figure, and a sermon on Catholic principles: it paralleled the growing Protestant liturgical and musical development.[83] At the same time migrants arrived in an increasingly democratic society after 1867 and 1884, had more support in associational networks whether Catholic or Protestant. Both were more willing to become political activists and sustain their interests. Education was but one battleground.

Catholic revivalism

For the Church, hard pressed for resources, plant and manpower, sought to mobilize folk religion and to win hearts and minds.[84] From the 1850s, Passionists, Franciscans, Jesuits, Rosminians and Dominicans conducted missions throughout Scotland. Their preaching, devotions, hymns and practices inculcated a disciplined faith in the parts of urban industrial life where traditional influences failed. A sense of sin encouraged more conservative social and political attitudes: self-denial and acceptance of the existing order in this vale of tears. Thrift, sobriety and hard work were dominant values. In capturing the nationalist soul, the Church appealed to ethnic loyalty and contained wilder elements: the futility of revolution, a theme of the international Church, reflected recent Irish experience. By acquiring property and the vote, migrants sought respectability, achieved status and safeguarded both their own and Catholic interests: both were concerned with survival. Papal policy, the background of the Irish clergy in Scotland and the modest success of many migrants made an attractive package of policies. Clergy and laity believed they gained. In this transformation the role of the priest, the parish and its institutions were strengthened and even exaggerated in forming a strong communal spirit.

There were, as suggested, tensions within Catholicism between Scottish and Irish faithful. Lay activism, if not control of funds and clerical appointments, in the early days in Edburgh and in Glasgow was a source of friction. Such clashes closely paralleled the trusteeism controversy in America. Patrick McGowan, labour leader, and William McGowan, one of the first professionally trained teachers and secretary of the Glasgow Catholic Association (1823), clashed with the Tory Bishop Scott on these and other issues. Similar complaints were heard in Edinburgh.[85]

Later the Conservative Robert Monteith, the distinguished wealthy Scottish convert, the driving force behind the Second Spring in Scotland, staunchly backed the British union, as did his son, a bitter opponent of Home Rule. Like the convert Oxford priest, Revd. George Angus, in Edinburgh, they looked askance upon Irish aspirations. Their Tory social ideas continued with the later Ayrshire Oxford convert, Sir David Hunter Blair, abbot of Fort Augustus. Social romanticism combined with British nationalism and a realistic assessment of the Catholic condition in Scotland. Converts like James Grant, founder of the nationalist Association for the Vindication of Scottish Right and the remarkable Marquess of Bute might be more sympathetic to *Scottish* identity but they were a minority.

The lifestyle of that élite was cosy, generously public-spirited but anti-pathetic to Irish nationalism and remote from working men's lives.[86] Reasserting fading social dominance of the secular world within a besieged, welcoming and deferential poor Catholic body was challenging, comforting and patronizing. They and the Scottish clergy contributed to the containment of wilder Irish aspirations.[87]

On occasion, the Scottish clergy seem to have been antipathetic to the Irish, to the exuberance of the Scottish Oxbridge converts and to the restoration of the Scottish hierarchy. The Irish were equally restive. In 1864, 22 Irish-born clergy drew up a memorial to Bishop Murdoch expressing their ethnic grievances and calling for a restoration of the Scottish hierarchy. They were dismayed by their Scottish confrères' lack of sympathy but, even more forcefully, they complained about unbusinesslike methods. A demand for an Irish bishop was mischievously added to their memorial in the *Free Press*. An Irish bishop, James Lynch, was appointed in 1866, but he was a protégé of Cardinal Cullen and hardly a radical nationalist.[88]

The real issue at stake was Scottish reluctance to overextend either organizational or financial commitments to a frequently remigrating flock. Contentions continued until Archbishop Manning's visitation in 1867. The tactless Lynch stepped down to be succeeded by an Englishman, Charles Eyre. A man of academic substance and financial resource, he later received an honorary degree from the University of Glasgow. Drawn from old English Catholic gentry stock, with one brother a Jesuit at Stonyhurst and the other a substantial Irish landowner, he held the mass of Catholics within his organizational and building revolution until his death in 1902. Well-regulated professionalism under canon law followed.[89] The restoration of the Scottish hierarchy in 1878 passed fairly quietly unlike in England in 1850. With Eyre as bishop, later archbishop of Glasgow, the new regime made for a fully Tridentine Church. Ultramontanism had arrived.

A new communal spirit was evolving. The migrants' increased rates of persistence, reflected in the growing marriage rates, expansion of schools, slow social advance and their increasingly ambitious liturgies and concerts mentioned above, which paralleled the growing Protestant liturgical and musical development, were part of that process.[90] The community now had real Scottish roots (see Tables 6.7 and 6.8).

To meet these demands, nuns were gradually brought into Scotland to staff day, night and Sunday schools. Thousands of children and adults attended these highly disciplined institutions: sheer numbers necessitated attention and order. Glasgow, Edinburgh and Dundee followed this pattern. To raise funds, Irish preachers like Revd. Thomas Burke OP — one sermon raised £235 at Bridgeton — or the celebrated Revd. Ignatius Spencer, the Passionist, gave popular charity sermons.[91] Their activities were part of that larger Catholic devotional and cultural revolution.

Table 6.7 Percentage of marriages according to the rites of various denominations (1853–1913)

Date	C of Scotland	Free Church	Utd Pres-byterian	R.C.	Episcopal	Other	Unstated	Irregular
1855	45.12	23.70	15.00	9.25	1.78	4.70	0.35	0.04
1856	47.55	22.40	13.87	9.42	1.73	4.74	0.12	0.17
1857	47.71	22.41	13.69	8.98	1.95	4.76	0.47	0.03
1858	46.32	23.66	13.77	8.63	1.93	5.26	0.30	0.13
1859	46.05	22.93	13.85	8.59	1.78	5.54	1.15	0.05
1860	45.73	22.95	13.36	8.75	1.95	5.73	1.45	0.08
1870	44.76	22.91	14.35	8.89	2.26	6.26	0.26	0.31
1880	46.02	21.53	12.17	9.53	2.85	6.85	6.24	0.13
1890	45.17	19.47	11.27	10.16	2.80	7.37	0.00	3.76
1900	45.00	14.50	8.54	10.24	2.97	7.40	0.00	5.90
		[Utd Free Church 5.45]						
1910	44.59	26.24		10.26	2.81	8.75	0.00	7.05
1913	42.55	2 5.1 3		11.76	3.30	8.15	0.00	9.06

Source: Registrar General Scotland Returns (1914). The figures again suggest a more settled, consolidating and even reluctantly accepted community in Scotland.

Table 6.8 Emigration from Glasgow to all destinations (1863–74)

Year	Total	Irish numbers	Irish percenage
1863	7,997	1,189	15.0
1864	10,394	3,444	33.1
1865	15,227	6,738	41.0
1866	12,253	4,877	25.2
1867	11,078	907	12.2
1868	12,447	1,075	8.5
1869	21,064	1,308	6.2
1870	23,774	589	2.4
1871	23,035	565	2.9
1872	23,193	908	3.9
1873	24,526	288	1.1
1874	19,766	1,055	5.3

Source: William West Watson (ed.) *Reports upon the Vital Statistics and Economic Statistics of Glasgow for 1865–75*, (Glasgow Corporation, Glasgow, 1868–75). Obviously the figures have severe limitations. Many Irish migrants may have gone from Glasgow to Liverpool or other ports before departure.

Catholic schools slowly evolved to meet the ever-increasing number of children of young Irish migrants, the future of the Church and of the nation. Catholic teachers had been trained in the first professional teachers' school in the world in Glasgow. That practice had ceased by the mid-century. By then teachers were being trained in England for service in

Scottish schools. From 1854, Catholic students were sent to Hammersmith, Wandsworth, Liverpool and Sussex. More than one-sixth of all teachers trained by the Catholic Schools Committee were for Scotland: by 1870 44 of 247 were Scottish teachers. Between 1854 and 1888, Hammersmith trained 33 teachers and between 1856 and 1888 Liverpool returned some 63 trained teachers to Scotland, an average of three per year. Only in 1894 did the sisters of Notre Dame open the first Scottish Catholic teacher training college in Glasgow.[92]

Numerous nuns were recruited from Ireland, France and elsewhere to help from the 1840s: their exact numbers and names are difficult to obtain. The Jesuits and Marists established schools for those aspiring to middle-class status in the mid-nineteenth century. A few children like the future archbishop of Glasgow, John Maguire, a son of Irish migrants, were sent to Stonyhurst. But as one clergyman complained, only a handful could aspire to residence in the middle-class West End of Glasgow. If commitment was immense, upward mobility was slow.

The Scottish Education Act (1872) made education compulsory for all children. Catholic schools, however, had to continue to rely largely on their own voluntary contributions. That necessity intensified migrant group identity, through weekly contributions, church collections, soirées, fairs, bazaars, charity sermons and the like. Publication of schools' religious examination and teacher training results injected competition, pride and pressure to improve. By 1876, 171 certificated teachers, 8 assistants and 357 pupil-teachers were in 102 institutions serving over 20,600 day children and 3300 night pupils. By 1894 there were 194 schools for 60,000 pupils and over one thousand teachers: less than 10 per cent were males. Catholic expenditure was £91,000.[93]

Such burdens on a poor community meant few highly qualified teachers, many pupil-teachers on low salaries and very limited access to secondary and even less higher education. Support from the British Catholic Poor Schools Committee and later from English Catholic teachers greatly helped. A system was up and running against all the odds.

Individuals might succeed but the Irish migrant community as a whole languished behind. Problems continued until the Education Act (1918) when, unlike England, local authorities took over responsibility for Catholic schools.[94]

Other children attracted Catholic concern. The neglected were frequently spirited away by proselytizing child-savers. One institution was accused of collecting, training and exporting several hundred children to the British colonies with scant regard to proper procedures. Similarly, adult poor were often subject to proselytism and refused access to their clergy even after the law admitted that right.[95]

Temperance

Catholic migrants shared some values of the host community. Catholic temperance societies tried to instil thrift, sobriety and discipline. Charles Bryson, a Catholic merchant in Edinburgh and Glasgow, a founder of the St Vincent de Paul Society, won good reports from the Protestant community. Catholics and Protestants joined in euphoric demonstrations. By 1840 some 7000 migrants were pledged in Glasgow alone. Ten thousand more were added in the following year. Two years later the numbers had almost doubled. The arrival in 1842 of Fr Mathew, the teetotal apostle, brought remarkable ecumenical support for temperance. Tens of thousands greeted him in Glasgow with special trains bringing thousands from across Scotland.[96] But with less sympathetic Protestants and other pressing problems, the drive declined by the 1850s. Archbishop Eyre later reinvigorated the movement and introduced the temperance League of the Cross into all parishes in his archdiocese. In this drive for respectability and the vote, Revd. Peter Forbes, St Mary's, Glasgow, recruited clergy from Ireland, taught in Youghal seminary for a year and organized savings and house purchase among his huge flock.[97] Not all migrants reached that ideal condition. Self-help was inadequate.

Social concerns

The poor migrant posed problems. Bishop Gillis, the Canadian-born vicar apostolic of the Eastern District responded with the Holy Gild of St Joseph in Edinburgh. Ecumenical in character, it held annual celebrations with good food and drink. It offered prizes for the best-kept houses and for hygiene; a burial society, insurance and unemployment benefits for men and, to a degree, women. Migrants were among beneficiaries in the closes of Edinburgh.[98]

The St Vincent de Paul Society had arrived in Scotland in 1846. Two years later it spread to Glasgow and through the country. By 1914 the Glasgow conference was spending about £10,000 p.a. in dealing with some 13,000 individual cases, or around 4 per cent of the total Catholic population in the city. As a critic said:

> ostensibly to benefit the poor, but it is in fact a religio-political organisation. It has local, central and general councils; quarterly meetings, conferences, fetes, pilgrimages; it has passports, fetes, pilgrimages and circular letters to its members. It adapts itself to all classes and conditions — addresses itself to the scholar, the soldier, the mechanic, the apprentice, the labourer — to the mother and the daughter, for all of whom it issues a suitable publication.[99]

Irish Catholics were unacceptable to many Scots: they were either perceived as Chartists, or strikebreakers, or politically indifferent and at odds with the Scottish working class. That distorted view needs correction. John Doherty, the Donegal-born spinners' leader, knew Patrick McGowan, the Glasgow Catholic textile leader: he worked closely with the Belfast spinners and English textile districts. While O'Connell was hostile to trade unions, the victimized McGowan defended the workers. Irish migrants were organized as early as 1852 as an effective political pressure group on parliamentary candidates. Slowly accepted, Irish miners were to the fore in the Lanarkshire coalfields from at least 1873 and responded to socialist ideas in the 1880s and 1890s.[100]

The late nineteenth century, then, was a turning-point for the Irish in Scotland. The decisive migrant experience was the Land League rather than the Famine. The third wave of migration formed a radical critique of society suggestive of its conservative origins. The firebrand, Revd. Patrick Lavelle, had visited the west of Scotland in 1864. Associated with the Glasgow *Free Press*, he encountered Bishop Murdoch's opposition. His was a specifically Irish appeal. He attacked irresponsible landlords, including a Glaswegian, Adam Pollock, who owned almost 30,000 acres in Galway. But his attack on proprietors found an echo in the Scottish Highlands and Islands.[101] Henry George, author of *Poverty and Progress*, was the second figure to influence Irish migrants and their Scottish hosts: his pamphlet, *The Irish Land Question*, was published in Glasgow in 1881. He was shocked by Glasgow: 'poverty and destitution that would appal a heathen ... they were better off a hundred years ago when their fathers were half naked savages.'[102] Like Laurence Gronlund, the author of *The Cooperative Commonwealth*, he influenced the Scottish Christian Socialist movement, a group associated with Michael Davitt, the English Land Restoration League and the American Christian Socialists.[103]

These links were part of an older intellectual connection. Since Daniel O'Connell, Irish and Scottish Liberals often made common cause. Revd. Michael Condon had contributed to *Young Ireland* and maintained his cultural associations with his homeland while assimilating into the Ultramontane Church; a migrant anxious to root himself in an increasingly attractive Scottish environment. In Blantyre, Daniel Gallagher, later a priest, taught David Livingstone: they corresponded until his death in 1873. But Irish nationalism grew in Scotland around John Ferguson. An Ulster Protestant, his Glasgow firm of Cameron and Ferguson published Lady Wilde's poems.[104] He claimed he had discovered Ireland and his Irishness in Glasgow. An early supporter of Isaac Butt, of the Land and Home Rule movement, he brought Parnell, Davitt and others to Glasgow. Ferguson, a Labour Party figure, was to be the driving force behind the Irish movement in Scotland until his death in 1906.[105] Nationalists had the sympathy of the Scottish miners' leader, Alexander McDonald, to his death in 1881.[106] Politically, the Irish usually remained committed to the Liberals and opposed to the Tories in most instances.

Links and alliances

The revival of Scottish and Irish Gaelic helped to develop further bonds between Irish and Highlanders: the destruction of the Highlanders' way of life was as horrendous as that of the Irish.[107] The North American tour of

John Murdoch, the Scottish Land League leader, and the writings of the Scottish-born journalist, James 'Boycott' Redpath, fostered its growth. From its first issue the Glasgow paper, the *Exile* (1884–85), sympathized with the Highlanders.[108] There were even expectations that the American leaders, Patrick Ford and John Boyle O'Reilly, would tour Scotland in 1884.[109] Davitt did visit the west of Scotland in 1884. His vote of thanks in Glasgow came from the former Barrhead priest, Revd. Thomas Keane, a relative of an editor of the *Free Press*: 'Highland lairds exercised a despotic power, greater in some respects than the slave owners of America.'[110]

Other connections flourished. Revd. Eugene O'Growney of Maynooth was honorary president of the Comunn Gailig Ghlasgcho, 1893–4. The *Glasgow Observer* had a weekly Gaelic column while the Irish National League ran classes in Gaelic. By 1900, some 17 branches flourished in the west of Scotland: soon there were 30. By 1908 the United Irish League claimed to have 25,000 members in 74 branches in Scotland. Patrick Pearse delivered the first of two addresses in Glasgow in 1902. Sinn Fein began to proselytize in Scotland: financial aid and arms were sent to Ireland before 1916 and beyond. Glasgow also provided refuge for P. J. Little's newspaper. In 1909 Captain Edward O'Meagher Condon, a veteran of 1867, came from America. In 1918 Sinn Fein quadrupled to 80 clubs in Scotland. The IRA reputedly had 20,000 men available in Scotland in 1920 while Constance Markiewicz addressed Scottish supporters in Glasgow. With Irish independence, interest waned. Irish nationalism had encouraged Scottish nationalists to establish their own party in 1920: many Republicans and Sinn Fein supporters in Scotland joined.[111]

Ulster Protestants were active in Unionist Scotland. Sir Edward Carson addressed large crowds in the autumn of 1913: 8700 allegedly signed the Ulster covenant. Unionists found support among Knox Clubs which rapidly grew in Scotland. Revd. James Brisby, minister of his Christian Union Church, Calton, organized support for Ulster in his *Scottish Protestant Review* and his Ulster Volunteers.[112] Dogged resistance and later overt antagonism continued as Tom Gallagher has shown in the interwar years. In more recent times, Revd. Ian Paisley found erstwhile support in Revd. Jack Glass but in recent times has established his own church near Ibrox stadium, home of Rangers FC.

Other cultural and social developments

By the end of the nineteenth century affluence was spreading or trickling down to the more settled Irish: their slow, upwardly mobile progress continued in the late nineteenth and early twentieth centuries. School board elections were part of that Irish education. Education, political awareness, organization, voting strength and the self-confidence to change the state to a more benevolent role helped.

The 1911 census suggests that although concentrated in unskilled areas, migrants saw some improvement. In 1884, 90 per cent of those working on the construction of the James Watt dock, Greenock, were reputedly Catholic. One observer believed migrants tended to bad company, slovenly children and preoccupation with Irish concerns. Devoid of cohesion and mutual improvement, they showed 'no ambition for social elevation in Scotland.'[113] Even as late as 1906, a Jesuit lamented a mere 12 Catholics were at Glasgow University.[114] Patrick Macgill's novels indicate the continued hardship of mobile, seasonal construction workers.[115] But the persistent population was slowly improving its condition.

The increasing market for religious objects and books, elaborate church extensions, particularly the virtual mass production of Peter Paul Pugin in the west of Scotland, pilgrimages to Rome and Lourdes from the 19870s, supposes an improving group. John Denvir found Duntocher, by Glasgow, a model community, 'with infinitely more domestic comfort and none of its wretchedness' than Ireland.[116] A. Connell, a leading figure in the Scottish branch of the Irish National League, was a prosperous Glasgow clothier. The father of the future Sir Denis W. Brogan, the renowned academic, a leading light in the intellectual Catholic Institute and a leading Gaelic Leaguer, was a successful tailor. Publicans were often Irish: in Greenock reputedly about one-quarter were Irish.[117]

Glasgow, a significant city of artists at the end of the nineteenth century, attracted a better type of migrant. John Lavery from County Down arrived to become one of the 'Glasgow Boys'. In his early days he associated with the Irish Impressionist, Frank O'Meara, (1858–88) and the Scot, Macaulay Stevenson.[118]

The Irish were far more urbanized in Scotland than in 1851: agrarian Wigtonshire had a third less Irish-born in 1891. Individual ascent was limited but group achievement was considerable. Like Davitt's new Ireland, they were more organized and assertive.

Popular sport was another indication. Clergy, from being 'merely mechanical apparatus', became involved in social concerns.[119] Catholic Young Men's Association and Temperance bodies proliferated throughout Scotland: Archbishop Eyre required a parish League of the Cross. By 1900 it had some 15,000 members. To prevent 'leakage' of youth from the Church, football rapidly developed: Mossend Emmet, Glasgow Hibernian, 'Harp' teams in Dundee, Falkirk, Stirling, Partick, Johnstone. Brass bands, glee clubs and 'improving' lectures followed recreational and reading rooms.[120] The foundation of the Edinburgh Hibernian club, initially for Catholic youths, by the abstainer, Revd. Joseph Hannan, and of Glasgow Celtic by Brother Walfrid, to raise funds for the poor were significant. The official opening of Parkhead was attended by Archbishop Eyre and Michael Davitt, the club patrons, with the planting of a sod from Donegal. These and more ephemeral clubs show moral concern and the need for identity, but also the growth of a publican and a small professional class among the migrants. Arguably even the clergy was becoming more 'professional' and less nationalist.[121] The Protestant Irish became identified with Glasgow Rangers with the arrival of Harland and Wolf, Belfast shipyard workers on the Clyde around 1905.[122]

Literary links expanded in the late nineteenth century. Oscar Wilde, enjoying popular success in Scotland, undertook several tours of the country. His close Scottish friend, Revd. Sir David Hunter Blair, an aristocratic Oxford convert, had forsaken his Ayrshire estates for the monastery.[123] Another devout Scottish Catholic friend, Robert Ross, was to work on the *Scots Observer*. Two other friends had Scottish ties: John Gray a priest in Edinburgh, and his associate, André Raffalovich, who subsidized his studies in Rome and later built a church for him in Edinburgh. His sister, Sophie, was to marry William O'Brien MP, the architect of the Irish Land Act (1903) which offered peasant proprietorship.[124]

Literary accomplishments, self-improvement and adaptation showed the subtle integration of the Irish on their terms into Scottish life. As in the United States, a lively nationalism for the home country showed the rootedness in the new home: but social activities were far more prominent than political concerns. The migrants gave considerably more to relief in France after 1870–1 than in several years to Fenian organizations. The Irish were increasingly scattered more through Scottish cities especially in Glasgow: a reflection of self-improvement and urban renewal.[125]

The social critic

If the Irish were identified with the victims of industrial life, they readily allied with the wider world of reform.[126] It was partly from self-interest, partly an evolution from Land League, Single Tax and papal social teaching to a conservative socialism — or more accurately to social justice rather than Marxism — that ultimately enabled an Irish Labour view to develop. Irish and Scottish (slum) landlord were one and the same. The ideas were laid in Revd. Hugh Quigley's novels attacking capitalism, Protestantism and Anglo-Saxonism.[127] That was further developed in Patrick Macgill's authentic working-class novels about Scotland, *Children of the Dead End* (1914) and *The Rat Pit* (1915).[128] Add discriminatory employment practices, and the transformation was complete. The argument was turned. Group self-consciousness and self-confidence had reached maturity in a democratizing Britain in the wake of franchise extension to 1918. Poverty was not inherent in the migrant Irish character but in an unjust vicious, economic system dominated by their ethnic and religious enemies: Irish critics cut through the rhetoric of the dignity of labour to the essential social issue.

James Connolly, with his mixture of socialism, nationalism and Catholicism, was a further indication of shifts taking place within the Irish migrant community in the latter part of the nineteenth century. He and his brother, John, were leading figures in the Scottish Labour Party and Scottish Socialist Federation. To him the Irish question was a social issue. His departure to Ireland, his American sojourn between several visits to Scotland (1901, 1902, 1903, 1910, 1911, 1913) emphasize the transatlantic nature of the Irish world in Scotland.[129]

In Glasgow, John Wheatley from Waterford established a Catholic

Socialist Society. It included William Regan of Rutherglen, member of the ILP and supporter of Connolly: Henry Somerville, a leading Catholic social movement figure, was closely associated. Archbishop Maguire of Glasgow warmed to their aims: he told a rally in the Albert Hall, London; 'the working man will rule the world.' As he said in another Glasgow lecture:

> How many inefficient men of high position have been buried in Westminster? When they had an inefficient Cabinet minister they sent him to the House of Lords. When they had an inefficient 'gentleman' they gave him a handsome pension and then when they had inefficient workman they sent him to the workhouse.[130]

The nature of Wheatley's socialism was and remains a matter of dispute. The Catholic *Glasgow Observer* felt he placed trade unionism before nationalism. Predictably, William Gallacher called him 'a Catholic who had outgrown religion.'[131] But both Wheatley and his archbishop were reflecting a radical Irish view of social justice.

Respectability

A variety of Catholic attitudes developed. The decline of family-dominated enterprises, the shared experience of depression and World War contributed. If the overwhelming bulk of Catholics supported Labour from the 1920s so other views gradually appeared. Other Catholics followed tradition in returning to the idyllic agrarian community. The influence of Ireland, smallholding and Chesterton and Gill could not revivify the old ideals.[132] More Catholics went to university and were entering the professions. John S. Phillimore, the first Catholic professor in the university of Glasgow since the Reformation, expressed that confidence.[133] That ebullience encouraged some to support the successful rectorial campaign of the Scottish Nationalist, Compton Mackenzie, at Glasgow University. But such new directions were stifled by anti-Irish sentiments of nationalist and Protestant elements in the 1920s amid the continuing mythology of Irish migration.[134]

The promised land?

After World War II such mentalities survived in Scotland until the mid-1960s but with increasing difficulty in an increasingly diverse ethnic Scotland. In a more tolerant post-imperialist age, with Irish migration a matter now of history, in a post-Holocaust Europe, such notions seemed outmoded. The growing indifferent, secularized ethos, a more relaxed, if not sophisticated, popular culture, a somewhat ecumenical religious atmosphere made Irish, Catholic or any other culture seem less alien. More educated Catholics changed their expectations and their Church in

Scotland as they became upwardly mobile. They benefited enormously from the welfare state: by 1970 about 40 per cent of students at Glasgow University came from Catholic, predominantly Irish backgrounds. In 1967, Glasgow Celtic of Catholic Irish origin won the European Cup and became a generally accepted 'Scottish' team at the very time sectarianism was re-appearing in Ulster.

Conservative 'Catholic-Irish' began to appear with the demise of sectarian Unionism in Scotland around 1965, the later election of the first Catholic Tory MP and the upward mobility of Catholic professionals. Urban strategy confronted Roman Catholics.

But by then Irish links were tenuous, more a shared memory, less a direct living link. Declining Scottish industry, the end of recruitment of Irish priests for the Scottish mission and the pull of south-eastern England made the Irish community less significant: Asian migration was more significant. The Irish were no longer a block on the road but a brick in the Scottish story. Numerically in decline, the Irish had arrived after a very long journey.[135]

Notes

1. Andrew Dewar Gibb, *Scotland in Eclipse*, Toulmin, London, 1930, p. 53.
2. *The Menace of the Irish Race to Scottish Nationality*, p. 2. See also George Malcolm Thomson, *Caledonia, or the Future of the Scots*, Kegan Paul, London, 1927.
3. H. J. Paton, *The Claim of Scotland*, Allen and Unwin, London, 1968, p. 178, quoted in J. F. McCaffrey, 'Roman Catholics in Scotland in the 19th and 20th centuries', *Records of the Scottish Church History Society*, 21 (1983), p. 277. See my 'Popery in Scotland: image and reality, 1820–1920', *Records of the Scottish Church History Society*, 22 (1986), pp. 235–57.
4. Cf. Frances Finnegan, *Poverty and Prejudice: a Study of Irish Immigrants in York, 1840–75*, Cork University Press, Cork 1982; T. Dillon, 'The Irish in Leeds, 1851–61', *Thoresby Society Miscellany*, 1,16 (1979), pp. 1–28; C. Richardson, 'Irish settlement in mid-nineteenth century Bradford', *Yorkshire Bulletin of Social and Economic Research*, 20 (1968), pp. 40–57; L. H. Lees, *Exiles of Erin: Irish Migrants in Victorian London*, Manchester University Press, 1979; Frank Neal, *Sectarian Violence: the Liverpool Experience, 1819–1914, An Aspect of Anglo-Irish History*, Manchester University Press, Manchester, 1988; David Fitzpatrick, 'A curious middle place: the Irish in Britain, 1871–1921', in R. Swift and S. Gilley (eds), *The Irish in Britain*, Pinter, London, 1989, pp. 10–59, among many others.
5. See his *The Irish in Scotland, 1789–1845*, Cork University Press, Cork, 1943; *The Irish in Modern Scotland*, Cork University Press, Cork, 1947; *The Celtic Story: the Story of the Celtic Football Club*, Stanley Paul, London, 1960; *The Navvy in Scotland*, Cork University Press, Cork, 1970. Callum G. Brown, *The Social History of Religion in Scotland since 1730*, Methuen, London, 1987, provides a fine recent overview.
6. Cf. J. Dillon to James Bryce, 24 Dec. 1903, quoted F. S. L. Lyons, *John Dillon*, Oxford University Press, London, 1968, p. 221.

7.   Cf. E. Bradford Burns, *Poverty of Progress: Latin America in the Nineteenth Century*, University of California Press, Berkeley, 1980; Judith Devlin, *The Superstitious Mind: French Peasants and the Supernatural in the Nineteenth Century*, Yale University Press, New Haven, 1987; Michael Hechter, *Internal Colonialism: the Celtic Fringe in British National Development, 1536–1966*, University of California Press, Berkeley, 1975, p. 113.

8.   Cf. J. F. C. Harrison, *Robert Owen and the Owenites in Britain and America: the Quest for a New Moral World*, Routledge, London, 1969; Ray Boston, *British Chartists in America*, Manchester University Press, Manchester, 1971.

9.   R. A. Billington, *The Protestant Crusade, 1800–1860*, Harper, New York 1938; John Higham, *Strangers in the Land: Patterns in American Nativism, 1865–1924*, Rutgers University Press, New Brunswick 1955; John Wolffe, *The Protestant Crusade in Great Britain, 1829–1860*, Oxford University Press, Oxford, 1991; Tom Gallagher, 'The Catholic Irish in Scotland: in search of identity', in T. M. Devine (ed.), *Irish Immigrants and Scottish Society in the Nineteenth and Twentieth Centuries: Proceedings of the Scottish Historical Studies Seminar, University of Strathclyde, 1989–90*, John Donald, Edinburgh, 1991, pp. 19–43.

10.   A. D. Gibb, *Scotland*, pp. 54, 61. Also J. R. Fleming, *A History of the Free Church of Scotland, 1875–1929*, T. and T. Clark, Edinburgh, 1933, p. 146; J. H. Paton, *The Claim of Scotland*, p. 178.

11.   Quoted in Hechter, *Internal Colonialism*, p. 285.

12.   David Kirkwood, *My Life of Revolt*, Harrap, London, 1935, p. 84. Also see especially p. 192 and p. 171. Glasgow 'workers laughed' at the Glasgow 'soviet' and 'went on with their jobs.'

13.   Cf. Walter Kendall, *The Revolutionary Movement in Britain, 1900–21: the Origins of British Communism*, Weidenfeld and Nicolson, London, 1969, p. 107; Alan B. Campbell, *The Lanarkshire Miners: a Social History of their Trade Unions, 1775–1874*, John Donald, Edinburgh, 1979, pp. 294, 300.

14.   James E. Handley, *The Irish in Scotland*, Cork University Press, Cork, 1945, pp. 284–6; Leslie Charles Wright, *Scottish Chartism*, Oliver and Boyd, Edinburgh, 1953; McCaffrey, 'Irish immigrants, and radical movements in the west of Scotland in the early nineteenth century', *Innes Review*, 39 (1988), pp. 46–60.

15.   See J. F. McCaffrey, 'The Irish vote in Glasgow in the late nineteenth century', *Innes Review*, 21 (1970), pp. 30–6; McCaffrey, 'Politics and the Catholic community since 1878', in D. McRoberts (ed.), *Modern Scottish Catholicism, 1878–1978*, J. S. Burns, Glasgow, 1979, pp. 140–55; and McCaffrey, 'Roman Catholics in Scotland in the nineteenth and twentieth centuries', *Records of the Scottish Church History Society*, 21 (1983), pp. 275–300; R. D. Lobban, 'The Irish community in Greenock in the nineteenth century', *Irish Geography*, 6 (1971), pp. 270–81; W. M. Walker, 'Irish immigrants in Scotland: their priests, politics and parochial life', *Historical Journal*, 4, 15 (1972), pp. 649–66; David McRoberts (ed.), *Modern Scottish Catholicism, 1878–1978*, J. S. Burns, Glasgow, 1979; W. Walker, *Juteopolis, Dundee and its Textile Workers, 1885–1923*, Scottish Academic Press, Edinburgh, 1979; B. Aspinwall, 'The Scottish dimension: Robert Monteith and the origins of Catholic social thought', *Downside Review*, 326, 97 (1979), pp. 46–68, and 'David Urquhart, Robert Monteith and the Catholic Church: a search for justice and peace', *Innes Review*, 31 (1980), pp. 57–70; Sheridan Gilley, 'Catholics and Socialists in Glasgow, 1906–1912', in Roger Swift and S. Gilley, *The Irish in Britain, 1815–1939*, Pinter, London, 1989, pp. 212–38; Ian S. Wood, 'John S. Wheatley, the Irish and the Labour movement in Scotland', *Innes Review*, 31 (1980), pp. 71–85; Brenda Collins,

'Irish emigration to Dundee and Paisley in the first half of the nineteenth century', in J. M. Goldstrom and L. A. Clarkson (eds), *Irish Population, Economy and Society*, Oxford University Press, Oxford, 1981, pp. 195–212; B. Aspinwall, 'The formation of the Catholic community in the west of Scotland', *Innes Review*, 33 (1982), pp. 44–57; Christine H. Johnson, *Developments in the Roman Catholic Church in Scotland, 1779–1829*, John Donald, Edinburgh, 1983; Bill Murray, *The Old Firm: Sectarianism, Sport and Society in Scotland*, John Donald, Edinburgh, 1984; B. Aspinwall and J. F. McCaffrey, 'A comparative view of the Irish in Edinburgh in the nineteenth century', in R. Swift and S. Gilley (eds), *The Irish in the Victorian City*, Croom Helm, London, 1985, pp. 130–57; Steve Bruce, *No Pope of Rome, Militant Protestantism in Modern Scotland*, Mainstream, Edinburgh, 1985; B. Aspinwall, 'The Welfare State within the state: the Saint Vincent de Paul Society in Glasgow, 1848–1920', in W. J. Shiels and Diana Wood (eds), *Voluntary Religion: Studies in Church History*, 23 (1986), pp. 445–59; J. F. McCaffrey, 'The stewardship of resources: financial strategies in the Glasgow District, 1800–1870', and B. Aspinwall, 'Broadfield revisited: some Scottish Catholic responses to wealth, 1918–1940', in W. J. Shiels and Diana Wood (eds), *The Church and Wealth: Studies in Church History*, 24 (1987), pp. 359–70 and pp. 393–406; T. Gallagher, 'A tale of two cities: communal strife in Glasgow and Liverpool before 1914', in R. Swift and S. Gilley (eds), *The Irish in the Victorian City*, Croom Helm, London, 1985, pp. 106–29; Gallagher, *Glasgow: the Uneasy Peace: Religious Tension in Modern Scotland, 1819–1940*, Manchester University Press, Manchester, 1987; Gallagher, *Edinburgh Divided: John Cormack and No Popery in the 1930s*, Polygon, Edinburgh, 1987; John F. McCaffrey, 'Irish immigrants' (1988), pp. 46–60; B. Aspinwall, 'The Irish priest abroad: Michael Condon in Scotland, 1848–78', *The Churches, Ireland and the Irish, Studies in Church History*, 25 (1989), pp. 279–97; Stewart J. Brown, ' "Outside the Covenant": the Scottish Presbyterian churches and Irish immigration', *Innes Review*, 1, 42 (1991), pp. 19–45; and Richard J. Finlay, 'Nationalism, race and the Irish Question in inter-war Scotland', *Innes Review*, 1, 42 (1991), pp. 46–67.

16.   Elaine McFarland, *Protestants First: Orangeism in Scotland*, Edinburgh University Press, Edinburgh, 1990, and Graham Walker,' Orange Order and Protestant working class life in Scotland, 1918–39', *International Review of Social History*, 37, 2 (1992), pp. 177–206.

17.   *Report from the Select Committee appointed to Inquire into the Origin, Nature, Extent and Tendency of Orange Institutions in Great Britain and the Colonies*, 1835, and McFarland, *Protestants First*.

18.   Handley, *The Irish in Modern Scotland*, 1947, pp. 310–12, and J. T. Ward, 'Some aspects of working class Conservatism in the nineteenth century', pp. 141–57, in John Butt and J. T. Ward (eds), *Scottish Themes*, Scottish Academic Press, Edinburgh, 1976.

19.   *Scottish Protestant*, 28 August 1851.

20.   See Robert S. Sylvain, *Clerc Garibaldien, Prêcheur du Deux Mondes, Alessandro Gavazzi, 1809–89*, 2 vols., Centre Pédagogique, Quebec, 1962; Basil Hall, 'Alessandro Gavazzi', *Studies in Church History, Church Society and Politics*, 12 (1976), pp. 305–56; and my 'Popery in Scotland: image and reality, 1820–1920', *Records of the Scottish Church History Society*, 22 (1986), pp. 235–67.

21.   *Glasgow Herald*, 16 July 1873, and 18, 19, 24, 25 March 1879; *Glasgow News*, 13 July 1874. I am indebted to Dr J. F. McCaffrey for these references. Also see I. G. C. Hutchison, *A Political History of Scotland, 1832–1924: Parties, Elections and*

Issues, John Donald, Edinburgh 1986.

22.   *Glasgow Evening Post*, 19 and 26 September 1835; *The Correspondence of Daniel O'Connell*, ed. Maurice R. O'Connell, Irish University Press, Shannon/Dublin 1972–80, II, 57; 5:327–28; 7:293–94; 8:72–3.

23.   Victor Walsh, 'A fanatic heart: the cause of Irish nationalism in Pittsburgh during the Gilded Age', *Journal of Social History*, 2, 15 (1982), pp. 187–203. Also Eric Foner, 'Class, ethnicity and radicalism in the Gilded Age: the Land League and Irish Americans', *Marxist Perspectives*, 1, 2 (1978), 6–55.

24.   W. D'Arcy, *The Fenian Movement in the United States*, Catholic University Press, Washington, DC, 1947, p. 374; K. R. M. Short, *The Dynamite War: Irish-American Bombers in Victorian Britain*, Gill and MacMillan, Dublin, 1979, pp. 125–54; Patrick Quinlivan and Paul Rose, *The Fenians in England, 1865–1872*, Calder, London, 1982; John Denvir, *The Irish in Britain*, Kegan Paul, London, 1892, pp. 112, 143, 205, 215; McCaffrey, 'Irish immigrants', *Innes Review*, 39 (1988). See the *Glasgow Herald* for a balanced view and London *Times*, March–May 1868, for savagery. His speech from the dock was a remarkably articulate performance. He is a classic Scottish case of 'not proven'.

25.   Condon Diaries, Glasgow Archdiocesan Archives. *Greenock Herald*, 17 March 1883.

26.   James Hunter (ed.), *For the People's Cause: From the Writings of John Murdoch, Highland and Irish Land Reformer*. The Crofters Commission, HMSO, Edinburgh, 1986.

27.   See W. Steuart [Richard] Trench, *Realities of Irish Life*, MacMillan, London, 1869, p. 282: 'The ould stock will not come by their rights at this time I fear, but there is a good time coming.'

28.   See my *Portable Utopia: Glasgow and the United States, 1820–1914*, Aberdeen University Press, Aberdeen, 1984.

29.   In Norristown, Pennsylvania; Patterson, New Jersey; Rammapool, New York. *Factory Commission 1833, First Report*, I, pp. 87, 103–4, 112.

30.   See Bernard Canning, *Irish-Born Secular Priests in Scotland, 1829–1979*, Bernard Canning, Greenock, 1979.

31.   *Second Report of the Commissioners of Religious Instruction*, 1837, pp. 16, 92, Hibernian Society, Minute Book, 1792–1824, Strathclyde Regional Archives, Mitchell Library, Glasgow. See David Stevenson, *Scottish Covenanters and the Irish Confederates: Scottish-Irish Relations in Mid-Seventeenth Century*, Ulster Historical Foundation, Belfast, 1981, for earlier links. Henry William Meikle, *Scotland and the French Revolution*, J. Maclehose and Sons, Glasgow, 1912; *First Report Factory Commission*, 1833, pp. 1, 12, 17; Norman Murray, *The Scottish Weavers, 1790–1850: a Social History*, John Donald, Edinburgh, 1978, p. 32; Graham Walker, The Protestant Irish in Scotland', in Devine (ed.), *Irish Immigrants*, pp. 44–66; J. G. Sims, 'John Toland 1670–1720, a Donegal heretic', *Irish Historical Studies*, 2, 16 (1989), pp. 304–20. Student listings can be found in *The Matriculation Album Glasgow University from 1728 to 1858*, Maclehose, Glasgow, 1913, and *A Roll of the Graduates of the University of Glasgow*, Maclehose, Glasgow, 1898, both edited by W. Innes Addition. Handley, *The Irish in Scotland*, pp. 3–79 gives an excellent synopsis.

32.   See my 'Was O'Connell necessary? Sir John Joseph Dillon, Scotland and the movement for Catholic emancipation', in David Loades (ed.), *The End of Strife*, T. and T. Clark, Edinburgh, 1984, pp. 114–36, and Handley, *The Irish in Scotland*, pp. 115–17.

33.   Sir J. J. Dillon to J. Menzies of Pitfodels, 4 Feb. 1813, Menzies Papers, Scottish

Catholic Archives, Edinburgh. Also Sir John Joseph Dillon to D. Scully, 28 May 1813, in Brian MacDermot (ed.), *The Catholic Question in Ireland and England, 1798–1822: the Papers of Denys Scully*, Irish Academic Press, Dublin, 1988, p. 458. See also pp. 451–2 and pp. 460–3.

34. *Catholic Directory*, 1831.
35. *Statistical Account, passim.* See *Report on the Irish Power in Great Britain*, appendix G, First Report for Inquiry into the Condition of the Poorer Classes in Ireland, 1835; Barbara M. Kerr, 'Irish seasonal migration to Great Britain, 1800–1838', *Irish Historical Studies*, 3, 12 (1943), pp. 365–80; J. Williamson, 'The Irish impact upon the British labour market during the Industrial Revolution', *Journal of Economic History*, 3, 46 (1986), pp. 693–720.
36. See James Clelland (ed.), *Enumeration of Districts of the City of Glasgow*, Hedderwick, Glasgow, 1821, p. 6. Gorbals, 1367; Bridgeton, 841; Calton, 718; Anderston, 604; St Mary's, 578; St James, 568; Blackfriars, 566, were above 500 Irish residents in their poorer areas.
37. Cf. Eric L. Hirsch, *Urban Revolt: Ethnic Politics in Nineteenth Century Chicago*, University of California, Berkeley, 1990, and J. Williamson, *Coping with City Growth in the British Industrial Revolution*, Cambridge University Press, Cambridge, 1990.
38. *The First Statistical Account*, Edinburgh, 1797, pp. 7, 35.
39. Thomas Wilkinson, *Some Account of the Last Journey of John Pemberton to the Highlands and other Parts of Scotland*, Brown, Philadelphia, 1811, p. 8. Other meetings had large peaceful crowds. Early Mormons had similar experiences. See my 'A fertile field: the early Mormons in Scotland', in T. L. Jensen and Malcolm Thorp, *The Early Mormons in Victorian Britain*, University of Utah Press, Salt Lake City, 1989, pp. 305–16.
40. See Patrick Gallagher ('Paddy the Cope'), *My Story*, Templecrone Co-operative Society, Dungloe, 1945; Michael MacGowan, *The Hard Road to Klondike*, Routledge, London, 1962; Patrick Macgill, *The Rat Pit* and *Children of the Dead End*, reprinted by Caliban Books, Ascot, 1982; *Report and Tables relating to Irish Migratory Agricultural and Other Labourers P.P.* 1902 Cd 850; *Report and Tables relating to Irish Migratory Agricultural Labourers*, 1906 Cd 286; Williamson, *Coping With City Growth*, Chapter 6, pp. 129–7.
41. Handley, *The Irish in Modern Scotland*, p. 260.
42. *Reports on the Sanitary Condition of the Labouring Population of Scotland 1842*, p. 73. See also Enid Gauldie, *Cruel Habitations: a History of Working Class Housing, 1780–1918*, Allen and Unwin, London, 1974.
43. *Reports on the Sanitary Condition*, pp. 244–5 and p. 252.
44. Handley, *The Irish in Scotland*, pp. 214–19, and *The Irish in Modern Scotland*, p. 255.
45. See Tables 6.5a and 6.5b.
46. Govan Parish Poor Board Records, 1879, Strathclyde Regional Archives.
47. Govan Parish Poor Board Records, 1879.
48. The case of Mary Helen McCottar or McQuillan, Govan Parish Poor Board Records, 1879, p. 38.
49. Barony Parish Poor Board Records, 1881, Strathclyde Regional Archives.
50. Handley, *The Irish in Modern Scotland*, p. 260.
51. See Owen Dudley Edwards, *Burke and Hare*, Polygon, Edinburgh, 1984, and *Scottish Protestant*, 60, 31 (July) and 62, 14 (August 1852) *re* the execution of the two Scanlan brothers at Cupar. The Glasgow *Free Press* had called the case 'judicial murder'.

52. Handley, *The Irish in Scotland*, pp. 40–1 and his *Irish in Modern Scotland*, pp. 72–4.
53. See Table 6.3
54. See Table 6.3, Denvir, *The Irish in Britain*, 1892, pp. 116, 446.
55. See Tables 6.3, 6.4 and data from the Censuses of 1861–1911; Brenda Collins, 'The origins of Irish immigration to Scotland in the nineteenth and twentieth centuries', in T. M. Devine (ed.), *Irish Immigrants and Scottish Society in the Nineteenth and Twentieth Centuries*, John Donald, Edinburgh, 1991, pp. 1–18.
56. As W. Walker, 'Irish immigrants in Scotland' (1983), implies. Elaine McFarland, *Protestants First*, 1990, emphasizes the Ulster origins of the membership.
57. *Irish Census General Report*, 1901, p. 437. Between 1841 and 1901 the Scots-born population had consistently risen from 0.11 to 0.68 per cent. Also see G. Walker, 'The Protestant Irish', p. 53.
58. Titles included the *Free Press*, 1851–68; *Northern Times*, 1855–7; *Irish Banner*, 1868; *Exile*, 1884–5; *Irish People's Friend*, 1910.
59. O. D. Edwards, 'The Catholic Press since the restoration of the hierarchy', in D. McRoberts (ed.), *Modern Scottish Catholicism 1878–1978*, J. S. Burns, Glasgow, 1979, pp. 156–82, especially 169–73.
60. See *Minutes of the Select Committee on Sites for Churches in Scotland*, 1837, pp. 335–57, 514–21, 1259–65.
61. See my 'Children of the dead end: the formation of the modern archdiocese of Glasgow, 1815–1914, *Innes Review*, 2, 47 (1992).
62. Cf. Frederich Charles Husenbeth, *The Life of Rt. Rev. John Milner, D.D.*, James Duffy, Dublin, 1862, p. 307.
63. Bishop Murdoch to Revd. Dr Kyle, 21 April and 20 August 1848, Blairs Papers, Scottish Catholic Archives, Edinburgh.
64. *Eighth Report of the Commissioners of Religious Instruction*, 1838, pp. 208–9, 316–17, 376–7.
65. *Scottish Catholic Directory*, 1851, p. 68; Glasgow Archdiocesan Archives, Annual Returns, 1858–60, WD/1, Glasgow Archdiocesan Archives.
66. See Depositors Books, 1851–65 and 1867–85, Glasgow Archdiocesan Archives.
67. J. Dawson Burn, *Autobiography of a Beggar Boy*, London, 1855, p. 4. His real father was an anti-popery weaver (p. 39).
68. Burn, *Autobiography*, pp. 19, 119. Comparable later experiences are W. H. Davies, *Autobiography of a Super Tramp*, Oxford University Press, Oxford, 1960, and Gordon M. Wilson, *Alexander McDonald, Leader of the Miners*, Aberdeen University Press, Aberdeen, 1982.
69. A. J. Cronin, *Shannon's Way*, Gollancz, London, 1948, pp. 46–7.
70. *Scottish Protestant*, 24 April 1852.
71. Bishop John Murdoch to Revd. Dr Smith, 18 October 1848, Blairs Papers, Scottish Catholic Archives, Edinburgh.
72. Annual Returns of Missions, Population and Temporalities, WD2/1, Glasgow Archdiocesan Archives, Glasgow.
73. *Second Report of the Commissioners of Religious Instruction*, 1837, pp. 36, 92, 94.
74. Handley, *The Irish in Scotland*, p. 313. See McCaffrey, 'The stewardship of resources', pp. 359–70.
75. Hibernian Society Minute Book.
76. *Report on the Sanitary Condition*, p. 252.
77. Robert Hay, *Catholicism Thirty Years Ago or the Reminiscences of the Last Years*

of Mrs Kelly, Chronicle Office, Rothesay, 1863. Distributed by Hugh Margey, Clyde St, Glasgow. A modern version was edited by David McRoberts in *Innes Review*, 14 (1963), pp. 64–71.

78. *Annual Reports of the Industrial School, Glasgow*, 1869–89, and *Jubilee Souvenir*, Glasgow, 1897.

79. Magnus MacClean (ed.), *Archaeology, Education, Medical and Charitable Institutions of Glasgow*, British Association, Glasgow, 1901, p. 184; Martha Skinnider, 'Catholic elementary education in Glasgow, 1818–1918', in T. R. Bone (ed.), *Studies in the History of Scottish Education*, London University Press, London, 1967; J. H. Treble, 'The development of Roman Catholic education in Scotland, 1878–1918', in David McRoberts (ed.), *Modern Scottish Catholicism*, 1979, pp. 111–39.

80. Annual Returns, Glasgow Archdiocesan Archives, Glasgow.

81. *Supplement Registrar General Scotland, Births, Marriages and Deaths During the Ten Years, 1861–70*, 1874, p. 39.

82. *Census*, 1931 data. See my article, 'Children of the dead end: the formation of the modern archdiocese of Glasgow', *Innes Review*, 47 (1992).

83. *Glasgow Herald*, 2 and 10 March 1868. Also the *Exile*, 22 November 1884. The quality of articles and debate in the *Glasgow Observer* in the first decade of the twentieth century was very high.

84. See my 'The formation of the Catholic community', *Innes Review*, 33 (1982), for details.

85. Cf. David Gerber, 'Modernity in the service of tradition: Catholic lay trustees and Buffalo's St. Louis Church and the transformation of European communal thought, 1829–55', *Journal of Social History*, 4, 15 (1982), pp. 655–84.

86. See David Oswald Hunter Blair, *A Medley of Memories: Fifty Years Recollections of a Benedictine Monk*, Arnold, London, 1919, p. 221; *A New Medley of Memories*, Arnold, London, 1922; *A Last Medley of Memories*, Arnold, London, 1936, pp. 109, 284.

87. See my 'Formation of the Catholic community', and 'The second spring in Scotland', *Clergy Review* (1981), pp. 66, 281–90 and 312–19. Monteith's son was to attack the Home Rule movement vigorously.

88. See Handley, *The Irish in Modern Scotland*, pp. 88–92; D. A. McRoberts, 'The restoration of the Scottish Catholic hierarchy in 1878', in his collection of essays, *Modern Scottish Catholicism*, 1979, pp. 3–29. A corrective to these clerical views is McCaffrey, 'Roman Catholics', *Records of the Scottish Church History Society*, 1983. See also V. A. McClelland, 'The Irish clergy and Archbishop Manning's Visitation to the Western District of Scotland, 1867', *Catholic Historical Review*, 1, 53 (1967–68), pp. 1–27 and pp. 229–50, and also his 'Documents relating to the appointment of a Delegate Apostolic for Scotland', *Innes Review*, 2, 8 (1957), pp. 93–8; and my 'Catholics to wealth'.

89. See my 'Formation of the Catholic community', 1982.

90. See my 'Formation of the Catholic community'.

91. E.g. *The Tablet*, 15 Nov. 1882. See my 'Formation of the Catholic community'; Emmet Larkin, 'The devotional revolution in Ireland', *American Historical Review*, 3, 77 (1982), pp. 625–52; and J. H. Murphy,' The role of the Vincentian Missions in the Irish Counter-Reformation of the mid-nineteenth century', *Irish Historical Studies*, 94, 24 (1984–5), pp. 152–71.

92. Catholic Schools Committee Papers, Liverpool University, and annual *Reports of Religious Examination of Schools*, 1878–9 onwards, archdiocese of Glasgow.

93. Catholic Schools Committee Papers. See Handley, *The Irish in Modern Scotland*, pp. 225–6, and T. A. Fitzpatrick, *Catholic Education in South West Scotland before 1972: its Contribution to the Change of Status of the Catholic Community of the Area*, Aberdeen University Press, Aberdeen, 1985.

94. James Darragh, 'The apostolic visitation of Scotland, 1912 and 1917', and Teresa Gourlay, 'Catholic education in Scotland since 1918', *Innes Review*, 1, 41 (1990), pp. 7–118 and pp. 119–31.

95. Handley, *The Irish in Modern Scotland*, pp. 252–9.

96. See Kathleen Tynan, *Life of Father Mathew*, Burns and Oates, London, 1908, and Patrick Rogers, *Fr. Theobald Mathew*, Browne and Nolan, Dublin, 1943, pp. 78–80.

97. See my article, 'A Glasgow pastoral plan', *Innes Review*, 1, 35, 1984, pp. 33–6.

98. *The Tablet*, 22 Feb. 1845; 18 Sept. 1847; 28 April 1848. Also see my 'Robert Monteith', *Downside Review*, 1979. Charles Dickens was invited to its annual gathering in 1842. It faded in the late 1840s.

99. Revd. Dr Alexander Duff, Edinburgh, in *Ultramontanism: a Full Report of the Great Public Meeting in the Interests of Civil and Religious Freedom, Glasgow, 7 October 1874*, Glasgow, 1874, p. 46. See my 'The Welfare State within the state: the St Vincent de Paul Society in Glasgow, 1848–1920', *Studies in Church History*, 23 (1986), pp. 445–59.

100. *Factory Commission, First Report*, 1833, I. 103–4; R. G. Kirby and A. E. Musson, *The Voice of the People: John Doherty, 1798–1854, Trade Unionist, Radical and Factory Reformer*, Manchester University Press, Manchester 1975; James Connolly, *Labour in Irish History*, (original edition Maunsel, Dublin, 1914) reprinted in *Labour in Ireland*, Maunsel, Dublin, 1917, pp. 145–58; Gordon Wilson, *Alexander McDonald*, pp. 202–3; A. B. Campbell, *The Lanarkshire Miners*, 1979, pp. 294, 300. Critics of the alleged inherent migrant conservatism have to explain their militancy in America. For example Grace Palladino, *Another Civil War: Labour, Capital and the State in the Anthracite Region of Pennsylvania, 1840–1866*, University of Illinois, Urbana, 1990, pp. 54–5.

101. See P. Lavelle, *The Irish Landlord since the Revolution*, W. B. Kelly, Dublin, 1870, p. 271.

102. *North British Daily Mail*, 23 Feb. 1884. See E. P. Lawrence, *Henry George in the British Isles*, Michigan State, East Lansing, Michigan, 1957.

103. *Christian Socialist*, July 1884.

104. R. Ellmann, *Oscar Wilde*, Knopf, New York, 1987, pp. 25, 627.

105. See Denvir, *The Irish in Britain*, pp. 265–77.

106. G. M. Wilson, *Alexander McDonald*, pp. 202–3.

107. See T. M. Devine's magisterial work, *The Great Highland Famine: Hunger, Emigration and the Scottish Highlands in the Nineteenth Century*, John Donald, Edinburgh, 1988.

108. See inaugural statement in the *Exile*, 30 Aug. 1884.

109. *Exile*, 18 Oct. 1884.

110. *Exile*, 15 Nov. 1884; J. Redpath, *Talks about Ireland*, P. J. Kenedy, New York, 1881; R. R. Greene, 'American Catholics and the Irish Land League, 1879–1882', *Catholic Historical Review*, 1, 25 (1949), pp. 19–42; T. W. Moody, 'Michael Davitt and the British Labour Movement, 1882–1906', *TRHS*, 5th series, 3 (1953), pp. 53–76; James Hunter, 'The Gaelic connection: the Highlands, Ireland and nationalism, 1873–1922', *Scottish Historical Review*, 54 (1974), pp. 178–204.

111. Handley, *The Irish in Modern Scotland*, pp. 261–301; R. J. Finlay, 'Nationalism, race, religion'.
112. See Walker, 'Protestant Irish', pp. 60–1 and his 'Orange Order', pp. 177–206.
113. *Exile*, 11 and 25 Oct. 1884.
114. Quoted in the *Bulwark*, April 1906.
115. See also David Fitzpatrick, 'A curious middle place' 1989, pp. 21–3.
116. Denvir, *The Irish in Britain*, 1892, p. 450.
117. *Exile*, 1884–5, and *Glasgow Observer* to 1914 contain numerous references.
118. John Lavery, *Life of a Painter*, Cassell, London, 1940; Roger Bilcliffe, *The Glasgow Boys: the Glasgow School of Painting, 1875–1895*, London 1985; Julian Campbell, *The Irish Impressionists: Irish Artists in France and Belgium, 1850–1914*, National Gallery of Ireland, Dublin, 1984, pp. 41–8, 64–7; Julian Campbell, *Frank O'Meara*, Dublin Corporation for the Hugh Lane Municipal Gallery, Dublin, 1989.
119. See Revd. Joseph Curry, 'Leakage from the Catholic Church in Great Britain', *Irish Ecclesiastical Record*, 12 N.S. (October 1890), pp. 914–26, especially pp. 924–5.
120. See *Exile*, 1884–5, and *Catholic Observer* for weekly reports. Some games ended in riots as a Bo'ness-Edinburgh Hibs game. The *Exile*, 20 Sept. 1884.
121. See my 'The Irish abroad: Michael Condon', pp. 279–97.
122. Handley, *The Celtic Story*, and Gerry Docherty and P. Thomson, *100 Years of Hibs*, John Donald, Edinburgh, 1975.
123. See David Oswald Hunter Blair, *In Victorian Days and Other Papers*, Longman, London, 1939, pp. 115–43.
124. Ellmann, *Oscar Wilde*, pp. 262–3, 275–83, 307–9, 387–96, 575–6; Brocard Sewell, *Two Friends, John Gray and André Raffalovich*, St Albert's Press, Aylesford, 1963, and *In The Dorian Mode, A Life of John Gray, 1866–1934*, Tabb House, Padstow, 1983; Jerusha Hull McCormack, *John Gray: Poet, Dandy and Priest*, Brandeis University Press, Hanover, NH, 1991, and Aspinwall, 'Broadfield revisited: some Scottish Catholic responses to wealth, 1918–40', pp. 393–406.
125. See P. Dougan, 'Irish life in Glasgow', *Catholic Bulletin*, 3 (1913), p. 730, quoted by David Fitzpatrick, 'A curious middle place', p. 52.
126. See Hirsch, *Urban Revolt, passim*, and David M. Emmons, *The Butte Irish: Class and Ethnicity in an American Mining Town, 1875–1925*, University of Illinois Press, Urbana, 1989, pp. 38–40, 50.
127. See Hugh Quigley, *The Cross and the Shamrock*, P. Donahoe, Boston, 1853.
128. See Patrick O'Sullivan, 'Patrick Macgill, the making of a writer', in S. Hutton and P. Stewart (eds), *Ireland's Histories: Aspects of State, Society and Ideology*, Routledge, London, 1991, and my 'Patrick Macgill, 1890–1963', *Contemporary Review*, 258 (June 1991), pp. 320–5 and my essay in *Studies in Church History*, 28, (1992), pp. 499–513.
129. See Samuel Levenson, *James Connolly*, Martin Brian and O'Keefe, London, 1973, pp. 21–43, 73, 79, 81–3, 104–5, 187–92, 196.
130. J. Wheatley, *The Catholic Workingman*, Catholic Socialist Society, Glasgow, 1909, p. 5. Also pp. 1, 12–14. He quotes Revd. Pries who described the deaths of seven Irish railway workers near Paisley, an incident which is very similar to one described by Patrick Macgill in his novel.
131. See Wheatley, *The Catholic Workingman*; Hubert Bland, *Socialism and the Catholic Faith*, Catholic Socialist Society, London, 1910; W. Gallacher, *Revolt on the Clyde*, Lawrence and Wishart, London, 1978 ed., p. 22, and *The Last*

Memoirs, Lawrence and Wishart, London, 1966. Also Gilley, 'Catholics and Socialists in Glasgow', and Ian S. Wood,' John Wheatley, the Irish and the Labour Movement in Scotland', *Innes Review*, 2, 31, (1980), pp. 71–85.

132.   See my 'Broadfield revisited'.

133.   John S. Phillimore, 'The prospects of the Catholic Church in Scotland', *Dublin Review*, 171 (1922), pp. 183–98.

134.   See Handley, *The Irish in Scotland*, pp. 352–3; and also S. J. Brown, and Tom Gallagher's studies on Edinburgh and Glasgow.

135.   On recent Scottish developments see David McCrone's excellent *Scotland: the Stateless Nation*, Polygon, Edinburgh, 1992.

7 From the cradle to the grave: popular Catholicism among the Irish in Wales

Paul O'Leary

In the mid-nineteenth century, Irish Catholicism underwent a basic transformation. From being a peasant religion based on a network of festal practices, it became a Mass-centred form of worship which accorded the clergy a role in popular culture they had not previously enjoyed. As this occurred, the clergy made strenuous efforts to impose orthodox 'Roman' practices upon everyday ritual, partly by enjoining the Irish to attend Mass regularly and the sacraments more frequently, and partly by reforming those popular religious rituals of which the Church disapproved. This chapter assesses the impact of this reforming zeal by examining the ways in which attitudes to the three central rites which define the 'borders of a Christian kinship'[1] — birth, marriage and death — underwent change among the Irish in Wales.

Irish migrants in Wales operated in a context substantially different from that inhabited by their countrymen and women in Scotland and England. The Welsh language, spoken by the vast majority of the host population in the mid-century, was the medium through which much of the business of everyday life was conducted. Equally important for the subject under discussion was the fact that the alienation of the Welsh from the anglicized Established Church had resulted not in wholesale irreligion but in the spectacular growth of the Nonconformist denominations. When the government conducted a religious census in 1851 it discovered that just over half the population of Wales had attended a place of worship and that three-quarters of these had worshipped at a Nonconformist chapel.[2] Given the way that intellectuals increasingly defined the essence of Welsh nationality in terms of a populist Protestant Nonconformity, Catholicism came to be seen exclusively in terms of an immigrant experience.[3]

Although it remained a minority religion in Wales, Catholicism had experienced a substantial rate of growth. Between 1773 and 1839 the number of practising Catholics increased by 735 per cent compared with a rate of 212 per cent in England, and this before the great influx of Famine Irish. In Wales the increase was almost completely attributable to the influx of Irish workers seeking work in the new industrial concerns of the country and they had outnumbered their Welsh co-religionists as early as the 1820s. The emergence of a Catholic culture identified closely with Irish migrants in a country whose majority religious culture was expressed through Welsh-speaking Protestant Nonconformity helped to define denominational constituencies clearly.

Under these circumstances, the Catholic Church should have been well placed to set about the onerous task of establishing parish networks and asserting its structures of authority and discipline in migrant communities. Only by achieving this could the Church ensure that Catholic values were transmitted from generation to generation.

Popular practice

Closer attention to the religious habits of the migrant Irish shows that they fell far short of the clergy's high expectations. Bishop Brown complained in a private letter that the neglect of Sunday Mass in south Wales was caused by the 'imperfect early religious training of many Catholics from Ireland',[4] an attitude shared by a number of his priests. When these views were made public, however, they were rarely accepted meekly by the congregation concerned. As late as 1910 the parish priest at Pontllanfraith in Monmouthshire was criticized for denouncing his congregation as 'the scum of Ireland and rotten Catholics'. One who heard the accusation believed that there would be a greater willingness to support a priest who 'would treat them as Irishmen and not as apostates'.[5]

The clergy were aware that the survival of Catholicism in a pluralist society depended upon the maintenance of a definite cultural boundary between Catholic and non-Catholic. This meant interweaving orthodox Catholicism with an ethnic Irish identity. In practice, many migrants refused to accept the authority of the priest and were resistant to attempts to reform their behaviour. The tensions which characterized the relationship between clergy and lay people had a history which extended at least as far back as the seventeenth century. In Ireland the Church had failed to establish the code of religious observance promoted during the Counter-Reformation. It was not until the mid-nineteenth century, with the upheaval associated with the Famine, that the Church found itself in a position to achieve the kind of reforms of popular practice envisaged two centuries earlier.[6] Similar attempts were made to transform the customs and rituals of the migrant Irish.

One way of assessing the impact of this impetus for reform is to calculate the frequency of Irish attendance at Mass. Levels of attendance had been low in pre-Famine Ireland, and the conditions in industrial south Wales were scarcely more propitious. Few meaningful statistics have survived, but where they do exist they are consistent with the low figures for rural Ireland.[7] However, attendance figures express only one aspect of religious culture. As Hugh McCleod has suggested, seeing Irish Catholicism from the viewpoint of the clergy alone can obscure some of the most salient aspects of the migrants' religious life.[8]

Even when contact with the clergy was infrequent, the Irish in Wales shared a culture which emphasized the difference between Catholic and non-Catholic. Irish friendly societies, Catholic schools and a variety of recreational institutions contributed to the creation of a more diffuse sense of loyalty to Catholicism. The success of the Church in exerting its authority and imposing its structures of discipline upon this religious culture can be seen by examining the rites associated with crucial points of transition — birth, death and marriage. It would appear that unlike continental Europe, baptism presented few problems for the Counter-Reformation in Ireland and there is no evidence to suggest that this was a contested area among migrants to Wales. By contrast, the rites surrounding death and marriage were the occasions for dispute.

Death

During the 1840s death was a migrant's close companion. Ships putting into the ports of south Wales disgorged large numbers of poor, diseased and often dying people. Newspapers recorded the horrifying conditions endured by the refugees from famine, many of whom had shared accommodation with animals as ballast in the holds of collier-ships returning to south Wales after delivering coal to Ireland. While not all of the Irish arrived in this condition, the exceptions were sufficiently rare for special note.[9]

For those who lost relatives either during or after the separation of 'exile', the psychological pain could be intense. This double separation of migration and death allowed little opportunity to recover emotionally. To one bereaved Irish woman the threat of removal to Ireland by the Poor Law authorities following the death of her husband was intolerable: 'My husband is dead and buried here and you cannot send me to Ireland.'[10] Under these conditions the punctilious enactment of rituals relating to the dead was a necessary step towards assuaging that pain. Here, also, the clergy believed that the Church should monopolize the ritual surrounding death.

Despite the clergy's disapproval since at least the seventeenth century the wake was flourishing in early nineteenth-century Ireland.[11] Catholicism had failed fully to establish a monopoly over the rites associated with the burial of the dead and popular practice embodied syncretic elements of pagan folk-belief and orthodox Christianity.[12] When the Irish emigrated they continued to 'wake' their dead. It was the feeling that the behaviour associated with these rituals was inconsistent with a Christian burial that fired the zeal of reforming priests. The observation of Thomas Crofton Croker while touring Ireland in 1824 pinpoints the issue well. 'The wake of a corpse,' he wrote, 'is a scene of merriment rather than of mourning.'[13]

When Joseph Keating recalled the death of his grandmother at the Welsh mining village of Mountain Ash in the 1870s he described an event similar to that observed by Crofton Croker in Ireland half a century earlier. It is the most detailed description of Irish wake ceremonial in Wales to have survived:

We played games and told tales of enchantments. When an Irish Catholic died in The Barracks [the Irish neighbourhood] — either a natural death at home or a violent death in the mines — all who could attended the wake. Our kitchen was crowded with men and women, young and old, till three o'clock in the morning. Two lighted candles were at my grandmother's head and another at her feet. On a table near her were saucers of red snuff and tobacco, and a dozen long and short clay pipes. We played Cock in the Corner,[14] Hunt the Button,[15] and told or listened to tales of leprechauns, giants and old hags — wonderful stories that had never been written or printed. The characters in them often arrived at lonely mountain tops, so bleak and far from anywhere else that in those places the cock never crew, the wind never blew and the 'divil' never stopped to put on his morning gown.

The tales enthralled me.

A few of the people on coming in would kneel beside the corpse. As soon as their prayers were finished they joined heartily in the games. We talked of everything except the dead. Good humour, humanity and religion were mixed together and the wakes brought relief and consolation to sorrow.[16]

Pat 'Kiker' O'Leary, born in Cardiff in 1890, also emphasized the gregariousness and play elements to be found in the wake. In addition, he emphasized the availability of alcohol. 'There were pipes and baccy and the quarts of beer flowed all night,' he recalled, 'to stop ourselves sleeping we played hunt the button.' This game entailed one of the company having to discover which of the others held a button in a clenched fist. On more macabre occasions the button would be found in the hand of the corpse itself.[17]

The conspicuous consumption of alcohol and tobacco were acts of sociability and a reaffirmation of group solidarity in the face of death. A Tonypandy publican who recalled supplying beer for an Irish wake in the years before World War I stressed the connection between the provision of alcohol and the financial pressures which befell a family at an unexpected crisis precipitated by death and the cost of a funeral:

The only time we ordered 4½ or 9 gallon casks was when an individual wanted it for a party; and a 4½ generally when an Irishman died and they used to have a wake ... And they used to have the lid of the coffin in the middle of the room and anybody who went there to the Irish wake, you see, would go there, have a drink of beer and they would put some money into the inside of the lid of the coffin to help bury him.[18]

The wake, therefore, acquired a financial as well as a cultural *raison d'être* and often the funeral would be delayed until enough money could be found to meet the expense. Providing alcohol at the wake became a way of raising funds as well as facilitating conviviality.

For their part, the Catholic clergy viewed the boisterousness of the wake celebrations with misgivings. These activities belonged to an alternative culture and denied a role for the priest in the ritual. As such they represented an implicit threat to the authority of the Church. While this state of affairs could be tolerated, if not condoned, in some other aspects of everyday life, the Church had a particular interest in ensuring that its own cere-monies were seen to dominate. After all, death was the final breach in the group's ranks, and ensuring that the Church dominated this ritual meant that Catholicism would play a key element in people's lives at a time of dis-orientating separation.

Priests, who were also concerned to inculcate the worldly values of sobriety, respectability and self-help, were appalled by what they consid-ered to be the excesses indulged in at wakes. Their anxiety derived from such stories as the 'Lazarus of Newtown'. On the third day of a wake in the Newtown, or 'Little Ireland' area of Cardiff, a young widow entered the room where her husband was laid out only to see him rising up. This 'miracle' was produced by three tipsy men who had tied a rope around the corpse and pulled it into a sitting position when the door opened. The event led to the parish priest prohibiting the drinking of alcohol at wakes.[19]

Prohibitory action had been taken far earlier at Newport. Speaking at the annual meeting of the Roman Catholic Association for the Suppression of Drunkenness, Fr Bailey recalled his arrival at the town:

> I well remember many of the painful scenes I witnessed at that time — drunken-ness at the christening, drunkenness at the marriage, drunkenness in the public streets, at most of the funerals and at all the wakes.[20]

But by 1867, he added 'drunkenness at wakes is entirely suppressed.' The success of attempts to suppress drunkenness varied from place to place and from time to time according to the strength of clerical discipline and the receptivity of the Irish to that discipline.

In this context the widely held belief that Irish women adhered more tenaciously to Catholicism than Irish men was reflected in the conviction that the 'grannies' or 'biddies' were, as one priest put it, 'the one strong conservative element ... the one link between the old life and the new.' They were, he insisted,

> the depositories of the faith and piety, the folklore and wake ceremonial and of the poetry ingrained in the Irish nature ... There are, doubtless, biddies now but not the real thing. They have never heard the cry of the banshee, or met real 'Little People', or confessed in Irish or cursed like 'Peggy Rhu'.[21]

As the Irish language was rarely passed on to the children of migrants, this plaintive celebration of a golden past is also a reminder that the intricate wordplay in Irish associated with much of the wake ritual did not survive.

Oral testimony[22] suggests that by the beginning of the twentieth century the wake had become little more than a pious vigil kept by the faithful, although there were exceptions. The Church attempted to assimilate pop-ular practices while imposing a strict morality and a more respectable code of behaviour, thereby cultivating an atmosphere where death without Catholic faith was, in the words of Bishop Hedley, 'a dreadful mystery, and after death a blank.'[23]

In contrast to the jocularity of the wake, the practice of accompanying the corpse to the grave by 'keening' (Irish *caoine*) entailed an ostentatious display of grief. At the end of the eighteenth century Arthur Young described this practice in the following manner: 'both men and women, particularly the latter, are hired to cry, that is to howl the corpse to the grave which they do in a most horrid manner.'[24] According to Thomas Crofton Croker, a quarter of a century later, the practice was in decline.[25] Whereas the wake took place inside the immigrant's home, keening was a public ritual, as ostentatious in its grief as the wake was in its merriment.

One of the few recorded cases of behaviour resembling keening in Wales occurred in Cardiff in 1862, when an Irish family was suffocated by the fumes of a charcoal fire. A newspaper reported that the other residents of the house were roused by 'the peculiar funeral wail of the startled and affrighted relative.'[26] However, this example does not replicate exactly the ritual described by observers of Irish life in the early nineteenth century, and the evidence suggesting that keening survived migration is scarce. The reasons for this are twofold. Firstly, in urban Wales the sensibilities of the Welsh could be offended by the re-enactment of such demonstrative grief in public, especially as the host society had, or was actively forming its own, less vocal, conventions about funerary display.[27] Secondly, the practice was already in decline in Ireland itself and so was unlikely to be doggedly retained by migrants.

Irish migrants were as meticulous about their choice of a place of burial in Wales as, reportedly, they had been in Ireland. In 1850 the Anglican vicar of Wrexham in north-east Wales found that his churchyard was 'rather crowded on the lower or eastern side, and has chiefly been appropriated for the burial of paupers and Irish residents, who would rather carry their dead to Chester, than not be allowed to bury in this old yard.'[28] With the opening of municipal cemeteries the question of where within the cemetery an interment should take place was taken out of the individual's hands. Cemeteries were divided territorially between the different denominations. When laying out the municipal cemetery at Cardiff in 1859 the Corporation not only allotted a large and well-situated division for Catholic use but also erected a substantial Catholic Mortuary Chapel with a vestry. Twenty years later additional land was set apart for Catholic use and in 1885 a bronze bell was added to the chapel at the Corporation's expense.[29]

While relations between the Corporation and Catholics at Cardiff were cordial on this subject, this was not the case everywhere. In 1884 the Local Board at Rhymni obtained permission from Whitehall to borrow £2500 to open a public cemetery. The Marquis of Bute, from whom the land was to be obtained and a convert to Catholicism, stipulated that separate sections were to be allotted to the Established Church and to the Catholic Church. In law this move required that the ground should be consecrated and a chapel built, a course of action which the Nonconformists on the Board resolutely opposed, and a great controversy ensued. In the end the motion was passed by the narrowest of margins.[30] Here again, the issue of choosing a burial place was assimilated to denominational rivalry.

When the body was safely despatched, the possibility of a return of the spirit had to be confronted. Many pre-Famine Irish peasants inhabited a cultural world populated by spirits and fairies, to whom were accorded alternately respect and fear. Stories about ghosts and other manifestations of the spirit world were woven into the very texture of agrarian life. Apparitions and visitations were not unknown among the Irish abroad. When faced with this question Bishop Hedley averred that Catholics should avoid telling or listening to ghost stories, as 'the great majority ... are either idle tales or misleading as regards the future state.'[31]

Changes in the way people thought about an afterlife are difficult to evaluate in the absence of any reliable testimony. However, it would not be unreasonable to assume that observers' comments about the decline of the Irish language among migrants and the lack of any major migration after the 1860s connote a distancing from thought patterns associated with the 'magical'. For the town-bred second and third generations, in particular, the spiritual world was more readily expressed through the sacraments of the Church than the world-view of a rural society they had not known. The clergy encouraged a mentality which accorded the sacraments a status set apart from the non-Catholic world around them. Marriage was a sacrament which, through intermarriage, threatened to admit the non-Catholic world. As a result of this potential for undermining the separateness of Catholicism, the Church expended considerable energy in its attempts to enforce orthodox behaviour.

Marriage

A great deal of the contemporary comment on the marriage customs of the Irish in Wales was coloured by entrenched assumptions about the migrants' sexual habits. Their overcrowded and insanitary accommodation was regarded by middle-class observers as the ideal breeding ground for a debased sexual morality. Public health reports, with their full panoply of scientific language and statistical tabulations, added their authoritative voice to such contentions. H. J. Paine, by no means a consistently hostile commentator on Irish migrant life, articulated the received view in his description of Irish overcrowding at Cardiff in 1854:

> the sexes live [in] and occupy the same rooms indiscriminately, hence early marriage and illegitimate births. Accustomed from a tender age to all kinds of privations, with no regard to comfort and decency, such people are little restrained by a sense of providence. A marriage of improvidence is with them the *rule* — a marriage of providence the *exception*.[32]

References to high rates of illegitimacy among the Irish should be treated with extreme caution. The illegitimacy rate in pre-Famine Ireland was regarded as uncommonly low and there is evidence that the Irish were notable for their underrepresentation in prosecutions for illegitimacy in at least one Welsh town.[33]

The Church considered an orthodox Catholic marriage to be desirable for a number of reasons. Doctrinally, the Church considered marriage to be a sacrament as well as a civil contract, a stance which prevented the acceptance of divorce.[34] In addition, in a society with a plurality of religions the potential for undermining Catholicism by intermarriage between Catholic and non-Catholic was always present, even if this threat was greatly exaggerated. Marriage within the Church would strengthen the ethnic solidarity of migrant settlements by creating a network of interlocking kinship groups and thus provide the basis for the transmission of the faith from generation to generation. However, marriage vows pledged before a Catholic priest had no civil standing before 1837, and so the hierarchy instructed the faithful to go through the Anglican service in addition to the Catholic service. According to J. R. Gillis, many Irish migrants to Britain disobeyed this injunction and satisfied their consciences by simply appearing before the Catholic priest.[35]

Priests — Welsh priests in particular — were faced with difficulties where individuals claimed that their course of action would have been acceptable in Ireland. For example, Fr Joseph Jones, ministering to a congregation in north Wales in 1846, enquired of the bishop whether it was possible to officiate at a private marriage in the bride's house without any prior publicity of the event 'as it is customary in Ireland'.[36] Reading the banns (publicly) was a customary way of involving kin and the wider community in marriage, and the attempt to restrict the service to a private, unannounced event clearly struck Fr Jones as being in some way improper. In 1855 Fr Lewis Harvard had to grapple with a thornier problem. Some years earlier, an Irishwoman in his congregation had been forced into taking part in a Protestant marriage service with an Irishman, although she never lived with him subsequently and never considered herself married. Now she wished to marry another man — could she do so? This was the question Harvard put to the diocesan vicar-general, who enquired why the woman had gone through with the service in the first place. Harvard replied:

> the presumption is, I should say, that the intention requisite for the validity of marriage may not have been possessed on the part of the woman. And this becomes more explicable when it is remembered that the marriage thus contracted in Ireland would not have been invalid. The woman not knowing the difference between circumstances of the two countries could well be under the impression that a marriage in a Protestant Church and before a Protestant clergyman would be invalid.[37]

These were vexing problems, but they were overshadowed by the more pressing issue of marriage between Catholics and members of another religion, that is 'mixed' marriages.

The church gave its approval for mixed marriages on the condition that the Catholic party was allowed free exercise of his/her religion and that any children would be baptized and brought up in the Catholic faith. This assurance was given on a voluntary basis and there was no means of enforcing it in law. The vast majority of such requests were granted speedily, but even Bishop Brown had to consult Rome on the propriety of a Jew and a Catholic marrying in church.[38]

It would appear that intermarriage between Irish and Welsh in the decades immediately after the Famine was relatively infrequent. Yet it is questionable whether endogamy was a realistic option in the long term, given the demographic imbalance between males and females in the Irish community. In all major towns in south Wales, and especially in the iron-producing town of Merthyr Tydfil, there was a predominance of Irish males over females.[39] In his study of the Irish in Cardiff John Hickey has shown that the last quarter of the nineteenth century was the crucial period for an increase in mixed marriages.[40] This was also the period when the debate on 'leakage' from the Church was at its most intense, an indicator of this being Bishop Hedley's influential pastoral letter on 'Mixed Marriages'. This was read out in all churches in the diocese and also published in pamphlet form. Occasionally, parish priests registered mixed marriages separately, but few, if any, did so consistently and the basis upon which the statistics were collected is often unclear. A more reliable impression of the incidence of mixed marriages may be obtained by a comparison of evidence gathered by parochial surveys in 1890 in response to enquiries from Rome.

Answers to a questionnaire circulated by the Sacred Congregation for the Propagation of the Faith to the parish priests of Newport, Cardiff, Merthyr Tydfil and Swansea were remarkably similar. They identified trends over the preceding decade and isolated points of particular importance.[41] At Newport it was estimated that one-fifth of marriages conducted in Catholic churches were mixed, but that 'not more than three or four' couples during the decade had deliberately broken their religious vows. In St David's parish, Swansea, only 41 out of 305 marriages conducted at the church were mixed, of which six couples refused to have their children baptized and there were ten cases where the non-Catholic partner was converted to Catholicism. At Merthyr there had been only 23 approved mixed marriages during the decade: 'some few parties have disappeared, but all we know have honourably fulfilled their engagements.'

These priests unanimously agreed upon the pivotal role of women in transmitting the faith to the children in a mixed marriage. At Newport it was believed that

> matters are worse when the mother is the non-Catholic. The children being mostly with her she cannot give them any true religious training, not having it herself.

At Cardiff, Mgr Williams was confident that a Catholic mother 'would usually procure the baptism of the child stealthily if opposition were made', while Canon Richards of Swansea insisted that 'a Catholic if good and even if careless will put into the child the instinct and some practical habits of the faith.' Canon Wade of Merthyr summed up prevailing clerical opinion when he wrote: 'it is more difficult to keep the children right when the mother is a non-Catholic, she having the complete early control of the children.' The matrifocal orientation of Irish migrant culture can be discerned in these statements, although as far as the religious education of children was concerned there was a compensatory stress on the establishment of separate Catholic schools which existed in nearly all parishes.

The priests who contributed to the survey of 1890 were acutely aware of the limitations of their personal experience, which concerned directly only those marriages conducted in their own churches. Mixed marriages occurred outside the Church also, without clerical approval. At Newport, Fr Cavalli conceded that it was difficult to give the precise number of such marriages 'as such parties carefully conceal the fact', although his enquiries led him to believe that there were four or five cases each year. A similar number was estimated for both Swansea parishes, while at Merthyr Tydfil the cases were believed to be in the region of ten per year. At Cardiff, Mgr Williams noted that few couples were married at the Registrar's Office because Church disapproval for mixed marriages was so rare, a significant point when it is remembered that civil marriages accounted for 43 per cent of the total at Cardiff in 1881.[42]

Each of the contributors to this survey of mixed marriages admitted the tentative nature of his conclusions, stressing that the mobility of members of the congregation did not permit precise statistical returns. Nevertheless, they convey the clear impression that this type of marriage was on the increase and that the Irish were less concerned than the clergy about the potential religious implications. Mgr Williams explained the popular attitude under such circumstances:

the Catholic party rarely gives up the faith in theory, but not infrequently does so in practise, and becomes indifferent, especially if he, or she, has a genuine love and admiration for the other party. The argument in the mind is that if Protestantism can produce a man (or a woman) as good as the party admired, it cannot be bad.

By the 1920s, a decisive change in attitudes to marriages had taken place. A Catholic magazine monitored the statistics of the largest parish in

Table 7.1 Marriages at St Peter's Church, Cardiff, 1920–2

	Total Marriages	Catholic	Mixed	Mixed as %
1920	88	47	41	46.6
1921	75	41	34	45.3
1922	58	28	30	51.7

Source: St Peter's Magazine, III, February 1923, p. 52

Cardiff and found that the birth rate of 40 per thousand in a congregation of between five and six thousand was 'a splendid tribute to the high standard of morality of our people.' Regarding marriage trends it found the statistics less encouraging (see Table 7.1). The editor drew his own conclusions from what became a trend in the interwar years:

> One feature of the marriage registers is the fact that for the first time in the history of our registers, mixed marriages have now passed the 50% mark. It is a matter of serious import. This intermarriage shows that whereas a generation ago our people did not as a whole mix with the people of this country, today the blending of the Irish and the Welsh is going ahead at a great pace.[43]

This survey of the changes in ritual practices surrounding death and marriage allows several tentative conclusions about the changes taking place in popular Catholicism among the Irish in Wales. The attempts of the clergy to impose upon their congregations a more rigorous form of religious piety met with only limited success. The Irish accepted those elements of religious dogma which were relevant to their lives and which did not contradict 'traditional' values. Innovations in religious practice did not wholly supercede pre-existing patterns of behaviour, but were superimposed upon them. Nevertheless, by a tortuous process of confrontation, conciliation and accommodation, the nature of religious ritual changed irrevocably in the seventy years after 1850, with the priest occupying a more defined and prominent role in popular culture.

Notes

1. John Bossy, 'The counter-reformation and the people of Catholic Ireland, 1596–1641', in T. D. Williams (ed.), *Historical Studies VIII*, Dublin, 1971, p. 162.
2. I. G. Jones, 'Introduction', in I. G. Jones and D. Williams (eds), *The Religious Census of 1851: a Calendar of the Returns Relating to Wales, Vol. I, South Wales*, University of Wales Press, Cardiff, 1976, pp. xi–xxxv; I. G. Jones, *Explorations and Explanations: Essays in the Social History of Victorian Wales*, Gomer Press, Llandysul, 1981; E. T. Davies, *A New History of Wales: Religion and Society in the Nineteenth Century*, Christopher Davies, Llandybie, 1981.
3. Paul O'Leary, 'Irish immigration and the Catholic "Welsh District", 1840–1850', in G. H. Jenkins and J. B. Smith (eds), *Politics and Society in Wales, 1840–1922: Essays in Honour of Ieuan Gwynedd Jones*, University of Wales Press, Cardiff, 1988, pp. 29–45.
4. Bishop T. J. Brown to the third Marquis of Bute, undated, Archives of the Archdiocese of Cardiff (AAC), box 123.
5. William Hill to Bishop Hedley, 12 June 1910, AAC, box 61.
6. Bossy, 'The counter-reformation'; Emmet Larkin, 'The devotional revolution in Ireland, 1850–1875', *American Historical Review*, 77 (1972); David W. Miller, 'Irish Catholicism and the Great Famine', *Journal of Social History*, IX (1975); Eugene Hughes, 'The Great Hunger and Irish Catholicism', *Societas* VIII (1978).
7. J. Hickey, *Urban Catholics*, Geoffrey Chapman, London, 1967, pp. 90–4; O'Leary, 'Irish immigration and the Catholic "Welsh District" ', pp. 40–3.

8. Hugh McCleod, 'Popular Catholicism in Irish New York, *c.* 1900', in W. J. Shiels and Diana Woods (eds), *The Churches, Ireland and the Irish*, Oxford, 1989, pp. 353–73.
9. On the Famine influx to south Wales see Paul O'Leary, 'Immigration and integration: a study of the Irish in Wales, 1798–1922', University of Wales PhD thesis, 1989, pp. 26–47.
10. Parliamentary Papers, 1854, XVII, Select Committee on Poor Removal, p. 492.
11. Sean O Súilleabháin, *Irish Wake Amusements*, Mercier Press, Cork, 1967, pp. 146–58; Bossy, 'The counter-reformation', pp. 162–4.
12. S. J. Connolly, *Priests and People in Pre-Famine Ireland, 1780–1845*, Gill and MacMillan, Dublin, 1982, pp. 100–20.
13. T. Crofton Croker, *Researches in the South of Ireland*, London, 1824, p. 170.
14. Probably a version of the game described as 'The Cockfight' in O Súilleabháin, *Irish Wake Amusements*, p. 45.
15. Described by O Súilleabháin, *Irish Wake Amusements*, pp. 116–17.
16. Joseph Keating, *My Struggle for Life*, London, 1916, p. 59. The last wake conforming in large part to this description at Mountain Ash occurred in the author's family in the 1950s.
17. John O'Sullivan, 'How green was their island?', in Stewart Williams (ed.), *The Cardiff Book ii*, Stewart Williams, Bridgend, 1974, p. 22.
18. Transcript of an interview with Mr Bryn Lewis, 28 January 1973, held at the South Wales Miners' Library, Swansea.
19. John O'Sullivan, 'How green was their island?', p. 23. Where the limbs of a dead person were bent by rheumatism or arthritis they would be tied down to straighten them; cutting the ropes would make the corpse sit up; O Súilleabháin, *Irish Wake Amusements*, p. 67.
20. *Monmouthshire Merlin*, 6 July 1867.
21. Canon J. W. Richards, *Reminiscences of the Early Days of the Parish and Church of St Joseph's, Greenhill*, 1919, p. 11.
22. Comments made by Maurice O'Brien, Cardiff. Interviewed by Paul O'Leary, 10 April 1982.
23. *Welsh Catholic Herald*, 20 June 1902.
24. Arthur Young, *A Tour in Ireland ... in the years 1776, 1777 and 1778, and brought down to the end of 1779* [1790], ed. by A. W. Hutton, London, 1892, Pt. 1, p. 249. On keening, see O Súilleabháin, *Irish Wake Amusements*, pp. 130–45.
25. T. Crofton Croker, *Researches in the South of Ireland*, pp. 172–3.
26. *Reformer and South Wales Times*, 14 February 1862.
27. Ruth Richardson, 'Why was death so big in Victorian Britain', in Ralph Houlbrooke (ed.), *Death, Ritual and Bereavement*, Routledge, London and New York, 1989, pp. 105–17.
28. G. T. Clark, *Report to the General Board of Health on a Preliminary Inquiry into the Sanitary Condition of the Inhabitants of Wrexham*, London, 1850, pp. 22–3.
29. *St Peter's Magazine*, VIII (1927), p. 138; J. H. Matthews, (ed.), *Cardiff Records*, IV, Cardiff, 1903, p. 511, and *Cardiff Records*, V, Cardiff, 1905, p. 94.
30. Thomas Jones, *Rhymney Memories*, Welsh Outlook Press, Newtown, 1938, p. 17.
31. Bishop Hedley to Mr Lilley, 6 January 1902. Archives of the Archdiocese of Cardiff.
32. H. J. Paine, *Annual Report of the Officer of Health to the Cardiff Local Board of Health*, Cardiff, 1854, p. 3.
33. K. H. Connell, 'Illegitimacy before the Famine', in his *Irish Peasant Society*, Clarendon Press, Oxford, 1968, pp. 51–86; H. A. Bruce, *Merthyr Tydfil in 1852*,

Merthyr Tydfil, 1852, p. 7.
34. Letter signed by the bishops of England and Wales, 11 April 1866. Printed in the appendix to the *Report of the Royal Commission on the Laws of Marriage*, Parliamentary Papers, 1867–8, XXXII, p. 43.
35. J. R. Gillis, *For Better, For Worse: British Marriages from 1600 to the Present*, Oxford University Press, Oxford and New York, 1985, p. 205.
36. Fr Joseph Jones to Bishop Brown, 16 November 1846, AAC, box 110.
37. Fr Lewis Harvard to Very Revd. J. Wilson, 1 March 1855, AAC, box 116.
38. 'In one case a dispensation was granted for a marriage that had been contracted with a Unitarian — but I know not whether a marriage with a Jew had been tolerated.' Brown to Fr Signini, 3 September 1863, AAC, unnumbered box.
39. Colin G. Pooley, 'Segregation or integration? The residential experience of the Irish in mid-Victorian Britain', in Roger Swift and Sheridan Gilley (eds), *The Irish in Britain 1815–1939*, Pinter, London, 1989, pp. 68–9.
40. J. Hickey, *Urban Catholics*, Geoffrey Chapman, London, 1967, pp. 122–4.
41. The following paragraphs are based on correspondence during April 1890 in AAC, box 51.
42. Olive Anderson, 'The incidence of civil marriage in Victorian England and Wales', *Past and Present*, 69 (November 1975), p. 72.
43. *St Peter's Magazine*, III (February 1923), pp. 52–3.

8 Incorporating and denationalizing the Irish in England: the role of the Catholic Church

Mary J. Hickman

Introduction

There have been many historians of the Irish in England and all have stressed that it is necessary to understand the relationship of Irish communities to Catholicism and the Catholic Church as an institution if the core of Irish Catholic experience in England is to be explained.[1] Broadly there seems to be agreement that by the end of the nineteenth century a close relationship existed between the English Catholic Church and Irish communities, notwithstanding continuing low church attendance. Either this relationship is depicted as beneficial for Irish communities in enabling the migrants to adjust to urban life and to develop a community life, or it is portrayed negatively in that the Catholicism of Irish communities is cited as segregating these communities from the indigenous population. In most of these accounts the Catholic Church is portrayed as determinate in the relationship. The segregationist policy of the Church is assumed to be an inevitable consequence of either a wish to build a jursidictional power base or to pursue its mission against lapsation at all costs.

Despite their useful characterizations of the relationship between the English Catholic Church and Irish communities, most of these accounts are locked within an insulated world of the history of the Irish in England. The accounts are written within frameworks bequeathed by either American sociology or Irish historiography. What is consequently absent is any sustained analysis of the society in England in which Irish migrants were settling, other than the occasionally proferred dichotomy between urban England and rural Ireland. For example, combining both an analysis of English society and of Irish migrants' experience enables a closer examination of the impact of anti-Catholicism and anti-Irishness on relations between the English Catholic Church and Irish communities. It also facilitates a fuller exploration of the role of the state in shaping Irish experience in England.

A review of relations between the Catholic Church and the Irish in England should therefore take account of the full circumstances and conditions which governed the formulation of the Catholic Church's strategies

towards the Irish. In this chapter an examination of the origins and formation of Catholic schools for the children of Irish migrants provides one
avenue for exploring the relationship of the Catholic Church, the British
state and Irish communities. In particular it will examine the extent to
which the Catholic Church was involved in the process of the incorporation of the Irish into national political culture and in the contestation of
Irish identity in England.

This approach will not only place an account of the schooling of the
children of Irish Catholic migrants in the context of the general project of
educating the working class in nineteenth-century England but will locate
the analysis of Irish experience within the general sociology of education.
Part of the project of the sociology of education is to explore how, under
the umbrella of mass education, schools acted as agencies of political
socialization rather than transmitters of literacy, skills and knowledge, and
what effect this had on the working-class child.

British state, anti-Catholicism and Ireland

The basis of relations between the Catholic Church and the British state in
the nineteenth century lay in the fact that the British national state was
founded on Protestantism and anti-Catholicism. It was the existence of the
neighbouring 'popish Irish' as well as an internal 'papist' enemy, which
underpinned national unity between England, Wales and Scotland. To be
a Catholic or to be a Protestant in Britain was not only to be infused with a
religious identity but was also to be politically constituted. The political
identity that accompanied a particular religious affirmation was a national
identity. Protestantism was the basis of the Union of England and Wales
with Scotland, and Catholicism from the sixteenth century onwards was
synonymous with 'the enemy'. The passage of the Relief Acts (which
gradually abolished the Penal Laws) towards the end of the eighteenth
century represented expedience at a time of war rather than a widespread
diminution in hostility to Catholicism.

It is important to remember the extent to which Roman Catholics were
viewed as a reviled minority in nineteenth-century British society. To
Protestants, Catholicism represented a body of superstitious beliefs, idola-
trous worship and vile practices. In addition 'Catholics were imagined to
be potential — and sometimes (as in Ireland) even actual — subversives of
the Protestant constitution.'[2] The corner-stone of this conception of the
Protestant constitution was the religious establishment. Full Catholic
emancipation was seen as undermining the indissoluble link between
religious and secular concerns. Not only was the Church of England, with
its established interests in Ireland, set against any further changes to the
constitutional position of Catholics, but so also were extensive tracts of the
Protestant revival (Baptists, Congregationalists, Presbyterians).

Geoffrey Best points out that these constitutional arguments were, in
reality, complicated by the fact that the Roman Catholic question was

largely an Irish question.[3] The widespread belief that Catholic loyalty to the Crown was of doubtful reliability was overlaid with the fear of rebellion in Ireland. An alliance between the Irish and British working class was a recurring fear throughout the first half of the century.[4] Eventually it was fear of rebellions and disorder in Ireland which united the Whig proponents of legislative change and many of their opponents in Parliament. Ireland had to be pacified and, faced with the mass mobilizations of the Catholic Association and with the threat of civil war looming, the usual military solution would not alone suffice. Catholics would have to be allowed access to Parliament, although it was accompanied by the disenfranchisement of all 40-shilling freeholders in Ireland, which secured the Irish landlords' interests. The Catholic Emancipation Act also included a list of continuing restrictions on Catholics, which involved the preservation of certain hallowed aspects of the Protestant constitution. Thus the monarch, the Lord Chancellor and the Lord-Lieutenant of Ireland had to be Protestant, and Protestant churches remained well established in Britain and Ireland.

In the aftermath of Catholic Emancipation the Tory Party's direct manipulation of anti-Catholicism and anti-Irish sentiment from the 1830s onwards not only fanned both of these hostilities but depended upon them as the base from which the Party's attacks on the Whigs were launched. Cahill (1957), commenting on the anti-Catholic campaigns of the Tories in the mid-nineteenth century, states that:

> Conservatism derived much of its appeal from the fact that conservatives linked their party ideology with British nationalism. Because of the close relationship between Protestantism and British nationalism, Conservative leaders, by treating the Irish question as a religious one, could capitalize upon the emotional complex which influenced the public mind. By their manner of presenting the Irish question, they directed the patriotic sentiments and feelings of the nation in favour of the conservatives and against the Whigs, Liberals and Radicals ... The fact that a No-Popery campaign based upon the Irish issue helped to unite the various interests within the Conservative party cannot be over-emphasized if the emotional force of Conservatism as an ideology is to be understood.[5]

In this sense, as O'Farrell has also pointed out, 'No-Popery' was available as a strategy because of the realities of British politics at the time.[6] Anti-Catholicism could always unite substantial elements of both Anglicans and Dissenters, even though the latter had formed part of the support for Catholic emancipation. In fact, both liberals and radicals, among whom Dissenters figured highly, were always susceptible to the 'Irish question' being presented as a religious one.

Edward Norman makes the point that British anti-Catholicism was unique, despite points of similarity with other equivalent European expressions of anti-Catholicism.[7] Norman argues that this was because it was peculiarly related to popularly subscribed precepts about the ends and nature of the British state. British anti-Catholicism was chauvinistic and almost general in the basis of its support. In contrast, European expressions of anti-Catholicism tended to represent varying class and regional discontents, and it was often inspired more by anticlericalism than opposition to the doctrines of the Church.

Although colonial racism and the ideology of the nation-state were separately generated, they became potently linked in the nineteenth century. Benedict Anderson, in a singular study of nationalism, argues that colonial racism was a major element in that conception of 'Empire' which attempted to weld dynastic legitimacy and national community. Colonial racism generalized a principle of innate, inherited superiority, thus conveying the idea that if, for example, English lords were naturally superior to other Englishmen, this did not matter because other Englishmen were no less superior to the subjected natives in the colonies.[8] During the nineteenth century, colonial racism and the convictions of the Protestant constitution combined to cement the federated state. A monolithic nationalism emerged by the end of the century, the allusions of which were able to bind together not only class to class but sect to church and periphery to centre. Due to their differing national aspirations and different religion it was not to prove possible to cohere the Catholic Irish to the United Kingdom on the same basis. In Britain the problem was: how were a necessary supply of surplus labourers, Irish migrants, to be incorporated into a national political culture which was premised on tenets hostile to their history, culture and identity?

The nineteenth century was a critical period because of the transformation of social relations caused by the processes of industrialization and urbanization. This produced new class forces and new class alliances. An important element in the situation was the existence of large numbers of Irish labour migrants in Britain looking for work to escape the economic devastation which faced them in Ireland. Irish migrants came to a society in which notions about 'Irish Catholics' were already constituted as significant constructs of British national identity and political culture. The arrival of Irish migrants and the revival of the Catholic Church may have been the catalyst for, but they were not the cause of, the nineteenth-century outbursts of anti-Catholicism and anti-Irishness. This was the context in which relations between the English Catholic Church and Irish communities were formed.

The English Catholic Church in the nineteenth century

Apart from employers, magistrates, Poor Law Guardians and, by the mid-century, the police, the institution within which the Irish Catholic migrants most often confronted the English middle class and aristocracy was the Catholic Church. English Catholics at the turn of the nineteenth century were small in number.[9] For the previous two centuries the leadership of English Catholics had been part of the inheritance of the landed and titled aristocracy and gentry who had remained with the Church. Many of them lived far from the capital; their strongholds were areas such as Durham,

Lancashire and Shropshire. The political leadership of English Catholics 'was drawn therefore from a squirearchy which except for religion was indistinguishable from the class which had governed England since the Glorious Revolution.'[10] When English Catholics contemplated Irish Catholics, possibly at Mass, packed into the standing-room area at the back of their churches, or traversing the countryside on their way to the next harvest, they were confronted with people who were distinguishable from themselves on every count except one, their religious denomination, Roman Catholicism.

English Catholics were alarmed at the arrival of Irish Catholics. They might share the same religion, although some doubted this, but differences of class and nationality were overriding. Derogatory views of the Irish and their religious practices were common among English Catholics.[11] Norman comments that the 'Old Catholic' gentry had settled their opinion of Irish Catholicism long before the increase in migration from Ireland in the mid-nineteenth century. One member of the Catholic gentry, Sir John Throckmorton, wrote in 1806, 'The religion of the low Irish forms a strange assemblage of strong faith and much superstition.'[12]

Although many of the prohibitions on Catholic religious practice were relaxed, restrictions on the participation of Catholics in public life remained in place after the second Relief Act became law in 1791. After the experience of the Penal era, and with continuing political suppression, it became paramount for many English Catholics to prove themselves 'an ultra-loyal minority'.[13] The attitudes of English Catholics to Irish migrants were similar to the attitudes of Protestants of the same class and nationality. These attitudes were transfused with an extra caution in the case of English Catholics. Their quest for legitimacy and respectability commenced rather than terminated with Catholic emancipation in 1829. Indebted though they were to the Irish campaign for the extension of Catholic political rights, English Catholics regretted that emancipation became largely an Irish issue,[14] and the presence of Irish migrants in Britain was not welcome. The necessity to prove their loyalty to the state was to be a decisive factor in their relations with the Irish migrants already swelling the ranks of Catholics in England by the end of the eighteenth century.

The anti-Irish hostility which was a crucial element in the attitudes of English Catholics was at odds with the fact that it was the migration of the Irish which enabled substantial expansion of the Church in England. It was the Ultramontane clergy who were in a position to attempt the resolution of this contradiction. For the Ultramontanes the Roman Catholic Church in England was part of a Catholic revival sweeping the Continent, in contrast to the 'Old Catholics' who subscribed to a specifically English Catholicism. The Ultramontanes were no less committed to demonstrating their loyalty to the British state, but their vision of what the Church should be more readily included the notion of a 'dutiful and religious' Irish congregation under the umbrella of Rome.[15] In this context the Irish responded more to Ultramontanism. This was not only because Ultramontane Catholics were active proponents of 'missions to the poor' but also because their fidelity to and championing of Roman authority was more acceptable to the Irish than an aristocratic English Catholicism.[16]

Bossy[17] argues that this alliance between the Ultramontane tendencies amongst the clergy and the Irish was one in which the latter were mere parish fodder for the aggrandizement of the episcopacy. This view marginalizes the significance of the Irish contribution. The Irish contribution to the Church, in the first instance, was numbers. By the 1840s it was clear that a substantial proportion of any growth of the Church would derive from the rapidly increasing numbers of Irish Catholic migrants and their descendants. Bossy estimates that the Irish contribution to the expansion of the Church by 1850 was 70 per cent. It is possible that his assessment is a conservative one. On any tabulation the Irish augmented the Catholic Church in England on a massive scale.

The arrival of Irish migrants transformed the social-class profile of Catholic congregations in urban areas,[18] and without this migration the Church would not have developed its reputation as the only major denomination with a close relationship with its working-class membership. It was the migration of large numbers of Irish Catholics to Britain which resuscitated the Catholic Church as an institution. New parishes had to be established, many churches and schools built and large numbers of priests recruited in order to cater for the rapid expansion of the Church's membership. The 'mission to the Irish' had been under way in a spasmodic and patchy fashion since the eighteenth century. However, from the 1830s onwards it became more systematic and was increasingly directed by an Ultramontane episcopacy.

State, Church and minority community

The 1830s and 1840s were a critical period for securing capitalist social relations in Britain. Education was an important means by which the long-term regulation and transformation of the working class was to be achieved. The Whig/Peelite political ascendancy which dominated government throughout the 1830s and 1840s wished to draw all working-class children into a national system of education, in order to produce the appropriate workforce and political subjects of the future.[19] However, education, more than any other sphere, was concerned with issues of the relationship between religion and the nation-state.

During the 1830s the contours of the problem concerning the education of the children of Irish migrants became apparent. In 1836 a report on *The State of the Irish Poor in Great Britain* appeared. The report noted what it viewed as a considerable improvement in the dress and personal appearance of Irish children after a short attendance in schools and factories. An English Roman Catholic priest stated in evidence

The children of Irish, born in Liverpool, generally go on well; they learn the habits of the English, are more careful and provident than those born in Ireland.

> They are willing and active. There is a decided amelioration in the English-born Irish; the longer they stay the more they improve.[20]

These comments indicated that it was thought that, in the right circumstances, the moral regulation of the Irish was possible and the second generation was the best place to begin.

In line with much contemporary thinking about the working class, education was posited by politicians, the Churches and civil servants as the means by which a transformation of the Irish could be achieved. In addition, it was claimed to be the primary means of securing the political loyalty of the Irish, a problem that did not arise in the same form with the other constituent sections of the working class. The loyalty of the Irish could be won only through a process of incorporation which involved denationalization. The concept of incorporation is used here to refer to the processes by which the state actively attempts to regulate the expression and development of the separate and distinctive identities of potentially oppositional ethnic groups, in order to create and sustain a single nation-state.

Anti-Catholic and anti-Irish hostility were crucial factors in determining the limits of central government action on education in the 1830s and 1840s. The anti-popery of the Anglicans in the late 1830s was a measure of the Church of England's crisis as a national Church; while the anti-popery of many Dissenters in the 1840s and after was a measure of their opposition to the privileged position of the Church of England, and also of their own inability to do more than restrain part of the Church of England's plans. Education was the issue through which these dilemmas were expressed, frequently couched in anti-Irish terms. The importance of this role of anti-Catholicism and anti-Irish hostility in determining the development of the education system has been underestimated.

The forces of anti-Catholicism and the fears of educating Irish Catholics with other working-class children produced a demand for separate schools for Roman Catholics. These demands were expressed at the level of municipal government and were at odds with the central government policy of developing a national system of education which included all children. The prejudice took the form of a fear of contagion. Even the most fierce anti-Catholic overcame their hostility to state funding of any Catholic enterprise in order to guarantee that Irish working-class children were not educated with their own children in interdenominational schools. In the end, the state successfully introduced grant aid for Catholic schools in 1847 against still significant opposition by stressing the dire educational need, and the consequences if neglected, of the poorest and most alien section of the population.[21]

A separate Catholic elementary schools system did not therefore develop because of the sectarian tendencies and ghetto mentality of the Catholic Church and Irish Catholics in Britain. Much of the hierarchy, including Cardinal Wiseman, in the first half of the nineteenth century would have accepted interdenominational schools as long as the Church retained full control of the religious instruction of Catholic children. Separate Catholic schools became inevitable because of the refusal of Anglicans to countenance mixed schools in which anything less than the Authorized Version of the Bible was used as the medium of instruction and because of fears of contamination by Irish Roman Catholics. What emerged by the middle of the nineteenth century, as a result of sustained opposition to the idea of interdenominational education as the basis of a national system, was an education system which segregated and differentiated sections of the working class according to religious denomination and ethnicity.

It was left to the Catholic Church in England to be the chief agency of the incorporation of the Irish population. Joseph Kay, brother of James Kay-Shuttleworth, the first Permanent Secretary of the Education Department, expressed the view that the prosyletization of Irish Catholics was doomed and that only Catholicism could influence this most destitute part of the population:

> What I mean is, that none but the lowest forms of Protestantism will ever affect an ignorant multitude; but that Catholicism is particularly designed for such a multitude; and what I do wish is, that if we may not have an educational system, whereby to fit our people for the reception of Protestantism, that we might again have Roman Catholicism for the people; believing as I do, that it is infinitely better that the people should be superstitiously religious, than that they should be, as at present, ignorant, sensual, and revolutionary infidels.[22]

In the context of rising immigration from Ireland, continuing activity against the Union in Ireland and of renewed Chartist agitation in Britain, the Catholic Church seemed the only agency that held out any hope of restraining and incorporating the Irish Catholic section of the working class.

For Irish children the consequences of government grants being extended to Catholic schools were that they were thus segregated and differentiated from the rest of the population. In other words, the Irish were integrated into a segregated system. Catholic schools became the institutional means of containing Irish children and the symbol of the differentiation of Irish Catholics from the indigenous working class, all of whom, whatever their other differences, shared Protestantism and British national identity. The working class were not solely determined by their class experience; religion and national identity were also important. The Catholic Church and Catholic school were local symbols of an 'enemy within' and were frequently attacked.

Educating the Irish in England

The Vicars Apostolic created the Catholic Poor School Committee (CPSC) in 1847 in order to receive government grant-in-aid. The bishops' intention was not only to provide the organizational framework for the transfer of government money to schools, but, to ensure the existence of a body under their supervision to deal with educational questions.[23] The Catholic bishops of England and Wales charged the CPSC with being responsible for the general interests of the education of the poor. From the outset of the committee's work the bishops stressed the high priority placed on the education of the poor:

> The children of the poor ... are at all times the object of our affection and solicitude, and justly, because on their religious education depends not only their own happiness, but also the well being of the Church and State.[24]

The presentation of the interests of the state, the Church and the Catholic poor as being mutually reinforcing was to be an insistent theme of Catholic education policy.

The name of the committee referred to the 'Catholic Poor' and the specification of the object of Catholic elementary education was the 'Catholic Poor'. For the English Church in the second half of the nineteenth century the term 'Catholic Poor' was their preferred means of distinguishing the Irish component of the Catholic population. In the official discourse of the Church concerning education from the 1840s onwards there is only an occasional reference to the fact that the Catholic poor were composed primarily of Irish migrants and their children. The term 'Catholic Poor' did not draw attention in public discourse to the fact that most of the Catholic poor were Irish. This indicates that in the middle of the nineteenth century a newly restored hierarchy, intent on building and expanding a unified Church, preferred to emphasize the class rather than the national differences within the Catholic body. Social class differences were more acceptable as part of the public profile of the Church than national differences.

However, distinctions were readily made between English and Irish Catholics. Indeed, many English Catholics, as opposed to the clergy, encouraged the highlighting of these differences. It was, for example, clear to all at the time that any references to the Catholic poor, especially in so far as they were perceived as a problem, were references to the Irish. For example, Feheney (1983), writing about the association between Catholicism and delinquency in Victoria London, comments:

> When the Victorians claimed a connection between Catholicism and crime they had of course Irish Catholics of the lower class in mind. Though there were at least three other distinct social groups among Irish Catholics ... the poor Irish made up 90 per cent of the quarter million Catholics in London.[25]

In line with their contemporaries, the Catholic Church put great faith in the powers of education to transform the working class, particularly a Catholic education. In its first report the CPSC asserted:

> It is now commonly allowed, even by persons whose opinions force them to explain away the fact, that the Catholic religion alone is qualified to influence the masses. What these masses now are, it is beside the purpose to describe.

Suffice it to say, that the education of the Catholic Church, and not one or all of the many devices which have been tried, or may be tried, can, and, as far as that education is diffused, will convert these masses into useful citizens, loyal subjects, and good men.[26]

The long-term transformation that Catholic schools were trying to bring about was described a year later in the *Catholic School*, a journal published by the CPSC during the first ten years of its existence:

A working man with a cottage and garden, his own freehold property, and Catholic county voters are charming pictures; and it would rejoice us to think that nothing worse ever became of our School Boys.[27]

The long-term aim of the Catholic authorities therefore was not just to produce good Catholics but also to produce a body of loyal, respectable working-class English Catholics of limited social mobility out of the Irish masses.

Although there were differences between middle-class and aristocratic English Catholics and within the clergy about the probity of accepting state aid for Catholic schools, there is no reason to suspect that they were anything but united on the need to elevate Irish life and on the efficacy of education for that purpose. But English Catholics were more likely to differ about how much contact they wanted with such a project concerning the Irish. The London Oratorians set up a ragged school whose aim was to raise the condition of Irish Catholics in London. Many others wanted no such direct contact. One English Catholic, writing in the *Contemporary Review* in the 1870s, describes the effect of the distance that existed between English and Irish Catholics:

English Catholics are more English than their countrymen in many national qualities, and they have joined less in the changes, political and social, of the modern world. Long training has strengthened in them a pride and reticence which shrinks from alliance, whether with converts of their own race or with the Irish who compose the numerical strength of their Church in England.[28]

However, the same writer bemoans the fact that insufficient recognition is given to the immense Catholic effort towards the Irish:

That the Irish do not figure yet more largely than they do in the criminal statistics of our great cities, that this alien million is not an advanced cancer in the English body politic, is due not to policemen, but to priests; not to 'necessary progress', but to the agents of Catholic charity.
... Apart from its dogmatic value, the use of Catholicism as social cement has probably been underestimated by the fairest sociologist who is not a Catholic; but it will every year gain larger acknowledgement as historic prejudices disappear and the science of human life is better understood.[29]

Thus the English Catholic Church, led by the clergy, set about the task of elementary education convinced of the necessity of transforming the children of Irish migrants and confident of the power of Catholic schooling to achieve their objectives: the production of useful citizens, loyal subjects, decent members of the working population and good Catholics.

As the number of Catholic elementary schools increased, what developed was a hierarchically organized system which united the Catholic body in England as no other enterprise did. The clergy and many of the English Catholic laity were convinced of the charitable necessity of educating the Catholic poor. The clergy were able to elicit the participation of Irish Catholics in the parish on the issue of the education of their children, if not any other issue. The whole enterprise was overseen by the bishops through the agency of the Catholic Poor School Committee (CPSC).

Incorporation and denationalization

A strategy of incorporation and denationalization would only be successful if sufficient numbers of the children of the Irish working class attended school and if there was a degree of uniformity across the country in the form and content of Catholic elementary education. After a massive school building effort in the final three decades of the century, the considerable shortfall in school accommodation which existed in 1870 was redressed and this is reflected in the increasing numbers of Catholic working-class children who did go to school by 1900.

These schools were largely paid for, and built by, their Irish parents. The evidence is that regardless of their own habits of Mass attendance the vast majority of Irish Catholic parents would not have sent their children to any but a Catholic school if one was available. The significance of education in the process of forming both what Irish Catholics became in England and of its impact on relations between the English Catholic Church and Irish communities has received too little attention in most previous accounts of the Irish in England, and thus the complexity of the Church's mission to its congregation has been underestimated.

The strengthening of Catholic identity became the principal rationale of Catholic elementary schools. This was a strategy designed not only to arrest lapsation but also to weaken Irish national identity. In the mid-nineteenth century, in addition to denominational instruction, schools were expected to provide some secular education. Under the arrangements agreed with the various churches in the 1840s, each denomination was given sole control of religious instruction, but the secular curriculum was subject to government inspection and direction. In Catholic elementary schools the greatest priority was placed on religious instruction and this dominated the curriculum. This set a pattern that was to continue throughout much of the next century.

For example, Steven Fielding, writing about Catholics in Manchester in the 1920s, quotes Dean Murray of St Wilfred's in Hulme praising his late headmaster for realizing that:

the true function of a Catholic teacher was to train the soul of the child for Heaven and that foundation of that training should be the moral teaching of Christ as explained and interpreted by the Catholic church. He had an intense love of his church ... He excelled in loyalty to the clergy and in respect for their office, and he instilled that into the children from their earliest years.[30]

Fielding comments that the most important effect of a Catholic education was that it emphasized the centrality of the Church to the individual at a very early age, placing him or her in contact with, and forcing acceptance of, its authority. This was achieved partly by the role accorded the parish priest, but also through the sustained effort injected into the transmission of religious knowledge compared with the periods of secular instruction.

Lynn Hollen Lees, in a brief consideration of the practices of Catholic schools, concludes that, whereas Catholics' secular education was turgid and flat, their religious education in the mid-nineteenth century was a multi-media effort combining the appeal of music, recreation and personal example. Lees points out that we do not know exactly what effects Catholic education had upon Irish workers' children, but she thinks it may be surmised that those who passed through the schools had their Catholic loyalties reinforced and grew in familiarity with the norms and messages of the Church.[31]

The diversity of religious education was encouraged by the hierarchy. Cardinal Wiseman had specifically advocated Italian-style missions for the Irish in London as providing a flamboyant ritual more likely to attract the Irish working class than the restrained practices of English Catholicism. Much later in the century Dr O'Reilly, the bishop of Liverpool, expressed his wish that Catholic schools avoid 'colourless religious teaching in which there is nothing distinctive and dogmatic.'[32] In mid-century the competition with proselytizing Protestant charitable schools, and later the competition of Board schools, were in part responsible for the concentration of the Catholic Church on religious education and the efforts expended to ensure that religion was a spectacular experience.

Considerable attention was also given in the schools to doctrinal instruction. Central to this was learning the catechism. In 1888, after education was made compulsory, the bishops gave detailed instructions to the clergy and Catholic teachers to heighten further the denominational content of the instruction given in Catholic schools. Priests were to conduct catechism classes in school hours; the clergy were to 'superintend and test the religious instruction given to Pupil-Teachers by masters and Mistresses of the schools'; there were to be annual retreats for teachers and pupils; 'objects and pictures of piety were to be placed in the classroom.'[33] Fielding considers that within the schools, religion, as a consequence, seemingly took priority over the rest of the pupils' education. At one school in Manchester, St Edmund's, whereas the government inspector complained about inadequate teaching standards in the secular subjects, the Diocesan Religious Inspector reported in 1928 that the 'children generally gave evidence of being carefully and efficiently trained in Religious Knowledge.'[34]

What took place in the schools was part of a greater plan for winning the continued allegiance of working-class parishioners. Archer (1986) describes how, by the end of the nineteenth century, most of the organizations that would provide the structure of the parish in the following century were founded:

> Ultimately there was an organisation for every stage of life. It started with the schools, for it was required 'on pain of sin' that Catholic children should go to Catholic schools, though there were never enough places for all those baptised as Catholics. Here, through the medium of the questions and answers of the catechism, the tenets of Catholicism were taught and, on Mondays, enquiries were made as to whether the children had attended mass. After school age, separate clubs for boys and girls took over, with a card for registering monthly communion, and on leaving those at the age of eighteen people were to enter the men's or women's Blessed Sacrament Guild.[35]

Other associations proliferated, amongst the most important being the Legion of Mary and the Society of St Vincent de Paul. Not only did this process of incorporation depend on a firm beginning in the school but often the school building served as the social centre for these activities.[36]

This emphasis on the religious education of the children of Irish migrants should not obscure the significance of the secular instruction they received. If overshadowed at first by religion, the teaching of other subjects was to take on greater importance, as it did in other elementary schools. The demand for Catholic pupil-teachers made it imperative even in the mid-nineteenth century that serious attention be given to the secular curriculum. Later the demands of public examinations would have an inevitable impact.

In all other aspects of the curriculum Catholic schools differed very little from other elementary schools for the working class. In the mid-nineteenth century Catholic pupils would have been given only an introduction to basic literacy. Lessons centred on reading, writing, arithmetic and religion. Pupils who stayed long enough to reach higher grades might in addition learn geometry or algebra, history, geography and English grammar.[37] There is little comment on the secular curriculum in the early reports of the CPSC. However, school books are discussed, and an examination of the recommendations of the CPSC gives an indication of what the CPSC considered was appropriate content for the education of Irish working-class children.

In the second issue of the *Catholic School* in 1848 the CPSC signalled that the long-term plan of the committee was to produce a series of school books 'adapted in all respects to the requirements of English Catholic Schools.' In the mean time the CPSC stated 'a general opinion prevails, that the publications of the Commissioners of National Education in Ireland form the best educational course procurable in the English language.'[38] The CPSC noted that the textbooks of the Irish Christian Brothers had been adopted by some schools, but it is clear the CPSC favoured the books of the Irish Commissioners.

The books of the Irish Commissioners came to be widely used in Britain because they were on the Committee of Council's (the Education Committee of the Privy Council) list and therefore grant aid towards their purchase was available. The Irish lesson-books are examples of direct state influence on the content of school books. The Irish Commissioners had been instructed to:

> Exercise the most entire control over all books to be used in the schools, whether in the combined moral and literary, or separate religious instruction; none to be employed in the first, except under the sanction of the Board, nor in the latter, but with the approbation of those members of the board who are of the same religious persuasion with those for whose use they are intended.[39]

In Britain, using the grant system as an incentive, the Committee of Council intended to have a similar influence over secular instruction as the National System of Education in Ireland.

By 1850 the Irish Commissioners had produced 41 titles. On this lengthy list were all the books schools required except for a history text. History was a subject too controversial for the Commissioners to be able to publish an agreed volume.[40] Each volume published had to have the approval of both the Anglican and Roman Catholic archbishops of Dublin. The fact that the Irish Commissioners' books had been approved by a Catholic authority undoubtedly explains why the CPSC favoured these books rather than others on the Committee of Council's list.

An examination of the content of these books gives some indication of the content of education in Catholic schools. J. M. Goldstrom describes the production of the books and points out that if the clamour of Protestants or Catholics was loud enough, an offending passage was removed. For example, references to Ireland proved offensive to some non-Catholics, and Irish geography, history and folklore all but vanished in later editions of the readers. It was this exclusion of references to Ireland that made the readers suitable for schools in England.[41] The object of the Irish Commissioners' books was to diffuse the major tensions in Irish life:

> These pious conservative textbooks were designed, among other things, to cool down two major tension areas in Irish national life: the tension between the Protestants and the Catholics and the tension between the British rulers and their Irish subjects. The books attempted to diffuse these conflicts by stressing Bible knowledge, Christian virtues and a common Anglo-Saxon heritage. They were, in fact, so successful in ignoring the specifics of the situation that they could be used in any school in British ruled territory.[42]

Various themes, the need to respect private property and to preserve the existing social order, were included in the books in a period when in Ireland agrarian outrages against enclosures were commonplace and when agitation against British rule was accelerating.

Most significantly, while the attitude to other nationalities in the textbooks is not hostile, their inhabitants tend to be stereotyped and emerge in none too favourable a light. But, as Goldstrom notes, by implication the English are normal, so normal that their characteristics need no comment. The ideas in the books stem from England and many of the positive examples of a good and advantageous life are based on stories set in England. These books had an obvious propaganda value in Ireland in the mid-nineteenth century. But because of these national characteristics, intertwined with the appropriate lessons in political economy, the books were considered suitable for use in England. The CPSC, concerned as they were with the possibilities of any Protestant bias, would have found nothing to remark upon in the absence of Ireland from the Irish lesson books.

From the beginning of the Catholic elementary system the content of the secular education of Irish working-class children in Britain, therefore, contained little reference to Ireland. What mention was made of Ireland in the new Catholic readers which replaced the Irish lesson-books primarily praised the Catholicity of the Irish as their outstanding feature.[43] These characteristics of Catholic schools curriculum were little changed over a century later.[44] Thus in the priority placed on religious instruction, in the effort which went into religious instruction and in the manner in which the religious pervaded all the rituals of school life, the identity of the children as Catholics was implanted and constantly reinforced. There was a corresponding silence in the curriculum content of Catholic schools about Ireland.

Catholic education and Irish identity

A consideration of the education of the Irish in Britain throws new light on the relationship between the Catholic Church and Irish communities. The evidence presented here suggests that the 'inward-looking, nationalist, Catholic ghetto' areas that many historians of the Irish in England describe were neither the end product of a plan of the Church nor the consequence, necessarily, of the migrants' unwillingness to integrate. Rather, both the strategy of the English Catholic Church towards its Irish congregation and the response of the migrants to their new environment have to be assessed in the context of the economic, political and social changes under way in nineteenth-century Britain. The demand for Irish labour, the paramount need for political stability and the establishment of class alliances combined with the role of anti-Catholicism and anti-Irish hostility, were crucial determinants of the experience of the Irish in Britain.

One consequence was the establishment of a system of separate Catholic schools which still exists today. This system of schools had long-term implications for both the 'integration' of the Irish in England and for Irish identity. Archer (1986), in a study of the Catholic Church in the north-east of England, highlights the extent to which Catholics were viewed as a 'race apart', and the most obvious symbol of this to many non-Catholics was the Catholic school. In an interview with one non-Catholic, who grew up between the two World Wars this century, he elicited the following observations:

we didn't mix you know really, you know at school or anything like this. They were very much at that time a separate community from non-Catholics. I suppose they had their affairs, like dances. I don't remember even mixing with them socially ... they were just a different type of people I think as far as I was concerned — like Jews you know.[45]

Archer cites many other examples of both the perception of the difference between Catholics and non-Catholics on both sides and of the means by which these differences were constantly regenerated. The separate institutions of the Irish Catholic parish, in particular the school, were central to this.

The schools became a crucial instrument in the contestation of Irish identity. As many previous accounts of Irish experience have attested, the clergy were frequently involved in a struggle with Irish groups involved in nationalist and later socialist politics. As Kevin Brehoney has commented, the values promoted in the area of the private, particularly by the Church, paralleled those of the dominant groups of British society, but especially those held by the Tory-Anglican bloc. The tension between those values and other aspects of the Irish identity, together with the political expression of that strain, requires further exploration.[46]

These tensions were explicitly referred to by a priest writing to *The Tablet* in 1885. Home Rule was the dominant political issue for Irish congregations at that time. The priest refers to the fact that his own congregation expected him to speak out on the subject. If he did not do so, he could experience opposition and lose touch with the people.[47] Apart from Cardinal Manning and Bishop Bagshawe of Nottingham, there were no expressions of support for Irish Home Rule by the Church authorities. Greene comments on the relative silence on the issue of the Catholic hierarchy and the Catholic press of the day.[48]

Bishop Goss of Liverpool, from an 'Old Catholic' family, was typical of the type of bishop the Irish encountered. Goss declared of Catholics in 1864:

We have been born on the soil and have all the feelings of Englishmen. And we are proud of the government under which we now live. We believe it to be the best, the most perfect government in the world ... We belong to the nation, in heart we are English, in purpose we are loyal.[49]

Goss was bishop of the diocese with the largest proportion of Irish Catholics in England. P. Doyle describes how Goss angered his Irish co-religionists by condemning Fenianism, which was strong in Liverpool, and when he said the Irish should abstain from drink and other vices. Goss considered that only by playing down their nationality could the Irish be accepted by society. At a St Patrick's night banquet in 1861 he asserted that he was proud to be an English subject and that he thought 'this country' was one of the greatest in the world; he went on, 'When I say this country I mean England, Ireland and Scotland, because it is perfectly chimerical to attempt to separate them — it is an impossibility.'[50] In this statement Goss denies the specificity of Irish national identity and encapsulates the gulf which persisted between English and Irish Catholics on the subject.

In this context, education became the only political issue to challenge Irish national politics amongst the Irish in Britain. The election of 1885 has been subject to particular attention by historians because during the course of it both Parnell, as leader of the Home Rule movement, and Cardinal Manning for different reasons urged the Irish and Catholics respectively not to vote for the Liberals. By the mid-1880s the franchise had been extended to much of the working class. It is, however, difficult to estimate how many Irish men would have qualified for the franchise and even more difficult to estimate how many would have exercised their newly acquired right. C. D. H. Howard, in a detailed examination of a number of constituencies in England in which the Irish and Catholic vote might be significant, concludes that the Catholic education issue determined the votes cast more than did Parnell's call for a boycott of Liberal candidates.[51] The Conservatives duly won the election and the Cross Commission was set up with Cardinal Manning as a prominent member. The recommendations of the Commission formed the main basis of the 1902 Education Act, which secured the rights of denominational schools within the state education system.

Either because of failing to qualify for the franchise or because of a disinclination to participate in the electoral system, it is certain that substantial sections of the Irish working class did not cast a vote in the 1885 election. However, it still remains indicative of the power of the educational issue that it may have had more influence on those who did vote than the claims of the Home Rule movement. What does seem to be suggested in this period is that Irish Catholics were prepared to defend the schools which they largely built. The argument here is that the long-term impact of the identification of the Irish communities with the parish school was important for the incorporation of the Irish and their continuing segregation and differentiation from the rest of the working class.

It is interesting to try and establish the impact of Catholic education in the contest over Irish identity in England. One contemporary account we have suggests the pressure experienced by the second generation to marginalize Irish identity. Tom Barclay, in his memoirs of a bottlewasher, recounts his childhood in Leicester in the 1850s and 1860s. After describing his mother's recitation of old bardic legends and laments he continues:

> But what had I to do with all that? I was becoming English. I did not hate things Irish, but I began to feel that they must be put away; they were inferior to things English ... Outside the house everything was English: my catechism, lessons, prayers, songs, tales, games ... Presently I began to feel ashamed of the jeers and mockery and criticism.[52]

This quotation indicates that 'becoming English' was not based on an inevitable process of cultural assimilation but on acquiring a perception of the inferiority of Irishness compared with Englishness. The cultural pressures to become English and reject Irishness that Barclay cites primarily emanated from the Catholic Church. When young, his world outside the house was defined by the Church and the school.

However, there was often resistance, and the Church could not preordain the manner in which Catholicism became part of the fabric of Irish community life. Robert Darwen has made the point that typical members of the Irish Catholic subculture might have been men who fitted the following description:

> As soon as they leave school they ceased to practise: true they were members of the Catholic club, drank Catholic beer and used the Church when they wanted to celebrate or grieve. They certainly were loyal, they would fight the Protestants: they would not dream of going to a non-Catholic Church: they would encourage their wives to pray to St. Anthony. It was a folk religion that endured while they felt culturally alienated from the English.[53]

There is some evidence that women were likely to remain more involved.[54] Darwen's description was written about a parish in one of the main Irish areas of Liverpool, a city which throughout the nineteenth century had particularly low Mass attendance figures. The contrast between the bishop, Goss, and his congregation could not have been greater and may partly account for both ostensible lapsation rates and for the manner in which Catholicism became part of the identity of Irish communities.

Conclusion

The main objective of this chapter has been to explore the origins and content of Catholic state elementary schooling for the Irish in England. This has been investigated in the context of the general project of educating the working class in nineteenth-century England. Examining the aims of the Catholic hierarchy, as articulated by the CPSC, reveals that both social class and national motives were intertwined in the formation of Catholic elementary school policy. Throughout the nineteenth century the interests of the state, the Catholic Church and the Catholic poor were presented by the bishops and the CPSC as harmonious. Catholic schools were to transform the Irish into useful citizens, loyal subjects, decent members of the working class and good Catholics. The control the Church exerted over the expansion of the Catholic elementary school system ensured that Catholic education was a more uniform experience than it might otherwise have been.

Catholic elementary school policy aimed both at arresting lapsation amongst the Irish and at incorporating them to the British 'body politic'. The incorporation policy was evident from early in the second half of the nineteenth century, with scant references to the Irishness of the Catholic poor being made in public by Catholic authorities. The examination of the expansion of Catholic schools shows that, in effect, the Irish paid for their own incorporation by funding and building the schools and sending their children to them. In the schools, incorporation of the Irish was attempted by strengthening their identity as Catholics and weakening their national identity. Religious education gave the schools their distinctiveness and there was a corresponding absence of information about Ireland in the curriculum content of Catholic elementary schools. Removing the history of Ireland was a chief means of incorporation, through denationalization, because it created a silence in the narrative of history.

The continuing segregation and differentiation of the Irish Catholic working class through their attendance at Catholic schools was ensured by the provisions of the 1870 Education Act, the political climate in which it was introduced and the response of the Catholic episcopacy to the Act. Catholic education was the one issue on which the Church was prepared to take an assertive public position, on the grounds of equality of educational opportunity. Irish Catholic congregations were drawn into the defence of the schools, to the extent of conflicting with their nationalist aspirations. Catholic schooling became the most successful aspect of the mission of the English Catholic Church to the Irish in Britain: successful in that the proportion of parents who sent their children to Catholic schools was higher than the proportion of Catholics who practised their religion. It was in the schools, therefore, that the best hope lay for transforming Irish Catholics. Catholic schools provided the context in which the complexity and contradictions of the relationship of Irish working-class Catholics to the English Catholic Church and to living in Britain were at their most acute.

Notes

1. J. A. Jackson, *The Irish in Britain*, Routledge and Kegan Paul, London, 1963; S. Gilley, 'The Irish', *History Today* (June 1985); L. H. Lees, *Exiles of Erin: Irish Immigrants in Victorian London*, Manchester University Press, Manchester, 1979; W. J. Lowe, *The Irish in Mid-Victorian Lancashire*, Peter Lang, New York, 1989; M. A. G. Ó Tuathaigh, 'The Irish in nineteenth century Britain: problems of integration', in R. Swift and S. Gilley (eds), *The Irish in the Victorian City*, Croom Helm, London, 1985.
2. E. R. Norman, *Anti-Catholicism in Victorian England*, George Allen and Unwin, London, 1968, p. 15.
3. G. F. A. Best, 'The Protestant constitution and its supporters, 1800–1829', *Transactions of the Royal Historical Society*, Vol. 13, 1958.
4. M. Elliott, 'Irish republicanism in England: the first phase 1797–9', in Thomas Bartlett and D. W. Hayton (eds), *Penal Era and Golden Age*, Ulster Historical Foundation, Belfast, 1979; J. Saville, *1848 the British State and the Chartist Movement*, Cambridge University Press, Cambridge, 1987.
5. G. I. Cahill, 'Irish Catholicism and English Toryism', in *Review of Politics*, Vol. 19 (1957), p. 64.
6. P. O'Farrell, *England and Ireland since 1800*, Oxford University Press, Oxford, 1975.
7. Norman, *Anti-Catholicism*, 1968.
8. B. Anderson, *Imagined Communities: Reflections on the Origin and Spread of*

Nationalism, New Left Books, London, 1983.
9. T. G. Holt, 'A note on some eighteenth century statistics', *Recusant History*, Vol. 10 (1969).
10. J. L. Altholz, 'The political behaviour of the English Catholics 1850–1867', *Journal of British Studies*, Vol. 4, 1 (1964), p. 90.
11. M. C. Bishop, 'The social methods of Roman Catholicism in England', *Contemporary Review*, Vol. 29 (1877); B. Ward, *The Sequel to Catholic Emancipation 1830–1850* (2 vols), Longman, London, 1915.
12. E. R. Norman, *The English Catholic Church in the Nineteenth Century*, Clarendon Press, Oxford, 1985, p. 21.
13. J. D. Homes, *More Roman than Rome: English Catholicism in the Nineteenth century*, Burns Oates, 1978.
14. Norman, *English Catholic Church*, 1985.
15. Norman, *English Catholic Church*, 1985.
16. A. Archer, *The Two Catholic Churches. A Study in Oppression*, SCM Press, London, 1986.
17. J. Bossy, *The English Catholic Community, 1570–1850*, Dalton, Longman, London, 1975.
18. J. F. Champ, 'The demographic impact of Irish immigration on Birmingham Catholicism 1800–1850', in W. J. Sheils and D. Wood (eds), *The Churches, Ireland and the Irish: Studies in Church History*. Vol. 25, Basil Blackwell, Oxford, 1989.
19. A. P. Donajrodski, *Social Control in Nineteenth Century Britain*, Croom Helm, London, 1978; P. Corrigan and V. Corrigan, 'State formation and social policy before 1871', in N. Parry *et al.* (eds), *Social Work, Welfare and the State*, Arnold, London, 1979; P. Richards, 'State formation and class struggle, 1832–48', in P. Corrigan (ed.), *Capitalism, State Formation and Class Struggle 1832–48*, Quartet, London, 1980.
20. Quoted in C. Jones, *Immigration and Social Policy in Britain*, Tavistock Books, London, 1977, p. 50.
21. M. J. Hickman, *Religion, Class and Identity: the State, the Catholic Church and the Education of the Irish in Britain*, Avebury Press, Aldershot, 1995.
22. *First Report of the Catholic Poor School Committee*, 1848, p. 55, housed at the Catholic Education Council, London.
23. Norman, *English Catholic Church*, 1985.
24. *First Report of the Catholic Poor School Committee*, 1848, p. 29.
25. J. M. Feheney, 'Delinquency among Irish Catholic children in Victorian London', *Irish Historical Studies*, Vol. 23, (1983), p. 320.
26. *First Report of the Catholic Poor School Committee*, 1848, p. 13.
27. *Catholic School*, Vol. XI (1849), p. 166, housed at the Catholic Education Council, London.
28. Bishop, 'The social methods of Roman Catholicism', *Contemporary Review*, Vol. 29 (1877), p. 603.
29. Bishop, 'Social methods', 1877, p. 607.
30. S. Fielding, 'The Labour Party and Catholics in Manchester 1906–38', *Working Papers Series*, Centre for the Study of Social History, University of Warwick, Warwick, 1988, p. 50.
31. Lees, *Exiles of Erin*, 1979.
32. Quoted in P. Pritchard, 'Churchmen, Catholics and elementary education: a comparison of attitudes and policies in Liverpool during the School Board era', *History of Education*, Vol. 12 (1983), p. 116.
33. Norman, *English Catholic Church*, 1985.

34. Fielding, 'Labour Party and Catholics', 1988, p. 50.
35. Archer, *The Two Catholic Churches*, 1986, p. 93.
36. See: Fielding, 'Labour Party and Catholics', 1988; W. J. Lowe, 'The Lancashire Irish and the Catholic Church 1846–71', *Irish Historical Studies*, Vol. 20, (1976).
37. Lees, *Exiles of Erin*, 1979.
38. *Catholic School*, Vol. II (1848), p. 27.
39. *Eighth Report of the Commissioners appointed by the Lord Lieutenant to Administer Funds Voted by Parliament for the Education of the Poor of Ireland for the Year 1841*, HC 1842, xxiii, p. 172.
40. J. M. Goldstrom, *The Social Content of Education 1808–1870 (a Study of the Working Class School Reader in England and Ireland*, Irish University Press, Shannon, 1972.
41. S. Repo, 'From Pilgrims Progress to Sesame Street: 125 years of colonial readers', in G. Martell (ed.), *The Politics of the Canadian Public School*, James Lewis and Samuel, Toronto, 1974, p. 121.
42. Goldstrom, *Social Content of Education*, 1972.
43. V. A. McClelland, 'The Protestant alliance and Roman Catholic schools, 1872–1874', *Victorian Studies*, Vol. 8 (December 1964), p. 176.
44. M. J. Hickman, *Religion, Class and Identity: the State, the Catholic Church and the Education of the Irish in Britain*, Avebury Press, Aldershot, 1995.
45. Archer, *The Two Catholic Churches*, 1986, p. 58.
46. K. J. Brehoney, 'Schooling the Irish in Britain', *Irish Studies in Britain*, Vol. 8, 1985.
47. T. R. Greene, 'The English Catholic press and the Home Rule Bill, 1885–1886', *Eire-Ireland*, Vol. 10, 3 (1975), p. 23.
48. Greene, 'English Catholic press', 1975.
49. P. Doyle, 'Bishop Goss of Liverpool (1856–1872) and the importance of being English', in S. Mews (ed.), *Religion and National Identity: Studies in Church History*, 18, Basil Blackwell, Oxford, 1982, p. 444.
50. Doyle, *Bishop Goss*, 1982, p. 445.
51. C. H. D. Howard, 'The Parnell manifesto of 21 November 1885 and the schools question', *English Historical Review*, Vol. LXIII (1947).
52. Lees, *Exiles of Erin*, 1979, p. 190.
53. R. Darwen, 'Why the Church fails the city', *Month*, Vol. 19, 7/8 (1986), p. 268.
54. See: R. Samuel, 'The Roman Catholic Church and the Irish poor', in R. Swift and S. Gilley (eds), *The Irish in the Victorian City*, Croom Helm, London, 1985; S. Fielding, *Class and Ethnicity: Irish Catholics in England 1880–1939*, Open University Press, Buckingham, 1993.

9 'A most unenviable reputation': the Christian Brothers and school discipline over two centuries

Barry M. Coldrey

A delegate to the 1947 General Chapter[1] of the Christian Brothers Institute prefaced his remarks on the topic 'Discipline in the schools' by referring to the 'most unenviable reputation' which the Congregation had acquired in its use of corporal punishment. On the question of reputation he was correct. Every novel, memoir, autobiography or oral reflection which makes reference to the Brothers refers to their fearsome discipline in the classroom. 'Irish Christian Brothers' should be rephrased 'International Child Beaters' according to one humorist.

Certainly most Christian Brothers have used corporal punishment in their classrooms over the last two hundred years. However, the Brothers were hardly unique educators in this regard. Yet, the image of the Institute is that its members were quite unusually and exceptionally severe, more unrestrained than teachers in general, more uncontrolled than members of other Religious Institutes serving the Catholic people.

This chapter will examine the issue to see where the truth lies in the images which surround the Brothers, and if their unique severity turns out to be a myth, it will attempt to locate the source or origins of the myth.

When Edmund Rice, a retired businessman, founded the institute, in Waterford, Ireland, in 1802, the Monitorial System of schooling was in vogue for educating the children of the poor. Throughout Europe, education at this time was neither compulsory, nor free, nor secular. With the Monitorial System, one trained teacher could organize the instruction of upwards of 150 pupils in one large room, with the assistance of senior pupils as teaching monitors. In effect, the master taught the monitors, 24 of them in an average room, and the monitors taught the classes of less advanced pupils. Each room was called a 'school'; the 'class' was the five to ten younger pupils instructed by a monitor. The curriculum focused on the '4 Rs' — with religion given a prominent place. The objective was basic literacy and numeracy.[2]

In the first extant outline of his system of education, Rice emphasized a mild, compassionate approach to teaching and children. He wrote: 'Unless for some faults which rarely occur, whipping is never inflicted.'[3] Such an attitude placed him well in advance of contemporary school discipline standards. Indeed, Rice and the first generation of Brothers had given much attention to the twin problems of organization and control of pupils. Considering the large numbers of pupils in each room, pupils from every class in society except the very rich, combined with the complicated manoeuvrings of the Monitorial System, this emphasis on discipline is understandable.[4]

The *Manual of School Government*[5] contains large sections on the various ways of correcting different kinds of pupils. Considerable use is made of prizes to encourage good behaviour and the general attitude to discipline, by the standards of Victorian England, is remarkably free of harshness. A Brother is expected to be a person who works for love and who evokes love:

> The more mildness, affection and kindness appear in his advices and remon-
> strances, the more they (the pupils) will profit by them.[6]

The schoolroom was to be a place of silence. The Brothers were trained to speak little and in a quiet voice. As far as possible they gave directions by signs rather than by words. At the same time the pupils were expected to learn most of their subjects by speaking rather than listening and the learning noise from the various classes was a matter for delicate control. The Monitorial System encouraged 'mechanical discipline' with military overtones.[7]

A good example of the military-type discipline used in a Brothers' school of the mid-nineteenth century is provided by a newspaper account of Br J. Maher in action at St Patrick's School, Liverpool, 1843:

> On entering the school ... the boys were ordered to make a bow, an act which
> was done with great uniformity. Then, at a given signal, made by a 'click' from
> a small instrument which the master held in his hand, the boys ranged them-
> selves around the room. At another 'click' and with almost military precision
> they turned around to show that their clothes were clean also; and at another
> signal they were all in an instant upon the forms.[8]

The Monitorial System demanded a military discipline for its efficient use but in the Brothers' case seems to have dispensed with the harsher corporal punishments. Rice and the first generation of Brothers, recruited from the small Catholic middle class, rejected to a large degree the floggings and general ill-treatment of minors which was the contemporary norm. In the earliest outline of his educational system which survives he had written:

> Unless for some very serious fault, which rarely occurs, corporal punishment is
> not allowed.[9]

By the 1820s the Irish Brothers were in touch with the headquarters of the French Brothers of the Christian Schools in Paris. It was from this source that they received two important disciplinary instruments — the wooden signal and the leather strap. This leather slapper — '13 inches long, 1.25 wide and 0.25 thick' — used only on the hand, was a mild instrument of discipline, in terms of contemporary schools in the British Isles.[10] In fact, use of the strap hardly qualified as corporal punishment at that time. Brother A. Dunphy wrote to the La Salle Brothers' Superior-General in 1826:

> The youth of this country are already deeply indebted to you. We have, from your example, banished all corporal punishment from our schools. Other masters are beginning to take the hint from us. I assure you, you have done no small good, even in the example you have given us in this.[11]

In addition, the use of the strap was carefully regulated — it was not to be given on a boy's writing hand and was normally to be one slap only. The official attitude of the Brothers to its regular use was very unfavourable:

> Blows are a servile form of chastisement and degrade the soul. They ordinarily harden rather than correct, and blunt those fine feelings which render a rational creature sensible to shame. If a master be silent, vigilant, even and reserved in his manner and conduct, he need seldom have recourse to this sort of correction.[12]

The early Christian Brothers, as an association, took a firm standard against severe corporal punishment. In the nineteenth century, British Royal Commissions on education praised them as good disciplinarians, but never faulted them for harshness. On the contrary, it was remarked, with some astonishment, that despite the size of the classes 'the children are kept in good order and the masters seldom have recourse to corporal punishment.'[13] That was in 1825.

In 1857 Br B. Duggan was examined before the Endowed Schools Commission in Cork. He admitted that corporal punishment had not been abolished but claimed that it was used only sparingly: 'my own opinion about it is that five or six boys receiving one slap on the hand in the day is quite sufficient to keep the school in order.' Duggan claimed categorically that boys were never flogged at the school.[14]

At the time of the 1881 Endowed Schools Commission, Mr Keys Moore inspected seven Christian Brothers' schools, and made the following comments to the Commission:

> The relation between teacher and pupil seemed all that could be desired, as there was perfect and prompt obedience without any sign of fear. The discipline was admirable, the Brothers being able to arrange the boys in any way desired almost with a word.[15]

In fact, we will see that the discipline reality in a Brothers' school at this early period could deviate from the sublime as contained in the theory of the *Manual* and the comments of Royal Commissioners, but not to the point where the Brothers were renowned as severe disciplinarians. This notoriety came somewhat later, and for a variety of reasons.

The nineteenth-century reality regarding corporal punishment in schools needs to be touched on, to place the Brothers' approach into context. The ferocious discipline of the great public schools educating upper-class youth, both before and after the reforms initiated by Thomas Arnold at Rugby in the 1840s, has been widely documented, and needs only to be touched on here. In the late eighteenth and early nineteenth centuries, children were seen as defective adults, the fruits of original sin, whose evil propensities were to be beaten out of them — 'Better whipped than damned' in the words of an American Puritan. In addition, flogging was common in the army and navy; not until 1866 did an Act of Parliament limit to 48 the number of lashes that could be given to a seaman for any one offence. Hanging, transportation and whipping were standard punishments throughout the penal system.

In schools, savage and uncontrolled beating remained the chief method of disciplining boys. Indeed, in the same month of the same year, May 1810, when Edmund Rice outlined his educational system, Dr John Keate, Headmaster at Eton, flogged a hundred boys in the Lower Fifth for disobeying a five o'clock holiday roll-call.[16] Even in mid-century, 60 strokes of the birch laid on a boy's buttocks or back was still permitted, though when John Moss, Headmaster at Shrewsbury for 40 years, gave a boy 88 strokes of the cane in 1874, questions were asked in the House of Commons.[17] However, the social class from which public school boys came was far removed from the world of the Christian Brothers in the nineteenth century.

On the other hand, boys in working-class circles were expected to accept the hardships of life at a very tender age. Obedience was the prime virtue expected in the young, and was enforced by 'reprimand, supported by the occasional blow'. Children were hit with sticks, cat-o'-nine-tails, belts and fists.[18] In the work place also, where child labour was common, work targets were maintained with severe corporal punishment. Discipline of children was similar throughout the British Isles among the major religious affiliations. Severity towards children was non-sectarian; nor did attitudes differ between social classes.

By contrast, in the Brothers' schools a kindly discipline seems to have prevailed normally, as the chronicler of St Wilfrid's, Preston, recorded:

> The Brothers seem in a wonderful way to have won the affections of the boys under them and in very large measure to have dispensed with anything in the nature of corporal punishment, but, on their leaving, the rod appears to have come into strong evidence again.[19]

In fact, there had been a shift in the Brothers' attitudes to corporal punishment, both in theory, and to an extent in practice, since Rice's death in 1844. The normal discipline standards in contemporary British education were drawing the Institute away from the ideals of its founder. In 1844 the Institute numbered some hundred men; it was soon to experience a rapid growth in post-Famine Ireland. Rice and his early followers had entered the Congregation as mature men, from secure middle-class backgrounds, and with some education. In the explosion of vocations to the religious orders after 1850, the normal recruit to the Institute became a young teenager. The demands from bishops, priests and people for more and more schools were insatiable. In time, training suffered; the *élan* and status of a small élite Institute became blurred with the advent of a Congregation of a thousand members by 1900. In addition, the Famine may have had its deleterious effect on manners and behaviour.

After Rice's death there was a shift in emphasis in the reprinted *Rules and Constitutions* and in the *Manual of School Government* regarding corporal punishment. In the original seventh chapter of the *Rules and Constitutions* (1832) there appears 'The Brothers shall be ever watchful that *they but rarely correct the Scholars by corporal punishments*; and that in whatever punishment they inflict, they be never prompted by any emotion of passion or impatience.' The italicized words were missing from the 1851 edition of the book. Moreover, the regulations about corporal punishment in the revised *Manual*, which came into force in 1851, contain no exhortation that punishment should be rare. On the contrary, the *Manual* lists offences that should be *severely punished* (my emphasis): lying, using obscene words, irreverent conduct in church or during prayers at school. Those who fight in school should be *punished very severely* (my emphasis). Lighter punishment, 'Slaps on the hands may be inflicted for many causes: as, for not being attentive at the lessons, at the prayers, or at catechism; for being idle in school; for not obeying the signal immediately; for having been too late, and for many and other similar causes.' Theory had changed.[20]

During the first 80 years of the institute's existence there was a single case where a Brother's severity towards a pupil led to his being charged with assault. The events are outlined in some detail in the annals of the O'Connell Schools. The case occurred in 1842 and the contemporary account bears a thorough citation:

The boy being disobedient and obstinate, the Brother took a wooden pointer just at hand and gave him some blows which left ugly marks on his flesh. The boy acquainted his mother when he went home with what had occurred, and she, seeing the state he was in, took him immediately to Jarvis Street Hospital. The doctor who happened to be in attendance was not a Catholic and, having seen the boy's condition, expressed his horror, and advised the woman to summon the master who had been guilty of such barbarity before a magistrate and have him punished for his cruelty. She did so, and the young man had to appear at the Police Court, at that time situated in Henry Street. Two magistrates presided in this court — Dr. Kelly, formerly Secretary to the National Board of Education, a Protestant, and a Mr. Duffy, a Catholic. The Brother Director took the precaution to fee counsel in order to make the best defence he could under the circumstances. But were it not for the high character of the schools, the general esteem in which the Brothers were held throughout the city, and especially the high personal regard which one of the magistrates (Dr. Kelly) had for Mr. Rice, the founder of the Schools, and which regard he expressed in open court from the bench, the culprit would, in all probability, have got six months imprisonment with hard labour.

As it was, he had to stand in the dock while receiving a severe reprimand from the Catholic Magistrate (Duffy) who, in conclusion, warned him that if ever again he was found guilty of the like offence he might expect the full penalty of the law. It may be added that during the writer's long experience in the Institute the above is the only case of its kind that had come under his notice in any of the schools.

The young Brother who was the defendant in the celebrated case continued to teach in the O'Connell Schools for another year but was then dismissed from the Institute, the curt comment 'Sent away; bad tempered' being added to his file.[21]

This remained a unique case for a long while.

The enthusiastic regard for the Brothers' schools which Royal Commissioners showed in 1857–8, 1870 and 1881 suggests that discipline practice did not radically change from that established in the pre-Famine period, at least beyond community tolerance. However, change there was. In Manchester, Br D. Phelan occasionally flogged boys in the accepted British tradition;[22] In Sunderland, a mother, in a celebrated incident, became very angry about the slapping of her lad;[23] and the visitation report on the Christian Brothers' school in Leeds, 1849, indicated that, 'slapping is used freely'.[24]

The memoirs of Edward O'Flynn, a Cork builder, who attended the North Monastery School in the late 1840s to early 1850s, gives a graphic and sympathetic portrait of his teachers, especially Br J. Wiseman, a vigorous Irish nationalist and author of a number of the Institute's first range of textbooks. However, O'Flynn makes it plain that Wiseman's discipline practices approximated to the contemporary British standard, and were a good distance from the standards of the 1832 Rules or their 1851 amendment. O'Flynn recalls that Wiseman 'made great use of the cane', flogging boys especially for lying or smoking.[25]

Another insight into the difficulty of applying the principle of 'no corporal punishment' may be gleaned from the following extract concerning CBS New Ross in the 1850s, soon after the school was established and after the Famine:

Punishment in the home was then more frequent and more severe than it is today. School chastisement, naturally, had to keep in line with it. Boys were much tougher. All of them did not then, as now, accept going to school as an inevitable fate. Not a few of them considered that it was up to the parents and Brothers to succeed in making them go. Legal compulsory attendance had not yet come. The exhortation to go to school as a moral duty was cynically dismissed by not a few schoolboys, as a very doubtful counsel of perfection. 'Mytching' (playing truant) was continuous among a certain set. Being contagious, its treatment demanded a certain ruthlessness in which parent and Brother collaborated frequently. The average age in a particular class was then much higher.[26]

In all this we are still a long way from the extraordinary notoriety of the

Christian Brothers in the matter of corporal punishment, referred to by L. B. Angus in his doctoral ethnography of the Christian Brothers, Newburyport, in 1988. Angus wrote: 'The firm, sometimes repressive or even brutal discipline which has historically been associated with the Brothers schools in Australia is legendary.'[27] The Brothers were deemed severe in their ordinary day schools and more severe in their orphanages and boarding schools. On their reputation, the evidence of novels and autobiographies abounds.

A sympathetic portrait of a Brothers' school in which discipline hardly warrants a mention is rare, the only two cases which come readily to mind being the recollections of C. B. C. Cahirciveen in the 1890s in Joseph O'Connor's *Hostage to Fortune*;[28] and Thomas Keneally's *National Times* article of 1977, in which he recalls his teenage years at St Patrick's College, Strathfield, New South Wales.[29]

On the other hand, M. Farrell in his novel *Thy Tears Might Cease* pictures his hero, Martin Reilly, in terror of the Brothers' harshness and in contempt at their ignorance.[30] In *The Hard Life*, popular Irish novelist Flann O'Brien paints a grim picture of education at CBS Synge Street, Dublin — the school a jail; the Brothers warders; the atmosphere sinister; and the discipline fearsome.[31] The tone of James Plunkett's *Farewell Companions* is light and humorous, but Uncle Charles's description of Christian Brothers teaching is scarcely flattering: 'Coax it into them or beat it into them, but they do the bloody job — that's the motto of the Brothers.'[32] Uncle Charles's tone is approving!

In his bitter memoirs, Irish statesman Noel Browne recalled his Brothers' schooling in the West of Ireland before World War II — 'the cruelly unbridled beatings which constituted discipline', though he admits that he was never punished himself.[33] Though his tone is somewhat lighter, Gay Byrne has similar memories of schooling at Synge St, Dublin, CBS[34] during the 1950s.

There is a strong sense in these books that the Brothers were exceptionally severe, especially from the 1920s to the 1950s, although it may be that the Brothers only seemed more severe since discipline practices were being modified in other schools. Many intellectuals recalling their education with other masters tend however to have similar comments. James Joyce's portrait of the Jesuits at Clongowes Wood scarcely requires mention; and Sean O'Faolain wrote of his schooling at Presentation Brothers College, Cork, that 'punishment was the sole spur (to achievement) within the school.'[35]

Herbert Moran in his provocative pre-World War II book, *Viewless Winds* mentioned his father's education in a rural National School where 'the master flogged in Latin verbs with a blackthorn stick.'[36] Frank O'Connor, in his autobiography, *An Only Child*, had a similar vision of his own National School education:

Tom Downey, the headmaster, combined the sanctimoniousness of a reformed pirate with the brutality of a half-witted drill sergeant. With him the cane was never a mere weapon; it was a real extension of his personality.[37]

Patrick Shea, in his memoirs, recalled the first phase of his education at Deerpark National School where the Principal 'taught by terror'; the Junior teacher's yellow cane 'stung half my body into throbbing agony' and the other assistant 'used his cane with chilling accuracy.' Plainly, in pre-war Ireland, the Christian Brothers had no monopoly of the use of corporal punishment in education.[38] Its wide and apparently accepted use in schools suggests wide acceptance, and extensive use in the home. This is the Brothers' image in Ireland and similar memories permeate past students' recollections in other parts of the world. The Brothers' image for severity permeates the memoirs of Australian Old Boys — as L. B. Angus recalled. Barry Oakley, one of Australia's significant dramatists of the post-war years, remembered his years at a Melbourne Brothers' school in the 1940s in an article for the *Secondary Teacher*. There was Brother Conroy who delivered regular 'leather fusillades' with his strap 'carried gunmanhandy in the hip pocket of his shabby black habit.' Conroy is said to have enjoyed handball after school, and this game 'along with six of the best' was his favourite sport.[39]

Laurie Clancy, a prominent university academic in Melbourne, appeared to have few fond memories of his secondary schooling at the Brothers' college in East St Kilda, Victoria. The Brothers in general were 'well-meaning dullards', 'highly neurotic and bigoted men'. When moved to his not infrequent anger, the form master waved his arms 'like some mad, blackwinged beast.' The strap is described:

> It was a vicious looking thing, about 12 inches long and consisting of six or eight black and brown thin strips of dried leather stitched amateurishly together. It was the stitching that was alleged to make it so painful.[40]

Novelist, Desmond O'Grady, a former pupil of another Melbourne Catholic college, relived his schooldays through his semi-fictional hero Kevin, in *Deschooling Kevin Carew*. 'Kevin felt fear and loathing when the Brothers adopted roughhouse methods,' he says.[41] The instrument which excited this fear and loathing in Laurie Clancy and Desmond O'Grady was the same slapper which the Irish Brothers acquired from the La Salle Institute in the 1820s, when it was considered such a mild instrument of discipline that its use did not qualify for the term 'corporal punishment' at all. Christopher Koch recalled its use by 'a bare-knuckle, old, working-class, Irish-Australian Brother' at St Virgil's College, Hobart, in the 1950s in his novel *The Doubleman*:

> The strapping that follows is agreed to be the worst anyone has seen: a sixer, the maximum. The Navvy (Brother Kinsella) says it's for insolence. His black form seems to rise from the floor as he brings the strap down: the reports are like gunshots. Gathering his strength for each cut, wet lower lip agape, his expression is that of a man on the verge of weeping. Grady's arm begins to shudder; and as he comes back down the aisle, bent over, his crossed hands in his armpits, his

face is blanched.[42]

However, in Australia from the 1930s to the 1950s, from which the above memoirs are culled, physical punishment was not confined to a Christian Brothers' school. The social historian, Helen Townsend, and the novelist, T. A. G. Hungerford, are two commentators who stress the near universality of strict, often physically enforced, discipline in the home and in the school. Townsend writes:

> Modern psychology had made little impression on the average Australian parent of the postwar era ... To many parents, it was clear that if children did the wrong thing, they should be punished, often physically. [Moreover] Twenty years ago, the cane ... was commonly used ... in public schools.[43]

Virtually all the commentators to whom reference has been made are sensitive, middle-class intellectuals, although many had humble working-class origins — hence their schooling at the Christian Brothers, an Institute founded for the special purpose of educating the poor and only exceptionally reaching out to the middle class. Creative writers, almost by definition, tend to be more intelligent and more sensitive than the average citizen, with an acute perception for accurate social commentary. However, their sensibility may not mirror that of the ordinary users of the Brothers' schools. Moreover, the writers seem to show little rounded knowledge of contemporary working-class social life, with its hard edge before the Western world experienced the broad-based affluence of the 1960s and the last quarter century. The Brothers' school was a working-class institution; its values reflected a working-class ethos. The Brothers disciplined children as the working class disciplined its young. It may be that the criticism of the Institute comes from a different class with different sensibilities.

On the other hand, during the 1980s, the Brothers have had their 'unenviable reputation' reinforced from an unusual and unexpected source. Self-conscious working-class Old Boys of the Congregation's residential institutions — Boys' Homes, borstals and orphanages — have circulated stories, often ghost-written by secular journalists, of mind-chilling severity at these homes during the interwar years and until the 1960s when childcare was reorganized throughout the Western world.

When the British government subsidized the establishment of industrial schools and reformatories, for illegitimate, abandoned, poverty-stricken and delinquent youth after the 1860s, Religious Institutes, among them the Christian Brothers, were quick to respond. Their response was immediate because the needs of these abandoned youth of the lowest levels of the working class corresponded with their charisms and vision to relieve the needs of the poor. However, the Brothers' inherited experience was with the regular instruction in day schools of working-class and lower middle-class Catholic youth, often poor but principally from regular family backgrounds. The boys who were placed in, or abandoned to, the Irish and later Australian and Canadian institutions came from the lowest level of the working class — a subculture with which the Brothers had had little experience.[44] The Institute's recruitment was heavily rural in Ireland, and from the respectable working class world-wide. The Christian Brothers were a working-class mission to the working class.

Institutional youth had regularly suffered acute deprivation before their admittance, a deprivation at which the Brothers could only guess because courses in childcare were very much a thing of the future — the 1960s, not the 1880s. The Brothers were normally trained as primary teachers, not as childcare professionals. In institutions Brothers and boys had one another's company around the clock. The work was especially tiring and stressful; recreation away from the institution was rare; holidays few; and the boys' moods and reactions differed from those with a stable family background. Bedwetting among the younger inmates, the result of basic insecurity and poor toilet training, was a pervasive problem, and no solution appeared to be available except primitive aversion therapy. It was likely that stress would lead to violence.

In *Nothing to Say*, Mannix Flynn painted a picture of grim severity at the Brothers' borstal at Letterfrack, Co. Galway — an institution for young urban delinquents on the remote and windswept Atlantic coast.[45] Flynn spent some years there during the 1960s where he claims 'the weather was as hard and cold-blooded as the Brothers.' In the late 1980s, accusations surfaced in Newfoundland (Canada) of a brutal regime in the Brothers' Mt Cashel orphanage near St John's. Fifteen years before Robert Connors charged that his brother had been kicked and slapped at the age of four or five for not making his bed properly;[46] and Shane Earle that he was 'brutally beaten' at the institution.[47] The *Gazette* (Montreal) summarized some of the accusations in an editorial:

> Christian Brothers spanked bare buttocks and punched boys in the head to keep discipline at the Mount Cashel orphanage. William Earle has testified that he was beaten regularly on his bare buttocks for breaking minor rules.[48]

In Australia, Brothers' institutions in Western Australia received similar accusations from ex-British child migrants, brought in under the Child Migration scheme in the late 1940s. Apart from regular discipline with the strap, Brothers are alleged to have flogged boys beyond the bounds of legal punishment, hit them with any instrument which came to hand — walking stick, truck fan belt, sheep stomach, open hand or fist — and imposed a rough-and-ready farmyard regime. Some of the stories are possibly fabricated or exaggerated, but others are undoubtedly true.[49]

The pupils were cheeky and uncontrolled, the times were hard, the staff untrained and government subsidies inadequate. However, discipline procedures diverged by a wide margin from the standards set by General and Provincial Chapters as we shall see, and by an equal distance from the principles set for his Congregation by its founder, Edmund Rice. When did these changes begin to occur and when did the Brothers' image for severity begin to be acquired?

The 1880s were the critical period, and the introduction of organized secondary education into Ireland was the critical factor, involving as it did 'payment by results'. In 1878 the British parliament passed the Intermediate Education (Ireland) Bill which allotted funds for the establishment of a board that would conduct examinations at four secondary levels and award prizes or scholarships to successful candidates as well as results fees to schools from which the qualifying students came.[50]

At that time the schools of the Christian Brothers were considered primary schools, though in fact for many years, work normally deemed 'secondary' was being taught to a significant minority of the pupils. Primary schools were not intended to send pupils for the Intermediate examinations, and the Act had been framed to exclude specifically the ordinary National schools from participation. However, a loophole permitted the Brothers to send candidates and they did so — with increasing success.

It was this success which, ironically, made the Congregation a significant and controversial factor in Irish education; and this role it has retained a century later. The Institute is both a 'significant' and 'controversial' factor in education. Over the 20 years, 1879 until 1900, the Brothers' schools dominated the Intermediate System, their pupils winning as much as 40 per cent of the prize money allotted in many years, and rarely less than one-third of the results' fees.

This success was bitterly resented by the headmasters and clientele of many of the established secondary colleges, because the Brothers were providing secondary education — free or at nominal rates — for a class of pupils deemed not to require secondary education for their stations in life. Moreover, the Brothers teaching the secondary work so successfully, as judged by their consistent results, had never been university trained. This galled many of the masters at established Protestant and Catholic middle-class colleges who were often graduates (in the case of Protestant staff), or priests (in the case of Catholic colleges). The charges against the Brothers were levelled with some venom: their pupils were not suited to secondary work; nor did they require it for their (lowly) vocations; the Brothers were untrained to teach higher classes, especially the classics; they were merely exploiting the pupils to make money for the Institute; they should cease doing so, and return to their *real* mission, that is, to primary education exclusively.

A corollary of the above view was that, since neither Brothers nor their pupils (the 'Paddy Stinks and Mickey Muds' of James Joyce's allusion) were appropriate for secondary education, the only explanation for their continued and aggravating success was that the Brothers were beating their pupils to qualify them beyond their real needs and abilities. Now there was a grain of truth in this; Brothers' discipline did become more urgent and severe in this period. However, discipline in all secondary schools was and remained severe. In fact, 'every' teacher was beating his pupils to facilitate success in the wonderworld of examinations where success promised so much — in this first flush of their modern use. The Brothers' reputation for severity dates from the 1880s, in their involvement in the Irish Intermediate examinations and in equivalent secondary work in other countries where they had schools and colleges. The Brothers never lost this image for severity.[51]

How did the Brothers' Executive react to these changed circumstances in the Brothers' role and image? Matters of school discipline do not appear to have been separately discussed at General Chapters between 1850 and 1896, which suggests that for most of that period these issues were no cause for concern. However, there were changes during the 1880s and at the 1896 General Chapter: a subcommittee was appointed to discuss the issue of 'Corporal Punishment in the Schools.' It appears to have treated the issue of school discipline exhaustively and produced a set of regulations for the Brothers which appear ahead of their times. Its Regulations and their Preamble are worth quoting in some detail:

> With a view to avoiding, as far as possible, the use of corporal punishment in the schools, the Chapter recommends the Brothers to encourage the spirit of emulation amongst the pupils by a judicious use of premiums and privileges.
>
> Every Brother of experience will know how to arouse this spirit; for many useful hints on the subject the attention of the novices is directed to the article 'Greater progress with less punishment' in the *Educational Record* for 1892. The following regulations are to be observed in regard to corporal punishment:
>
> (a) No instrument of punishment is to be used in the schools except a strap of leather, that is not to exceed 13 inches in length, 1.25 inches in width, and 0.25 inch in thickness. In junior schools the strap is to be of smaller dimensions; and in each case the strap is to be supplied by the agent for the sale of our books, Dublin.
>
> (b) No child shall be punished on any part of the body save on the palm of the hand.
>
> (c) Corporal punishment is to be administered by the Brothers only. Assistant teachers and monitors are not allowed to strike the pupils, and Brothers in charge of schools must not permit their assistants and monitors to have straps, sticks or pointers in class unless when they are necessary for pointing on maps or blackboards.
>
> (d) Corporal punishment is not to be administered for separate home lessons. Punishment is to be reserved until all the home lessons under examination shall have been examined.[52]

There were additional regulations banning punishment for failure to answer questions, 'degrading punishments' such as kneeling in front of the class, detention of pupils during recess without the express leave of the principal or the infliction of more than five slaps on any one pupil in any school day.

There things rested and there are no references to Brothers and corporal punishment in the Superior-General's Letter Books over the next four years. However, at the General Chapter of 1900, while no special subcommittee on 'School Discipline' was appointed, the Committee on the Schools did consider the matter, and its comments suggest that the issue had not been fully resolved, that is, that the incidences of corporal punishment had not declined as they were meant to do. It noted in its Report to the Chapter:

It is generally complained that the use of the slapper in the schools is excessive. As the slapping is given chiefly for failure in Home Lessons and for incorrect work in sums, it is recommended that the Home Lessons should be suited to the Junior Classes and consist of what has been taught in school.[53]

The regulations on corporal punishment were fine tuned, and Chapter directed that anything savouring of cruelty or injustice towards the children should be eschewed. The Chapter noted a recent common law decision which reaffirmed the right of a teacher *in loco parentis* to inflict 'moderate and reasonable' punishment on a pupil, but stressed that there were limits beyond which the law would not countenance severe punishment of minors.

The files of the Superior-General, M. T. Moylan, 1900–5, show only two letters in which Moylan or an Assistant wrote criticizing a Brother for using unjust and/or excessive punishment of one of the boys in his class. In November 1901 he wrote to a Brother Alban as follows:

> Though I wrote to you so short a time ago on the necessity of treating the boys with much kindness and observing great prudence when obliged to resort to punishment I very much regret that an instance of very severe punishment alleged to have been inflicted by you within the last two or three days has just been brought under my notice.

Moylan reminded Br Alban that he had been 'extremely imprudent' and 'absolutely unjust' in requiring a boy to come to the monastery after school hours to weed the monastery garden. The boy had not appeared and had been severely punished the following day in class, 'entirely in excess of what the Rule permits' as the Superior-General said. He concluded 'a more signal instance of injustice to a boy I do not remember to have ever heard.'[54]

In the second letter, one of the Assistants, T. I. O'Neill, wrote to a Br Joachim, in May 1905, that his punishment of certain boys in his class had been excessive:[55]

> We have looked into the matter of your severity towards some boys in your school — have heard both sides — and we have no hesitation in saying that you have been altogether too severe in your punishments. I need scarcely say that such conduct will not be tolerated, and if there is any repetition of it, the matter will be of serious consequence to you.

There is no further comment in the archives on either of these two matters. Meanwhile at the General Chapter of 1905, some ten years after the matter of corporal punishment had been raised seriously and urgently, school discipline was further discussed. 'Abuse of corporal punishment existed in some schools', although in others 'the Act is being carried out in the proper spirit and with the best results.'[56] It is difficult to know how accurate this statement was, since most of the Brothers' schools had sections devoted to preparation of pupils for the Intermediate examinations and the enthusiasm for excellent results had by no means abated.

At the conclusion of each Chapter the recently elected Superior was accustomed to write to all the Brothers concerning the deliberations of the recent meeting. After the Chapters of 1896, 1900 and 1905 corporal punishment and school discipline figured strongly in these Circular Letters,[57] and then the emphasis disappeared for many years. In Ireland, especially, political questions came to the fore and the national turbulence made school discipline a low priority for Chapter deliberations.

Over twenty years later a major revision of the *Directory and Rules* of the Institute included two pages on 'Conduct the Brothers are to Observe in Correcting the Pupils' and the principles outlined are along lines similar to those first published in detail at the 1896 Chapter. There is a new emphasis on the Brothers' role in residential schools, since boarding schools were prominent in the Congregation's ministry in Australia, and industrial schools had special prominence in the Institute's work in both Ireland and the Antipodes. In these institutions, the 1927 *Rules* enjoined the Brothers to especial care for the pastoral welfare of the pupils:[58]

> As the Brothers hold the position of parents in regard to the children in these schools, every effort should be made to make the school as much as possible resemble a home; in this way a nice family tone and spirit will be cultivated and much good thereby effected.

In 1933 Superior-General J. J. Hennessy required all principals to see that the children in their respective schools were 'treated with kindness' and that punishment 'should be the exception, not the rule, in the classes.'[59] It is plain that the problem did not disappear, since it was at a somewhat later General Chapter that a delegate, for the first time, remarked on the 'unenviable reputation' of the Brothers in the question of school discipline. This came after more than a half-century of ceaseless exhortation from Chapters, Superiors-General and appropriate sections of the *Rules and Constitutions* for corporal punishment to be minimized.[60] These exhortations and regulations were honoured in the breach by many Brothers most of the time. The way official Congregation policy was ignored by the Brothers is the main finding of this study.

There is something fascinating that this should be so, since the Brothers were dedicated to the ministry of the schools and to the Religious life with its three vows of poverty, chastity and obedience. Since most Brothers were ignoring the repeated admonitions of higher Superiors on school discipline, there must have been weighty reasons why this was so. Until some years after World War II general discipline practice remained severe in schools in the English-speaking world. The Brothers were simply part of this world, with the educational, social and political ideas of their times. Admonitions of the Brothers' executives fell on deaf ears since the Brothers actually teaching in school were part of a long tradition in which corporal punishment was accepted as a normal mode of disciplining students.

Moreover, the Brothers since their foundation had, as one of their primary thrusts, encouraging the social mobility of their deprived, working-class pupils — with the explicit or tacit support of generations of ambitious parents. The education of deprived students for social mobility by means of examination success almost required severity in the class-room.[61] This dilemma between admonitions to kindness and restraint in dealing with boys in school, and the requirements for examination success many Brothers never solved. By means of severe discipline, Brothers, often working class in background themselves, imposed middle-class values on their pupils, to facilitate their entry into middle-class society by way of achievement in school. The imposition of sacrifices on their young was the way people in the severely deprived subculture raised themselves.

In addition, most Brothers, until the 1960s, faced enormous classes of turbulent pupils, with few resources in their day-to-day work in the schools. These problems were accentuated in residential institutions. Punishment was necessary to keep schools and institutions functioning at all, since the nature of the staff/student ratio did not admit of a great deal of freedom for student self-expression. Edmund Rice's zeal for compassion for the poor was side-tracked by the pressures among the deprived themselves for upward social mobility which required, at school level, an intense driving concentration on examination success with pupils under severe control by the Brothers in the thrust for academic achievement. In this quest for social mobility the Brothers had the support of their working-class clientele.

Notes

1. The words 'Institute', 'Order' and 'Congregation' are used interchangeably when reference is made to the Christian Brothers as an organization. The term 'General Chapter' refers to the sexennial meeting of elected delegates from Brothers around the world to discuss the progress and policy of the Congregation and to make appointments.
2. The early part of this chapter is informed by the following work which is not well known outside the Institute, i.e. W. L. Gillespie, *The Christian Brothers in England, 1825–1880*, Burleigh press, Bristol, 1975, pp. 30 ff.
3. M. C. Normoyle, *A Companion to 'A Tree is Planted': the Correspondence of Edmund Rice and His Assistants, 1810–1842*, privately printed, Rome, 1977, p. 3.
4. J. E. Kent, 'The educational ideas of Edmund Rice, founder of the Presentation and Christian Brothers', unpublished MEd thesis, University College, Cork, 1988, p. 90.
5. *The Manual of School Government*, Dublin, 1832, pp. 13–15; 178–9; 187–204. See also *Rules and Constitutions of the Society of Religious Brothers*, Dublin, 1832, Ch. VII.
6. *Manual*, p. 201.
7. J. J. Sullivan, 'The education of Irish Catholics, 1782–1831', Unpublished PhD thesis, Queen's University, Belfast, 1959, pp. 232–3.
8. *Liverpool Journal*, 28 January 1843, p. 4.
9. Rice to archbishop of Cashel, 9 May 1810, Archives of the Christian Brothers, Via della Maglianella, 375, Roma 00166 Italy; hereafter cited as Generalate Archives.
10. Minutes of General Chapters, 1841, No. 5, Generalate Archives.
11. Dunphy to Superior-General, La Salle Brothers, 28 July 1826, de La Salle

232   Barry M. Coldrey

Archives, Via Aurelia, 476, Rome, 00165.
12. *Manual*, p. 193.
13. *First Report ... Irish Education Enquiry*, HC 1825 (400), xii, p. 85.
14. *Report of Her Majesty's Commissioners appointed to Inquire into the Endowments. Funds and Actual Condition of all Schools for Purpose of Education in Ireland. HC 1857–58. Evidence taken before the Commissioners, HC Vol. 1, 1857–58. (2336–II)*, xxii, Part 11, 1, p. 79.
15. *Report of the Commissioners ... Schools Endowed for the Purpose of Education in Ireland*, HC 1881, Vol. 1. (Cd. 2831), p. 128.
16. J. Gathorne-Hardy, *The Public School Phenomenon 597–1977*, Hodder and Stoughton, London, 1977, p. 41. Books on the public schools relevant to this section are legion, and include J. A. Mangan, *The Games Ethic and Imperialism*, Viking, Harmondsworth, 1986; and J. A. Mangan, *Athleticism in the Victorian and Edwardian Public School*, Cambridge University Press, Cambridge, 1981.
17. Gathorne-Hardy, *Public School Phenomenon*, p. 108.
18. J. Benson (ed.), *The Working Class in England 1875–1914*, Croom Helm, London, 1985, p. 4. The following are simply two of the increasing literature on the history of childhood: J. Walvin, *A Child's World: A Social History of English Childhood, 1800–1914*, Penguin, Harmondsworth, 1982; M. Hewitt and I. Pinchbeck, *Children in English Society*, Routledge & Kegan Paul, London, 1973.
19. J. H. Wright, *Notes on the History of Wilfrid's School, Fox St., Preston, 1814–1914*, Preston, 1915, p. 48.
20. W. A. O'Hanlon, 'Brother T. J. Wiseman and his Contemporaries', *Christian Brothers Educational Record*, Rome, 1980, p. 147.
21. The account, written by Brother J. A. Grace, is in the House Annals of the O'Connell Schools, Richmond Street, Dublin. See also: D. Blake, 'John Austin Grace (1800–1886) educator', unpublished PhD thesis, University of Hull, 1986, p. 186 ff.
22. Notes of Visitation, i, Manchester, 1848, Generalate Archives.
23. Gillespie, *Christian Brothers in England*, p. 66.
24. Notes on Visitation, i, Leeds, 1849, Generalate Archives.
25. O'Hanlon, 'Br. T. J. Wiseman', p. 149.
26. J. Donovan, *The History of Christian Brothers School, New Ross, Co. Wexford, 1849–1949*, Freedom Press, Wexford, 1959, cited in D. S. Blake, 'The Christian Brothers and education in nineteenth century Ireland', unpublished Med thesis, University College, Cork, 1977, p. 167. See also: P. Crosbie, *Your Dinner's Poured Out*, O'Brien Press, Dublin 1981. Crosbie recalls that at the opening of CBS North Brunswick St, Dublin, 1869: 'practically all the boys were barefooted. They were an unruly lot, as none had ever been to school before.'
27. L. B. Angus, *Continuity and Change in Catholic Schooling*, Falmer Press, London, 1988, p. 21.
28. J. O'Connor, *Hostage to Fortune*, Dublin, 1983.
29. T. Keneally, 'Memories of a Catholic boyhood', *National Times*, 3–8 October 1977, pp. 18 ff.
30. M. Farrell, *Thy Tears Might Cease*, Hutchinson, London, 1963, pp. 93–8.
31. F. O'Brien, *The Hard Life: an Exegesis of Squalor*, Grafton, London, 1961, p. 25.
32. J. Plunkett, *Farewell Companions*, Coward, McCann and Geoghegan, New York, 1977, p. 30 (Arrow Books, London, 1978).
33. N. Browne, *Against the Tide*, Gill and Macmillan, Dublin, 1987, p. 31.
34. G. Byrne, *The Time of My Life*, Gill & Macmillan, Dublin, 1989, p. 10.
35. S. O'Faolain, *Vive Moi: An Autobiography*, Rupert Hart-Davies, London, 1965, p. 96.

36. H. Moran, *Viewless Winds*, Peter Davies, London, 1939, p. 167.
37. F. O'Connor, *An Only Child*, Macmillan, London, 1961, p. 139.
38. P. Shea, *Voices and the Sound of Drums*, Blackstaff, Belfast, 1981, p. 14.
39. B. Oakley, 'Years of sawdust, the crack of the whip', *The Secondary Teacher*, February 1967, p. 13. On the other hand, Julian Morris (Morris West) in his first novel, *Moon in My Pocket*, Sydney, 1946, while critical of many features of the religious life as lived by the Brothers, does not stress severity in school as being one of their quite numerous faults. R. Blair, *The Christian Brothers*, Currency Press, Sydney, 1976.
40. L. Clancy, *A Collapsible Man*, Outback Press, Fitzroy, 1975, p. 55.
41. D. O'Grady, *Deschooling Kevin Carew*, Wren, Melbourne, 1974, p. 15.
42. C. Koch, *The Doubleman*, Triad, London, 1986, p. 38.
43. H. Townsend, *Baby Boomers: Growing up in Australia in the 1940s, 50s and 80s*, Brookvale, NSW, 1988, p. 81.
44. At this time, primary education was not compulsory in Ireland and such children frequently went to no school at all.
45. M. Flynn, *Nothing to Say*, Ward River Press, Dublin, 1983, p. 67. See also: P. Touher, *Fear of the Collar*, O'Brien Press, Dublin, 1991.
46. *Globe and Mail* (Toronto), 17 November 1989, p. A 10.
47. *Globe and Mail*, 22 November 1989, p. A 5.
48. *Gazette* (Montreal), 23 September 1989, p. B 4.
49. L. P. Welsh, *Geordie — Orphan of the Empire*, Perth, 1989; also L. P. Welsh, *The Bindoon File*, Perth, 1990.
50. These matters are discussed thoroughly in B. M. Coldrey, *Faith and Fatherland: The Christian Brothers and the Development of Irish Revolution, 1838–1921*, Gill and Macmillan, Dublin, 1988, pp. 87–109.
51. Arnold Lunn discusses fear-driven examination success in the Brothers' School in Brisbane (Australia) in the years after World War II in A. Lunn, *Over the Top with Jim*, Macmillan (Aust.), Brisbane, 1991.
52. Minutes, General Chapter 1896, unpublished MS, Christian Brothers Archives, Rome.
53. Minutes, General Chapter 1900, unpublished MS, Christian Brothers Archives, Rome.
54. Moylan to Br Alban, 30 November 1901, Letter Books, M. P. Moylan, Superior-General, Christian Brothers Archives, Rome.
55. O'Neill to Br Joachim, 1 May 1905. Letter Books, M. P. Moylan, Superior-General, Christian Brothers Archives, Rome.
56. Minutes, General Chapter, 1905, unpublished MS, Christian Brothers Archives, Rome.
57. *Circular Letters of Superiors-General of the Brothers of the Christian Schools of Ireland*, Dublin, 1934, pp. 122; 191.
58. *Directory and Rules of the Congregation of the Brothers of the Christian Schools in Ireland*, Dublin, 1927, p. 298.
59. *Circular Letters*, p. 309.
60. Minutes, General Chapter, 1947, unpublished MS, Christian Brothers Archives, Rome.
61. This question of the Christian Brothers and their influence on the upward mobility of Irish and Australian Catholics will be dealt with in another paper.

10 The Irish dimension of an Australian Religious Sisterhood: the Sisters of St Joseph

Janice Tranter

It is no surprise to find the widespread influence of Irish women in Australia through foundations of Religious women's congregations from Ireland. The first Religious women in the Australian colony were the Irish Sisters of Charity, opening their Sydney foundation in 1838. Within a few decades there were many foundations from Ireland by Sisters of Mercy, Presentation Sisters, Dominicans and Brigidines, to name the largest groups.[1] The Irish influence is larger than may appear: at least one congregation of non-Irish origin made their Australian foundation with all Irish personnel.[2]

What is surprising is the large Irish membership in the Australian founded Sisters of St Joseph, from its two separate foundations in the nineteenth century, till now. This chapter explores the Irish dimension of this sisterhood, highlighting the Irish background of the founder and his role in enabling the Sisters to forge their new identity in their new land. It examines the Irish contribution in the two early Josephite foundations, indicates the subsequent flow of new Irish members and explores the missionary impetus of the Irish Sisters.[3]

Origins of the sisterhood and the Irish background of the founder

In March 1866 33-year-old Julian Tenison Woods, parish priest of 22,000 square miles of south-east South Australia, and colonial-born Mary MacKillop, ten years younger, launched a new religious institute at Penola, the small town at the centre of his parish. MacKillop was born in Melbourne, Australia, of Scottish parents. Woods, however, though born and raised in London, had Irish parents of Irish and Anglo-Irish tradition. His father, James, the son of a Cork businessman, was Catholic, though non-practising in Julian's childhood and youth. In Burke's *Landed Gentry in Ireland* he was listed as Queen's Counsel, though he never practised as a barrister, but migrated to London, married in the Catholic St-Georges-in-the-fields Chapel, Southwark, and worked on *The Times*. His literary ability was shared by his sons, five of whom, including Julian, were also journalists, three in Australia.[4] MacLysaght interestingly notes that 'Woods' was a mistranslation of the Irish 'O'Cuill', a distinguished literary family, two of whom were mentioned in the annals.[5] Julian Woods' mother, Henrietta Tenison, was Anglican, the daughter of the Rector of Donoughmore in the present parish of Donard, Co. Wicklow.[6] Her Tenison forebears numbered five more in the Anglican clergy, including an archbishop of Canterbury and a bishop of Ossory. The Woods' London household welcomed many literary and professional visitors, including the Irish poet, Gerald Griffin, his brother, James, Tom Steel, the companion of O'Connell and, especially admired by young Julian, the Irish William Russell, special correspondent on *The Times*.[7]

In 1857, two years after coming to Australia, Julian Woods was ordained priest in St Patrick's, Adelaide. As a child he had most ambivalent denominational affiliations, sometimes not knowing what religion he was. Although sent regularly to the Anglican Church, he was inclined towards the Catholic, he said, through the reverence with which his father spoke of his earlier frequent reception of the sacraments in Ireland. So, at the age of 16, on his own initiative, Julian received his first communion in the Catholic Church. Both parents had impressed on him one particular Christian attitude: 'to assist all in distress was a thing which God and man demanded as a positive duty.' 'Nothing,' he said, 'was so thoroughly engrafted into his mind, until really it became part of his nature, as a spirit of self-sacrificing benevolence.' He recalled his mother, especially, going to 'extraordinary lengths' to assist the poor, and his father 'constantly repeating, "he that mocketh the poor reproacheth his Maker."'

When Woods was sent after ordination to his huge bush parish, 'the spiritual destitution' of the outlying districts struck him 'with terrible reality'. In ten years of travelling around his scattered flock, he 'was constantly brooding over the establishment of a religious order of teaching Sisters', whose members would live in remote areas, far from 'the consolations of religion', and provide, through elementary schools, a sound and truly religious education for the children of the poor, widely scattered Catholic settlers.[9] Woods encapsulated the essence of his vision in the *Rules* for the new Institute: 'the Sisters shall recognise in the children committed to their charge,' he wrote, 'the person of the Infant Jesus.' In the towns, he continued, as well as teaching poor children, the Sisters could care for orphans and destitute persons, but the schools were 'the first care'.[10] In his conception of the Institute at Penola and in his extraordinary efforts to found the Institute at Adelaide, and later at Perthville, near Bathurst, Woods lived out a Christian predilection for the poor learned from his Irish parents, who had seen, at first hand, the impoverished condition of their Irish people.

When Woods visited Ireland in 1850 in the immediate aftermath of the Famine, what impressed him to the degree of improving his 'idea of human nature' was 'the spirit of cheerful kindliness that reigned everywhere in spite of such poverty and suffering.'[11] This unquenchable and seemingly unwarranted optimism resonated with a trait in his own character, a trait he sought to instil into the Sisters.

Noting the Irish influences on the founder is not to overstress them. There were other strong influences: his pursuit of priesthood, despite family opposition; his love of the Eucharist; the Oxford Movement; his period as a Passionist in England and with the Marists in France, especially under the direction of Peter Julian Eymard; the Sisters in the Auvergne, who overturned his notion of nuns and gave him the idea for his own Institute; his unsought path to Australia; his affirmation living among the Jesuits; his meeting with Mary MacKillop, their shared zeal for God and their common goal, in which the new Institute was born; his lifelong enthusiasm for natural science.

Although Woods had, as he said, great 'sympathy and love' for the Irish, he saw himself as a migrant who identified with Australia: 'we have made it our home', he often said, in lectures throughout Australia.[12] Deeply identified with his adopted land, he directed his Institute towards its children. Whether Irish or colonials, the Sisters were to teach in such a way that 'the little ones of the Church' could be 'the means of drawing God's blessing upon all, and the seeds of the future perfection of their generation.'[13] Working with him was MacKillop, sound, intelligent and unwaveringly identified with the Institute. In this way, with MacKillop, Woods offered the Sisters a firm identity in their new land. Woods was sufficiently identified with the Irish, however, to be chosen to speak at the Hobart centenary of Daniel O'Connell's death.[14] Woods's brother, James, who had migrated with his wife, Catherine Griffin, the poet's niece, was a writer for the Adelaide *Irish Harp*.

Early development of the sisterhood and early Irish membership

I now draw on Marie Foale's study to consider the early development of the Institute of St Joseph and the extent, background and contribution of its early Irish membership. I also refer to some significant colonial Sisters who had the immediate Irish influence of Irish parents.

In September 1866 the Irish bishop of Adelaide, Lawrence Bonaventure Shiel, gave the parish priest of Penola a new appointment, making Woods his Secretary and Director General of Catholic education in the diocese, so in June 1867 the infant Institute moved to Adelaide, starting its mission there with three members. With Woods's extraordinary effort and enthusiasm and MacKillop's unstinting involvement, the new Institute expanded rapidly. By the end of August 1871, 127 young women had joined the Institute; 81, that is 64 per cent, were Irish. The Irish and Irish-Australian together comprised 90 per cent of the Institute. Foale traced the migration of 46 of the Irish Sisters, showing 27 had migrated with and 19 without their families.[15]

As British settlement in South Australia commenced only in 1836, it is not surprising that there were many migrants in the Institute's early years. What is surprising is the Institute's growth. In 1866 the Catholic proportion of South Australia, mostly among the poorer people, was 14.5 per cent,[16] far lower than in eastern Australia. In a major bicentennial Australian study, J. Jupp summarized the situation: 'Catholics and the Irish-born were always weakest in South Australia.'[17] No one would have predicted the growth of a new Catholic sisterhood here. Besides, Woods, who wrote the Rules, instructed the Sisters and, with huge effort, reorganized the educational provision for the diocese, had other large pastoral responsibilities. Another factor was that Shiel was overseas for two and a half of the Institute's first four years.[18] There was no other Religious women's congregation in Adelaide till December 1868. This largely Irish-based sisterhood, therefore, was a remarkable, pioneering venture.

In studying the Sisters of the first four years, Foale concluded that their 'most notable characteristic ... taken as a group, was their ordinariness': there was nothing exceptional about their family background, social standing or education. Nineteen Sisters had migrated as single women, 14 of them 'almost certainly' working as servants before joining the Sisters. Fifteen of the 19 remained in the Institute, contributing to its life and work. One spent her life caring for children in an orphanage run by the Sisters.[19]

The 'ordinary' women made many remarkable contributions in the Institute. Of nine who came from Irish farm labouring families north of Adelaide, two Irish sisters from the one family held many responsible positions in the Institute. One, in leadership roles for most of her life, was also appointed by MacKillop to deputize for her in long absences.[20] Another of the nine, referred to further below, was Hyacinth Quinlan. Born of Irish parents in the South Australian Armagh, near Clare, she joined the Sisters in 1868, and in 1872 was sent with two other Sisters to open a foundation in Perthville, a small village in the distant diocese of Bathurst. In 1876, in difficult circumstances, the 25-year-old Quinlan took a vital role in establishing a second separate Institute, when the alternative was that the Institute would no longer remain in the diocese.[21] Another of the nine became 'something of a legend' for her care of poor men who came for a meal to the Providence.

Versatility, as shown at the Providence, was another feature of the 'ordinary' Sisters, whether Irish or colonials. Woods had discovered many homeless, old women, 'poor creatures', he said, who never found families they migrated to join. The Providence, established at his initiative on the style of that at Ars,[22] offered care to poor, old women, girls and children ineligible for the orphanage. The Sisters also ran an orphanage and a refuge to care for women released from prison and in similar need, a difficult task requiring great 'gentleness and patience',[23] so there was plenty to do for Sisters who did not teach. At first, however, experienced Sisters, including two Irish Sisters who were teachers, were needed at these charitable institutions.

Most of the Irish Sisters, like the colonials, became teachers. A major experiment of October 1867 was the first rural foundation, 75 kilometres from Adelaide and nearly half that distance from the local priest. Launched by two mature women, one Irish, both with teaching experience, its success led rapidly to other branches, not always with mature, experienced teachers. By July 1868 the Sisters taught in eight schools, some in scattered rural or mining districts without a resident priest. By August 1871 there were 123 Sisters, many in tiny communities of two or three Sisters. They were responsible for 43 schools and four institutions.[24] As well, a branch community was sent to Queensland in December 1869.

Woods described the early Sisters as 'virtuous and disinterested, with the most earnest zeal for the work' and 'just the subjects that were needed, except in one particular', their lack of education, a lack he felt keenly as 'a serious drawback ... for a teaching order'. How did these poorly educated Irish and colonial women become teachers? In their eagerness and tenacity, 'all their spare time,' explained Woods, 'was devoted to study.' Their tutors were MacKillop and the other experienced teachers; Woods gave encouragement and whatever practical help he could, and with MacKillop sought to place one experienced teacher in each school.[25] Many had natural ability, responding well to instruction and guidance. Woods's claim that they overcame their lack of education was supported by the Apostolic Commission appointed to investigate the Adelaide Church in 1872: it found no cause for complaint in the Sisters. At the end of the enquiry, one of the Commissioners, Bishop Matthew Quinn, an experienced educator, concluded plans for three Sisters to open a foundation in his diocese of Bathurst.

Among the relatively few well-educated women, six, including four Irish women, had joined the Institute by mid-July 1868. Three of the four became significant leaders: Josephine McMullen was Provincial of two provinces in eastern Australia and a member of the order's advisory council; gracious, artistic Monica Phillips was Novice Mistress and Provincial for many years in South Australia; Bernard Walsh, a solicitor's daughter from Galway, followed MacKillop as the second Superior General, a position she held for 12 years.[26] A few accomplished Irish women, therefore, who joined the Institute in its founding year, had notable roles in its later leadership.

Near collapse then new growth of the sisterhood and Irish membership in this period

In September 1871, while Woods, at the request of the bishop of Bathurst, was missioning and seeking a location for a foundation of the Sisters in Bathurst diocese, the Institute was threatened with extinction and the Irish Sisters, like the rest, were swept into the confusion: MacKillop was excommunicated by Shiel, nearly half the Sisters were dismissed or left and 17 of the schools were left without Sisters. At the word of Archbishop Polding of Sydney, Woods was ordered to remain missioning in eastern Australia, hundreds of miles from Adelaide, while the foundation he had striven to establish seemed about to perish. The orchestrated opposition to Woods and the Sisters was kept in the public eye by the Adelaide *Irish Harp*, which openly criticized Bishop Shiel and supported the Institute and its founder. The protagonist was a young Irish priest, Charles Horan, bent on revenge against Woods for revealing to the Vicar General the grave misdeeds of Horan's friend, another priest.[27]

A weapon of Woods's opponents was the Institute's style of community. There were no 'choir' and 'lay' Sisters as in European orders, where choir Sisters chanted formal prayer and undertook the order's ministry, such as teaching, while lay Sisters did the manual tasks. All in the new Institute were to share the household tasks. Woods was operating out of a new concept of Religious life, as seen in post-revolutionary France; he was in a new society where growing egalitarianism favoured this concept. Woods and MacKillop were at a touchstone of social change, with the choir/lay division finally removed from Religious communities by Vatican II. Although the issue was deeper than the style of community, the Irish and colonial Sisters supported the Institute as it was, and despite severe opposition, their new style was retained.

In February 1872, five months after imposing the excommunication, Shiel withdrew it, without explanation. He died a week later. The 52 disbanded Sisters, including 29 Irish Sisters, were free to return. Two-thirds of all and two-thirds of the Irish Sisters returned, a significant indication of the homogeneity of the Irish with the colonial Sisters.[28] One remarkable Irish Sister who returned was Lawrence O'Brien, aged 17 at MacKillop's excommunication. She maintained firm identity with the sisterhood, becoming Provincial in two provinces, then Superior General for over 12 years.

Out of what appeared to be the Institute's early demise, unanticipated growth emerged. Despite further searing trials, which revealed the strength of Irish Sisters in key positions, the Institute steadily expanded in Australia and, from the 1880s, in New Zealand. In the 1880s the congregational base was transferred from Adelaide to Sydney, where all new candidates were received.

A significant source of these was the vast missionary journeying of Woods in eastern Australia. Between 1872 and 1874 inclusive, for example, as well as founding another sisterhood,[29] he recruited 35 candidates, including 18 Irish women,[30] for the Queensland branch. MacKillop had also been recruiting. After travelling to Rome to have the Institute's Rule approved, she visited Ireland, returning to Adelaide in January 1875 with 15 Irish candidates,[31] the first of many to follow to this sisterhood much later.

While each year after 1871 brought new candidates, the Irish proportion fell, as Table 10.1 shows, by the end of the 1880s, a pattern reflecting the fall in Irish migration.[32] The proportion of Irish candidates on the Sisters' register dropped from 64 per cent in September 1871 to 52 per cent by the end of 1889, and 49 per cent by the end of 1891.[33] Between 1 September 1871 and the end of 1890 there were the same number (127) of Irish and Australian candidates. The founder's death, on 7 October 1889, occurred at a turning-point.[34] Woods had come as a migrant among migrants and founded a largely Irish-based Institute. He died as the flow of migration dropped and a strongly Australian membership emerged. The new Institute, begun in formative times, achieved local identity just as Australians were claiming national identity. At the end of 1891, 25 years after the Penola beginnings, the total number of candidates registered was 429; the Congregation had foundations in New South Wales, South Australia, Western Australia, Victoria and New Zealand. From its Sydney base the Congregation continued to expand, but with fewer Irish members, till the death of the co-founding Mary MacKillop, on 8 August 1909, when there were 650 living members.[35] Soon another Irish flow began.

Table 10.1 Places of birth of Sisters entered in Adelaide and North Sydney registers in given years

Year of entry	Ireland f	cf	Australia f	cf	England f	Scotland f	N. Zealand* f	f
1 Sept. 1871 to end of								
1887	107	–	90	–	11	5	9	9
1888	5	112	7	97	–	–	–	–
1889	9	121	11	108	–	–	–	–
1890	6	127	19	127	1	–	2	–
1891	2	129	9	136	–	–	–	–
Total	–	129	–	136	12	5	11	9

Note: * Other. Places of birth for these are listed as: three unknown, one at sea and one each in Poland, Germany, India, Africa and South Africa
f = frequency
cf = cumulative frequency
Source: Register of the Sisters of St Joseph, North Sydney

Unexpected developments; Irish recruitment

Along with expansion from Adelaide then Sydney, there were two off-shoots from the Adelaide group after 1872, both begun in small, unpromising ways, and both fruitful. The Irish dimension was significant in both.

An offshoot from Adelaide

Before the 1871–2 Adelaide crisis, a disruptive group of six Sisters (three Irish), claimed to be visited by visions.[36] After the crisis, their Sydney-born leader, daughter of an Irish schoolteacher and his wife, returned to Sydney where she adopted the name Gertrude Abbott, and lived with a small group, mainly ex-Sisters. The group later included Abbott's sister from the Adelaide Institute and a Perthville ex-Sister, Juliana Dowling, whose father was an Irish artist.[37] When Woods returned ill to Sydney after three years in South-East Asia, he was given a home among this community for two years till his death. Abbott, assisted by others, especially an Irish ex-Sister,[38] then cared for poor, unmarried, pregnant mothers. She extended her work, establishing St Margaret's Maternity Hospital, training large numbers of nurses and tending many more mothers. After her death, the hospital expanded in the care of the sisterhood she had left.

Another offshoot: a second Institute based mainly on Irish recruits

The first foundation from Adelaide to New South Wales was made in 1872 to Perthville, Bathurst diocese, at the request of Bishop Matthew Quinn. The founding community of three, one Irish, one Scottish and colonial Hyacinth Quinlan, daughter of Irish parents, grew to 28 Sisters in six schools by January 1876. Fifteen of the new candidates were recruited by Woods in missionary journeys, and nine by Quinn in Ireland. In mid-February, the Perthville branch was halved, and a second Institute, separate in government from Adelaide, was launched.

In September 1874 Quinn had met MacKillop in Ireland, soon after MacKillop gained Roman approval for the new Institute. Quinn had supported the move for Roman approval, but insisted the Institute have diocesan, not centralized government. He saw the bishop as the Superior, with the Sisters identified with a diocese, like the Sisters of Mercy, without coming and going vast distances from one diocese to another. He also insisted their Rule should not preclude Sisters from teaching instrumental music, which Woods and MacKillop considered would deflect the Sisters from the poor. Quinn valued music in worship and knew its popularity: by the 1870s, his post-gold rush diocese was not the same as that of South Australia in the 1860s. The new Catholic migrants of the east were not so poor and expected music to be taught. As one of several migrant governesses observed with surprise, 'the commonest people have a piano and have their children taught to play.'[39]

Meeting MacKillop in Ireland, Quinn learned Rome had approved the order's centralized government, and, in Press's words, 'Quinn girded for battle.' 'If the Sisters that I brought from Adelaide choose to go back, they can,' he wrote to Mgr Kirby at the Irish College in Rome, 'and I will form my own subjects, according to the necessities of my own diocese.'[40] While MacKillop recruited for Adelaide, Quinn recruited for Perthville. Nine responded to Quinn, migrating to Perthville in three groups.[41] Quinn returned to Bathurst in October 1875, determined to have his separate Institute. On Christmas Eve he offered the Perthville Sisters the choice of returning to Adelaide or remaining as members of a diocesan Institute.

In February 1876, 14 Sisters left for Adelaide and 15 remained, namely Quinlan, from Adelaide, the nine from Ireland and five from the local area.[42] All they had were Quinlan's teaching and example, Quinn's encouragement and their own generosity and perseverance. The diocesan Institute did not look promising. Within a few years, one of the nine died, another of the nine and two of the five left.

In December 1884, Quinn marvelled after seeing the diocesan Institute flourish. Speaking of the Sisters at Perthville's annual prizegiving and entertainment, he declared: 'Their very existence is marvel.' A month later, on retreat among his clergy and sensing his immanent death, he addressed his priests, recommending to them 'important matters' he had undertaken, naming one such matter as the Sisters of St Joseph. Within days he was dead.[43] At the end of 1884 there were 127 entries in the Perthville Register. Forty-two, that is, 33 per cent, were Irish and both parents of at least 28 others were Irish; at least another ten had one Irish parent.[44] Altogether, 63 per cent were Irish or had the influence of Irish parents. These Sisters had opened schools in 24 locations in the Bathurst diocese, closing some to re-open them elsewhere, following mining and railway settlements. As well, 13 Sisters from Perthville were sent to found three Institutes in other dioceses, in Wanganui, New Zealand (1880), Goulburn (1882) and Lochinvar, Maitland diocese (1883). In 1887 another founding community was sent to Tasmania, all four[45] new Institutes expanding and enduring, so there was, as at Adelaide, prodigious growth.

Tenison Woods and the growth of the second Institute

The reason for the growth of the Perthville Institute rests in Tenison Woods. Missioning in Tasmania, Woods was recalled by Quinn to Bathurst diocese to preach missions, instruct the Perthville Sisters and rewrite their Rule, incorporating the changes Quinn required.[46] The Irish Quinn made decisive moves to create the Institute, his Irish group provided its nucleus and Quinlan kept the group viable till Woods arrived; spirit and growth came with Woods. Woods arrived at Perthville on Easter Day 1877 and his arrival, repeated visits and subsequent work provide the reason for the strong, rapid expansion of the second Institute. For the next five and a half years, till his missionary period ended, many young women, including Irish migrants, found their direction to Perthville through him. In this period there were probably only two more recruits from Ireland.[47] Woods's five and a half years of direct influence on the Perthville Sisters left a close bond with them and recognition as 'founder', a bond and recognition passed on at Perthville and the Institutes founded from there.

When Woods completed the revision of the Rule, he attached, as an 'Explanation', the 1867 Rule with what Woods described as changes 'in some few matters of detail', 'but no change whatever ... in its spirit.'[48] He also gave the Sisters virtually the same written instructions on the spirit of the Rule as at Adelaide.[49] Quinn's approval of the Rule affirmed the new institute.

The Irish and other Sisters learned this Rule and their new identity above all in Woods's eight-day preached retreats for the assembled Institute, and in the ceremonies of reception of new members and profession of novices that usually concluded the retreats. There were three retreats for the whole

Institute between Easter 1877 and 1880 (In 1880 Woods preached two retreats to accommodate the growing community). Between the retreats, Irish and colonial Sisters were missioned to near and far rural places, challenged to live their new identity away from the Perthville base. One of the 1881 founding community to the diocesan outpost, Bourke, 570 kilometres from Perthville, was an Irish Sister, professed only in 1880. In January 1882, Woods again preached two eight-day retreats to accommodate all the Sisters. Between the retreats was a ceremony of reception of seven new members (one Irish), and profession of four novices (two Irish). Woods's retreats educated the heart and consecrated for mission. His influence strengthened the Irish and colonials for their expanding mission.

Notable leadership by the Irish of the second Institute

Young Irish Sisters who experienced Woods's influence were notable in the leadership and expansion of the Perthville Institute. The group sent from Perthville in 1882 to found the Institute at Goulburn was led by 23-year-old Irish Sister Evangelist Duggan with four companions, three of whom were Irish. The average age of the four Irish was 21. In 1883, two Irish and two colonial Sisters were sent to found an Institute at Lochinvar in the Maitland diocese. The superior, 23-year-old Irish Joseph Dirkin, had professed her vows only in 1882; her 22-year-old Irish companion, Aloysius Cahill, had arrived at Perthville during the January 1882 retreats, following Woods from Brisbane. In seven years' leadership, Dirkin opened ten more foundations and initiated a strong musical tradition. These Irish Sisters decisively took up the challenge offered in this mobile missionary Institute.

This statement is especially true of Quinn's nine Irish recruits of 1875. Their contribution, much more significant than their numbers suggest, calls for a closer view. There were three in the first group: a 25-year-old, whose father was a bootmaker, one slightly younger and an 18-year-old, whose father was a builder.[50] The next group, four candidates from farming families in Cork, had travelled as assisted passengers among the single women, an unusual feature for candidates for religious orders, who, in keeping with their usual background in the upper and upper middle class, travelled first or second class.[51] The shipping list shows all four claiming an earlier Irish candidate for the Sisters of Mercy as their relative in the colony, and registering their occupation as 'dairymaid'. The youngest turned 16 on the voyage; two sisters were 16 and 21; the other volunteer was 17.

Quinn's last two recruits of 1875 were a 21-year-old from a well-known farming family at 'Turrenbawn', near Millstreet, Co. Cork, and a 43-year-old, whose father was a shopkeeper in Co. Kerry. The younger, Benedict Hickey, learned of the Institute when invited by the Presentation Sisters to hear Quinn's address at Millstreet, her former school. She persisted in her desire, despite her relatives' pressure to join some well-established order, not 'the new Institute', to which she was attracted.[52] Hickey and her older companion travelled second class, with three women migrating to be lay Sisters with the Sisters of Mercy. In first class were three professed Sisters of Mercy and 11 other candidates for the Sisters of Mercy, all to be choir, not lay Sisters. When the group reached Bathurst, Hickey again resisted encouragement to join her cousins there, and continued with her companion to Perthville.

Four of Quinn's nine recruits helped found new Institutes. The youngest 'dairymaid', Duggan, led the Goulburn foundation; the bootmaker's daughter, Francis McCarthy, led the foundation to Tasmania in 1887. One of McCarthy's founding community was Hickey's 1875 companion. They were joined by another 1875 recruit in 1892. Another, Rose Hartnett, aged 25, was appointed to the important role of Novice Mistress till her death in 1881.

The most remarkable contribution of the nine was made by Benedict Hickey. Apart from Quinlan, who had a founding role in the second Institute, Hickey, as Sr Benedict, became the significant leader in the Institute's founding decades. For all but 18 years from 1881, when she was 27, till 1941, when she died, still in office, Hickey was in the Institute's key position of leadership. McCarthy, chosen by Hickey as her Assistant in 1881, held Hickey in high regard. McCarthy herself was recognized for her zeal, prayer, love of the Eucharist, and her humour and simplicity. There is record of a miracle worked in her lifetime through her prayer over a wounded child.[53] The community she led to Tasmania opened three more foundations in four years. In 1927, she wrote of her old friend, with whom she had professed her religious vows 40 years before: 'if anyone deserves praise and honour for work well done and of long duration without a halt, it is our dear kind humble Sr M. Benedict. Many a time I thanked God for sending her to us and sparing her so long.'[54] Sisters still recall Hickey's strict exterior, but several saw it veiling a genuine, caring heart,[55] and recall her humble ways, sharing the manual tasks, including floor-scrubbing, when she did not have the responsibilities of leadership.

Evangelist Duggan at Goulburn also left a strong impression. Living till 1951, she is still remembered by many. She opened six new houses in her ten years as Sister Guardian, and held responsible positions after this. She was witty, astute, 'nobody's fool', in clear command when decisions were to be made when local priests may not have shared her views. She appreciated education and refinement and made up for her small stature with a fiery disposition.[56]

The one who stood beside the nine from Ireland was Hyacinth Quinlan. Faced with the choice to return to Adelaide or stay at Perthville, at personal cost,[57] she chose to remain to pass on the Josephite tradition to the new members. This she did till Woods arrived in 1877, and as Sister Guardian till 1880, when she led a foundation to New Zealand. In 1891 she transferred to Tasmania, where she was Sister Guardian for three terms, establishing the centre of the Institute at New Town, Hobart, where she died in 1933. By then the fruit of her decision was clear: as shown in Table 10.2 there were 950 entries in the combined registers of Perthville and its four offshoots. Through the instrumentality of this colonial daughter of Irish parents, the Josephite tradition was passed on through Perthville and the four groups founded from there.

Table 10.2 Candidates entered in registers at Perthville and its four offshoots by given dates

Place (Founding year)	7 Oct 1889*	31 Dec 1891>	31 Dec 1901<	8 Aug 1909+	12 Sept 1933#
Perthville (1872/1876)	160	160	185	206	298
Wanganui, NZ (1880)	23	30	71	92	192
Goulburn (1882)	31	34	48	59	163
Lochinvar (1883)	32	39	85	108	232
Tasmania (1887)	8	15	36	46	65
Total	254	278	425	511	950

Notes:
* Death of Julian Tenison Woods
> 25 years after origin of Institute at Penola
< 25 years after separation of Perthville foundation
+ Death of Mary MacKillop
# Death of Hyacinth Quinlan

Further Irish recruitment

Having considered the earlier Irish membership, this section now indicates subsequent Irish membership at Perthville, in the groups founded from there, and in the Sydney-based group. It notes parents' responses to daughter's migrating, some significant Sisters and enters the hearts of Irish Sisters, discovering what prompted them to migrate and remain in this sisterhood.

Perthville

At Perthville ten of the 59 candidates between 1885 and 1900 were Irish migrants living in Australia. Between 1926 and 1930, Irish membership grew when 18 migrated to join the Sisters, invited by Bishops O'Farrell, Norton and two priests of Bathurst diocese. One priest spoke so 'glowingly' of the Perthville Sisters that three migrating to the Bathurst Mercies joined the Josephites instead.[58] Both O'Farrell and Norton had sisters in Irish convents and through these, several recruits learned of 'the wonderful work of the Bathurst Sisters of St Joseph.' In school, they prayed for the Perthville Sisters; in the reception room of Dungarvan Mercy Convent they saw the large photograph of Perthville's professed Sisters and novices. When the invitation came, Perthville sounded familiar.[59]

For the parents, however, Perthville was not familiar. While no parents opposed their daughters' decision, their attitude was the same: Australia was a very, very distant place. They valued the decision to be a nun. Several had daughters in convents in Ireland, England and France, but the choice to go so far away was different. It saddened them; they thought it 'crazy'; they queried their daughters' capacity for such a decision.[60] The parents of one offered her a holiday in America if she would change her mind. In another family the tension was resolved when the father, filling in a form for his departing daughter, read out the question, 'Is there a history of insanity in the family?' 'Not till now', a visiting friend remarked wryly. All parents accepted the decision in an attitude of religious faith.

Wanganui, New Zealand

In the Wanganui group, all Irish candidates are believed to have lived locally before joining the Sisters.[61] The pattern of Irish membership reflected the fall in Irish migration: between 1880 and 1891, 11 of the 28 candidates were Irish; from then till 1924 there were only 11 more Irish candidates, while total membership grew at a higher rate. There has been one Irish candidate since.

As at Adelaide and Perthville, early Irish members became significant. The most remarkable was Columba McWilliams, joining the Sisters in 1886. She became bursar, Mother-General and Novice Mistress, showing capable leadership. In 1883 a young Irish Sister, another Josephite and Mother Joseph Aubert travelled to a Maori mission, two and a half days' canoe-trip from Wanganui, working here till 1884, when Aubert found candidates for her new order.[62]

Goulburn

In the Goulburn Institute the Irish Sisters 'made a tremendous contribution despite their small numbers.'[63] Irish Sisters filled the position of Sister Guardian till 1899. By the end of 1891 eight of the 34 new members were Irish, three probably directly from Ireland. Another six arrived from Tipperary in 1892, after Bishop Lanigan's next trip home. Six Irish candidates later joined the Institute, four directly from Ireland.[64]

As a group, the Irish Sisters lived their conviction of 'all for the love of God'. They were noted for their earnest spirit in whatever they did, teaching, household tasks, visiting the sick and poor, bent on making a success of it. Their total severance from their families and their lived faith has challenged the rest of the community.[65]

Lochinvar

The Lochinvar Institute in the Maitland diocese has had the smallest number of Irish Sisters of all Josephite groups. The district was the earliest settled after Sydney and by 1860 had a higher than average proportion of free, Irish Catholic settlers. As the area was settled so early, there were few young Irish migrants when the Sisters came to the district. Members were not sought in Ireland, as there were sufficient local candidates. Some Sisters have forebears among the earliest local Catholics, Irish convicts working for British or Scottish landowners: many have forebears among the more numerous Irish free settlers.

Of the 127 candidates by 1913, two were Irish. In 1914 two Irish women who migrated to join the Sisters came to Lochinvar. They transferred with a Josephite community from Ballarat, Victoria, led by Dowling.[66] Another Irish candidate joined later. While the groups at Perthville, Wanganui, Goulburn and Lochinvar all had significant early Irish membership, in 1991, out of the combined total of approximately 450 Sisters, there were nine (0.02 per cent) Irish Sisters.

Tasmania

In the smaller Tasmanian Institute,[67] serving a smaller population, Irish membership in 1991 was 13 per cent. The significant early Irish candidate was Columba Cahill, sister to the founding member at Lochinvar. Her Novice Mistress was the Irish Stanislaus Doyle, later Sister Guardian. A capable, kind, good-humoured woman with zeal for the Institute and care for the needy, Cahill was elected Sister Guardian seven times. This office was also held by Irish Dirkin, transferring to Tasmania from Lochinvar, and Quinlan, transferring from Wanganui.

Irish membership grew between 1933 and 1947 when 12 volunteers migrated from Ireland, invited by Archbishop Hayden of Hobart. On reaching Tasmania, most were aged between 16 and 20 and had spent an initial period at the Callan Sisters of Mercy Missionary School, an institution some found 'tougher than the novitiate'. For some parents, distance from Australia was made less daunting through relatives or friends in the Institute; for others, the decision brought grief. Ten of the 12 Sisters remained in the Institute; one, Celsus McCarthy, became Sister Guardian; some, including McCarthy, were among the first in the Institute to gain university degrees.[68]

Sydney

In the large Sydney-based group, some Irish candidates since 1891 migrated alone or with families, but a far larger number migrated through the zeal of an Irish priest and the Josephite Juniorate in Newmarket. In 1991

210 Irish Sisters formed 15 per cent of this group's membership.

In 1910 Irish Fr Edward O'Carroll brought a group of volunteers from Ireland to the Sydney novitiate. Having met the Josephites in rural Queensland, he visited MacKillop in Sydney in 1909 on his way to Ireland. Before O'Carroll reached Ireland the saintly MacKillop had died, but her request that he return with Irish candidates had abundant results. Deeply impressed by MacKillop and the order, he visited Ireland twice more by 1920, each time returning with candidates for the Sydney novitiate.[69] In the third or fourth group, arriving in 1923, there were 22 candidates.[70] Fifty-two came in the largest group, in 1925.

The next year, the Irish Lawrence O'Brien, Superior General, travelled to Ireland to prepare for an Irish juniorate, a venture determined by the 1925 congregational chapter. After purchasing Newmarket Manor in Co. Cork and organizing renovations, O'Brien returned to Australia, sending a community to Ireland in 1927. From then till 1973, Newmarket became a bountiful source of volunteers for the Sydney Josephite novitiate.[71]

Twenty-five candidates reached Sydney in 1928, followed by 19 in 1929, thence an annual group till the outbreak of World War II.[72] Between 1947 and 1950, at least three small groups migrated, bringing professed members who completed their novitiate in Newmarket during the war, and new candidates. In the 1950s there was a steady flow of candidates till 1959, when no group came, as the candidates were considered too young. Numbers dropped in the 1960s, reflecting a pattern in novitiates in Western society. In 1971 the congregational chapter decided to close Newmarket and its Sydney Juniorate.

These migrations, part of the massive Irish missionary endeavour, are open to further research. Here, even a brief comment indicates the notable contribution of the Irish in the Sydney-based Josephites. Till 1931, the majority of the Superior Generals and councillors were Irish. Columbkille Browne, held in high regard, served as a congregational councillor for 40 years. Two Irish Sisters of remarkable scholarship were Kevin Herron and Maria Kieran Herron, the latter helping initiate the Sisters' Teachers' Training School.[73] Frances Therese Delaney, one of O'Carroll's group of 52, was Novice Mistress or Assistant Novice Mistress for a total of 33 years. Others were significant as Provincials for repeated terms in Australia and New Zealand.

According to two from O'Carroll's 1923 group, most of his volunteers were in their twenties, with few in mid-teenage years. The early Newmarket groups were similar, with probably more in their latter teenage years.[74] After 1925 O'Carroll continued an intermittent presence in Dublin, where he held weekly sessions of instruction and prayer on love of the Sacred Heart, attended by a small group of young women. He gained many volunteers by visiting homes and schools, telling of the Australian order; several took the initiative to meet him. The Newmarket Sisters also visited homes and schools, speaking of their order; again, several volunteers met the Sisters on their own initiative. Instead of a campaign of persuasion that the large numbers could indicate, the Irish women interviewed, of various ages, communicated the strong individuality of their choice and their capacity to make a choice.[75] Several also told of Irish aunts in the order, providing insight into earlier Irish Sisters. One knew the Irish volunteers brought before 1900 to Western Australia by Bishop Gibney. These endured poverty and severe living conditions in extreme heat and arid land, living first in tents and having to buy water.[76]

The strength of their choice was matched by the shock and grief of their parents. It was the same story told by the Irish Sisters of Perthville and Tasmania, with the added impact of greater numbers. The Sisters' words convey best their parents' responses. 'To be a nun was wonderful, but why go to the other ends of the earth?' 'My mother's face went deadly white'; 'she said I couldn't go, but I knew I would'; 'it was like dropping a bombshell in the family'; 'my father thought I was infatuated'; 'my mother kept questioning me about leaving when I was so young'; 'I did not know till later how much grief it caused her'; 'they were sad, as it was so far away'; 'they were upset, they thought they'd lose track of me altogether.' The huge problem was total separation, as there was no prospect of returning, unless they left the order. The young, as one Sister said, 'could not know what it means for a parent to part with a child.' All parents, in deep, generous faith, accepted their daughter's decision. 'If this is what you want, we give our permission,' quoted one Sister. They assured them of love and welcome if they were not happy and wanted to return. 'You can always come home.' Many did not, and never saw their parents again. Sometimes O'Carroll helped: ' "God is asking for your daughter. How could you refuse?" My mother liked that.'

A few parents were pleased, as they had close relatives in the order and in Australia. One dying mother knew her sister in Australia would look after her daughter. The separation was eased for the growing number who had some contact or relative in the order, but, till the changes after Vatican II, the separation remained total: until then, the Irish Sisters did not visit home.

Mission and identity

The Irish Sisters who migrated this century to the Josephite sisterhood came from varied backgrounds, several having relatively rare opportunities for advanced education, others more usual opportunities. However diverse their background, their common interest was 'to go to the missions' and this attraction was stronger than the security of their families.

To enter the hearts of these Sisters, whether at Sydney or Perthville or its offshoots, it is essential to capture the contemporary Catholic attitude to 'the missionary countries'. Australia was then considered one of the 'foreign missions', a country little touched by Christianity, where the Gospel needed to be sown. In the Irish volunteers was a longing to give their life 'for the missions'. 'I was all for the missions'; 'mission was in my mind.' The fact that Australia was so remote, so unknown, 'at the other ends of the earth', made its missionary pull all the stronger for these women. 'My brother joined the Cistercians and so did a sister, but I wanted to go to the missions.' Several in Perthville, Tasmania and Sydney had wanted to go to China. Many spoke of the attraction of the Columban missionary magazine, *The Far East*. 'If I wasn't a Josephite,' said one, 'I would be a Columban.'

Some Sisters communicated the actual moment of attraction to the order, or of deciding on a missionary life. The moments were rain on water, indelible impressions in the heart. All were already led with a sense of a missionary calling, then something triggered their sense of where and how they were called to go.

There was something in the Sisters' responses that was different from just the notion of religious consecration, of being set apart for God. There was a sense of being set apart and sent for God. These women expressed an out-going urge to go to others for the sake of the Gospel. 'We weren't sure what we were coming to, but we wanted to share our faith with the Australian people, and this is what we are doing.'

They admitted the cost, but passed over it. Several still choked with the memory of the initial loneliness, but their decision had not changed: 'I knew I was right then, and I know I am right now.' Australian Sisters referred to the war years when the Irish longed for news from home.

Woods wrote to MacKillop at the palpable beginning of their Institute, 'Everybody says, "What can you expect of colonial girls? ..." Without St Joseph, I know what I should expect, but with him and his Divine Foster-son, I am sure of placing the work right amid the Holy Family, and they will do what we can't.'[77] Woods and MacKillop's order was fashioned with a sense of the tenderness of the Infant Christ. They had to overcome notions of religious life as an ossified product of a former society; they wanted their order to communicate the tender love of God in a way that suited their new world, in the ancient land of Australia.

In colonial Australia, 'at the other end of the earth', they founded an order where the missionary energies of young hearts could find expression and be channelled. In the new order hundreds of Irish migrants and Irish missioners gained their new identity. They were to be, Woods explained, like Joseph, 'the poor man, the humble man, upon whom the child Jesus loved to rest', who 'fled into the desert to save the infant Jesus from His enemies.' They were to live away from 'the consolations of Religion ... for the sake of the little ones for whom Jesus suffered.' Woods 'firmly believed' this Joseph-like way was the one 'in which the mystery and sacrifice of Our Lord was to be reproduced in our own days to meet the wants of our adopted country.'[78]

In 1991, 125 years since the order was founded, descendants of Irish migrants formed the majority in the Josephite sisterhood. In the same year, Irene McCormack, one of these descendants, was executed where she worked with her own Sisters and the Columbans among the poor of Peru. In 1995 the co-founding MacKillop was beatified, nearing the Catholic Church's highest recognition. There have been Irish women in the six

Josephite groups from their separate years of foundation until now. By their faith and missionary generosity they have brought an added dimension to the Josephite sisterhood.

Notes

1. *National Statistical Survey of Religious Personnel: Australia — 1976,* Conferences of major superiors, 1976, p. 27. I acknowledge the Irish Sisters who provided information and inspiration, assistance of congregational archivists and secretaries, Srs Evelyn Pickering, Benedetta (Sydney), Patricia Dunne, Paula Wilson (Perthville), Mary O'Dea (Goulburn), Cyril (New Town), Genevieve, Anne Burke (Wanganui) and invaluable reference from M. Rosa MacGinley PBVM, whose major historical study, *Institutes of Women Religious in Australia,* is due for publication, 1996. Records of correspondence and interviews referred to below are in author's possession, unless otherwise stated.
2. The French Good Shepherd order.
3. This develops my paper, 'The Irish base of an Australian religious sisterhood', in *Irish Australian Studies, Papers Delivered at Sixth Irish–Australian Conference,* Philip Bull *et al,* La Trobe University, Victoria, 1991, pp. 228–43.
4. Julian was the best known and most prolific, writing books, articles and over 170 documents, most in scientific journals. See Mary MacKillop, *Life of Rev. J. E. T. Woods,* (1903), ed. Margaret Press, Harper Collins, Melbourne, 1996; Margaret Press, *Julian Tenison Woods: 'Father Founder',* Collins Dove, Melbourne, 1994; Isabel Hepburn, *No Ordinary Man, Life and Letters of Julian E. Tenison Woods,* Sisters of St Joseph, Wanganui, 1979; Anne Player, 'Julian Tenison Woods, the interaction of science and religion', MA thesis, 1990, Australian National University.
5. Edward MacLysaght, *More Irish Families,* O'Gorman Ltd., Galway, 1960, pp. 201, 282.
6. Revd. P. Semple, Donard, to Sr Brigid Linehan, 4 March 1900.
7. J. E. Tenison Woods, 'Memoirs', Vol. I, dictated typescript, St Joseph's Archives, Lochinvar, pp. 4, 6–7, 18–9, 39.
8. Woods, 'Memoirs', Vol. I, pp. 6–7.
9. Woods in *Freemans Journal,* 14 April 1877; 'Memoirs', 2, p. 24.
10. J. E. Tenison Woods, *Rules for the Institute of St Joseph,* Adelaide, 1868 (written 1867).
11. Woods, 'Memoirs', 1, p. 63.
12. J. T. Woods, 'Ten years in the bush', Passionist Archives, Sydney. See *Australasian Catholic Record,* lxvi, 3, (July 1989), pp. 259ff.
13. Woods, *Rules,* paragraph 6.
14. *Mercury* (Hobart), 6 August 1875.
15. Marie Therese Foale, *The Josephite Story,* St Joseph's Generalate, Sydney, 1989, pp. 34, 37.
16. Margaret Press, *From our Broken Toil, South Australian Catholics, 1836–1906,* Archdiocese, Adelaide, 1986, pp. 12, 178. Cf Oliver MacDonough, 'Emigration from Ireland to Australia, pp. 121–38', in Colm Kiernan (ed.), *Australia and Ireland, 1788–1988,* Gill and MacMillan, Dublin, 1986.
17. J. Jupp, The making of the Anglo-Australian', in James Jupp (ed.), *The Australian People,* Angus and Robertson, 1988, p. 58.

18. Foale, *The Josephite Story*, pp. 78, 198.
19. Foale, *The Josephite Story*, pp. 36–7, 48.
20. Calasanctius Howley.
21. The baptismal register (per M. Foale) gives 20 August 1850 as Quinlan's birth date.
22. Woods visited St John Vianney there.
23. Woods, 'Memoirs', Vol. 2, pp. 30–2.
24. Foale, *The Josephite Story*, pp. 42–3.
25. Woods, 'Memoirs', Vol. 2, pp. 29, 34; Press, *Woods*, p. 96.
26. Foale, *The Josephite Story*, pp. 30–6.
27. As a result of Woods's action, Horan's friend was dismissed from the diocese. Foale, *The Josephite Story*, pp. 58ff; Press, *Woods*, pp. 122–9. The vengeful manoeuvering of Fr Charles Horan was 'the determining factor' in MacKillop's excommunication and the Sisters' disbandment. Paul Gardiner, in comprehensive official document on MacKillop, *Positio Super Virtutibus*, Rome, 1989, pp. 339–340. See Paul Gardiner, *An Extraordinary Australian, Mary MacKillop*, Dwyer, Newtown, 1993, pp. 85, 88, 97ff.
28. Proportions derived from Foale, *The Josephite Story*, pp. 98, 202ff.
29. In the Sisters of Perpetual Adoration, an uncloistered contemplative group Woods founded in Brisbane, 11 of the first 25 candidates were Irish. In 1991 9 per cent were Irish.
30. Foale, *The Josephite Story*, pp. 222–3. One, Baptista Molloy, was Superior General from 1910 to 1918. The Sisters left Queensland in 1880, returning in 1900.
31. Mother Mary of the Cross, 'A brief sketch of the Institute, June 1885, *Resource Material, Sisters of St Joseph of the Sacred Heart*, No. 3 (1980), p. 66.
32. Cf. Jupp, *The Australian People*, p. 58; D. Fitzgerald, 'Irish Immigration, 1840–1914', in Jupp, *Australian People*, p. 564.
33. Derived from Foale, *The Josephite Story*, p. 37, and Table 10.1.
34. Woods died aged 56. There were 384 on the Register of Sisters, 199 Irish, 142 Australian and 43 others (mainly English, Scottish and New Zealanders).
35. William Modystack, *Mary MacKillop*, Rigby, Adelaide, 1982, p. 269. MacKillop died aged 67.
36. Foale, *The Josephite Story*, pp. 61–6. Woods trusted them, despite their extraordinary claims.
37. William Paul Dowling (transported for his part in a revolutionary Irish society in London) and his daughter knew Woods in Tasmania.
38. Magdalen Foley trained as a nurse and completed a pharmacy course for this work. Margaret Press, *Sunrise to Sunrise: The History of St Margaret's Hospital. Darlinghurst 1894–1994*, Hale & Iremonger, Marrickville, 1994, pp. 13–21; Chris Cunneen, Gertrude Abbott, in Bede Nairn and Geoffrey Serle (eds), *Australian Dictionary of Biography*, 7, 1979; Abbot's sister later joined an English apostolic Passionist order. George O'Neill, *Life of the Reverend Julian Edmund Tenison Woods*, Sydney, 1929, pp. 370–2.
39. Patricia Clarke, *The Governesses: Letters from the Colonies, 1862–1882*, Hutchison, Victoria, 1985, p. 141.
40. In Press, *Woods*, pp. 172–3. See Margaret Press, 'Sisters of St Joseph — diocesan variety', *Australasian Catholic Record*, LXIV, 3 (1972), pp. 193–215; Foale, *The Josephite Story*, pp. 128–132, 220.
41. Janice Tranter, 'Julian Tenison Woods, his role as founder of the sisters of St Joseph of Lochinvar', *Journal of Australian Catholic Historical Society* (1990), Sydney, pp. 45–58.

42. Information on Perthville Sisters is from Perthville Archives, unless otherwise stated.
43. *Record* (Bathurst), 18 December 1884, 2 February 1885. Quinn died on 17 January 1885, aged 63.
44. Migration details have been located for 24 of the 42 Irish: of the 17 who migrated to join the Sisters, 13 had paid passages and 4 were assisted immigrants; another 6 were assisted immigrants, 5 as single women, 1 with her family; 1 was a remittance passenger. At least another 2 came with families. Of the 127, 25 left the sisterhood; of the 42 Irish, 10 left. See also Tranter, 'Irish base', 1991.
45. Two foundations did not endure. Four Irish Sisters opened a foundation in Ballarat diocese in 1891. In 1900 two returned to Perthville; the others, led by Irish Gonzaga Delaney, transferred to Sydney. In 1901 another group transferred to Sydney from the remote Wilcannia diocese. A group of Perthville Sisters, finding themselves in a newly formed Wilcannia diocese when diocesan boundaries changed, tried to maintain a separate institute, but isolation led them to amalgamate with Sydney.
46. Woods had been told his official direction of the Sisters had ended. See Press, *Woods* p. 164.
47. In 1880 Bishop Lanigan of Goulburn sought recruits in Ireland to train at Perthville for his diocese. Mary Murphy and Mary Cahill, later in the founding community to Goulburn, migrated in December 1880.
48. Julian Edmund Tenison Woods, *Rules and Instructions of the Institute of the Sisters of St Joseph*, Printed at the *Record* office, George Street, Bathurst, 1878, p. 33.
49. J. E. Tenison Woods, *A Book of Instructions for the Use of the Sisters of St Joseph of the Sacred Heart*, n.d. (est. 1870s), Brisbane.
50. For shipping details for the nine, see Tranter, 'Irish base', 1991.
51. The author knows of no others migrating to Australia as assisted passengers to join a religious order.
52. File, 'Benedict Hickey', Perthville Archives.
53. *Standard* (Tasmania), 15 February 1940; Josephite Archives, New Town. (Early Josephite convents in Tasmania had no chapel.) Inspired by the parish crib, she wrote: 'Grant, O infant Jesus, that I may be like that shepherd, without a head to reason or rebel; like that cow without horns, to escape hurting anyone; and without feet, like your little image here, so as not to be able to run away from Thee. Amen.'
54. S.F. to My dear Sr M. Anthony, July 1927, Archives, New Town.
55. Irish Sisters interviewed referred to her 'outstanding leadership ... with the interests of every Sister at heart', her interest in their personal happiness and in their families and her stress on 'doing all for the love of God, with no half-measures.'
56. Written memoirs, Sr M. Tarcisius, Goulburn Superioress General, 1963–75. (Tarcisius' mother was Irish.) Duggan used to speak of applying to lease land from Samuel McCaughey, a prominent Protestant landowner. On being asked in which banks she had security, she replied 'the banks of the Murray' (the river in required land).
57. Her family were in South Australia; she had a sister in the Adelaide Institute.
58. Irish Sister Peter Griffin, of three companions. Note: In those days many Sisters bore the names of male saints.
59. From Irish Sisters Declan, Fidelis, Martha, Peter; Memoirs, Sr Brenda.
60. Most of the 18 were aged between 16 and 20.

61. From Sr Bega Downing, who migrated in 1916, joining the Sisters in 1919.
62. Sisters of Compassion.
63. Sr Tarcisius.
64. From Sr Mel Gough who migrated in 1920.
65. Sr Tarcisius.
66. Bridget Daly and Sarah Bolger migrated in 1900 to join Delaney's Ballarat community, but, finding these leaving for Sydney, they joined Dowling's community, founded nearby from Tasmania. Dowling, who helped care for Woods in his final illness, joined the Tasmanian Josephites after Woods's death.
67. Over 50 members.
68. From Srs Kieran, Brigid, Colman, Malachy and Philomena.
69. *Congregation of the Sisters of St Joseph of the Sacred Heart*, Westmead, 1919, p. 778.
70. From group members and photograph.
71. In the same period O'Brien initiated the process for MacKillop's beatification. Kathleen Burford, *Unfurrowed Fields: A Josephite Story*, St Joseph's, North Sydney, 1991, pp. 111–12, 116–18, 231–2.
72. This lists some groups. Where known, numbers remaining in congregation are in brackets.

O'Carroll's groups

1923	22	(19)
1925	52	(?)

Newmarket groups

1928	25	(21)
1929	19	(?)
1931	7	(7)
1932	23	(19)
1934 Jan.	10	(9)
1934 Nov.	10	(10)
1936	10	(10)
1937	7+?	(7)+?
1938	10	(10)
1939	12	(12)
(World War II)		
1947 i	7 professed	(6)
	3 candidates	(2)
1947 ii	3 professed	(3)
	3 candidates	(3)
1949	1 professed	(1)
	2 candidates	(0)
1951	10	(4)
1958	13	(10)
1963	3	(2)

73. Browne and one Herron migrated before 1910, Herron's sister with O'Carroll.
74. These 18 Irish Sisters, listed with year of arrival in Sydney, provided the information on these groups:

Justina Lynam	1923	Teresita Heffernan	1938
Lelia Cotter	1923	Ellen Keane	1938
Columba O'Mahoney	1928	Ellen Barry	1939
Clement Higgins	1931	Mary Keane	1947
Aloysius Smyth	1932	Elizabeth Dowling	1947
Marie Mida Tobin	1934	Nora McGrane	1949
Ailbe Rahilly	1934	Margaret Lambert	1951
Kevin Furlong	1936	Eileen Lambert	1958
M. Catherine Ryan	1937	Julia Joyce	1963

75. Of the 18 above, eight met O'Carroll or Newmarket Sisters on their own initiative.
76. M. Mida Tobin.
77. 12 June 1867, *Mary and Julian, Their Letters, 1862–1868*, St Joseph's, North Sydney.
78. Woods, *Freeman's Journal*, 14 April 1877.

Index

The reader's attention is drawn to the indexer's note on page 222 of *Patterns of Migration*, Volume 1 of *The Irish World Wide*.